Contents

Introduction   vii
Explanatory Notes   xix
Maps   xxiii

1   Setting the Stage   1
2   Opening Moves   23
3   Germany Enters the Fray   47
4   Stabilising the Middle East   69
5   Malta under Siege   93
6   Turning Point   115
7   Masters of the North African Shores   139
8   Italy Subdued   165
9   Supporting the Southern Flank   191
10 Victory on the Peripheries   211
11 Britannia's Sea, Victory in the Mediterranean   229
12 The Triumph of British Maritime Power   247
Appendix 1 Timeline of Significant Global Events during
            World War II   267
Appendix 2 Wartime Biographies of Prominent Royal
            Navy Officers Who Served in the Mediterranean Theatre   275

Selected Bibliography   281
Endnotes   285
Index   309

Introduction

The large body of crystal blue water separating the European continent from Africa has been called many names throughout history. The ancient Egyptians referred to it as *Wadj-Wer*. The ancient Israelis primarily referred to it as *HaYam HaGadol* (Great Sea) in the Hebrew Bible. In classic Persian texts, it was referred to as *Daryāy-e Šām* (the Western Sea or Syrian Sea). The ancient Greeks had many names for this body of water, including *Hē Thálassa* (the Sea), *Hē Megálē Thálassa* (the Great Sea), *Hē Hēmétera Thálassa* (Our Sea) or *Hē Thálassa Hē Kath'Hēmâs* (the sea around us). The Romans followed suit initially calling it *Mare Magnum* (Great Sea) or *Mare Internum* (Internal Sea), but eventually settled upon *Mare Nostrum* (Our Sea) with the rise of the Roman Empire. Ancient Arabic literature agreed with this sentiment generally referring to it as *Baḥr al-Rūm(ī)* (the Sea of the Romans or the Roman Sea). Of course, in the modern western world, we have come to refer to this expanse of water as the Mediterranean Sea.

Stretching approximately 2,500 miles from east to west and varying in width from a few dozen to several hundred miles north to south, the Mediterranean Sea encompasses an area of roughly 965,000 square miles. While this clearly represents an immense regional presence, the Mediterranean is actually quite small compared to the world's great oceans, making up only 0.7 percent of the world's ocean surface. Another interesting fact regarding the Mediterranean is that it is almost entirely landlocked with its only natural access to the world's outer oceans being the Strait of Gibraltar located on the extreme western side of the sea. This strait, which is a mere 8.1 miles across at its narrowest point, is positioned between the Iberian Peninsula and Morocco and provides a direct connection to the Atlantic Ocean. In 1869 the Mediterranean gained a second access point to the outer world when a European consortium completed and opened the Suez Canal through the Isthmus of Suez, thus connecting the Eastern Mediterranean to the Indian Ocean via the Red Sea. In turn, this development allowed the Mediterranean to become a viable transportation artery between the Atlantic and Indian Oceans.

While its relative size compared to the world's oceans is limited, the Mediterranean's impact upon history has been immense. For more than three millennia, the region served as the focal point for the formation and advancement of western civilization. Aided by the relative ease of maritime travel, the abundance of sustenance garnered from the sea and its generally temperate climates, the Mediterranean helped transform many of the region's peoples from small, primitive, tribal cultures into the larger, highly organised and structurally complex social entities prevalent in our modern world. This included the rise of several great nations and empires, including the long succession of Egyptian dynasties, the Greek city-states and the Assyrian, Babylonian, Persian, Carthaginian, Macedonian, Roman, Byzantine, Moorish and Ottoman Empires. Along with these rich cultures came a corresponding rise in language, agriculture, economics, trade, transportation, science, mathematics, architecture, art, literature and social organisation. The region also served as the birthplace for several great religious movements, three of which (Judaism, Christianity and Islam) remain dominant in the world today. Much of this progress was aided by seaborne trade and migration that spread people, commerce, knowledge and culture throughout the area.

Sadly, these developments also spurred the rise of large-scale, highly organised and technically complex warfare as the region's history is replete with armed conflict. Not only was this strife common on land, but the Mediterranean Sea became the birthplace of organised naval combat. In 1210 BC a Hittite fleet under the command of King Suppiluliuma II defeated a rival Cypriot fleet off Cypress in what is acknowledged to be the first recorded naval battle in history. It would not be the last as a succession of varying powers vied for control over these coveted waters. Over the next two and a half millennia, scores of similar battles were fought across the length and breadth of the Mediterranean as well as around its many islands and coastal areas. Many of these had decisive results, helping to facilitate the rise or fall of numerous nation states and empires. Many more were less pivotal in their outcomes, but still represented a life-or-death struggle for the participants involved. A common denominator in all was a sea bottom strewn with remnants of sunken ships and the tinging of crimson blood in the otherwise clear blue waters of this contested sea.

While a full accounting of these various engagements is beyond the scope of this text, it is worthwhile to highlight some of the key battles. In 480 BC a Greek fleet under the command of Themistocles defeated a substantially larger Persian fleet under Xerxes the Great off Salamis, thus helping to blunt the ongoing Persian invasion of Greece and saving much of Europe from potential Persian domination. Two centuries later in 260 BC, a Roman fleet commanded by Consul Caius Duilius defeated a similarly sized Carthaginian fleet under Hannibal off Mylae, Sicily, thus signalling the rise of Rome as a naval power. Over the next six decades the Romans won additional victories including at Ecnomus in 256 BC, the Aegates Islands in 241 BC and Ebro River in 217 BC, which eventually solidified Rome's dominance over the central and Western Mediterranean and helped facilitate the demise of Carthage as a regional power. In 190 BC a Roman/Rhodian fleet under Eudamas defeated a Syrian fleet under Polyxenidas at Myonnesus. This battle allowed the Romans to push into Asia Minor and expand their empire eastward while securing Roman dominion over the entire Mediterranean.

Although there would be ongoing challenges, the Romans retained this dominant position for the next six centuries, thus truly transforming the Mediterranean into *Mare Nostrum* (Our Sea). Given this lack of external foes, the Roman's spent part of this period confronting each other as various factions within the ruling elite competed for power and control over the empire. In the 1st century BC this rivalry erupted into open warfare between three competing leaders; Octavian in Rome, Antony in the east and Sextus Pompey in Sicily, Sardinia, Corsica and Achoria. Recognising that whoever controlled the Mediterranean also controlled the empire, much of this fighting took place at sea, and there were a number of notable naval battles fought between the opposing sides. Amongst these were at Cumae in 37 BC and at Mylae and Naulochus in 36 BC that helped secure Octavian's ascendancy over Pompey. Then in 31 BC a western fleet under Octavian decisively defeated an eastern fleet under Anthony and Cleopatra at Actium, Greece. With this victory, Rome reasserted its authority over the entire empire, thus facilitating an age of *Pax Romana* (Roman Peace) that would last for the next 200 years.

The eventual demise of Rome in the 5th century AD saw a return to naval conflict in the Mediterranean as new powers sought to fill the void left behind by the dying regime. What remained of the empire predominantly presided in the east with its capital located in Constantinople. For about 100 years, this eastern (Byzantine) empire maintained a degree of control over the Mediterranean allowing it to reconquer much of the territory lost in the west, but in the 7th century a new threat emerged as an immense army of Muslim Arabs invaded the region from the east. Motivated by a call for holy war, it only took these Arabs a few years to capture most of the Asian and African territories bordering the Mediterranean Sea, and in AD 674 they actually put Constantinople itself under siege. While this siege was eventually lifted in 678, this began a period of reoccurring conflict between Islam and European Christianity that would last for the next 900 years. Beyond this, the period also saw a high degree of internal strife as a variety of new kingdoms and states arose from the ashes of the older orders in Europe to confront each other. Many of these conflicts centred in the Mediterranean where countless battles were fought between the competing sides. Of these, the most significant occurred in 1571 when a large Christian fleet under Don John of Austria defeated a similarly sized Ottoman (Muslim) fleet off Lepanto, Spain. This victory halted Ottoman expansion into the Western Mediterranean and signalled a transition point from which Europe finally began a period of decisive ascendancy over its Muslim rivals.

The battle and period also saw another important change. For roughly 3,000 years, the Mediterranean region had served as the cradle and focal point for western civilization. By the 16th century, this distinction was no longer true as regional power increasingly shifted to the nations of Western and Northern Europe. Part of this transition was due to advancements in maritime technology and the nautical exploration that had brought about the discovery of the Americas and other distant destinations. These events largely reoriented European ambitions outward into the Atlantic and the world beyond, as opposed to inward towards the predominantly landlocked Mediterranean. Soon, the various nations of Western Europe were travelling the world's oceans establishing colonies in distant lands and amassing great wealth for themselves through the exploitation of these colonies as well as through increased global trade. A second factor helping to facilitate this shift was an industrial revolution that occurred in some of these same Western European countries that transformed them into major manufacturing centres and technological leaders. Thus, while history continued in the Mediterranean, it was increasingly overshadowed and affected by events occurring in the greater world.

As if to emphasise this point, a new major competitor in the form of the British Royal Navy soon joined the contest for power and influence in the Mediterranean. In many respects, the inclusion of Britain into this region was an odd development. Unlike the other powers that had vied for control over this region through the ages, the British had no direct land connection to the Mediterranean Sea. Instead, the British homeland was an island located some 600 direct miles away (at the closest point) on the edge of Northwest Europe. Given European geography, Britain's only access to the Mediterranean, short of crossing through France or Spain, was via the sea through the strait of Gibraltar, which was located some 1,200 miles from the nearest British port. Perhaps even more astonishing was the fact that during most of the previous 3,000 years when Mediterranean societies such as the Egyptians, Greeks, Romans and Arabs had controlled vast empires and excelled in technology, architecture and culture, the British Isles were populated by primitive, tribal people barely in the Iron Age. Throughout much of this history, Britain was beset by invaders, including the Romans who occupied part of the island for about 400 years, as well as various Germanic tribes, the Vikings, Danes and Normans. Yet, despite this turmoil, a unified nation eventually emerged starting with England and then later expanding to all of Great Britain (following England's unification with Scotland in 1707) that transformed this seemingly backwater island into a great global power.

The precipitous rise of Britain was largely tied to its success at sea and ability to exercise effective maritime power. Like the nation itself, this maritime prowess had modest origins, but quickly proved to be decisive. One of its first impacts occurred in 1217 when an English fleet of about 40 ships defeated a French force twice its size during the battle of Sandwich, thus helping to end a short-lived French occupation of Southern England. Then in 1337 the upstart English nation went to war with France, a country roughly three times its size in terms of population. Early in this conflict, in 1340, an English fleet won a smashing victory over a larger French fleet off Sluys in Flanders, thus ensuring that the succeeding warfare would be waged on French soil. In the latter half of the 16th century, English privateers routinely attacked Spanish treasure ships and outposts, thus expanding English reach throughout the world's oceans, but antagonizing the powerful Spanish nation. These actions, as well as other provocations, eventually prompted Spain to attempt an invasion of England in 1588. In August of that year an improvised English fleet of about 200 ships under Admiral Lord Howard scored a decisive victory over a Spanish fleet of 130 (mostly larger) ships at Gravelines, thus thwarting this invasion attempt.

At the time of this battle, Spain had been considered the most powerful nation in Europe, and the English victory began a period of prolonged English/British ascendancy while Spain went into a period of concurrent decline. Over the next three centuries, England/Great Britain transformed itself from a small island nation perched on the edge of the European continent to a premier world power with an empire spanning the globe. A number of factors contributed to this transformation, but none was more important than the effective exploitation of sea power to establish and maintain colonies, facilitate trade, fuel economic enterprise and exert national influence. This was no easy task as England, and later Great Britain, engaged in an extensive series of wars against its European competitors, namely Spain, the Netherlands and France. While far from universally successful, the overriding trend throughout these conflicts was one of growing British expansion and ascendancy. In keeping with this, the British won numerous naval victories throughout this period, including at Cadiz in 1596, Portland, Gabbard Bank and Scheveningen in 1653, Santa Cruz in 1657, Lowestoft in 1665, La Hogue in 1692, Vigo Bay in 1702, Cape Finisterre in 1747, Lagos and Quiberon Bay in 1759, Cape St. Vincent in 1780 and the Saints in 1782.

Britain's expansion into the Mediterranean began in the early 1700s during the War of the Spanish Succession. In 1704 an Anglo-Dutch force seized Gibraltar at the entrance to the Mediterranean Sea. Despite a long siege, these British and Dutch forces retained control over Gibraltar for the duration of the war. Part of this success was facilitated by British naval victories at Vélez-Málaga and Cabrita Point in 1704 and 1705 that repelled a French attempt to regain Gibraltar and then broke a French blockade that allowed supplies and reinforcements to arrive at the besieged outpost. At the conclusion of hostilities, Britain attained permanent sovereignty over Gibraltar through the Treaty of Utrecht in 1713. In the succeeding years, Spain engaged in numerous diplomatic and military efforts to regain control over Gibraltar, but the prized territory remained firmly under British administration, thus providing the Royal Navy with an important staging base and access point to the Mediterranean Sea. With this, the British extended their influence deeper into the region, and in 1718 they won their first major fleet action in the central Mediterranean when a force of some 20 British warships under Admiral George Byng engaged and largely destroyed a similarly-sized Spanish squadron off Cape Passero, Sicily. While not all subsequent battles would have the same triumphant result, Britain was now clearly a viable competitor within the region.

From a global perspective, by 1793 Britain had established itself as the world's premier naval power in terms of its size, professionalism and capability, with France a close second and Spain and the Netherlands now relegated to the status of secondary powers. Over the next two decades this position was sorely tested as Britain began a long period of near-continuous warfare against France fuelled by that nation's revolution and subsequent rise of Napoleon. During much of this conflict, Spain and the Netherlands aligned themselves with France, thus producing a combined fleet twice the size of Britain's. Yet, despite this adversity, the British Royal Navy acquitted itself quite well winning a string of stunning victories including off Ushant in 1784, Cape St. Vincent and Camperdown in 1797, Copenhagen in 1801 and Cape Trafalgar in 1805. While most of these battles occurred in the Atlantic, a number of engagements were also fought in the Mediterranean. In terms of the latter, the most important occurred in 1798 when a British squadron under Rear-Admiral Horatio Nelson destroyed a larger French force off Aboukir Bay, Egypt. This victory, which later became known as the battle of the Nile, gained Britain control over the Mediterranean and forced France to abandon its ambitions in Northeast Africa. Two years later, the British scored a less ostentatious, but perhaps more enduring, success when they seized Malta from the French. That same year the British made Malta a protectorate, thus effectively incorporating it into the British Empire and securing for themselves an important naval base in the central Mediterranean.

When the Napoleonic Wars finally ended in 1815 with the Anglo-Prussian victory at Waterloo, Europe went into a period of relative peace and stability that lasted almost a full century. Given this circumstance, the Royal Navy enjoyed a similar respite from hostilities. In fact, during the next 99 years it only participated in one major naval battle, which occurred in 1827 when a combined force of British, French and Russian warships destroyed a larger Ottoman-Egyptian fleet at Navarino Bay in Greece. Devoid of significant European commitments, the Royal Navy turned most of its attention to consolidating, expanding and policing the British Empire while concurrently ensuring freedom of navigation for global British trade. Within this framework, the British also continued expanding their power and influence within the Mediterranean and Middle East. A key success in this occurred in 1875 when the British government attained partial ownership over the recently built Suez Canal. Then in 1882 the British helped suppress the Urabi revolt in Egypt, thus effectively putting themselves in control of the canal. This arrangement was formalised in 1888 when the Convention of Constantinople declared the canal a neutral zone under the protection of Britain. Through this and their retention of Gibraltar, the British now effectively exercised control over both access points to the Mediterranean Sea.

While Britain and much of the rest of the world basked in this period of relative peace, stability and growing prosperity sometimes referred to as Pax Britannica, a new nation emerged in the Mediterranean region. In the millennium and a half since the collapse of the western Roman Empire, the Italian peninsula had devolved into a series of small city states, republics and other independent entities. In the mid-1800s these various elements underwent an arduous, and often violent, unification process that resulted in the creation of the Kingdom of Italy in 1861. Over the next decade this fledgling kingdom expanded further with the annexation of Veneto and the Papal States, thus fully uniting the Italian peninsula under a centralised government located in Rome. Given its size and population, Italy immediately became a major nation within Europe, although it still markedly lagged behind some of its more prosperous contemporaries, namely Great Britain, France and the newly created state of Germany, in terms of its power and influence. Only time would tell how well this new Italian state would fair in the ever-changing vortex of European and global politics.

To this point, by the beginning of the 1900s, political tension and rivalries within Europe threatened to unravel the stability that Pax Britannica had garnered over the previous century. As tensions mounted, the various European nations paired off in differing alliances to counter perceived adversaries. In 1914 war finally erupted and quickly escalated into a conflict of unprecedented proportions that initially pitted the Entente Powers consisting of the British Empire, France and Russia against the Central Powers of the German, Austro-Hungarian and Ottoman Empires. This was primarily a ground war with the naval contribution overwhelmingly focused on supply and blockade operations carried out by the two major naval antagonists, Britain and Germany. In this, there were only a handful of materially significant naval battles, including Heligoland Bight and the Falkland Islands in 1914, Dogger Bank in 1915 and most notably Jutland in 1916. Beyond this, the naval conflict primarily settled upon the execution of submarine and mine warfare. In many respects, this was a gruelling and unspectacular duty, but in the end the Royal Navy and British merchant marine prevailed in all their objectives and performed an essential role in supporting the Entente war effort.

While this colossal conflict was primarily centred in Northern Europe and the Atlantic, the fighting quickly spread to the Mediterranean region. Much of this focused on British efforts to confront the Ottoman Empire, but in 1915 Italy joined the war on the side of the Entente alliance. This action was the result of an agreement (the Treaty of London) signed between the Allied powers and Italy that promised the latter substantial territorial gains after the war. Over the next three years the Italian army fought a series of costly battles along its northern border with Austria, while the Italian navy participated in a blockade against the Austrian-Hungarian fleet in the Adriatic. In this latter regard, there were no major naval battles, but both sides used light units, including submarines, motor torpedo boats and saboteurs to inflict periodic damage against the other. Finally, in the autumn of 1918 the Italian army, with British and French support, scored a decisive victory over the Austrian-Hungarians at Vittorio Veneto. At roughly the same time, the British scored a similar success against the Ottoman Turks in Palestine and Syria. These victories, along with similar triumphs in Western Europe, quickly compelled the Central Powers to sue for peace, thus bringing the war to an abrupt end in November 1918.

As the various nations in Europe emerged from the smoke of this colossal contest, which eventually became known as World War I, many faced immense questions and challenges regarding their future directions. For the victors, Britain and France, little satisfaction was gained from the spoils of war, which now included control over lost German and Ottoman territory in Africa and the Middle East. Instead, both nations emerged from the conflict in a state of immense social and financial exhaustion. The situation was even worse for many other countries as the collapse of the German, Russian, Austro-Hungarian and Ottoman Empires left much of central and Eastern Europe consumed by revolution, civil war and regional strife. Results in Italy were only marginally better as the war had inflicted a substantial cost upon the nation for very little gain. Unlike the British – who gained control over Iraq, Palestine and Jordan – and French – who controlled Lebanon and Syria – the Italians had little to show for their wartime expenditure as the Allies reneged on many of the territorial guarantees made in the Treaty of London. This outcome, plus severe post-war economic conditions, caused great strain and consternation within the Italian government and populace alike.

Nor was this a unique reaction. A common sentiment affecting much of the world during this time was a revulsion against the waste and carnage of World War I, resulting in a widespread pacifistic movement. This, plus severe financial constraints, caused many governments to pursue disarmament and internationalism as a means to supplant war. The primary vehicle for this effort was the League of Nations; an association of nation states created in 1919 to maintain the peace through collective security and conflict arbitration. This period also saw the first attempt at arms control with the adoption of the Five-Power Naval Limitation Treaty, also known as the Washington Treaty, in 1922. The main provision of this treaty set limits on the total capital ship tonnage allowed to each nation, with Britain and the United States each allocated 525,000 tons, Japan allocated 315,000 tons and France and Italy each allocated 175,000 tons. A similar arrangement covered aircraft carriers, with Britain and the United States allotted 135,000 tons compared to 81,000 tons for Japan and 60,000 tons for France and Italy. Germany was not part of this agreement, but was nevertheless restricted to a small, token naval force as a result of the previously signed Treaty of Versailles. Through these and other related actions, the major powers were able to slash their competing defence budgets over the next decade. A prime example of this was Great Britain, which reduced its naval expenditures from £334,091,000 and £154,084,000 in 1918 (the last year of the war) and 1919 to just £50,164,000 in 1932.[1] In keeping with this, the British government adopted a 'ten-year rule' stating there would be no major wars in the next ten years, thus eliminating the need for large standing forces.

Yet, despite these noble intentions and optimistic projections, the facade of internationalism quickly unravelled as new potential adversaries rose in Asia and Europe. As early as 1920 the British government recognised the growing menace

Table 0.1 British Naval Expenditures, Staffing and New Construction between the Wars

Year	Naval expenditures	Average naval staffing	New warships authorised				
			Battleships/ battlecruisers	Aircraft carriers	Cruisers/ minelayers	Destroyers/ escorts	Submarines
1919	£154,084,000	176,087	-	-	-	-	-
1920	£92,505,000	124,009	-	-	-	-	-
1921	£75,896,000	127,180	-	-	-	-	1
1922	£57,492,000	107,782	2	-	1	-	-
1923	£54,064,000	99,107	-	-	-	-	-
1924	£55,694,000	99,453	-	-	5	2	-
1925	£60,005,000	100,284	-	-	4	-	-
1926	£57,143,000	100,791	-	-	3	-	6
1927	£58,123,000	101,916	-	-	1	11	6
1928	£57,139,000	100,680	-	-	-	13	4
1929	£55,988,000	99,300	-	-	1	9	3
1930	£52,274,000	94,921	-	-	3	13	3
1931	£51,015,000	92,449	-	-	3	13	3
1932	£50,164,000	89,667	-	-	3	13	3
1933	£53,444,000	89,863	-	-	3	14	3
1934	£56,616,000	91,351	-	1	4	15	3
1935	£64,888,000	94,259	-	-	3	13	3
1936	£80,976,000	99,886	2	2	7	24	8
1937	£78,259,000	107,040	3	2	7	22	7
1938	£96,396,000	118,167	-	1	10	-	3
1939	£99,429,000	120,000	-	1	3	94	-

Source: Stephen Roskill, *Naval Policy Between the Wars, Volume I: The Period of Anglo-American Antagonism 1919–1929* (New York: Walker and Company, 1968).
Note: The 1939 data only reflects figures accrued prior to the outbreak of the war.

that Japan posed to its Southeast Asian empire. Then in 1922 Benito Mussolini and his Fascist party emerged from the post-war turmoil of Italian politics to assume control over the Italian government. Preaching a form of revolutionary nationalism that envisioned the creation of a new Roman Empire, Mussolini quickly consolidated rule over the nation and then cautiously embarked upon a foreign policy designed to expand Italian power and influence throughout the region. A decade later Adolf Hitler and the Nazis came to power in Germany possessing an even greater aspiration for territorial expansion, along with a depraved view of racial politics. Almost immediately, Hitler began to rearm Germany in defiance of the Treaty of

Versailles. Sadly, the Allied powers of Britain and France failed to decisively respond to these growing threats, although the British did finally begin a belated rearmament programme in 1936. Even in the face of flagrant provocations such as an Italian invasion of Abyssinia (present-day Ethiopia) in 1935, the German occupation of the Rhineland in 1936 and the German annexation of Austria and the Czech Sudetenland in 1938, the Allies took no direct action. Instead, they largely pursued a policy of appeasement in the hope they could moderate the dictators' appetites for expansion. However, in 1939 when Hitler occupied the rest of Czechoslovakia and then made territorial demands against neighbouring Poland, the Allies finally realised the abject futility of further appeasement and made public guarantees to help defend Polish independence. After 21 years of often turbulent peace, Europe again braced itself for war.

In this, they did not have long to wait. On 1 September 1939 Germany launched a full-scale invasion of Poland, thus prompting Britain and France to honour their defensive guarantees and declare war against Germany two days later. Initially, this war was confined to Northern Europe as Mussolini, who had formally allied himself

On the eve of the Mediterranean conflict the British faced a powerful adversary in the form of the Regia Marina (Italian Royal Navy), which possessed some 270 combatant warships and submarines including the battleship *Conte di Cavour* pictured here. (Luigi Rollino, CC BY 2.5 IT, public domain)

with Hitler through the Rome-Berlin Axis Agreement and the subsequent Pact of Steel in 1936 and 1939 respectively, nevertheless chose to remain neutral. Still, many observers speculated that it was only a matter of time before the war migrated south into the Mediterranean region. If this occurred, it would almost assuredly pit the forces of the British Empire against those of the Kingdom of Italy. In this regard, the pending conflict promised to be a clash of competing naval traditions. On one side, there was Britain, the world's reigning maritime power with a heritage of naval success stretching back four centuries. On the other, there was the upstart Italian state, which lacked a recent naval legacy, but could trace its lineage back to the ancient Romans who had once dominated these waters. Only time would tell which tradition prevailed, but two things seemed certain: the timing for this pending conflict rested with Mussolini and, as it had done so many times in the past, the tranquil blue waters of the Mediterranean Sea would once again serve as a contested battleground.

Explanatory Notes

British Forces/Operations

Throughout the text I will often use the term British to describe all British-related forces and operations. This is done for the sake of simplicity and is not meant to undermine or omit the invaluable contributions made by Imperial, Commonwealth and other Allied formations. An exception to this is in discussing specific units or ships, where I will generally identify the nationality involved. When Britain went to war, it did so as the head of a great global empire and Commonwealth of Nations and not simply as the United Kingdom. Accordingly, the subsequent British war effort was a collective enterprise in which Imperial and Commonwealth formations usually comprised a portion (and often a sizable portion) of the British order of battle. Examples of Imperial forces included Indian and East/West African formations while Commonwealth contingents included units and servicemen from Australia, Canada, New Zealand and South Africa. Beyond this, the British also employed elements from the various conquered European nations such as Greece and Poland. Invariably, these foreign elements were incorporated into the British force structure and were armed and supported by the British.

Main vessel categories

- Principal warships – major combat vessels ranging from battleships to fleet minesweepers broken down into 12 class groupings as specified in Chapter 11 of my book *The Longest Campaign, Britain's Maritime Struggle in the Atlantic and Northwest Europe, 1939–1945*. With the exception of certain aircraft carriers, these were purpose-built warships and not conversions from civilian vessels. A brief synopsis is presented here:

    - <u>Battleships and battlecruisers</u>. Displacing between 22,000 and 42,000 tons and possessing a primary armament ranging from 11- to 16-inch guns.
    - <u>Pocket battleships, pre-dreadnought battleships, armoured cruisers and monitors</u>. Large-gunned warships that existed outside the

parameters of the standard battleship/battlecruiser displacing between 7,200 and 13,200 tons and armed with 10- to 15-inch guns.

o Fleet aircraft carriers. Displacing between 11,000 and 36,000 tons and carrying between 20 and 80 aircraft.

o Escort carriers. Displacing between 7,800 and 18,000 tons and carrying between 10 and 30 aircraft.

o Heavy cruisers. Displacing between 8,000 and 14,000 tons and typically armed with 8-inch guns.

o Light cruisers and anti-aircraft cruisers. Displacing between 3,000 and 11,000 tons and usually possessing a main armament consisting of 5- to 6-inch guns.

o Destroyers and large-class torpedo boats. Displacing between 900 and 2,600 tons and possessing a main armament of 4.1- to 5.9-inch guns.

o Escort destroyers, small-class torpedo boats and general-purpose escorts. Displacing between 600 and 2,000 tons and possessing a main armament consisting of 3.9- to 5-inch guns.

o Corvettes, cutters and large-class sub-chasers. Displacing between 600 and 1,000 tons and armed with 3.9- to 4-inch guns.

o Submarines. The standard size of most Second World War-era submarines was between 600 and 1,600 tons, but there were classes that were smaller or larger, thus producing an overall range of between 150 and 2,600 tons.

o Minelayers. Displacing between 450 and 2,600 tons and armed with 3- to 5.5-inch guns.

o Fleet minesweepers. Displacing between 500 and 900 tons and armed with 3- to 4.7-inch guns.

• Merchant/commercial vessels – civilian vessels used for trade or other commercial purposes such as fishing.

• Minor warships/auxiliaries – small, coastal combatants of less than 500 tons (such as motor torpedo boats or MAS boats), military support vessels and commercial vessels adopted/converted to perform military tasks.

Vessel sizes

The two primary means used to delineate vessel size are displacement and gross registered tonnage. Displacement refers to a vessel's actual weight as measured by the amount of water it displaces when afloat. Gross registered tonnage refers to a ship's internal volume measured as one ton equalling 100 cubic feet of capacity. In both cases, the resulting measurement is expressed in tons. All principal warship tonnage is an expression of displacement while that for merchant/commercial vessels is a calculation of gross registered tonnage. Minor warships and auxiliaries can reflect either. Finally, submarine displacement can be measured both surfaced and submerged. Unless otherwise specified, submarine tonnage reflects surface displacement.

Armament

- Other than light weapons, the size of most naval guns is expressed in inches reflecting the interior diameter of the barrel.
- Torpedoes are similarly measured in inches reflecting the diameter of the torpedo.
- Main armaments are expressed as guns for surface warships (reflecting the largest guns carried), torpedo tubes (TT) for submarines and aircraft capacity for aircraft carriers.
- At times in the text, I will list the tonnage and main armament for certain vessels in the following manner: *Giovanni Berta* (644 tons, 2 × 3-inch guns).
- Aircraft bomb loads are expressed in pounds.

Loss presentation

Loss tallies are often presented showing the number of vessels lost and their corresponding tonnage. In terms of merchant/commercial vessels, these tonnage figures reflect gross registered tons. However, in the case of military vessels, tonnage figures can be a combination of both displacement and gross registered tons based upon the vessel types involved. While mixing these calculation methods is not ideal, I found it to be the most practical way to present the information reflecting the primary source data.

Loss calculation

A number of parameters are used in determining vessel losses and assigning credit for these losses.

- Losses are only attributed to vessels that were a total loss to the losing participant. This breaks down into two categories:

    ○ Vessels that were sunk, destroyed or irretrievably damaged as a result of military action, scuttling or non-combat related causes. Vessels that were sunk in shallow water, but subsequently raised, repaired and put back into service are not included in this category.
    ○ Vessels that were captured during the course of the war or surrendered at the conclusion of hostilities.

- Sole British Successes consist of all Axis vessels that were lost solely or overwhelmingly as a result of British action. This includes vessels that were crippled or put out of action by British forces and subsequently scuttled. It also includes Axis ships that were scuttled to avoid action with British forces or seized by force of arms.
- Partial British Successes consist of Axis vessels that were lost due to the activities of British forces in conjunction with other Allied forces. This includes vessels that were lost as a result of direct, collaborative action as well as those lost through more indirect means such as scuttling to avoid capture by Allied forces or surrender at the end of hostilities.
- British Forces are defined as all military forces (naval, air and ground) affiliated with the United Kingdom, the British Empire and the British Commonwealth. This includes Allied forces operating British vessels and equipment within the British force structure, but does not include American, Free French or other Allied forces operating their own equipment in affiliation with the British.

Maps

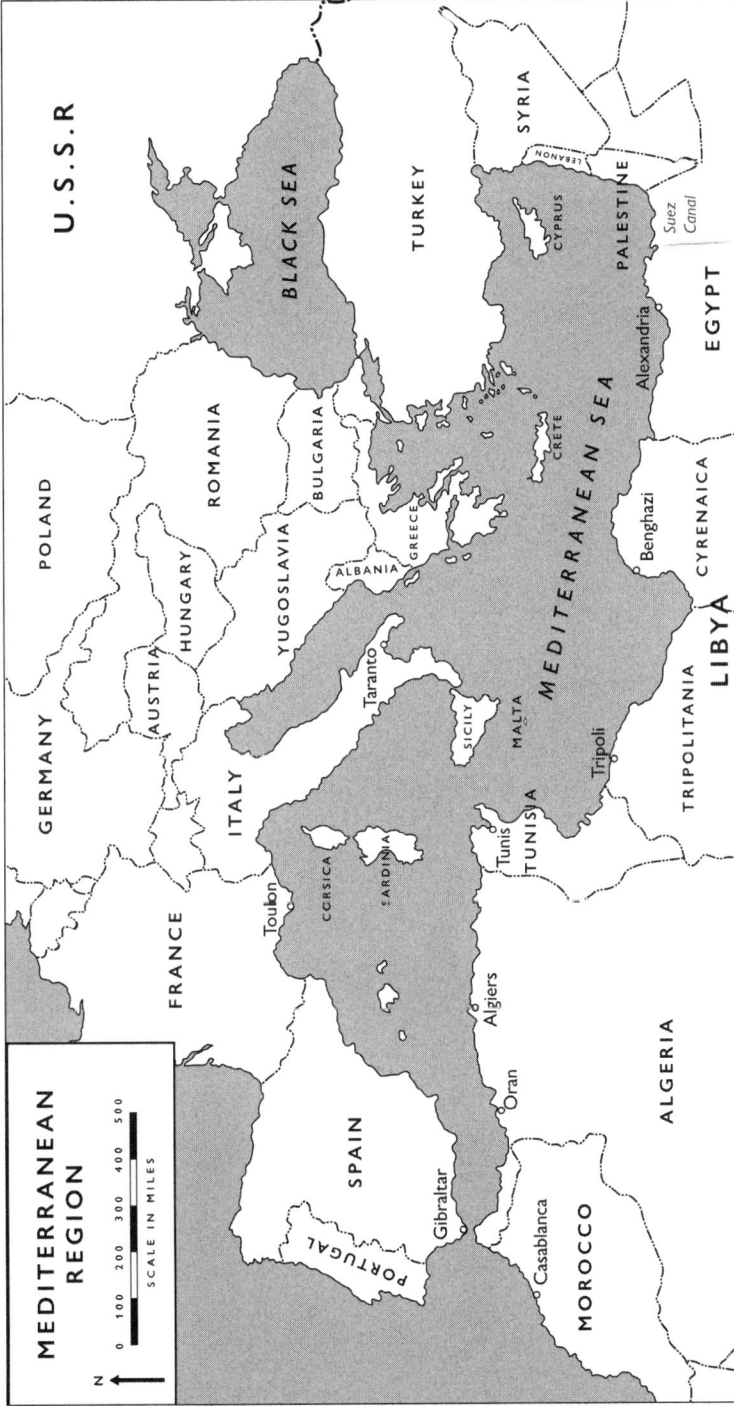

MEDITERRANEAN REGION

SCALE IN MILES
0 100 200 300 400 500

U.S.S.R

POLAND

GERMANY

FRANCE

ROMANIA

HUNGARY

AUSTRIA

YUGOSLAVIA

BULGARIA

ALBANIA

BLACK SEA

TURKEY

SYRIA

LEBANON

CYPRUS

PALESTINE

Suez Canal

EGYPT

ITALY

GREECE

CRETE

Alexandria

MEDITERRANEAN SEA

Benghazi

CYRENAICA

LIBYA

Taranto

SICILY

MALTA

Tripoli

TRIPOLITANIA

Toulon

CORSICA

SARDINIA

Tunis

TUNISIA

SPAIN

PORTUGAL

Gibraltar

Oran

Algiers

Casablanca

MOROCCO

ALGERIA

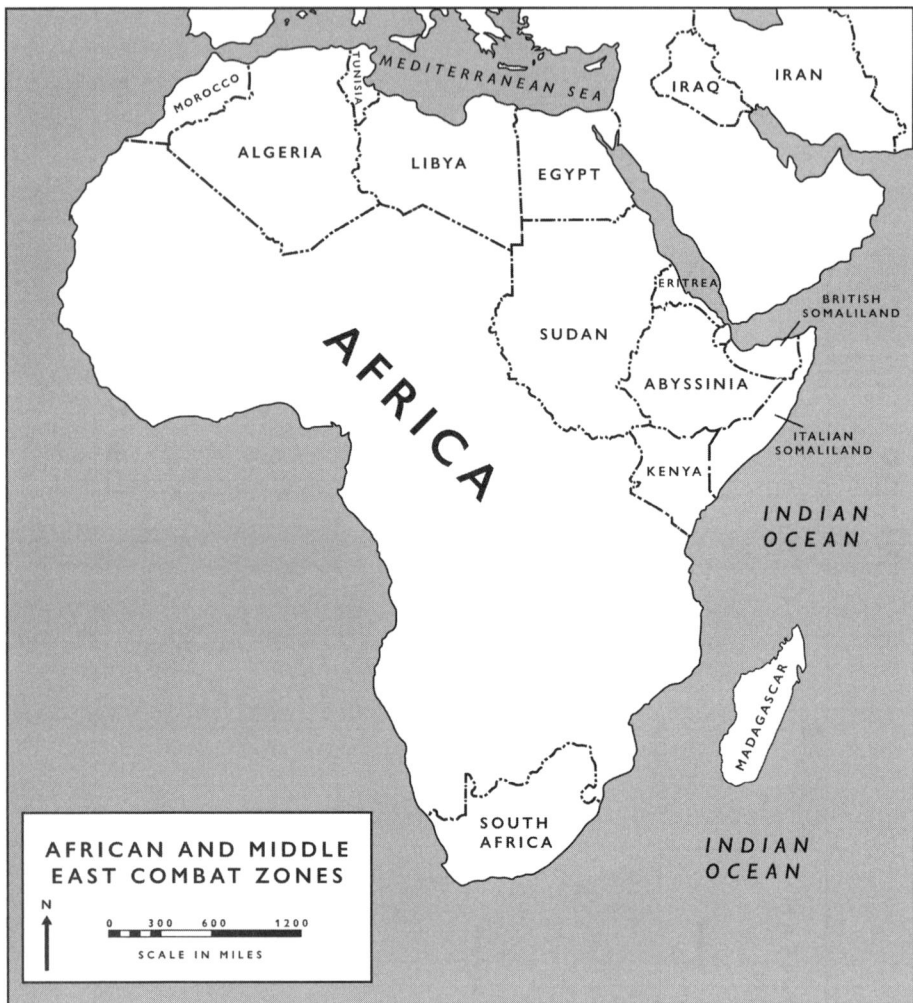

AFRICAN AND MIDDLE
EAST COMBAT ZONES

N

0   300   600   1200

SCALE IN MILES

Salonika

GREECE

TURKEY

AEGEAN SEA

Piraeus
Athens

Leros

Kos

Rhodes

MEDITERRANEAN
SEA

CRETE

EASTERN MEDITERRANEAN
FEATURING GREECE AND THE
NORTH AFRICAN BATTLE REGION

N

0   35   70   105   140   175

SCALE IN MILES

Benghazi

Tobruk

Bardia

Sidi Barrani

Alexandria

Sollum

Mersa Matruh

El Alamein

LIBYA

EGYPT

El Agheila

Trieste

Venice

Fiume

YUGOSLAVIA

Genoa

La Spezia

LIGURIAN
SEA

ITALY

ADRIATIC SEA

CORSICA

Rome

Anzio

Naples

Salerno

Taranto

SARDINIA

TYRRHENIAN SEA

Palermo

Messina

SICILY

Syracuse

Bizerte

PANTELLARIA

Tunis

MALTA

TUNISIA

LAMPEDUSA

ITALY AND
SURROUNDING WATERS

N

30   0   30   60   90

SCALE IN MILES

Tripoli

LIBYA

CHAPTER I

Setting the Stage

When Italian dictator Benito Mussolini opportunistically declared war against Britain and France on 10 June 1940, the timing could not have been worse from a British point of view. Nine months earlier Britain had reluctantly entered into armed conflict against Nazi Germany to counter that nation's expansionist policies. At the time, British officials had scant enthusiasm for the undertaking, but they could take solace in three bulwarks to help defend their island nation. The first of these was geography, as the nations of France, Belgium and the Netherlands provided a physical barrier between Britain and Germany. The second was Britain's alliance with France and the presence of the French army, which was arguably the most powerful army in Europe. The last was the Royal Navy, which despite two decades of shameful neglect and downsizing, still constituted the largest navy in the world, far exceeding that of its German rival, the Kriegsmarine. Unfortunately for the British, by the time Mussolini delivered his wartime declaration to an enthusiastic crowd in Rome's Piazza Venezia, two of these bulwarks had largely disintegrated while the third was under great duress. In terms of the former, by the middle of June the Netherlands and Belgium had already fallen while France was destined for a similar fate in just a matter of days. This calamity was the result of a month-long campaign in which the Germans had roundly defeated the combined strength of the French, Belgian and Dutch armies while compelling the British Expeditionary Force to conduct a seaborne evacuation from northern France. In the process of doing so, and in conjunction with concurrent operations underway in Norway, the Germans had inflicted heavy losses upon the Royal Navy, including 28 principal warships sunk and dozens more damaged to varying degrees.[1]

The surrender of France, which officially occurred on 22 June 1940, put the British in a highly precarious situation. Britain had entered the war as part of an alliance confronting a single adversary. Now with the events just described, Britain abruptly found itself devoid of European allies and facing two powerful assailants. Making matters worse, Italy's entry into the conflict meant that Britain now faced the prospect of a two-front war with one front focused in Northwest Europe and the Atlantic while the other centred in the Mediterranean and Middle East. Of these two fronts, the former was by far the most important, thus promising to be a priority for available resources. This was true because for the first time in 135 years, Britain faced the very real threat of invasion and conquest. Against a German enemy that possessed some 160 divisions and over 3,000 combat aircraft in its order of battle, the British could only muster 29 understrength and ill-equipped divisions and a few hundred fighter aircraft to defend their island nation. Fortunately, the situation was much better for the Royal Navy, but given its recent heavy losses and unrelenting requirements to defend British seaborne commerce in order to sustain the nation's long-term viability, even this force found itself hard pressed to meet its many obligations.

Given this reality, British forces in the Mediterranean and Middle East understood they were largely on their own and would have to make do with what they had for the immediate future. This constituted a perilous situation as a review of the competing forces within the theatre clearly put the British at a distinct numerical disadvantage. Starting first with the navy, on the eve of Mussolini's wartime declaration, British naval forces in the Mediterranean consisted of the battleships *Warspite*, *Malaya*, *Royal Sovereign* and *Ramillies*; the aircraft carrier *Eagle*; nine light cruisers; 21 destroyers and six submarines. By comparison, the Regia Marina (Italian Royal Navy) boasted a strength of six battleships, one old armoured cruiser, seven heavy cruisers, 12 light cruisers, 61 destroyers, 69 torpedo boats and 115 submarines either on hand or nearing completion.[2] The vast bulk of this sizable Italian fleet was located in the Mediterranean with the only exception being a squadron of seven destroyers, two torpedo boats and eight submarines stationed in the Red Sea. Thus, the Regia Marina outnumbered the British Mediterranean Fleet in every warship category other than aircraft carriers, and in some cases this numerical advantage was substantial. Of course, the British could always send additional reinforcements into the Mediterranean, but given the situation already described; these reinforcements were likely to be limited.

Nor was this numerical imbalance unique to the navy. Both the Italian army and the Regia Aeronautica (Italian Royal Air Force) significantly outnumbered their British counterparts in the region. In terms of the former, the Italian army entered the conflict with a nominal strength of more than 1.6 million men spread between 73 divisions and several lesser units. Added to this were a further 300,000 men in various 'Blackshirt' militia formations.[3] Of the forces most directly confronting the British, the Italians possessed some 250,000 men in Libya, of which the bulk were organised into two field armies consisting of 14 divisions. The situation was much the same in the East African colonies of Eritrea, Abyssinia and Italian Somaliland, where the Italians maintained a total military force of some 290,000 men.[4] Although not as well equipped as their German counterparts, these African-deployed units possessed several hundred tanks and armoured vehicles and upwards of 2,000 assorted

At the beginning of the Mediterranean conflict the Regia Marina outnumbered the British Mediterranean Fleet in most warship categories. Likewise, many of the available British ships were older and less capable than their Italian counterparts. Pictured here are the aircraft carrier *Eagle* and battleship *Malaya*, which both saw service in the early Mediterranean Fleet. (Marshall, J. G. (Lt), Royal Navy official photographer, public domain)

artillery pieces. Against this human and materiel threat, the British could only muster some 36,000 troops in Egypt, 27,500 troops in Palestine and about 20,000 miscellaneous military and security personnel in Sudan, Kenya, British Somaliland and Aden.[5] For the most part, these British formations were only partially equipped and/or lacked proper training and organisation for modern warfare. Likewise, sizable portions of these forces were required to perform internal security duties and were spread across vast expanses of territory, making them less accessible to counter massed Italian incursions.

In regards to the balance of air strength, the situation was equally bleak. At the onset of hostilities, the Regia Aeronautica possessed 313 aircraft in Libya and the Dodecanese and 325 aircraft in East Africa.[6] The Italians further possessed over a thousand aircraft stationed in Italy, Sicily and Southern Europe that were available to intervene in the Mediterranean or reinforce operations in Africa if called upon to do so. Together, this constituted a front-line strength of 1,753 aircraft.[7] Likewise, as additional aircraft were produced by Italian industry, they could also be injected into the conflict with little difficulty. The British countered this with only 205 aircraft in Egypt and Palestine and 163 aircraft in Sudan, Aden and Kenya.[8] This small force comprised at least 15 different aircraft types, of which most were obsolete designs ill-suited for modern combat operations. Beyond this, it would take considerable effort to deliver additional aircraft into the theatre, assuming any were available to be sent. The British also suffered from a territorial disadvantage that put many key British bases and logistical centres within range of local Italian airfields, while their own airfields were ill positioned to strike back against crucial Italian power bases in Italy or their primary African port of Tripoli.

Fortunately for the British, these many numerical and circumstantial weaknesses were counterbalanced by numerous shortcomings on the Italian side, as all three branches of the Italian military suffered varying degrees of technical and operational deficiencies. These problems were least prevalent in the Regia Marina, but even this service possessed its share of proficiency issues. On the positive side, many Italian warship classes were generally equivalent, and in some cases superior, to their British counterparts in terms of basic design and construction. However, when it came to higher level technologies, such as radar, Asdic (sonar) and range-finding equipment, the Italians were in a significantly inferior position. Likewise, standards of Italian gunnery and night fighting proficiency markedly lagged behind that of the Royal Navy. The Regia Marina also suffered from a lack of aircraft carriers or an internal air arm. Even though most of the Mediterranean was within range of shore-based aircraft, poor cooperation between the air force and navy often resulted in inadequate air coverage for fleet defence, reconnaissance and strike functions. The Italians were also constrained by limited oil stocks that threatened to restrict fleet operations if the conflict became protracted. The same held true for Italy's weak industrial base, which was ill prepared to meet the rigors of a long war in terms of materiel support, new ship construction and naval repairs.

Complicating these materiel deficiencies, the Regia Marina lacked the same degree of professionalism, technical competence and aggressive spirit more prevalently found in the Royal Navy. A number of factors contributed to this reality. First, the Italians recruited their officers and seaman from a population far less affiliated with seafaring and technology than their British counterparts. Likewise, unlike Britain, which enjoyed a long and proud naval tradition, Italy possessed a far less abundant naval heritage. In its recent history, the Regia Marina had only engaged in one noteworthy naval battle, which occurred in 1866 off Lissa during a short-run war against the Austrian-Hungarian Empire. The Italians lost this battle. By comparison, the Royal Navy had a 400-year history of triumph and expansion that gave the British a sense of pride, confidence and professional expectation. Similarly, despite Mussolini's many machinations about transforming Italy into a second Roman Empire, it was unclear how many of his countrymen embraced the martial qualities of their distant ancestors. Instead, a sizable portion of the Italian population held ambivalent or even hostile attitudes about the war. Inevitably, these attitudes permeated much of the military. While this mentality was far less prevalent in the Regia Marina than in the army, it still had the potential to be a negative drag on morale and motivation.

When coupled with its technical and structural shortfalls, these cultural and personnel deficiencies portended to impede the Regia Marinas' performance in the upcoming conflict. While individual crews from various ships and units were certainly capable of displaying great bravery and skill, it was unclear to what degree the Regia Marina as a whole would be able to emulate these same qualities. One manifestation of this was the adoption of a defensive mentality on both the strategic and operational level that might dissuade Italian commanders from seizing or pressing the initiative. This lack of aggressiveness was further exacerbated by an absence of an overall strategic plan as opportunism and blind ambition had driven many of Mussolini's earlier decisions without benefit of a coordinated strategy. In fact, Italy's top military leaders had advised against going to war and were thus surprised when Mussolini decided to do so. This impetuousness would remain a factor as the war progressed. While these combined factors did not preclude the likelihood of Italian success given their great numerical and geographical advantages, they did bring a greater degree of parity to the competing sides than one might have initially surmised.

Turning now to the surface fleet, the Italians possessed a battle line consisting of six capital ships with two others in the early stages of construction. Four of these were vintage vessels of the *Cavour* and *Andrea Doria* classes that dated back to World War I. These veteran warships were smaller, possessed less armour protection and were less heavily armed than their contemporary British counterparts. On the other hand, both classes had undergone extensive modernisation during the inter-war years and were thus capable of speeds exceeding that of most British capital ships. Likewise, despite their smaller calibre guns, the *Cavours* and *Andrea Dorias* were actually capable of out-ranging many of the less modernised British battleships. Of course, this latter advantage was only useful under conditions of good visibility and proficient fire control. The remaining ships of the Italian capital fleet were the new battleships of the *Littorio*-class. These exceptional warships displaced over 40,000 tons, were armed with nine 15-inch guns and were capable of speeds approaching 30 knots. As such, the *Littorios* held the enviable position of being able to outfight or outrun every capital ship in the British inventory.

Filling out the bulk of the Italian surface fleet were a variety of cruisers, destroyers and escort vessels. Paramount amongst these were three classes of heavy cruisers that displaced between 10,000 and 12,000 tons and sported eight 8-inch guns. The Italians also possessed a single armoured cruiser that was employed as a coastal defence vessel and was armed with four 10-inch and eight 7.5-inch guns. Augmenting these powerful warships were a number of light cruisers, including the venerable Condottiersi-class, which were reputed to be the fastest cruisers in the world. However, these speeds were only achieved through the use of unrealistic trial conditions and by sacrificing armour protection. Likewise, by the summer of 1940, years of service had taken their toll on these vessels, thus reducing their actual speeds to levels comparable with other cruiser classes. This was not the case with a new

Capitani Romani-class of ultra-light cruisers, which were under early construction and were truly capable of speeds in excess of 40 knots.

In terms of lesser vessels, the Regia Marina possessed a number of destroyer and escort classes that were generally comparable in size, armament and capability to their British counterparts. These Italian destroyers came in a number of classes, ranging from 970 tons on the low end to upwards of 2,000 tons for the larger variants, and typically possessed a main armament consisting of 4.7-inch guns. Beyond this, the Italians also maintained a number of torpedo boat classes that were essentially small, destroyer-type warships displacing between 600 and 900 tons and armed with 3.9- or 4-inch guns as well as torpedo tubes (as the name would suggest). Although ill-suited for largescale fleet operations, these torpedo boats were well suited to serve as escort vessels and coastal attack craft in the confined waters of the Mediterranean. Germany, France and Japan also used torpedo boats as a designation for small, destroyer-type warships, but this classification was not used in the Royal Navy or the United States Navy.[9]

Table 1.1 Characteristics of Selected Italian Surface Warships

	Tonnage	Main armament (guns) (in)	Maximum speed (knots)
Cavour-class battleships	25,902	10 × 12.6	28
Andrea Doria-class battleships	26,100	10 × 12.6	27
Littorio-class Battleships	40,700	9 × 15	30
San Giorgio-class armoured cruiser*	9,470	4 × 10	22
Trento-class heavy cruisers	10,340	8 × 8	35
Zara-class heavy cruisers	11,327–11,713	8 × 8	32
Condottieri-class light cruisers**	5,109–9,441	8–10 × 6	34–37***
Capitani Romani-class light cruisers	3,686	8 × 5.3	40
Sauro-class destroyers	1,058	4 × 4.7	35
Navigatori-class destroyers	1,913	6 × 4.7	38
Soldati-class destroyers	1,620–1,830	4 × 4.7	38
Palestro-class torpedo boats	862	4 × 4	27
Spica-class torpedo boats	620–670	3 × 3.9	34

Note: Covers all classes of Italian battleships but only covers selected cruiser and destroyer-type classes.
* San Giorgio was in use as a coastal defence vessel at the opening of hostilities.
** The Condottieris were built in five groups, thus accounting for the wide range in tonnage, armament and speed.
*** The Condottieris attained speeds in excess of 40 knots during trials, but were incapable of reproducing this level of performance under operational conditions.

Supporting this formidable surface fleet was the world's largest combatant submarine force, which in the summer of 1940 was twice the size of the concurrent German U-boat arm. However, despite its immense numbers, the Italian submarine fleet was plagued by qualitative and operational deficiencies that significantly reduced its overall effectiveness. First, the Italians tended to build large and ungainly boats that were slow in diving and had cumbersome underwater performance. In terms of the former, Italian submarines often took two or three times longer to execute dives than their German counterparts. This tendency could easily prove fatal when encountering patrolling aircraft or escort vessels. Likewise, the oversized conning towers on many Italian submarines made them more susceptible to visual or radar detection. Italian submarines also lacked sophisticated detection and fire control equipment. This latter problem was made worse by faulty doctrine that called for Italian submarines to operate individually, remain submerged during the day and wait for targets to come to them. Finally, many Italian submarines suffered from insufficient ventilation that hindered functionality in the often-sweltering climates of the Mediterranean and Red Sea. For that matter, the Mediterranean was not a particularly conducive area for submarine operations. Unlike the North Atlantic, with its grey and murky water, many locations in the Mediterranean featured clear blue water that rendered shallow submerged submarines visible to overhead aircraft. Of course, both sides were susceptible to this condition, but the large and unwieldy boats of the Regia Marina were particularly vulnerable to this phenomenon.

Of the sizable number of submarines available to the Regia Marina during the summer of 1940, the most modern came from the *Marcello*, *Brin*, *Liuzzi* and *Marconi* classes. These were large, ocean-going boats that all possessed a surface displacement of 1,000 tons or greater and were armed with eight 21-inch torpedo tubes and one or two 3.9-inch deck guns. An even larger submarine, the *Cagni*-class, was under construction and would attain operational status during the first half of 1941. With a surface displacement of 1,654 tons and a main armament consisting of 14 17.7-inch torpedo tubes and two 3.9-inch deck guns, these *Cagni*-class boats were designed to perform extended anti-commerce patrolling in the waters outside of the Mediterranean. In terms of smaller variants, the Italians also possessed a series of coastal submarines of which the *Perla* and *Adua* classes were the newest and most prevalent. These boats displaced between 680 and 687 tons (surfaced) and were armed with six 21-inch torpedo tubes and a single 3.9-inch deck gun.

At this time, it is also useful to briefly describe the technical limitations universal to all submarines during this era. A more accurate name to describe these early submarines was submersibles, since they were only capable of operating submerged for short periods of time. This was due to their limited battery capacity that powered their electric motors for underwater propulsion and their inability to regenerate breathable air. Likewise, while submerged operations provided submarines with stealth, this came at a heavy cost, including reduced handling and speed performance, severely restricted visibility and an inability to transmit and receive radio communications. As such, submarines spent much of their time operating on the surface using diesel engines for power and propulsion. These same diesel engines recharged the batteries used for underwater operations.

Turning now to the Royal Navy, the bulk of Britain's battle line consisted of the *Queen Elizabeth*- and *Royal Sovereign*-class battleships. Armed with eight 15-inch guns, these vessels were the most powerful ships afloat in their day, but that had been 22 years earlier. Now, at the onset of the Mediterranean conflict, more modern designs surpassed these veteran warships. Nevertheless, despite their age, these were well-tested fighting ships still capable of providing much valued service. This was particularly true of *Warspite*, *Valiant*, *Queen Elizabeth*, *Barham* and *Malaya*, which had all undergone extensive or partial modernisation. Britain's two most modern battleships, *Nelson* and *Rodney*, had been completed in 1927. These ships were heavily armed with nine 16-inch guns and possessed good armour protection. However, British designers had compromised speed and some ship handling characteristics in order to attain these attributes while still complying with the tonnage limitations set forth in the 1922 Washington Treaty. Closing out the battle line, the British had five *King George V*-class battleships under construction. These were stoutly designed ships with excellent armour protection and reasonably good speed. Less advantageous was the ships' main armament of ten 14-inch guns mounted in two quadruple and one twin gun turrets. Although capable of outranging their un-modernised counterparts, the shells fired from these 14-inch guns were lighter and less destructive than comparable 15- and 16-inch shells, and the class's quadruple gun turrets were initially prone to technical problems. Eventually, the British would resolve many of these reliability issues, but this would take time. Still, despite their armament deficiencies, the *King George V*-class was a welcome addition to the Royal Navy, and the first of these new warships was only a few months away from commissioning.

The British augmented their battleship force with three battlecruisers. Of these, *Hood* was the largest and most redoubtable, displacing some 42,100 tons and armed with eight 15-inch guns. Capable of speeds in excess of 30 knots, *Hood* was arguably the world's most powerful warship and enjoyed the status of being the pride of the Royal Navy. However, despite its imposing size and graceful lines, *Hood* possessed a dangerous deficiency. In order to attain its impressive speed, British designers had sacrificed armour protection. Accordingly, *Hood* was susceptible to enemy fire and was particularly vulnerable to high angle plunging shot. The remaining battlecruisers, *Renown* and *Repulse*, were capable of similar speeds, but only possessed three-quarters of *Hood*'s tonnage. Likewise, these latter battlecruisers were less heavily armed with a main armament consisting of only six 15-inch guns, and both vessels had similar deficiencies in armour protection as their larger counterpart. Of the three battlecruisers, only *Renown* had received significant modernisation during the inter-war years when it was extensively rebuilt from the hull up.

Beyond these capital ships, the British possessed several cruiser and destroyer classes. In terms of the former, the *Leander*-class was particularly prevalent in the Mediterranean during the early stages of the war. Built in the early 1930s, the *Leanders* displaced between 6,980 and 7,270 tons and had a main armament of eight 6-inch guns. Augmenting this was the newer Town-class, which displaced between 9,100 and 10,000 tons and had a main armament of 12 6-inch guns. Following this was the Colony-class, which maintained the same armament as the 'Towns' but had a reduced displacement of only 8,800 tons. Finally, the British had a new cruiser type under construction called the *Dido*-class. These were smaller cruisers primarily designed for an air defence role. They displaced between 5,450 and 5,770 tons and were armed with eight or ten 5.25-inch dual purpose guns.[10] As for destroyers, the British had no fewer than 17 different classes of these indispensable vessels at the beginning of the war, with additional classes under development. At the larger end of this spectrum were the Tribal, *Javelin*, *Kelly* and *Laforey* classes, which ranged in size from 1,690 to 1,920 tons and carried six to eight 4.7-inch guns and four to ten 21-inch torpedo tubes. On the other end of the spectrum were the new Hunt-class

Table 1.2 Characteristics of Selected British Warships

	Tonnage	Main armament (guns) (in)	Maximum speed (knots)
Queen Elizabeth-class battleships	30,600–32,700	8 × 15	24
Royal Sovereign-class battleships	29,150	8 × 15	21.5
Nelson-class battleships	33,900	9 × 16	23
King George V-class battleships	36,700	10 × 14	28.5
Hood-class battlecruiser	42,100	8 × 15	31
Renown-class battlecruisers	32,000	6 × 15	29
County-class heavy cruisers	9,750–10,000	8 × 8	31–32
Leander-class light cruisers	6,980–7,270	8 × 6	32.5
Town-class light cruisers	9,100–10,000	12 × 6	32
Colony-class light cruisers	8,800	12 × 6	33
Dido-class light cruisers	5,450–5,770	8–10 × 5.25	33
Tribal-class destroyers	1,870	8 × 4.7	36
Javelin-class destroyers	1,690	6 × 4.7	36
Laforey-class destroyers	1,920	6 × 4.7	36
Hunt-class escort destroyers	907–1,050	4–6 × 4	27

Note: Covers all classes of battleships/battlecruisers but only covers selected cruiser and destroyer-type classes.

escort destroyers, which were just beginning to enter service. Displacing between 907 and 1,050 tons and possessing a main armament of four or six 4-inch guns, the 'Hunts' were well suited to perform coastal operations and convoy defence roles in the limited confines of the Mediterranean.

In terms of submarines, the British had 12 different classes at the beginning of the war, but like their Italian counterparts, most (such as the recently produced T-class) were too large to ideally operate in the clear waters of the Mediterranean. An exception to this was the S-class, which was produced in three different groupings (and two subgroupings) ranging in size from 737 to 842 tons. Armed with six or seven 21-inch torpedo tubes and a 3- or 4-inch deck gun (depending upon the grouping), these S-class boats enjoyed a sturdy design with reasonable handling characteristics and a quick diving interval. A follow-up class of even smaller submarines, the U-class, was under construction at the time. Possessing a surface displacement of just 646 tons and usually only possessing four 21-inch torpedo tubes along with a 3-inch deck gun, these U-class boats lacked range (which was not a major impediment in the Mediterranean) and armament, but compensated for this with stealth and a reliable design that was easily maintained. A final submarine type worth noting was the 1,810-ton *Grampus*-class. These boats were specially designed for mine-laying and could carry 50 mines as well as six 21-inch torpedo tubes and one 4-inch deck gun.

The one category of warship in which the British had complete dominance over the Italians was the aircraft carrier. At the onset of the Mediterranean war, the British had six of these valuable warships on hand with six more under construction.

Table 1.3 Characteristics of Selected Axis and British Submarines

	Displacement (tons) surf/subm	Speed (knots) surf/subm	Main armament
Axis			
Adua-class	680/844	14.0/7.5	6 × 21in TT, 1 × 3.9in gun
Brin-class	1,000/1,246	17.3/8.0	8 × 21in TT, 1 × 3.9in gun
Marconi-class	1,176/1,466	17.8/8.2	8 × 21in TT, 1 × 3.9in gun
Cagni-class	1,654/2,136	17.0/8.5	14 × 17.7in TT, 2 × 3.9in guns
Type VIIC (German)	749/851	17.7/7.6	5 × 21in TT, 1 × 3.5in gun
British			
T-class	1,326/1,575	15.3/9.0	10 × 21in TT, 1 × 4in gun
S-class (2nd group)	768/960	13.8/10.0	6 × 21in TT, 1 × 3in gun
U-class	646/732	11.3/10.0	4 × 21in TT, 1 × 3in gun
Grampus-class	1,810/2,157	15.8/8.8	6 × 21in TT, 1 × 4in gun

However, only one of these, *Eagle*, was actually present in the Mediterranean at the time. Displacing 22,600 tons, *Eagle* was capable of carrying 21 aircraft, but only had a complement of 18 aircraft currently available for use. Of the remaining carriers, *Ark Royal* was arguably the most capable with a maximum speed of 31 knots and the ability to operate over 60 aircraft. *Furious*, *Hermes* and *Argus* had smaller aircraft capacities, with the latter two being ill-suited for anything other than trade protection and ferrying duties. The newest carrier in Britain's inventory was *Illustrious*, which had just entered service the month before. This was the first of four *Illustrious-* and two *Implacable*-class aircraft carriers under construction. These vessels featured an armoured flight deck that afforded them a great deal of protection while still maintaining a maximum operating capacity of between 55 (*Illustrious*) and 81 (*Implacable*) aircraft. The British had a final carrier-type vessel, *Unicorn*, under construction. Technically, *Unicorn* was designed to be an aircraft repair ship, but with its flight deck and capacity to carry 35 aircraft, it could be used as a conventional carrier if needed.

A similar warship class, which was not currently in use or under construction, but would eventually see service in the Mediterranean was the escort carrier. Essentially, escort carriers were small aircraft carriers built along modified commercial designs. Generally displacing between 7,800 and 11,800 tons depending upon the class, these escort carriers could accommodate up to 28 aircraft, although British variants usually only operated about half this number when on tactical operations. The first escort carriers would not become available for Mediterranean service until the closing months of 1942, but thereafter these versatile warships would perform a number of useful functions including aerial defence, anti-submarine patrolling, offensive strikes, naval gunfire spotting and aircraft ferrying activities. Eventually, these escort carriers

Table 1.4 Characteristics of British Aircraft Carriers

	Tonnage	Normal aircraft capacity	Main defensive armament	Maximum speed (knots)
Ark Royal-class	22,000	60	16 × 4.5in guns	31
Furious-class	22,450	36	12 × 4in guns	30
Eagle-class	22,600	21	9 × 6in guns	24
Hermes-class	10,850	15	6 × 5.5in guns	25
Argus-class	14,000	15	light AA guns	20
Illustrious-class (building)	23,000	55	16 × 4.5in guns	30.5
Implacable-class (building)	23,450	81	16 × 4.5in guns	32
Unicorn-class (building)	14,750	35	8 × 4in guns	24

Note: The *Illustrious* and *Implacable* classes only had design hanger capacities for 36 and 48 aircraft respectively, but were able to expand this to 55 and 81 aircraft using deck parking arrangements.

would exist in far greater numbers than their larger fleet carrier counterparts, and they would see service in every maritime theatre of the war where they would often augment or fill in for the larger carriers.

Of course, whether fleet or escort carriers, these ships were only as effective as the aircraft they carried. At the onset of the war the Fleet Air Arm (FAA) only possessed 232 first-line aircraft with another 191 earmarked for training.[11] This was not enough aircraft to fully provision each of the British carriers while still maintaining necessary shore establishments. Exacerbating this shortage was a limited number of trained pilots and aircrews within the FAA organisation that barely gave the British the ability to fully utilise the aircraft they had. By the summer of 1940 the situation had hardly improved, and the British invariably had to operate their carriers with reduced air complements. This was the result of several factors, including reduced British defence budgets during the interwar years, a command structure during most of that period that had limited the FAA's development and ongoing resource priorities that favoured the Royal Air Force (RAF) over the FAA. While this situation would progressively improve, it would not be until the latter stages of the war (1944–1945) that the British were truly able to operate their carriers at full capacity. Until then, they would have to make do with what they had.

Nor was quantity the only factor limiting British naval aviation as the FAA also suffered from a lack of modern aircraft designs. The most prevalent aircraft in the Navy's inventory at the time was the Fairey Swordfish torpedo-bomber. A biplane designed in 1934 but looking more suited for World War I service; the Swordfish was laboriously slow with a top speed of only 139 miles per hour and a limited range of only 546 miles. Still, with its ability to carry an 18-inch torpedo or 1,500-pound bombload, the Swordfish had the potential to be a formidable combatant if used under favourable conditions. The British had a successor torpedo-bomber, the Fairey Albacore, nearly ready for FAA service, but this aircraft's performance was only moderately better than that of the Swordfish and thus did not constitute a major improvement. In terms of defence, the British had a new carrier-borne fighter, the Fairey Fulmar, coming into service with a top speed of 280 miles per hour, a range of 800 miles and an armament of eight .303 machine guns. Given these attributes, the Fulmar constituted the best FAA fighter of its day, but its performance still lagged behind that of many contemporary shore-based designs. Yet, against unescorted Italian bombers and reconnaissance aircraft, the Fulmar would prove to be an effective foe.

The same sentiment was true for the entire FAA. Despite its many limitations, the British benefitted from the fact that they faced an enemy that had no similar capabilities. While both sides possessed warships that carried floatplanes for reconnaissance purposes, these aircraft were limited in numbers and awkward to use. By comparison, the presence of British carrier-borne aircraft provided British fleet commanders with dedicated capabilities that their Italian counterparts did not

Although technically obsolete and looking like a relic from an earlier era, the Swordfish torpedo-bomber served the entire duration of the war and accumulated the best combat record of any Fleet Air Arm strike aircraft, including the destruction of over two dozen principal warships and 150,000 tons of merchant shipping, most of which occurred in the Mediterranean. (Beadell S. J. (Lt), Royal Navy official photographer, public domain)

have. Amongst the roles these carrier-borne aircraft could fulfil were expanded and more agile reconnaissance (given their greater numbers and ease of use), naval gunfire spotting, maritime strike and aerial defence for the fleet. Against this, Italian naval commanders had to depend upon a separate service to carry out all aviation strike and defence functions for the fleet as well as to fulfil the bulk of their reconnaissance needs. Even under ideal conditions, this arrangement was bound to be less responsive than the dedicated and immediately accessible air contingents available to the British.

Making matters worse, there were a number of factors that served to degrade the Regia Aeronautica's ability to support maritime operations. At the forefront were different command structures and overly bureaucratic lines of communication that impeded efficiency and delayed responsiveness. The Regia Aeronautica also suffered from poor aircraft designs that tended to be inferior to their top line British and German counterparts and lacked anything strictly dedicated to maritime strike operations. Similarly, the Regia Aeronautica's preferred method of attack was high-altitude bombing, which proved to be far less effective against ships than dive or torpedo bombing. Finally, poor bombsights, limited radio equipment, a lack of modern navigational aids and training, and limited night flying capabilities all served to impede effective cooperation between the Regia Marina and Regia Aeronautica. Eventually the Italians would remedy some of these deficiencies, including the deployment of a torpedo-carrying version of the Savoia-Marchetti SM.79 bomber, but the Regia Aeronautica would continue to struggle in meeting the navy's needs. Thus, while the Italians possessed substantial numbers of aircraft ringing the proposed Mediterranean battleground, it remained to be seen how effectively these aircraft could be used.

For its part, although heavily outnumbered and generally lacking in modern aircraft designs itself, the local Royal Air Force Middle East (RAFME) enjoyed a number of institutional advantages, both real and potential, that would likely pay dividends in the upcoming conflict. This included a superior ground support infrastructure that provided the British with a degree of sustainability and flexibility not matched by their more rigid and cumbersome Italian counterparts. As such, despite having to operate on a logistical shoestring far from its primary sources of materiel resupply, the RAFME attained higher aircraft serviceability rates and was capable of sustaining a more robust operating tempo than the Italian air units in Africa. The British also benefited from superior command and control, intelligence, reconnaissance and early warning capabilities. In terms of maritime operations, although far from perfect, the British were also more adept at inter-service cooperation. Finally, and perhaps most importantly, the RAFME was well led, confident in its abilities and aggressive in its operational outlook. Thus, notwithstanding the numerical imbalance, the British intended to challenge the Regia Aeronautica from the onset of hostilities and had plans in place to support the army and navy in their concurrent endeavours.

Assuming it was able to hold out long enough and Britain did not fall in the interim, the RAFME could also look forward to receiving improved aircraft types as the conflict developed. In terms of maritime applications, the most capable aircraft within the RAFME at the time was the four-engine Short Sunderland flying boat. With a maximum range of 2,980 miles and a 2,000-pound bomb load, the Sunderland was an effective maritime patrol and anti-submarine aircraft, but it only existed in small numbers within the theatre. The British would soon augment this with the arrival of American-built, twin-engine Martin Maryland bombers to fulfil a photo-reconnaissance role. In terms of potential anti-shipping weapons, the British had a number of improved aircraft types on hand or under development in Britain, including the Bristol Blenheim Mk IX light bomber, the Vickers Wellington medium bomber, the Bristol Beaufort torpedo-bomber and the Bristol Beaufighter fighter-bomber. Of these, the Beaufort was a dedicated maritime strike aircraft while the rest were multipurpose aircraft capable of fulfilling this function if called upon to do so.

Table 1.5 Characteristics of Selected Italian and British Aircraft Involved in the Maritime Conflict

	Roles	Top speed (mph)	Range (miles)	Maximum ordnance load (lbs)
Italian				
Savoia-Marchetti SM.81	Medium bomber	211	1,200	4,415
Savoia-Marchetti SM.79	Medium bomber, maritime strike	267	1,180	2,756
Cant Z.1007bis	Medium bomber	283	1,243	2,430
Fiat BR.20	Medium bomber	286	1,860	3,527
Cant Z.506B	Maritime patrol	226	1,700	2,650
British				
Fairey Swordfish	Naval torpedo-bomber	139	546	1,610
Fairey Albacore	Naval torpedo-bomber	161	930	1,610
Short Sunderland	Anti-submarine, patrol	210	2,980	2,000
Vickers Wellington	Medium bomber, maritime strike	235	2,200	4,500
Bristol Blenheim Mk IV	Light bomber	266	1,460	1,320
Bristol Beaufort	Maritime strike	265	1,600	1,605

Rounding out the British fleet hierarchy were a number of diverse warship types in terms of size and function. The first of these consisted of two classes of monitors, the *Erebus*- and *Roberts*-class, that were on hand or under construction for the Royal Navy. Of the various navies engaged in World War II, the Royal Navy was the only one to utilise these unique vessels. With a displacement ranging between 7,000 to 8,500 tons and a main armament consisting of two 15-inch guns in a single turret, these specialised warships were designed to perform shore bombardment duties, but could also be used in a coastal defence role. A second notable warship type was the *Abdiel*-class fast minelayer. Displacing 2,650 tons and armed with six 4-inch guns, these highly versatile warships were capable of high-speed transits of 34 knots or greater and could deliver 165 mines per sortie. The first of these valuable vessels would come into service in early 1941. In terms of anti-submarine escort vessels, the British maintained a variety of types ranging from unassuming trawlers to purpose-built corvettes and sloops. Soon to become a mainstay of this force was the Flower-class corvette, which displaced between 925 and 1,110 tons and was armed with a single 4-inch gun as well as anti-aircraft guns and depth charges. Finally, the British possessed a number of minesweeper classes typically ranging in size from between 600 to 900 tons and armed with 3- or 4-inch guns.

Turning now to the war goals of the competing adversaries, the Italians were motivated by the prospect of territorial and geopolitical expansion. From the onset of Mussolini's rise to power in 1922, both he and his Fascist party espoused a desire to establish a 'New Roman Empire' in which Italy became the dominant power in the Mediterranean region. Mussolini believed that the Mediterranean was rightfully 'an Italian lake' or *Mare Nostrum*, but he also considered it to be a prison in which Britain and France controlled the access points. Through direct conquest and the exertion of geopolitical power, Mussolini hoped to establish Italian dominance in the area and gain unfettered access to the outside world. As part of this, he also desired colonial expansion as a means to bolster Italy's economic prosperity, attain valuable resources and provide living space for Italy's surplus population. At the onset of the Second World War, Italy's colonial holdings were relatively small and impoverished compared to those of Britain and France. These Italian colonies primarily consisted of Libya in North Africa and Eritrea, Abyssinia and Italian Somaliland in East Africa. Now, with France in the process of collapsing and Britain expected to follow suit shortly, Mussolini believed the time was right to force concessions upon these nations and fulfil his dream of a New Roman Empire.

For the British, who directly or indirectly controlled substantial portions of Africa and the Middle East, the initial goal was to preserve mastery over critical territory in the face of expected Italian aggression. In particular, the British recognised two regional possessions warranting essential retention. The first was the Persian Gulf area, which contained vast oil fields representing a major prize for whichever side possessed them. The second was the Suez Canal and passageway through the Red Sea, which served as a vital transportation link between Europe and the Indian Ocean. By retaining control over this vital waterway, the British could logistically maintain their own position in the Middle East, deny Italy maritime access to their East African colonies and hold open the eventual prospect of reopening the Mediterranean to Allied shipping. While initially defensive in their outlook, the British planned to take the offensive as soon as conditions allowed. This was in line with pre-war British planning that envisioned an ultimate goal of destroying all Italian forces in Africa and then using Africa as a staging area to attack Italy directly and drive it out of the war.

While these objectives were laudable in the long term, the British still had to contend with the immediate here and now, which was far from a satisfactory situation. Despite their many qualitative issues, the Italians still had the fundamental advantage of superior numbers. In terms of the maritime conflict, it therefore seemed reasonable to surmise that the Regia Marina might drive the less numerous British out of the Mediterranean. In fact, just after Italy's declaration of war, the British Admiralty contemplated a voluntary withdrawal from the Eastern Mediterranean. However, Prime Minister Winston Churchill quickly vetoed this proposal, and the British Mediterranean Fleet remained on station in Alexandria. This turned out to be an insightful decision as the Italians were disinclined to press their numerical advantage. Instead, the Italian Naval High Command contented itself with securing the Adriatic and Tyrrhenian Seas, maintaining open sea routes to North Africa and providing support to the Dodecanese. The adoption of these limited objectives effectively established a situation where the Italians tried to maintain dominance in the central Mediterranean while the British controlled the eastern and western fringes with strongholds in Alexandria and Gibraltar. It also set the conditions by which the upcoming naval campaign would become a struggle of competing supply and interdiction operations.

For the Italians, this manifested itself in a requirement to maintain a substantial and continuous flow of supplies and reinforcements to their forces in Africa. Positioned just a few hundred miles away from mainland Italy, this did not seem like an unduly difficult task. However, there were two major factors that complicated, or at least had the potential to complicate, this seemingly simple assignment. The first of these was the poor state of the Italian merchant navy. On the eve of the Mediterranean war, Italy possessed a merchant fleet consisting of 786 ships grossing some 3,318,129 tons.[12] Unfortunately for them, Italian authorities failed to provide adequate warning to their deployed merchant ships regarding the pending hostilities. As such, 212 Italian merchant ships worth 1,216,637 tons were caught outside of the Mediterranean while others were located in British-controlled areas within the region.[13] In the hours and days immediately following Italy's wartime declaration, British and affiliated forces seized no fewer than 25 of these valuable vessels worth 149,867 tons and sank or forced the scuttling of a further nine vessels worth 58,266 tons.[14] Of the remaining displaced merchant ships, a handful successfully ran the Allied blockade to make it back to the Mediterranean while many more took refuge in Italy's East African colonies or ended up in the German-occupied French Atlantic ports. However, most found themselves marooned in various neutral ports predominantly in the Americas and Asia. Here they would idly languish and play no part in the Italian war effort.

Thus, at the very onset of the Mediterranean conflict, Italy had already suffered a significant strategic reversal with the effective loss of one-third of its merchant fleet. Making matters worse, these lost vessels represented a disproportionate percentage of Italy's larger and more capable merchant ships. Of the 574 commercial ships that remained available for use in the Mediterranean, many were too small or old to be ideally suited for convoy work or supply runs to Africa. The Italians were able to partially compensate for this loss with the presence of 56 German merchant ships previously trapped in the Mediterranean. However, even with this addition, total Axis merchant strength (of ships of 500 tons or greater) in the Mediterranean amounted to just 2,305,005 tons.[15] Unless the Axis could wrest control of Gibraltar or the Suez Canal away from the British, their only source of additional merchant shipping rested with new construction or the seizure of foreign vessels. This prospect did not bode well for the Italians given their inadequate shipbuilding industry. Finally, adding insult to injury, most of the Italian ships caught outside of the Mediterranean would eventually find themselves pressed into Allied service as a result of subsequent British action or when the United States and its Latin American allies entered the war.

The second potential complication to Italy's North African supply operation was the British colony of Malta, three small islands of which Malta and Gozo are the largest, located some 60 miles south of Sicily. With a combined area of just 122 square miles, Malta is hardly noticeable on most maps. Yet, in 1940 this little island group possessed a population of some 260,000 residents and a long history as an important British military base. For almost a century and a half Malta had served as the home port for the British Mediterranean Fleet. However, due to its close proximity to Italian airfields in Sicily, the British had opted to move the fleet to Alexandria in 1939. With this departure, Malta was left with only minimal defences and no appreciable offensive power. Nevertheless, assuming the British could build-up and maintain viable forces on Malta, the little colony was ideally positioned to menace Italy's crucial lines of communication to North Africa. Therefore, Malta held the potential to become a major disruption to Italian logistical operations, but this would require the expenditure of significant resources and effort to achieve this. As such, Malta represented both an opportunity and a burden for the British.

In terms of the latter, the British had their own set of logistical challenges to contend with. Foremost amongst these was the arduous task of providing reinforcements and materiel support to their forces in Egypt and Palestine. Realising the impracticality of conducting regular supply runs through the central Mediterranean given Italy's dominance in this area, the British opted to route their logistical operations around the Cape of Good Hope and through the Red Sea. By doing this, the British bypassed the main areas of danger posed by the Regia Marina and Regia Aeronautica, but added an additional 8,000 miles to each trip, thus putting increased strain upon their already over-stretched shipping situation.[16] Likewise, this diversion significantly delayed their ability to rapidly build-up and sustain forces as most convoys travelling from Britain or North America took between ten and 13 weeks to complete. A lesser maritime power would have been incapable of doing this over a prolonged period, but Britain's sizable merchant fleet, which at the end of June 1940 consisted of 3,535 ocean-going vessels worth 20,477,000 tons, and worldwide logistical infrastructure made this a feasible option.[17] While this arrangement addressed Britain's main Middle East supply situation, it was not a workable solution for Malta. If the British planned to hold and transform Malta into a base for offensive action, they would have to conduct reinforcement and supply operations deep within enemy-dominated seas against a potential gauntlet of enemy opposition. Given Britain's weak numerical position in the Mediterranean, this seemed a particularly daunting task.

Fortunately for the British, they had a bold and aggressive leader in the form of Vice-Admiral Andrew Cunningham, the Commander-in-Chief of the British

Mediterranean Fleet. Andrew Browne Cunningham was born the third of five children to Daniel and Elizabeth Cunningham in Rathmines on the south side of Dublin on 7 January 1883. Although born in Ireland, his parents were actually Scottish. The son of a renowned physician and academic, young Cunningham received his early education at Edinburgh Academy and the Naval Preparatory School of Stubbington House. At age 14 he entered the Royal Navy as a cadet aboard the training ship *Britannia* at Dartmouth, where he received high marks in mathematics and seamanship. In 1899 Cunningham embarked upon his first sea assignment as a midshipman on the cruiser *Doris*, and the next year he saw his first combat action as part of the naval brigade during the Boer War. Thereafter, he advanced in rank and held a number of duty positions, eventually attaining his first command of a torpedo boat in 1908. During World War I Cunningham commanded the destroyer *Scorpion*, which took part in the Gallipoli campaign, thus earning him promotion to commander and a Distinguished Service Order (DSO). After further service in the Mediterranean, Cunningham transferred home and ended the war as part of the Dover Patrol where he earned a bar to his DSO.

During the interwar years, Cunningham held a number of varied duty assignments and continued to advance in rank. As commander of the destroyer *Seafire* in 1919, Cunningham participated in a British naval expedition to the Baltic that checked Soviet encroachment on the newly independent Baltic States and earned him a second bar to his DSO and promotion to captain. In 1922 he took command of the 6th Destroyer Flotilla followed a year later by command of the 1st Destroyer Flotilla. After various administrative assignments, Cunningham had a short stint as commander of the recently-built battleship *Rodney* in 1930 and was later promoted to rear-admiral and made Aide-de-Camp to the King in 1932. The next year Cunningham returned to sea duty as Rear-Admiral (Destroyers) in the Mediterranean and, upon promotion to vice-admiral in 1936, became commander of the Battle Cruiser Squadron and second-in-command of the Mediterranean Fleet in 1937. In 1938 Cunningham returned to Britain to become Deputy Chief of the Naval Staff, but this assignment did not last long as he returned to the Mediterranean in June 1939 to assume command of the Mediterranean Fleet.

Hoisting his flag on the battleship *Warspite*, Cunningham embraced this new assignment with determination and vigour. Forged by over 40 years of naval service, including a sizable portion spent at sea, Cunningham personified the notion of a fighting admiral. Not a particularly meticulous administrator or planner himself, Cunningham's strongest attributes were his seaborne prowess and tenacious desire to come to grips with the enemy. Yet, despite his aggressive nature, Cunningham also possessed strong common sense and keen situational awareness that assured that his actions, while often bold, never bordered upon foolhardiness. He was not easily rattled and often showed great personal courage and calmness in the face of adversity. Like many of his peers, Cunningham was a demanding taskmaster, but he also had a good eye for talent and had no qualms about delegating and sharing the workload. In doing so, he espoused loyalty and confidence in the men around him and was capable of displaying great diplomacy when situations required. Finally, although a navy man his entire adult life, Cunningham was not blindly naval-centric in his outlook. Rather, he understood the role the navy played in conjunction with the other services and was willing to cooperate, and when necessary, sacrifice in pursuit of joint strategic and tactical goals.

With the commencement of hostilities in the Mediterranean, Cunningham was eager to meet the challenge. Undeterred by his limited resources, he was determined to deny undisputed command of the central Mediterranean to the Italians or allow them unimpeded access to their forces in North Africa. Instead, he intended to seek out and directly challenge the Italians wherever he could. This was in keeping with similar aggressive strategies adopted by all of the British service chiefs within the theatre. While the British would clearly start the war on the defensive, they planned to exercise a highly aggressive defence in their approach to the Italians. To this end, the British hoped to use audacious and decisive action as a means to unnerve and

Vice-Admiral, and later Admiral of the Fleet, Sir Andrew Cunningham served as the Commander-in-Chief of the British Mediterranean Fleet during the first half of the war and was a key architect of the ultimate Allied victory within the theatre. (Ware, C. J. (Lt), Royal Navy official photographer, public domain)

dissuade the Italians from effectively utilising their numerical advantage. Part of this British bravado was based upon the confidence they had in themselves, and part was based upon a contempt they had for their adversary. Only time would tell if these sentiments were justified. In the end, it would largely come down to Admiral Cunningham, his peers and the men under their collective commands to thwart Mussolini's dream of transforming the Mediterranean into *Mare Nostrum* and instead exploit this vital body of water for their own use as Britannia's Sea.

CHAPTER 2

Opening Moves

Italy's declaration of war, while unwelcome, came as little surprise to the British, who responded quickly to this development. Within hours of Italy's wartime declaration, Admiral Cunningham sortied a large portion of the British Mediterranean Fleet into the central Mediterranean to test the Regia Marina's reaction. At the same time, a squadron of British cruisers and destroyers carried out a bombardment of the port of Tobruk in Italian-controlled Cyrenaica (eastern Libya). During the course of this latter attack the British ships engaged the old armoured cruiser *San Giorgio* and sank the gunboat *Giovanni Berta* (644 tons, 2 × 3-inch guns) for no loss to themselves. The operation of the main fleet was less successful with no Italian ships located. Making matters worse, early on the morning of 12 June the Italian submarine *Bagnolini* torpedoed and sank the attending light cruiser *Calypso* south of Crete. Thus, in little more than 24 hours, both sides had suffered their first naval losses in the new Mediterranean war, but the British had clearly come off worse in the exchange. Yet, despite this result, both Cunningham and his naval commanders remained undaunted in their offensive spirit, and eight days later British cruisers and destroyers participated in a follow-up bombardment of the Libyan port of Bardia on the night of 20/21 June.

Activities in the air were much the same with more encouraging results. Throughout Africa the small, but aggressive, British and Commonwealth air components reacted with good results against their numerically superior opponents. This trend was highlighted on 11 June when RAF Blenheim light-bombers caught the important El Adem airfield in a state of unpreparedness and destroyed or damaged 18 Italian aircraft on the ground. That same day British bombers destroyed 780 tons of irreplaceable aviation fuel at Massawa, thus putting Italian air units in East Africa at an immediate disadvantage. In the days and weeks that followed, the British continued this onslaught as RAFME aircraft made regular strikes against Italian airfields, troop concentrations, ports and infrastructure targets. While not all universally successful, these raids had a general debilitating effect that rattled the Italians and kept them off balance. Meanwhile, in terms of the maritime conflict, on 12 June Blenheim bombers attacked *San Giorgio* in Tobruk harbour and claimed damage on the old armoured cruiser. Later that month RAF aircraft scored their first success against the Italian merchant fleet when they sank the 440-ton vessel *Maria*.

British air power also played a small, but essential, role in the first open-ocean surface engagement of the Mediterranean war. On 28 June RAF Sunderland reconnaissance aircraft from Malta located three Italian destroyers some 50 miles west of Zante as these vessels were ferrying an artillery unit to Tobruk. Based upon the subsequent sighting reports, the British 7th Cruiser Squadron, which happened to be in the area covering British convoy operations to Malta and the Aegean, altered course to intercept the Italian warships. At 1830 hours this British force, commanded by Vice-Admiral John Tovey and consisting of the cruisers *Orion, Neptune, Sydney, Liverpool* and *Gloucester*, came into contact with the Italian destroyers and commenced fire three minutes later at a range of 18,000 yards. The Italian destroyers immediately took to flight, and a running battle ensued. Eventually, the British succeeded in slowing the Italian leader, *Espero*, which then turned to cover the withdrawal of its two compatriots. In a one-sided contest, the British quickly overwhelmed and sank the brave *Espero*, but its sacrifice was not in vain as the other two destroyers made good their escape in the fading light.

Unfortunately for the Italians, this proved to be a short-lived reprieve for one of these destroyers as the FAA soon joined the fray and made its presence felt in an appreciable way. As previously mentioned, Admiral Cunningham's sole aircraft carrier, *Eagle*, initially possessed a complement of some 18 Swordfish torpedo-bombers. When the carrier was in port these aircraft became available for shore-based operations. This is precisely what happened on the evening of 5 July when nine Swordfish from No. 813 Squadron departed a forward airstrip at Sidi Barrani to attack shipping in Tobruk harbour. Despite their limited numbers, this proved to be a highly effective undertaking as the attacking British aircraft dropped seven torpedoes that sank the destroyer *Zeffiro* and the merchant ships *Manzoni* and *Serenitas* (3,955 and 5,171 tons respectively) and seriously damaged the destroyer *Euro* and the 15,354-ton troopship *Liguria*. The next day British cruisers and destroyers followed up this success with a repeat bombardment of Bardia, thus continuing the navy's aggressive posture.

For their part, the local British ground forces also moved assertively to establish moral ascendency over their more numerous Italian foes. This was particularly true along the Egyptian–Libyan frontier, where elements of the British 7th Armoured Division engaged in a series of offensive patrols, hit and run raids, ambushes and various deception efforts to keep the Italians off balance and give them the impression that the British were stronger than they really were. Often advancing over open desert, these British raiding parties penetrated as far west as Tobruk, and in the first two months of operations the British seized three Italian border outposts, destroyed or seized considerable equipment, including a small Italian mechanised force, and collected some 800 prisoners for minimal loss to themselves.[1] More importantly, these actions helped freeze the Italians in place as they declined to take any meaningful offensive action themselves. The situation in East Africa was somewhat less satisfactory as the Italians were able to make minor territorial gains along the borders of Sudan and Kenya, but here too the heavily outnumbered British forces acquitted themselves well. An example of this occurred on 4 July when a British defence force, outnumbered by a factor of at least ten to one, inflicted 117 casualties on the Italians for the loss of just ten of their own at Kassala in southern Sudan.[2] Once again, through aggressive patrolling and deception efforts, the British dissuaded the Italians from advancing beyond these minor gains along the Sudanese and Kenyan borders.

Against these various British moves, the Italians, who were the initiators of the war, were largely caught off guard and showed little inclination to take the initiative or exploit their numerical advantage. Instead, the Italians generally limited their initial offensive activities to mine laying, air strikes and submarine operations that proved to be fairly ineffective. The first of these actually began before the official commencement of hostilities. Beginning on 6 June Italian vessels laid a series of defensive mine barrages around strategic Italian and overseas locations culminating in the placement of 10,988 mines by 10 July. Then, during the period of 8–12 June other Italian vessels laid the first offensive barrages consisting of 2,508 mines in the Sicilian Channel.[3] The Italians would continue this effort in the succeeding weeks and months, eventually laying a total of 54,457 mines during the duration of the war, including 16,134 laid during the first six months.[4]

While this was underway, the Regia Aeronautica began its bombing campaign against Malta on 11 June. In the days and weeks that followed, the Italians conducted a continuous series of raids designed to pummel the beleaguered colony into a state of complete impotence. Malta's original defence against this onslaught rested with four obsolete Gladiator fighters and 42 assorted anti-aircraft guns. However, the British quickly found that their Italian attackers were easily deterred when confronted by opposition and preferred to bomb from high altitudes, thus reducing accuracy. As such, despite their frequency, the actual damage inflicted during these early raids was not significant. Air operations in Africa were even less consequential as the Regia Aeronautica typically declined to carry out heavy attacks against Alexandria or other major military installations, but instead concentrated on minor raids, reconnaissance and patrol activities.

This same lack of success held true for Italy's submarine effort. Notwithstanding *Bagnolini*'s triumph over *Calypso*, the Regia Marina's debut to submarine warfare was generally a costly and unproductive affair. This was highlighted by the loss of ten Italian submarines during the first three weeks of hostilities. Of these, British escorts and surface warships accounted for *Galileo Galilei*, *Evangelista Torricelli*, *Luigi Galvani*, *Liuzzi* and *Uebi Scebeli* while the British submarine *Parthian* dispatched

Diamante. Two others, *Argonauta* and *Rubino*, were lost to British Sunderland aircraft from No. 230 Squadron. Finally, the French sloop *La Curieuse* sank *Provana* (prior to France's capitulation), while *Macalle* was lost due to accidental causes. A contributing factor to some of these losses was Britain's initial ability to read the Italian naval codes. This was further assisted by intelligence seized from two of the dispatched submarines that provided the British with selected patrol locations. In return for these heavy losses, Italy's submarine force only succeeded in sinking the British destroyer *Khartoum*, the sloop *Pathan* and three merchant ships worth 18,132 tons, in addition to the aforementioned *Calypso*.[5] This represented an insupportable exchange rate made worse by the negative impact these losses had on Italian morale and confidence. This problem was particularly evident in the Red Sea where four out of the eight submarines stationed there were lost during the period in question.

While this denoted an early defensive victory for the British, their own initial submarine operations were hardly more successful as Cunningham's small submarine force struggled to attain meaningful results under dangerous conditions. Like their Italian counterparts, these original British submarines, which were designed for operations in the Pacific, were too large to be properly suited for the Mediterranean theatre. Likewise, the British were handicapped by the same water visibility conditions that plagued the Italians. As such, during their first month of Mediterranean operations three British submarines (*Odin*, *Grampus* and *Orpheus*) were lost to Italian surface escorts for the return of the previously mentioned Italian submarine *Diamante* and the 5,968-ton merchant ship *Loasso*. This latter vessel was sunk in a minefield laid by the British submarine *Rorqual*. French submarines were also active for a short period prior to France's capitulation, and mines from one of these sank a second Italian merchant ship worth 1,642 tons.[6]

Notwithstanding the initial poor performance of their submarines, the British had reason to be satisfied with the general trend of events in the Mediterranean conflict thus far. However, when viewing the war as a whole, British authorities had far greater matters to concern themselves with than the opening salvos of this regional struggle. Paramount above all other considerations was the defence of the United Kingdom, which now faced the prospect of potential invasion from powerful German forces stationed just a few dozen miles across the English Channel. Fortunately, in evaluating this threat, British defence planners could take some solace in the poor state of the Kriegsmarine (German navy). The Germans had started the war at a substantial numerical disadvantage compared to the Royal Navy, and this situation had only worsened during the intervening period. This latter decline was due to the heavy attrition suffered by the Kriegsmarine during the first ten months of the war (mostly at the hands of the Royal Navy), which included the loss of a pocket battleship, one heavy cruiser, two light cruisers, 12 destroyers, two torpedo boats, one escort destroyer, one minelayer, three fleet minesweepers and 23 U-boats (submarines).[7] Beyond this, a number of German warships were laid up due to battle damage or other necessary repairs, including the battlecruisers *Gneisenau* and *Scharnhorst*, the pocket battleships *Lützow* and *Admiral Scheer* and the heavy cruiser *Admiral Hipper*.

Given these factors, the British considered the probable composition of the invasion fleet likely to be arrayed against them. Assuming the Germans were able to enact their repairs quickly, British Intelligence estimated that the Kriegsmarine would only be able to muster a maximum force of two battlecruisers, two pre-dreadnought battleships, two heavy cruisers, at least two and possibly four light cruisers, seven to ten destroyers, 16 torpedo boats, eight escort vessels, 40 to 50 U-boats and a similar number of motor torpedo boats to support a potential invasion.[8] Against the power of the Royal Navy, weakened and overcommitted though it was, this force hardly seemed sufficient for the task. As a potential remedy for this German shortfall, the British also considered the possible contributions that other naval powers might make. The most obvious of these was Italy with its sizable fleet. Although expected to retain the vast majority of their naval assets in the Mediterranean, the British could not entirely discount the possibility that Italian ships might participate in a German invasion. To counter this potential threat, the British were now compelled to send a battle squadron to Gibraltar to defend the Western Mediterranean and deny the Italians access to the Atlantic Ocean. This squadron, designated Force H, was commanded by Vice-Admiral James Somerville and initially consisted of the battlecruiser *Hood*, the battleships *Resolution* and *Valiant*, the aircraft carrier *Ark Royal*, two light cruisers and 11 destroyers.

The necessity of this latter action highlighted a second major concern confronting the British. With the fall of France, British officials were haunted by the prospect that Germany might gain access to a sizable portion of the French fleet. During a meeting of the Supreme War Council on 12 June Admiral François Darlan, the Commander-in-Chief of the French navy, had assured British authorities that the French fleet would never surrender and would withdraw to Canada if necessary. However, when the Admiralty requested fulfilment of this withdrawal pledge six days later, Darlan reversed himself and stated that the fleet would remain under French control in French waters. British appeals to the French president failed to change this decision. To make matters worse, on 22 June the British learned that Article 8 of the draft armistice agreement between Germany and France called for the bulk of the French fleet to be collected in specified French ports for demobilisation and disarmament under German or Italian control. The only exception to this would be those vessels deemed necessary to safeguard French colonial interests. Although this same article also stipulated that Germany had no intention of using these warships for its own purposes, the British government was understandably sceptical of German assurances.

At the time the French fleet was spread over a wide area. From a British point of view, the most secure portion of this fleet consisted of those vessels sheltering in British ports. This included the veteran battleships *Courbet* and *Paris*, four destroyers, six torpedo boats, seven submarines, 12 sloops, one minelayer and nearly 200 auxiliary and minor vessels. Outside of Britain, the vast majority of the French fleet was stationed in a variety of African bases. The most powerful portion existed in the twin Algerian ports of Mers-el-Kébir and Oran. The former included the French capital ships *Dunkerque*, *Strasbourg*, *Bretagne* and *Provence*, the seaplane tender *Commandant Teste* and six destroyers, while ten assorted destroyers/escort vessels and four submarines were present in the latter. In Alexandria, a French squadron consisting of the battleship *Lorraine*, three heavy cruisers, a light cruiser, three destroyers and a submarine coexisted with the British Mediterranean Fleet. In Dakar and Casablanca, the French maintained the incomplete battleships *Richelieu* and *Jean Bart*, along with a sizable number of lesser warships. Finally, in the French West Indies, the French possessed the aircraft carrier *Béarn* and two cruisers.

Throughout this period French authorities repeatedly espoused a commitment to scuttle their ships before allowing them to fall under German control, but the British remained understandably concerned given the stakes involved. Under the provisions of the newly signed armistice agreement, German forces occupied Paris and the northern half of France, including the French Atlantic ports, while a semi-independent French government located in the spa town of Vichy administered the southern portion of the country and France's colonial possessions. Given these arrangements, British authorities were justifiably dubious regarding the Vichy government's willingness and/or ability to withstand German pressure or act contrary to German interests. Recent events and intelligence reports bolstered these concerns. Lord Dillon of the British mission in Algeria reported that French morale was low and that the attitude within the navy was uncertain. An effort to persuade former French ministers to create an émigré government in North Africa came to naught when French authorities refused to meet with the British delegation sent to negotiate the matter. Finally, and of greatest concern, the British received intelligence indicating that the Germans might have gained access to the French naval codes, thus giving

Table 2.1 Characteristics of French Capital Ships

	Number of vessels	Tonnage	Main armament	Maximum speed (knots)
Courbert-class battleships	2	22,189	12 × 12in guns	20
Bretagne-class battleships	3	22,189	10 × 13.4in guns*	20
Dunkerque-class battlecruisers	2	26,500	8 × 13in guns	29.5
Richelieu-class battleships (building)	2	38,000	8 × 15in guns	30
Béarn-class aircraft carrier	1	22,146	40 aircraft	21.5

*During the inter-war years the *Bretagne*-class battleship *Lorraine* underwent a major rebuild that reduced its main armament from ten to eight 13.4-inch guns. The remaining battleships in this class also underwent rebuilds but retained their original armament schemes.

them the ability to communicate directly with French naval units in the name of the Vichy government.

Fearing that the balance of maritime power might be significantly altered if Germany gained control over the French fleet, the British government resolved to take decisive action before this threat could materialise. In particular, the British sought to deny the Germans access to the French capital ships and other major surface combatants. Therefore, on 27 June the British War Cabinet authorised the execution of Operation *Catapult*, the simultaneous seizure, neutralisation or destruction of French warships located in Britain, Africa and other accessible areas. This decision was made and received with great reluctance, and the overwhelming aspiration was that the mission could be carried out with a minimum of violence and bloodshed. This sentiment was certainly true regarding many of the naval officers charged with executing the assignment, including Admiral Somerville, whose Force H was tasked to deal with the main French Fleet at Mers-el-Kébir and who viewed the entire matter with great distaste.

Still, despite their personal reservations, these officers were resolved to fulfil their duties, and on 3 July Operation *Catapult* commenced with simultaneous actions taken in Britain, Alexandria and Mers-el-Kébir. In Britain the results were overwhelmingly positive as British boarding parties successfully took control over 220 French warships, including the battleships *Courbet* and *Paris*, with a minimum of violence and only a handful of casualties sustained on both sides. The British achieved a similar satisfactory outcome in Alexandria, where after long negotiations, Admiral Cunningham convinced his French counterpart, Admiral René-Émile Godfroy, to immobilise and demilitarise his squadron. In accordance with this agreement, the French ships later discharged their fuel oil, surrendered the breech-blocks of their guns and reduced their staffing levels to skeleton status, thus voluntarily submitting themselves to effective British custody.

Sadly, the situation at Mers-el-Kébir proved more problematic. Early on the morning of 3 July Force H arrived off the French port, and Admiral Somerville sent Captain C. S. Holland, a fluent French speaker, to deliver a British ultimatum to the French commander, Admiral Marcel-Bruno Gensoul. In this, the British offered Gensoul four options regarding the disposition of his force. First, the French could join the British and continue the fight against the Germans and Italians. Second, they could sail with reduced crews to any British port and be interned with the crews being repatriated. In both of these options, the British pledged to restore the ships back to France at the conclusion of the war or pay full compensation if they were damaged. Third, they could sail to a French West Indies port and demilitarise their ships or entrust them to the United States. Again, the crews would be repatriated. Finally, they could scuttle their ships in place within six hours.[9] Unfortunately, Admiral Gensoul refused to see Holland, but did take possession of the ultimatum. After several hours of fruitless waiting, Gensoul finally agreed to meet with Holland, but their discussions went nowhere. Meanwhile, the British observed the French vessels raising steam and making preparations for departure. Likewise, signal intercepts passed on to Somerville indicated that the French Admiralty had ordered reinforcements to converge on Mers-el-Kébir. Realising that time was running out, Somerville sent one final appeal to Gensoul to accept Britain's terms by 1730 hours or he would be forced to sink the French ships.

When no response was forthcoming even after an additional grace period of 24 minutes, Somerville reluctantly ordered his squadron to open fire, commencing at 1754 hours. For 15 minutes *Hood*, *Valiant* and *Resolution* rained down a heavy bombardment on the stationary French ships. Assisted by spotter aircraft from *Ark Royal*, the British capital ships quickly scored hits with devastating effect. On their third salvo a British 15-inch shell hit the French battleship *Bretagne* detonating its aft magazine. The resulting explosion ripped through the 22,189-ton warship causing massive fires from bridge to stern. In little more than ten minutes *Bretagne* rolled over and sank to starboard taking 977 of its 1,133-man crew with it. While this was underway, the British continued to score hits on the other French warships. The battlecruiser *Dunkerque* received at least four heavy calibre hits, which disable its steering, cut electrical power, silenced two guns from No. 2 gun turret and wrecked a boiler. Another British shell blew open *Provence*'s stern and set the battleship ablaze. A similar event occurred on the destroyer *Mogador* when a shell blew off the vessel's stern. As a result of this damage, all three of these latter warships beached or grounded in shallow water.

At 1810 hours Somerville ordered a cease-fire to give the French crews an opportunity to evacuate their ships. At about the same time Force H made a turn to seaward to avoid the increasingly accurate return fire coming from French shore batteries. These actions inadvertently coincided with the breakout departure of the relatively undamaged battlecruiser *Strasbourg* and five destroyers. This fleeing force was soon joined by additional warships out of Oran. By the time this departure was confirmed to Somerville, these French ships were already well underway, and the British found themselves out of position to enact a likely intercept. Despite this, Somerville ordered an immediate pursuit of the fleeing ships. To improve his chances, he launched a couple of Swordfish air strikes from *Ark Royal* in an attempt to hit and reduce *Strasbourg*'s speed, but these strikes failed to attain any hits, and the battlecruiser and its accompanying destroyers increasingly pulled away in the gathering darkness. Opting against a potential night action, Somerville broke off the pursuit and ordered Force H back to Gibraltar. Meanwhile, *Strasbourg* and its accompanying escorts continued their journey arriving at Toulon in Vichy-controlled France on the 4th.

Over the next few days, the British continued operations against a handful of selected French vessels and targets of opportunity. On 4 July the British submarine *Pandora* sank the French sloop *Rigault de Genouilly* off Algiers. Two days later Force H returned to Mers-el-Kébir to deliver a coup de grace against *Dunkerque*, which was reported to be only moderately damaged. Three waves of Swordfish aircraft from *Ark Royal* carried out the attack claiming at least four torpedo hits on *Dunkerque*. However, it appears that the only ships actually hit and sunk by these torpedoes were the 780-ton auxiliary French patrol vessel *Terre Neuve* and a tug lying alongside the battlecruiser. In a freak occurrence, one of the last British torpedoes struck the sunken *Terre Neuve* and detonated its depth charges, causing a massive underwater explosion that ripped open 40 metres of *Dunkerque*'s hull and caused severe shock damage to its engine mountings. *Dunkerque* was now truly immobilised and would never again be made fully operational. A similar incident occurred on 7/8 July when a small British force featuring the aircraft carrier *Hermes* arrived off Dakar to neutralise the nearly completed *Richelieu*. An initial attempt to drop depth charges under the battleship's stern failed, but a subsequent Swordfish attack scored a single torpedo hit that caused enough damage to render *Richelieu* immobile for several months. Finally, the British were able to use diplomatic pressure and the denial of fuel oil to keep the aircraft carrier *Béarn* and other French warships stranded in the West Indies.

With the conclusion of these actions, the British halted their assault against the French Fleet. In less than a week the British had accomplished their overriding

Beyond the Italians, the British also had to contend with the threat of the Vichy French fleet falling under Axis control. Pictured here (pre-war) is the battlecruiser *Hood*, which led the bombardment against the French naval base at Mers-el Kébir. (Photographer: Allan C. Green, Restoration: Adam Cuerden, public domain)

objective by removing a sizable portion of the French navy from the potential clutches of the German enemy. This was particularly true regarding the main units of the French battle line. With the exception of *Strasbourg*, all of France's operational or near operational capital ships had either been seized, sunk or otherwise neutralised. The operation also had a major psychological benefit regarding a nominal ally and a potential adversary. During a time when many observers were privately or openly questioning Britain's resolve, Operation *Catapult* sent a clear message that the British were determined to carry on the fight and were willing and able to do whatever was necessary to act in their own defence. This demonstrated commitment reassured the United States, which also recognised Nazi Germany as a potential threat, that Britain was still a country worth supporting. As such, the United States, despite its official position of neutrality, increasingly implemented measures to assist the British war effort. Meanwhile, Britain's bold action had an equally important impact upon the Spanish government. At the time Germany was actively lobbying Spain to come into the war against Britain. Had this happened, Britain's position in the Mediterranean would have been severely undermined if not rendered completely untenable. However, the Spanish government resisted German pressure to do so realising that Britain was still a power to be reckoned with.

On the other hand, the success of Operation *Catapult* came at a heavy cost as Franco-British relations immediately deteriorated to a dangerous level following the attack. Many officials in the Vichy government and French military were outraged and shamed by what they saw as an unprovoked and treacherous act of aggression by a former ally. The loss of 1,297 French naval personnel and 351 wounded at Mers-el-Kébir only served to increase this anger. Fortunately, the Vichy government limited its response to this provocation to an ineffective retaliatory air strike against Gibraltar and the suspension of diplomatic relations. Nevertheless, the potential for further hostilities was always present. Likewise, the French were now more prone to cooperate with the Germans, or at least less inclined to resist their pressure. On the other hand, few French were now willing to cooperate with their former British allies. This factor was particularly relevant outside of France where the overwhelming majority of French colonial possessions remained loyal to the Vichy government. As such, many of these possessions, including some located in strategically important areas, were now at best apathetic or at worst tacitly hostile towards British interests. The same held true in the military where the vast majority of French officers felt duty bound to support the Vichy government. By comparison, a fledgling Free French movement under the leadership of General Charles de Gaulle attracted few volunteers to carry on the war alongside Britain.

With the matter of the French fleet now resolved, the British turned their attention back to their primary Italian enemies, and on 9 July the two sides engaged in their first major fleet action of the Mediterranean war. At this time both sides were at sea supporting concurrent convoy operations. For the British, this included most of the

Mediterranean Fleet, which was divided into three forces. The leading element (Force A) consisted of five cruisers and a destroyer; the centre (Force B) consisted of the battleship *Warspite* and five destroyers; and the rear (Force C) consisted of the slower battleships *Malaya* and *Royal Sovereign*, the aircraft carrier *Eagle* and ten destroyers. Opposing them was a large composite Italian fleet consisting of the battleships *Giulio Cesare* and *Conte di Cavour*, six heavy cruisers, ten light cruisers and 32 destroyers. Forewarned by a series of sighting reports from aircraft and submarines as well as signal intelligence, Cunningham manoeuvred his forces to enact an intercept of the enemy fleet as it was returning to Italy. In doing so, his ships endured several heavy air attacks from the Regia Aeronautica, but generally escaped serious damage from the high-altitude bombing. The sole exception to this was the cruiser *Gloucester*, which took a bomb hit on its compass platform.

At 1447 hours on 9 July Cunningham's persistence in the face of this continuous harassment was rewarded when his forward cruisers sighted smoke on the horizon. Minutes later this smoke materialised into a van of enemy cruisers and destroyers that opened fire at 1520 hours. The British quickly followed suit, and a long-range duel ensued. At 1526 hours *Warspite* arrived on the scene, forcing the Italian cruisers to retreat, but at 1550 hours the balance changed once again as the two Italian capital ships came into sight. For the next few minutes, the opposing capital ships engaged each other at ranges varying from 24,000 to 27,000 yards. Then at 1559 hours *Warspite* scored a large calibre hit on the Italian flagship *Giulio Cesare* that temporarily reduced its speed to 18 knots. This development quickly convinced the Italian commander, Admiral Inigo Campioni, to break off the engagement and withdraw towards the Italian mainland. Over the next several minutes the Italians executed a progressive withdrawal under the cover of smoke, and by 1650 hours the fighting was over. Thereafter, Cunningham pursued the retreating Italians to within 25 miles of the Calabrian coast, but failed to renew the engagement and eventually turned away in the face of the continued Italian air threat.

So ended what became known as the battle of Calabria to the British or the battle of Punta Stilo to the Italians. In terms of materiel damage, the battle was a fairly insignificant event. Other than *Giulio Cesare*, the only ships to suffer meaningful damage were the aforementioned *Gloucester* and the Italian heavy cruiser *Bolzano*, which was hit by three 6-inch shells. Nevertheless, the British considered the battle a moral victory having driven off a numerically superior enemy from the scene of the fighting while gaining confidence in their ability to operate in the face of incessant Italian air attacks. Nor did the British exit the battle entirely empty handed. As a postscript to this action, on 10 July *Eagle* launched a strike of nine Swordfish to attack a concentration of Italian warships reported to be in the Sicilian harbour of Augusta. Arriving over the target at dusk, the British found the harbour to be largely devoid of targets, but still managed to sink the Italian destroyer *Leone Pancaldo* (which was ultimately raised and put back into service in December 1941) and damage a fleet tanker.

On 19 July the British and Italians fought their third running surface engagement in as many weeks. In this case the Australian light cruiser *Sydney* and five destroyers encountered the Italian light cruisers *Bartolomeo Colleoni* and *Giovanni delle Bande Nere* off Crete's Cape Spada. After initially engaging four of the British destroyers, the Italian cruisers were put to flight when *Sydney* and the fifth British destroyer arrived on the scene. In a running battle *Sydney* scored a number of well-placed hits that immobilised *Bartolomeo Colleoni* and allowed the destroyers *Ilex* and *Hyperion* to close on and sink the disabled cruiser with torpedoes. Meanwhile, *Sydney* continued to pursue *Giovanni delle Bande Nere*, but the Italian light cruiser eventually made good its escape despite receiving further hits from *Sydney*'s guns. For its part, *Sydney* only received one superficial hit during the engagement. That night six Swordfish from *Eagle*'s No. 824 Squadron departed Sidi Barrani to attack Tobruk in the belief that *Giovanni delle Bande Nere* might have taken shelter there. As it turned out, *Giovanni delle Bande Nere* was not present having proceeded to Benghazi instead. Still, the British aircraft were able to find worthwhile targets for their torpedoes as they sank the Italian destroyers *Nembo* and *Ostro* and the 2,333-ton merchant ship *Sereno* in the Gulf of Bomba near Tobruk.

British *Leander*-class cruisers provided valuable service during much of the Mediterranean war. Pictured here is HMAS *Sydney*, which played the central role in destroying the Italian light cruiser *Bartolomeo Colleoni* during the battle of Cape Spada. (Allan C. Green, public domain)

While these celebrated actions were underway, both the British and Italians continued their all-important supply and reinforcement operations. Of particular importance to Britain's naval effort were actions to reinforce and *sustain* Malta and the Mediterranean Fleet. In early August Force H from Gibraltar conducted Operation *Hurry*, which provided Malta with 12 Hurricane fighters flown off from the old aircraft carrier *Argus*. Coinciding with this, Swordfish from *Ark Royal* carried out a combined air strike and mining operation against the air base and harbour at Cagliari on Sardinia's southern coast. One month later the British undertook an even more ambitious task when they embarked upon Operation *Hats* to simultaneously provision Malta and sail a number of major naval units directly through the Mediterranean to reinforce the Mediterranean Fleet. This was an elaborate operation requiring almost the full strength of Force H and the Mediterranean Fleet, but the British were handsomely rewarded for their efforts. At no significant loss to themselves, the British delivered some 40,000 tons of cargo and provisions to Malta, including additional anti-aircraft guns, ammunition and associated equipment. At the same time, they successfully transferred the battleship *Valiant*, the new aircraft carrier *Illustrious* and the anti-aircraft cruisers *Coventry* and *Calcutta* to Cunningham's command. Finally, at various times throughout the operation the carriers *Ark Royal*, *Illustrious* and *Eagle* each conducted air strikes against Italian airfields at Elmas, Kalatho and Maritza respectively.

Nor were these supply movements particularly unique. Throughout the period a series of Italian convoys successfully landed in North Africa bringing supplies and reinforcements to their already considerable forces stationed there. Meanwhile, the British began the slow and arduous task of building up their forces in the Middle East by way of the Red Sea Route. All of these operations were carried out with little or no loss to the vessels involved. One reason for this was the continued inability of either side's submarine force to attain significant success. From July through September, Italian submarines only sank three merchant ships worth 8,374 tons along with the British destroyer *Escort*.[10] Against this, they lost two of their own number. Of these, three Swordfish from *Eagle*'s No. 824 Squadron, but operating from Sidi Barrani, sank the submarine *Iride* and the 1,976-ton depot ship *Monte Gargano* in the Gulf of Bomba on 22 August. One month later the Australian destroyer *Stuart*, with support from a No. 230 Squadron Sunderland, sank the submarine *Gondar* off Alexandria. Britain's small submarine force fared slightly better during this period sinking seven merchant ships worth 20,413 tons and the Italian torpedo boat *Palestro* (including some vessels sunk by submarine-laid mines).[11] However, these meagre results cost the British two submarines (*Phoenix* and *Oswald*) in return, both of which were sunk by Italian escort vessels.

With this influx of men and supplies, the large Italian forces in Africa finally yielded to Rome's continued urging and went on the offensive after several weeks of inactivity. In August some 26,000 Italian troops departed their garrisons in East

Africa and invaded neighbouring British Somaliland. Woefully outnumbered, the British quickly realised they had no viable prospect of holding the impoverished colony and instead conducted a skilful fighting retreat inflicting 2,052 casualties on the invading Italians. Then, before the Italians could entrap them, the British successfully evacuated some 7,000 soldiers and civilians by sea. Total British losses for the short campaign amounted to just 260 casualties.[12] Later in September the Italian Tenth Army, consisting of some 100,000 men, crossed the Egyptian border and advanced into northwest Egypt. Once again, the British were too weak to firmly oppose this incursion and instead yielded ground while conducting minor harassing operations. As it was, the Italians only advanced some 60 miles into Egypt before halting at Sidi Barrani on the coast. Once there, they erected a monument commemorating their accomplishment and went onto the defensive establishing a series of fortified camps south of that location. Their intention was to secure the area and build up their logistics before continuing their methodical advance towards Mersa Matruh, but they showed no apparent haste in getting this done.

At approximately the same time the British embarked upon their own limited offensive on the other side of Africa. Sadly, the recipients of this action were the Vichy French and not the Italians. Encouraged by French Equatorial Africa's (Chad, Cameroon and French Congo) recent decision to join General de Gaulle's Free French movement, the Allies sought to entice or compel Dakar in Senegal to do the same. In doing so, they hoped to bring further momentum to the Free French effort and eliminate a potential threat to Britain's main North-South Atlantic shipping route that accommodated most of the supply traffic to the Middle East. Accordingly, the Allies assembled an assault force under the command of Major-General N.M.S. Irwin, consisting of 3,670 Free French and 4,270 British troops on 11 transport ships. The naval contingent for this expedition consisted of the battleships *Barham* and *Resolution*, the aircraft carrier *Ark Royal*, four cruisers, ten destroyers and five sloops (three of which were Free French).[13] This force, commanded by Vice-Admiral John Cunningham (no relation to Vice-Admiral Andrew Cunningham), departed Britain on 31 August.

After a short stopover in nearby Freetown, the Allied force arrived off Dakar on a foggy 23 September morning. Hoping to avoid bloodshed, a French delegation under the authority of General de Gaulle entered the harbour to try and open negotiations with Vichy authorities, but this mission was met by gunfire. A direct appeal by de Gaulle over the radio was equally unsuccessful. Then at 1000 hours a Vichy shore battery opened fire on a British destroyer facilitating a response in kind. This quickly degenerated into a wider melee as additional units joined the fighting and a handful of Vichy vessels attempted to leave the harbour. In the naval combat that followed, the British destroyers *Inglefield* and *Foresight* sank the Vichy submarine *Persée* while the Australian cruiser *Australia* reduced the Vichy destroyer *L'Audacieux* to a beached, burning wreck. As this progressed, General de Gaulle made further attempts to resolve the conflict peacefully, but the Vichy authorities remained intransigent and promised to oppose any landings with force. Finally, at 1730 hours the Allies attempted a landing at Rufisque Bay on the east side of Dakar, but thickening fog and a breakdown in communications soon rendered this a failure.

Over the next two days the British conducted a series of naval bombardments in an attempt to reduce Dakar's coastal defences, which included the immobilised battleship *Richelieu*. In this, they scored at least one heavy calibre hit on *Richelieu*, which was often shrouded in smoke screens, and sank the nearby 4,482-ton merchant ship *Tacoma*, but otherwise failed to inflict meaningful damage. By comparison, *Resolution* and *Barham* were both hit by return fire, but likewise suffered minimal damage. Meanwhile, on the 24th the destroyer *Fortune* sank a second Vichy submarine, *Ajax*, as it was attempting to attack the fleet. Then on the 25th the Vichy submarine *Bévéziers* succeeded in torpedoing *Resolution*, thus forcing the battleship to withdraw in a badly damaged state. This development prompted Churchill to cancel the operation, and the Allied fleet withdrew having accomplished nothing for their efforts. Fortunately, there was little loss of life associated with this debacle, and no British ships were sunk. Nevertheless, *Resolution* would be out of service for a year. Vichy losses were higher, amounting to 184 dead and 379 wounded (both military and civilian) along with two submarines and a merchant ship sunk and a destroyer heavily damaged.[14]

Sadly, the operation's main cost was the further deterioration it caused to the already strained relations between Great Britain and the Vichy regime. To emphasise this point, on 24 and 25 September Vichy bombers from Morocco attacked Gibraltar in reprisal for the Dakar assault, but failed to cause serious damage other than the destruction of the trawler *Stella Sirius*. This proved to be part of an ongoing low intensity conflict that would continue to exact a small but steady toll of casualties, the majority of which fell upon the Vichy French. An example of this occurred two months later when Free French forces, with British support, seized control of Libreville in Gabon, the last territory in French Equatorial Africa still under Vichy jurisdiction. During the course of this operation the British sloop *Milford* forced the scuttling of the Vichy submarine *Poncelet*, while the Free French sloop *Savorgnan de Brazza* sank its Vichy counterpart *Bougainville* in a rare case of two ships of the same class engaging each other. The ongoing conflict also manifested itself in the regular seizure of Vichy merchant ships. From June 1940 through February 1942 British and affiliated forces seized no fewer than 46 ocean-going French merchant ships worth 285,958 tons and forced the scuttling of two additional vessels worth 8,376 tons.[15]

While this struggle constituted an unfortunate diversion for the British, the Italians were soon embroiled in a secondary campaign of their own. In 1939 Italy had occupied the small Balkan country of Albania. Now in the autumn of 1940, Mussolini greedily eyed Albania's southern neighbour, Greece, as a potential target for easy conquest. Putting these ambitions into effect, on 28 October Italian forces crossed Albania's mountainous border and began an invasion of Greece. However, Mussolini's expectation for an easy victory quickly came to naught as his ill-prepared units encountered stronger than anticipated opposition. Far from being an easy conquest, the outnumbered Greeks defended their homeland with great zeal, and in just a few weeks succeeded in throwing back the Italian invaders. In little more than a month the Italians were summarily expelled from Greek territory and actually surrendered control over part of Albania. Thereafter, the situation stabilised as exhaustion and logistical constraints curtailed further large-scale operations.

For the British, this course of events provided them with a new, if limited, European ally in the war against Italy. Although the Greeks possessed little offensive power, their continued resistance forced the Italians to divert increasing numbers of units to the Balkan front, thus splitting their war effort. In early 1941 this included several divisions sent to Albania in preparation for a new spring offensive to be launched in March. This also required the diversion of corresponding air and sea assets to support this build-up. Beyond this point, the Greeks provided little further benefit to the British. With their minor air force and navy, the Greeks were incapable of playing a significant role in the maritime conflict. Likewise, they lacked the strength and inclination to provide any direct support to British operations in the Middle East. Finally, since Greece was not at war with Germany at the time, the Greeks refused to fully coordinate with or accept large-scale support from the British to avoid provoking a German intervention. By comparison, the British lacked sufficient strength in the Middle East to provide decisive assistance or effectively use Greek territory as a platform to attack Italian and German interests. Thus, despite their close proximity in the Mediterranean theatre, the British and Greeks largely waged independent conflicts against a common Italian enemy.

Nor was the Greek campaign the only diversion to impact the Regia Marina. In a rare case of direct cooperation between the two Axis partners, in August 1940 Italian submarines began operating in the Atlantic from the German-controlled French port of Bordeaux. Initially, these Italian boats conducted patrols between the Azores and Spain, but in subsequent weeks these patrols ventured further north. By the end of November, 26 Italian submarines had passed through the Strait of Gibraltar to assist the Germans in waging mercantile warfare against Britain's vital seaborne lines of communication. In this, the Italians attained a greater degree of success than they did in the Mediterranean, but this level of performance still lagged behind that of their German counterparts. From August 1940 through February 1941 Italian submarines operating in the Atlantic sank 26 Allied and neutral merchant ships worth 110,921 tons along with two minor vessels.[16] This cost the Italians four submarines in return, of which *Faa di Bruno*, *Nani* and *Marcello* were lost to British escorts while *Tarantini* was sunk by the British submarine *Thunderbolt*.

Returning now to the maritime struggle in the Mediterranean, in September and October the Mediterranean Fleet received a steady stream of reinforcements. Of these, none was more important than the arrival of the aircraft carrier *Illustrious* with its air group of 18 Swordfish and 15 Fulmars. Although limited in numbers, the Fulmar's introduction to the Mediterranean Fleet finally gave Cunningham a viable fighter defence against Italian bombers and reconnaissance aircraft. As confirmation of this point, from September 1940 through January 1941 *Illustrious'* Fulmars claimed 29 aerial victories.[17] Meanwhile, on 15 September Cunningham set out to test his new carrier's offensive power when he dispatched it along with the battleship *Valiant* and a cruiser/destroyer escort to raid Benghazi. On the night of 16/17 September this force arrived some 100 miles north of Benghazi, and *Illustrious* launched a strike of nine bomb-laden Swordfish with a further six Swordfish earmarked for mine laying. Attacking in bright moonlight, the bombing Swordfish sank the Italian destroyer *Borea* and the merchant ships *Gloria Stella* and *Maria Eugenia* (5,490 and 4,702 tons respectively), while the mining aircraft laid their charges unobserved in the harbour entrance. Over the next few days these latter mines sank the destroyer *Aquilone* and two patrol vessels and damaged a third merchant ship. There were no British losses for this operation, but the cruiser *Kent* was damaged by an aerial torpedo following a subsequent bombardment of Bardia.

In October the British attained further success when their forces fought two surface engagements in conjunction with varied convoy operations. The first occurred during the second week in October when the British successfully delivered a four-ship supply convoy to Malta while returning three empty merchant ships back to Alexandria. Early on the morning of the 12th a mixed force of Italian destroyers and torpedo boats attacked the cruiser *Ajax* off Cape Passero as the latter was providing flank security for the returning British ships. Despite being outnumbered, the lone British cruiser effectively defended itself, sinking the torpedo boats *Ariel* and *Airone* and severely damaging the destroyer *Artigliere*. With the coming of dawn other British ships arrived on the scene, and the cruiser *York* finished off the crippled *Artigliere*. For its part, the gallant *Ajax* did not sustain substantial damage despite being hit by several 3.9-inch and 4.7-inch shells. Eight days later on the night of 20/21 October the British fought a second action in defence of a 32-ship convoy passing through the Red Sea. Attacked by four Italian destroyers out of Massawa, the convoy's escort, which included the cruiser *Leander* and the destroyer *Kimberley*, successfully repelled the attack and drove the destroyer *Francesco Nullo* aground. The next morning *Kimberley* finished off the crippled *Francesco Nullo*, but was itself damaged by Italian shore batteries.

While these engagements represented meaningful success against the Regia Marina, in October the British made preparations for a far greater coup against the Italian battle fleet. As far back as 1935, the British had devised plans for a carrier-borne strike against the Italian naval base at Taranto. Now with the arrival of *Illustrious*, Cunningham felt himself strong enough to make such an attempt. His original intention was to attack Taranto on the night of 21 October (the anniversary of the battle of Trafalgar) with 30 Swordfish from *Eagle* and *Illustrious*. However, this plan soon went awry when a hanger fire on *Illustrious* required a postponement of the operation. The British reset the strike date to the next satisfactory moon period of 11 November. Unfortunately, a breakdown in *Eagle's* aviation fuel system due to shock damage from earlier bombing attacks forced the old carrier out of the operation at the last minute. Undaunted by this latest complication, Cunningham departed Alexandria with *Illustrious* and the remainder of the Mediterranean Fleet on 6 November. On board the carrier were 24 Swordfish, including five recent transfers from the incapacitated *Eagle*.

Acting in conjunction with a series of concurrent convoy operations to Malta, Greece and Alexandria, which included the transfer of the battleship *Barham* and other naval reinforcements to the Mediterranean fleet, Cunningham carefully manoeuvred his attack force into position to carry out the strike against Taranto, code-named Operation *Judgment*. Italian aircraft soon found and attacked the British fleet, but *Illustrious'* Fulmars were able to hold these attackers at bay. Meanwhile, reconnaissance aircraft from Malta provided the British with up-to-date intelligence regarding the disposition of ships and defences at Taranto. On the eve of the attack this reconnaissance revealed that all six Italian battleships and a handful of cruisers were present in Taranto's outer harbour, the Mar Grande, while multiple additional cruisers and destroyers occupied the inner harbour, the Mar Piccolo. Defences consisted of 21 anti-aircraft batteries along with 84 heavy and 68 light machine guns. Beyond this, the harbour possessed 22 searchlights, 4,200 metres of anti-torpedo netting and 27 barrage balloons.[18] Fortunately for the British, this defensive coverage was not entirely complete, and they were able to devise routes through the gaps. On a less positive note, contaminated fuel cost *Illustrious* three Swordfish, reducing the available strike force to just 21 aircraft. Of these, the British planned to arm 11 with torpedoes while the remainder were armed with various combinations of bombs and flares. These latter aircraft were to attack shipping in the Mar Piccolo and lay flares to silhouette the capital ships in the outer harbour for attack by their torpedo-carrying counterparts.

Early on the evening of 11 November Cunningham detached *Illustrious* and a screen of cruisers and destroyers to proceed forward and commence the attack. Arriving at a position some 170 miles southeast of Taranto, *Illustrious* launched its first wave of 12 Swordfish beginning at 2035 hours, with a second wave of nine Swordfish following about 50 minutes later. It took two hours for the lumbering Swordfish to travel the distance to Taranto, where they were met by an intense umbrella of anti-aircraft fire. Undeterred by this reception, the British aircraft carried out their attacks with great courage and skill and attained a remarkable degree of success given their limited numbers. This was particularly true in the Mar Grande where the torpedo-armed aircraft of the first wave scored two hits on the battleship *Littorio* and a single hit on *Conte di Cavour*. The second wave attained similar results, scoring two more hits on *Littorio* (only one of which exploded) and a single hit on the battleship *Caio Duilio*. While this was underway, the bombing aircraft scored hits on the cruiser *Trento* and destroyer *Libeccio* (both of which failed to explode), caused splinter and shock damage to other ships, struck an Italian seaplane base and damaged fuel storage tanks. This was all accomplished for the loss of just two Swordfish, and the remaining aircraft successfully returned to *Illustrious* by 0250 hours on the 12th.

With the coming of dawn, both sides began the process of assessing the damage. In most obvious terms, all three battleships hit the night before now laid sunk, or partially sunk, in the shallow waters of the Mar Grande. Of these, *Conte di Cavour* was in the most serious state. Although only hit by a single torpedo that exploded under its keel, *Conte di Cavour* suffered extensive structural damage and massive internal flooding. Within a matter of hours internal bulkheads gave way to the rising water, and the distressed battleship settled on the harbour bottom. While the Italians would eventually raise *Conte di Cavour* in July 1941, the stricken vessel would never be fully repaired or put back into service, and was thus a total loss. The remaining two battleships, *Littorio* and *Caio Duilio*, suffered less extensive damage, but would still be out of service for four and six months respectively. Likewise, a number of lesser vessels, including the cruiser *Trento*, three destroyers and two auxiliaries suffered varying degrees of light to moderate damage, while two Italian aircraft were destroyed on the ground. Finally, there was random havoc caused throughout the harbour area, much of which was the result of errant anti-aircraft fire, which included the expenditure of 6,854 × 3.05-inch, 313 × 4.02-inch and 1,430 × 4.09-inch shells during the raid.[19]

When it was all added up, the raid on Taranto represented a resounding British victory. For the price of just two Swordfish lost during the attack, the Royal Navy altered the strategic balance in the Mediterranean. With one battleship rendered a permanent loss and two others temporarily out of service, the Regia Marina suddenly found itself outnumbered by Cunningham's battle line. This turn of events prompted the Italians to temporarily transfer their remaining battleships, along with several cruisers and destroyers, from Taranto to the less accessible port of Naples. In doing so, the Regia Marina lessened its ability to respond to British operations in the Eastern Mediterranean. For their part, Churchill and the British hierarchy used the raid's results to boost morale and confidence during a period when good news was often in short supply. Finally, adding insult to injury, Cunningham augmented Operation *Judgment* by concurrently dispatching a cruiser squadron under Vice-Admiral H. D. Pridham-Wippell into the Strait of Otranto to search out Italian shipping. This effort was rewarded when the British force, consisting of the cruisers *Orion*, *Ajax* and *Sydney* and the destroyers *Nubian* and *Mohawk*, encountered a four-ship convoy proceeding from Valona to Brindisi. After driving off the convoy's escort, the British squadron destroyed all four merchant ships worth 16,938 tons for no loss to themselves.

The arrival of the modern aircraft carrier *Illustrious* had a great impact on the early Mediterranean conflict. This was highlighted in November 1940 when aircraft from *Illustrious* neutralised half the Italian battle line at Taranto. (Commander Joseph C. Clifton, U.S. Navy, public domain)

While these operations earned great notoriety, the British also enjoyed considerable success on less celebrated activities during the waning months of 1940. Of particular importance was the continued flow of men and materiel to and within the theatre. By this time, the invasion threat against Britain had waned, and the British were free to send increased resources into the region. From the last week in August through the end of the year, the British successfully transported some 76,000 men from the United Kingdom and another 49,400 men from India, Australia and New Zealand, along with vast amounts of equipment and supplies to Middle East Command.[20] With the arrival of these vital reinforcements, Britain's military position in the region improved significantly. Although still outnumbered, the British were in a much better state to engage the Italians and even devised plans to go onto the offensive. Meanwhile, during the same period the British continued to sustain and build up Malta. In early November, this included the arrival of an infantry battalion, two 25-pounder field batteries, one tank troop and two heavy and one light anti-aircraft batteries (some 2,150 troops in all).[21] Later that month Force H and *Argus* conducted another operation to fly additional Hurricane fighters to Malta. However, in this case the fighters were launched too far out given the weather conditions, and only four out of the 12 aircraft dispatched actually reached the island, with the remainder crashing due to fuel exhaustion.

During the last week in November the British carried out another complex series of convoy movements under the designation Operation *Collar*. A key component of this operation was the running of three fast (16-knot) merchant ships carrying tanks and other key provisions, along with four Flower-class corvettes that had been converted to perform minesweeping duties directly through the Mediterranean to Malta and Alexandria. Concurrently, the British dispatched the battleship *Ramillies* and two cruisers to proceed from Alexandria to Gibraltar. The British covered the western portion of these movements with the battlecruiser *Renown*, the aircraft carrier *Ark Royal*, two cruisers and nine destroyers under the command of Vice-Admiral Somerville. On 26 November an Italian force consisting of the battleships *Vittorio Veneto* and *Giulio Cesare*, six cruisers and 14 destroyers departed Naples and other proximate ports in a bid to intercept the convoy. The next morning a reconnaissance aircraft from *Ark Royal* located elements of the Italian force south of Sardinia and issued a warning to Somerville. In response, Somerville manoeuvred the convoy out of jeopardy while he rendezvoused with the *Ramillies'* force and then turned to intercept the oncoming Italians. At 1215 hours the two sides came into contact, but after an hour-long indecisive engagement, the Italians promptly withdrew and retired back towards Italy. For his part, Somerville declined to pursue the fleeing enemy given his overriding responsibility to protect the convoy, which successfully concluded its passage.[22]

Meanwhile, on the eastern side of the Mediterranean, Cunningham carried out his desired tasks with little effective interference from the Italians. During Operation *Collar* this included the running of convoys to Malta and Crete while *Eagle* and *Illustrious* conducted diversionary raids against Tripoli and Leros. This trend continued into December as the British successfully executed another series of shipping movements throughout the region, resulting in the delivery of 55 merchant ships without a loss.[23] The British also conducted a number of wide-ranging offensive sorties during this period in which they operated in a state of near impunity from Italian intervention. Particularly active during this time was the aircraft carrier *Illustrious*, which carried out a succession of air strikes against Bardia, Rhodes, Stampalia and Tripoli and conducted a strike by nine Swordfish against an Italian convoy east of Sfax that sank the merchant ships *Norge* and *Peuceta* (6,511 and 1,926 tons respectively) on 21 December. Meanwhile, on the night of 18/19 December the battleships *Warspite* and *Valiant* ventured deep into enemy-controlled waters and carried out a bombardment of the Albanian port of Valona with no interference from the Regia Marina or the Regia Aeronautica.

This lack of opposition highlighted Britain's growing ability to operate at will throughout the Mediterranean. During the period in question the Italians failed to sink a single British merchant ship within the theatre despite a near constant flow of convoys to and from Malta and Greece. Nor was this lack of success limited to the Italian surface fleet or the Regia Aeronautica. Italy's sizable submarine force also failed to have a meaningful impact upon the struggle. During the final three months of 1940 Italian submarines operating in the Mediterranean only succeeded in sinking the British destroyer *Hyperion* and the submarine *Rainbow* for the loss of six of their own number. Of the latter, British destroyers sank *Berillo*, *Lafolè* and *Naiade* while surface warships working in conjunction with two London flying boats from No. 202 Squadron accounted for *Durbo*. The remaining two Italian submarine casualties, *Gemma* and *Foca*, were lost due to accidental and unknown causes. Of course, the British still had to take considerable precautions when conducting their shipping movements, but the Mediterranean was becoming increasingly accessible to their ambitions.

By comparison, the British made minor, but tangible, progress in their own interdiction efforts against the Italians. In addition to the various Italian merchant ships already described as lost through air and surface actions, British and Greek submarines added a further eight merchant ships and three minor vessels worth 36,570 tons sunk during the final three months of the year.[24] Likewise, mines laid by the British submarine *Rorqual* accounted for the destruction of the Italian torpedo boats *Calipso* and *Fratelli Cairoli* in December. On the other hand, one Greek and four British submarines were lost in the Mediterranean from October through December. These casualties consisted of the aforementioned *Rainbow* and the submarines *Triad*, *Regulus*, *Triton* and *Proteus* (Greek), which were all lost to mines, unknown causes and Italian surface vessels. Meanwhile, the British scored additional successes with RAF aircraft, aerial mines and surface vessels. When combined together and going back to the beginning of the conflict, these British and Allied assets accounted for the loss of 66 Italian, German and affiliated merchant ships worth 168,821 tons in the Mediterranean during the period of June through December 1940. Other causes, including the seizure or forced scuttling of vessels at the onset of hostilities, accounted for an additional 38 Axis merchant ships and minor vessels worth 84,631 tons that were lost in the Mediterranean during the same period.[25] Concurrent Italian construction only produced two vessels worth 7,136 tons to compensate for these casualties.[26] Returning vessels that skirted the British blockade and various foreign merchant ships that came under Italian control during this time provided further replacements. Still, these additions failed to fully keep pace with losses, and by year's end the total amount of Mediterranean-based merchant shipping (500 tons or more) available to the Italians was down 99,025 tons compared to the starting total at the beginning of the conflict.[27]

When viewed together, Britain's status in the Mediterranean was clearly on the ascendancy, but the campaign was still young with many challenges yet to overcome. In terms of the maritime conflict, the British had thus far inflicted heavier losses upon the Italians than they themselves had suffered in both military and commercial shipping, but these losses had not reached prohibitive levels. This was particularly true regarding the Axis merchant fleet, which had only lost about 4.3 percent of its accumulated regional tonnage since the beginning of the campaign. Nor was the depletion of the Axis shipping pool decisive in its own right. Instead, it was only important to the extent it impacted the overall strategic and military situation in the Middle East. The immediate prizes for this struggle were Africa and the Persian Gulf. In this regard, the British had made great progress in fulfilling their own logistical needs, but had been woefully inadequate in impeding the ongoing Italian supply operations to Africa. During the last seven months of 1940 the Italians successfully transported some 29,000 men and 298,000 tons of materiel to Libya with only about 1.7 and 2.3 percent of the original dispatched totals lost in transit respectively.[28] Thus, while the Italian merchant fleet was a slowly wasting asset, this attrition had not had an appreciable impact upon the supply situation yet.

Fortunately for the British, these Italian logistical successes were soon offset by a major British victory on the battlefield. Bolstered by the steady flow of reinforcements and supplies to the region, the British Western Desert Force, consisting mainly of the 7th Armoured Division and the 4th Indian Division[29] and commanded by Lieutenant-General Richard O'Connor, launched an attack against the Italians at Sidi Barrani on 9 December. This assault was immensely successful as the British exploited gaps in the Italian lines and rolled up their defences in a piecemeal fashion. Within three days Sidi Barrani was once again in British hands, and the remnants of the defeated Italian forces were streaming back towards Cyrenaica. The monitor *Terror* and two gunboats added to this rout by firing some 220 15-inch and 600 6-inch shells at the retreating Italian formations as they congested the coastal road.[30] The Regia Marina made no attempt to counter these bombarding warships or to provide comparable support to their own ground forces, thus ceding the battlefield to the British. The result was an Italian defeat of immense proportions as the British captured some 38,300 prisoners, 73 tanks, 237 guns, over 1,000 vehicles and large stocks of supplies for the loss of just 624 casualties to themselves.[31]

This was the beginning of Operation *Compass*. Although originally envisioned as a large-scale raid lasting no more than four days, the wholesale collapse of the Italians and the bonanza of captured vehicles and supplies it netted offered the British an opportunity to continue their offensive. On 16 December the Italians abandoned Sollum, their last remaining outpost on Egyptian territory, and withdrew to Bardia on the Libyan side of the border. The British followed this retreat and quickly advanced to the outskirts of Bardia. Here they paused to make preparations for an assault against the strongly defended port. A major factor complicating this advance was the need to withdraw the 4th Indian Division for service in East Africa. Replacing this tested formation was the 6th Australian Division fresh from forming up in Palestine. While the Australians traversed the 350 miles from the Nile Delta to the outskirts of Bardia, the British made logistical preparations for the coming assault, which was tentatively scheduled for early January.

So as the year ended, the British had reason for great satisfaction and continued caution regarding their recent performance and standing in the Middle East. Seven months earlier the situation had been significantly more precarious. Grossly outnumbered by the Italians on land, sea and air, Britain's position in the Middle East had been far from secure. Thankfully, the Italians had failed to exploit their initial numerical advantages, and the British gained valuable time to strengthen their defences and bring in reinforcements. Then taking bold and aggressive action, the British had facilitated a series of successes, both small and large, that progressively tilted the struggle in their favour. Now with the advent of a new year, the British still faced a numerically superior enemy, but their fortunes were undisputedly on the rise. In the Mediterranean, North Africa, and even East Africa, where the British were preparing to go onto the offensive, the British clearly held the initiative. Yet, the British were also aware of a great danger looming on the horizon. With each Italian reversal, it only seemed a matter of time before Germany intervened to rescue its beleaguered Axis partner. When, where and to what extent this might occur was still uncertain, but there was growing consensus that German intervention was inevitable. To this end, the British were determined to use what time they had available to exploit their burgeoning ascendancy over the Italians and better position themselves to meet the expected German onslaught when it came. Only providence would tell if this would be enough.

CHAPTER 3

Germany Enters the Fray

On 6 January 1941 four merchant ships along with the cruiser *Bonaventure* and the destroyers *Jaguar*, *Hereward*, *Hasty* and *Hero* departed Gibraltar and set sail for the central Mediterranean. This was the beginning of Operation *Excess*, Britain's latest attempt to send supplies and reinforcements to Malta and Greece. Like so many recent undertakings of this nature, Operation *Excess* consisted of a complex series of shipping movements. At its core was the passage of the merchant ship *Essex* to Malta with 4,000 tons of ammunition, 3,000 tons of seed potatoes and a deck cargo of 12 crated Hurricane fighters. *Essex*'s three sailing companions, the freighters *Clan Cumming*, *Clan MacDonald* and *Empire Song*, would then proceed on to Piraeus and deliver valuable supplies to the Greeks. Meanwhile, from the Eastern Mediterranean the cruisers *Gloucester* and *Southampton* and two destroyers were tasked to transport 500 military and RAF personnel to Malta while a second convoy of two merchant ships delivered additional provisions to the besieged colony. Finally, eight empty merchant ships were scheduled to depart Malta and proceed to Alexandria. Providing overall security for this orchestrated set of manoeuvres was Force H and the Mediterranean Fleet.

Despite its varied complexities and the myriad of dangers arrayed against it, Operation *Excess* was far from a unique undertaking. During the previous seven months the British had successfully executed a number of similar convoy movements through the Mediterranean. In doing so, they had transformed Malta from a state of near defencelessness to a point where the colony was increasingly capable of offering effective resistance. By the beginning of 1941 Malta's air contingent had grown to a strength of 20 Hurricane fighters, 12 Swordfish torpedo-bombers, 20 Vickers Wellington medium bombers, six Short Sunderland flying boats and five American-built Glenn Martin Maryland reconnaissance bombers.[1] Likewise, in December the submarine *Upright* had arrived at Malta. This was the first of the new U-class submarines to enter the Mediterranean conflict, with additional boats soon to follow. At only a third to half the displacement of the currently employed submarines, these U-class boats were exceedingly better suited for Mediterranean operations than their larger counterparts. Of course, Malta's burgeoning relevance was contingent upon Britain's ability to keep the small island group supplied. To this end, Operation *Excess* was entirely successful as all personnel and materiel movements were accomplished without loss.

The same could not be said for some of the naval forces supporting the operation. On the morning of 10 January, the Italian torpedo boats *Vega* and *Circe* attacked the Gibraltar-originated convoy south of Pantelleria. After launching an ineffective torpedo salvo, the two torpedo boats quickly found themselves heavily engaged by the British escorts. In a matter of minutes *Bonaventure* and *Hereward* sank the hapless *Vega* while *Circe* was forced to retreat in a damaged state. Admiral Cunningham and the Mediterranean Fleet arrived on the scene just as the British ships were delivering the coup de grace against *Vega*, but this rendezvous was quickly marred when the attending destroyer *Gallant* lost its bow to a mine. The British towed the badly damaged destroyer to Malta, where it was declared a total constructive loss on 20 January. In doing so, the British split their forces and deprived the fleet of valuable anti-aircraft support that would soon be sorely missed.

At midday, after repelling a low-level torpedo-bomber attack, British radar identified a large formation of enemy aircraft approaching the fleet at an altitude of 12,000 feet. Accustomed to ineffective Italian high-altitude bombing, the British were not unduly alarmed by these approaching aircraft as the carrier *Illustrious* launched Fulmar fighters to intercept the attackers. However, before these fighters, or other fighters that were already airborne, could attain the correct altitude, the enemy formation arrived over the fleet and began a deadly attack. Tragically for the British, these were not Italian aircraft, but rather German Junkers Ju 87 Stuka dive-bombers. These aircraft were part of Fliegerkorps X, a specialised Luftwaffe anti-shipping unit that had recently arrived in the Mediterranean. Proceeding with lethal precision, the German aircraft targeted *Illustrious* with a rain of bombs that quickly scored at least five hits and one near miss on the exposed aircraft carrier. Such an onslaught would have surely destroyed a lesser protected vessel, but *Illustrious'* armoured flight deck and fire prevention/suppression systems saved the ship from destruction. Nevertheless, the carrier was heavily damaged and proceeded with great difficulty to Malta, which was 75 miles away. During the course of this tortured journey, *Illustrious* endured further air attacks and received another bomb hit and two more near misses. Finally, at 2215 hours the battered carrier arrived at Parlatorio Wharf in Malta's Grand Harbour and immediately began the process of undergoing emergency repairs and tending to its casualties, which consisted of 126 dead and 91 wounded.[2]

The calamity that had befallen *Illustrious* signalled Germany's long-expected intervention into the Mediterranean war. Alarmed by Italy's growing misfortune and the threat this situation posed to his southern flank; Hitler had begrudgingly consented to send forces south to bolster his troubled ally. The arrival of Fliegerkorps X was the first tangible result of this decision. Then on 11 January Hitler issued Directive No 22 authorising the establishment of a German military force in Libya with deployment scheduled to begin on or about 20 February. In the meantime, Fliegerkorps X continued its onslaught against the Mediterranean Fleet. On the 11th German bombers attacked the British cruisers *Gloucester* and *Southampton* as the latter were withdrawing from Malta. Hit by at least two bombs, *Southampton* was damaged beyond salvation and had to be scuttled. During the same period the Germans launched a series of raids against *Illustrious*, as the carrier lay exposed in Malta. These raids inflicted further damage on the immobilised aircraft carrier as well as the surrounding area, but failed to decisively curtail repair operations. On 23 January the carrier was finally deemed seaworthy enough to attempt a passage back to Alexandria. Departing Malta that evening, *Illustrious* successfully made this transit arriving in Alexandria on the 25th. The carrier then underwent further repairs before it was dispatched to the United States for a full refit.

While the departure of *Illustrious* and the arrival of Fliegerkorps X represented a dangerous turn of events for the British in the Mediterranean, it would take time before the Germans were fully integrated into the theatre. In the interim, notwithstanding these misfortunes, the overall trend in the region continued to favour the British. This was particularly true in North Africa where the Western Desert Force, now renamed XIII Corps, continued its offensive against the Italians. On 3 January Australian and British forces launched their long-awaited assault against the Italian stronghold of Bardia. RAF aircraft and various naval ships assisted this operation with bombing and gunfire support. On the morning of the assault this included the big guns of the Mediterranean Fleet as the battleships *Warspite*, *Valiant* and *Barham* carried out a 45-minute bombardment during which they fired 246 15-inch shells, 270 6-inch shells and 240 4.5-inch shells at Italian positions north of the Bardia–Tobruk road.[3] Thereafter, the monitor *Terror* and various gunboats provided intermittent fire support as the Australian and British troops successfully breached the Italian defences and raced deep into their interior positions. Once again as at Sidi Barrani, the Regia Marina made no attempt to intervene in the fighting, and by 5 January it was all over as Italian resistance collapsed and the British seized firm control over Bardia. During the three-day battle the Italians lost over 40,000 men killed or captured (mostly captured), along with over 400 guns, 130 tanks and several hundred motor vehicles. Corresponding British/Australian losses for the action numbered just 456 casualties.[4]

Not content to rest upon its laurels, XIII Corps continued its offensive with utmost haste. On 22 January Tobruk fell after undergoing extensive naval and air bombardment and an assault by the 6th Australian Division. In the process, another 25,000 Italian prisoners, 208 guns and 87 tanks went into the bag for the cost of just over 400 British/Australian casualties.[5] In addition to these military losses, the British found a dozen ships sunk in the harbour, including the 15,354-ton troopship

Liguria and the burning wreck of the armoured cruiser *San Giorgio*, which had opted to scuttle itself rather than attempt a breakout against blockading British warships. Likewise, large quantities of supplies were captured intact in the various warehouses along the docks, and it would only take the British two days to make the harbour ready to receive shipping. Continuing the advance, Australian forces captured Derna unopposed on 29 January, and Benghazi fell eight days later. Meanwhile, elements of the 7th Armoured Division crossed the desert south of Jebel Akhdar on Cyrenaica's western frontier and entrapped the remnants of the retreating Italian Tenth Army at Beda Fomm. After three days of desperate fighting, the Italian forces surrendered on 7 February and another 25,000 prisoners along with large quantities of equipment (including over 100 tanks and 100 guns) fell into British hands.[6]

This final success proved to be a fitting end for Operation *Compass* as exhaustion and logistical constraints forced the British to halt their offensive. Taking stock of the situation, it was clear the British had won a significant victory. During the ten-week campaign a British force, which never exceeded more than two under-strength divisions, had advanced some 500 miles, driven the Italians out of Egypt and conquered Cyrenaica. In the process of doing this, the British annihilated an entire Italian army consisting of ten divisions, took some 130,000 prisoners and destroyed or captured over 380 tanks and 845 guns.[7] Thousands of additional Italians were killed or wounded, many of which succumbed to British naval gunfire as bombarding warships devastated their positions and retreating columns along the coastal road. British casualties for the operation amounted to just 500 dead, 1,373 wounded and 55 missing.[8] Losses in the air were equally lopsided as 58 Italian aircraft were destroyed in aerial combat, 91 were captured intact and no fewer than 1,100 were found wrecked or otherwise disabled by the advancing British forces, while British losses relating to the operation numbered just 26 aircraft.[9] Finally, in addition to the cruiser *San Giorgio* and troopship *Liguria*, Britain's conquest of Cyrenaica cost the Regia Marina many installations and depots along with some 50 small auxiliary vessels that could not be evacuated in time or had to be sacrificed in last minute support operations.[10]

Nor was this Britain's only success during this period. In January the British launched two disparate campaigns to conquer Italian East Africa. The first of these was an offensive out of Sudan by the 4th and 5th Indian Divisions under the command of Lieutenant-General William Platt against Italian-controlled Eritrea. In the first fortnight of operations, British forces captured the important centres of Agordat and Barentu in northwest Eritrea along with 6,000 prisoners, 80 guns, 26 tanks and 400 trucks.[11] However, progress abruptly stalled when British forces assaulted the main Italian defensive position at Keren on the Asmara Plateau. This began a protracted battle lasting several weeks as the British slowly reduced the Italian defences in the formidable location. Meanwhile, a thousand miles to the south, Lieutenant-General Alan Cunningham (the brother of the Mediterranean Fleet's Admiral Andrew

Cunningham) launched an offensive out of Kenya with the 1st South African and the 11th and 12th African Divisions against Italian Somaliland.[12] Despite harsh terrain and climatic conditions, Cunningham's forces made good progress against largely ineffective Italian opposition and quickly captured the important port cities of Kismayu and Mogadishu on 14 and 25 February, along with some 30,000 prisoners and large quantities of supplies and equipment.[13] From there, Cunningham redirected his forces northward and began an invasion of Abyssinia.

Supporting this southern offensive was Force T consisting of the aircraft carrier *Hermes*, the cruisers *Shropshire*, *Hawkins*, *Capetown* and *Ceres* and the destroyer *Kandahar*. These ships provided fire support for Cunningham's advancing formations and blockaded Axis merchant ships caught in Italian Somaliland's southern ports. On 10 and 11 February eight Italian and two German merchant ships attempted to breakout of Kismayu. They left behind three Italian merchant ships of 16,758 tons that were scuttled on the 12th. Of the merchant ships attempting to breakout, five vessels worth 28,055 tons were located by Swordfish from *Hermes* and subsequently captured by the cruiser *Hawkins* as the latter arrived upon the scene. At roughly the same time the British discovered the 590-ton German *Askari* and the 6,861-ton Italian *Pensilvania* off Mogadishu and destroyed both with bombs and gunfire. Finally, on the 14th the 7,021-ton German *Uckermark* scuttled itself when intercepted by British warships. The only ships to actually avoid the British blockade were the Italian *Duca degli Abruzzi* and *Somalia*, which successfully reached Diego Suarez in Vichy-controlled Madagascar.[14]

Meanwhile, in the Red Sea another 30 Axis merchant ships languished in and around the Eritrean port of Massawa. In February and early March the new British aircraft carrier *Formidable* launched a series of air strikes against these vessels and other nearby targets as it passed through the Red Sea en route to the Mediterranean. During one of these attacks on 13 February *Formidable*'s Albacore aircraft sank the 5,723-ton Italian merchant ship *Moncalieri* at Massawa. A fortnight later the 7,669-ton Italian *Giuseppe Mazzini* was sunk by bombs at nearby Dalac Island. During this same period and throughout March a handful of Axis ships attempted to break out of the Red Sea and proceed to various locations, including Japan and South America. A few of these attempts were successful, but most either turned back or were lost to British naval units. Of the latter, on 27 February the New Zealand cruiser *Leander* intercepted and sank the Italian auxiliary cruiser *Ramb I* (3,667 tons, 4 × 4.7-inch guns) west of the Maldives. Five days later the German merchant ship *Coburg* and the prize tanker *Ketty Brovig* (7,400 and 7,031 tons respectively) scuttled themselves when approached by the cruisers *Canberra* and *Leander* southeast of the Seychelles. Then, on 24 March the 8,516-ton German merchant ship *Oder* scuttled itself when intercepted by the British sloop *Shoreham* in the Strait of Perim. Finally, on 1 April the British destroyer *Kandahar* intercepted and forced the scuttling of the 4,188-ton *Bertrand Rickmers* in the same area.

Beyond the fulfilment of these interdiction efforts, the Royal Navy also performed a number of important support functions. This included the prompt opening of captured ports in Italian Somaliland and the subsequent delivery of reinforcements and supplies through these ports to help sustain the British advance into Abyssinia. Then on 16 March a naval force (designated Force D) consisting of the cruisers *Glasgow* and *Caledon*, the destroyers *Kandahar* and *Kingston* and a number of auxiliaries landed two Indian army battalions and a Somali native unit on both sides of Berbera, the capital of British Somaliland. This undertaking, designated Operation *Appearance*, was entirely successful as the Italian opposition largely disintegrated in the face of the British landings and corresponding naval gunfire support. Berbera was promptly captured, followed shortly thereafter by the rest of British Somaliland, and the British were able to quickly put the port back into service, thus supporting part of the 11th African Division's materiel needs and reducing its logistical tail by some 500 road miles.[15]

As momentous as these various developments were, the main focus of the regional naval struggle remained in the Mediterranean. Despite the unwelcome appearance of the Luftwaffe, which continued to exact a deadly toll, including the destruction of the minesweeper *Huntley*, monitor *Terror* and destroyer *Dainty* from 31 January through 24 February, the British endeavoured to maintain an aggressive posture throughout the theatre. At no time was this more evident than during the period of 6–11 February when Admiral Somerville brought Force H right to the threshold of the Italian mainland and carried out a bombardment of the key commercial/military port of Genoa. Arriving unopposed off Genoa on the morning of the 9th, the battleship *Malaya*, battlecruiser *Renown* and cruiser *Sheffield* fired 273 15-inch shells, 782 6-inch shells and 400 4.5-inch shells against the harbour's docks, shipyards and marshalling areas.[16] Three Swordfish from *Ark Royal* provided spotter support for this barrage while a further 18 aircraft concurrently attacked an oil refinery at Leghorn and laid mines in La Spezia harbour. Of the 55 ships located in Genoa at the time, four freighters and the old training ship *Garaventa* were sunk while 18 other vessels suffered varying degrees of damage. The bombardment also caused widespread mayhem to the port and 144 fatalities.[17] By comparison, Force H was able to extricate itself and return to Gibraltar without undue loss or interference.

Admiral Cunningham's expanding submarine force and the FAA also enjoyed several successes during this period. In terms of the former, British submarines sank 13 Axis merchant ships worth 38,712 tons in the Mediterranean during the first three months of 1941. Added to this, on 25 February the submarine *Upright* sank the Italian light cruiser *Armando Diaz* 60 miles east of Sfax, Tunisia. One month later *Rorqual* sank the Italian submarine *Pier Capponi* off Sicily. Finally, mines laid by *Rorqual* accounted for the Italian torpedo boat *Generale Antonio Chinotto* and the merchant ships *Verde* and *Ticino* (1,432 and 1,470 tons respectively).[18] The only

Allied loss during this time was the Free French submarine *Narval*, which was sunk by an Italian torpedo boat off Tobruk. The same could not be said for the Italian submarine force, which in addition to the aforementioned *Pier Capponi*, lost *Neghelli* and *Anfitrite* to British escorts in January and March. Meanwhile, on 27 January Swordfish from No. 830 Squadron stationed at Malta scored their first success with the destruction of the 3,950-ton German merchant ship *Ingo* off Tunisia. Twenty days later aircraft from the same squadron sank the 4,920-ton Italian *Juventus* off Kuriot Island. Then in March six No. 815 Squadron Swordfish from the recently evacuated *Illustrious* began operations from a primitive airstrip at Paramythia in Greece. During the period of 12 March through 15 April these aircraft flew a number of nocturnal raids against Italian shipping in Valona harbour and sank three merchant ships worth 11,846 tons, severely damaged a fourth worth 3,539 tons and destroyed the torpedo boat *Andromeda*.

A development of a less positive nature occurred on 11 February when a small convoy of three German ships arrived safely in Tripoli. Although modest in its scope, this constituted the first of many such operations as the Germans deployed a small, but capable mechanised force to North Africa. There, they joined the equivalent of six Italian divisions still intact in Tripolitania (western Libya). This move caught the British at a time when their own limited resources were stretching to accommodate yet another mission, the expected deployment of an expeditionary force to Greece as the Greek government was now open to this proposition. Likewise, the British were compelled to withdraw and refit units that were worn-out from their recent participation in Operation *Compass*. As such, by March two newly arrived and untested formations, the 9th Australian Division and the incomplete 2nd Armoured Division, were entrusted with the defence of Cyrenaica. The British justified this arrangement with the belief that it would take until May before the Germans were ready for large-scale operations.

Meanwhile, in early March the British, with concurrence from the Greek government, began deployment of their expeditionary force to Greece. At the time the British already had some 4,200 men stationed in Greece, and they planned to increase this force fifteen-fold to include the 6th Australian Division, 2nd New Zealand Division and the 1st Armoured Brigade, with proposed follow-up formations including the 7th Australian Division and a Polish brigade. Throughout March and early April the British carried out a series of convoys under the designation of Operation *Lustre* that successfully transported 58,364 troops to Greece without significant loss.[19] They accomplished this despite attempted interference from Axis aircraft, submarines and the Italian surface fleet. This latter threat materialised in late March when the Regia Marina, under pressure from the Germans and with the promise of German air support, authorised a strong sortie into the Aegean. This operation commenced on 26 March as a powerful Italian force, under the command of Admiral Angelo Iachino and consisting of the battleship *Vittorio Veneto*, six heavy cruisers, two light cruisers and 13 destroyers, departed various Italian ports and proceeded eastward in search of British shipping.

Signal intercepts forewarned Cunningham that something was underway. This included a series of messages on 25–26 March that revealed increased Axis reconnaissance and other air activities over the Eastern Mediterranean in preparation for a special operation to be carried out on the 28th.[20] Cunningham surmised that a large-scale air attack or surface raid into the Aegean was indicated, and he adjusted his forces to meet the pending threat. First, on the evening of the 26th he cancelled the departure of a southbound convoy from Piraeus and ordered a northbound convoy to reverse course under the cover of darkness. Concurrently, he ordered Vice-Admiral Pridham-Wippell's Force B, with the cruisers *Orion*, *Ajax*, *Perth* and *Gloucester* and four destroyers, to position itself southwest of Gavdo Island. Then on the afternoon of the 27th a Sunderland flying boat located three Italian cruisers and a destroyer heading on a south-easterly course some 75 miles east of Sicily. This information provided further evidence of Italian intentions, and on the evening of the 27th Cunningham sortied the Mediterranean Fleet out of Alexandria and proceeded towards the south of Crete. Flying his flag on the battleship *Warspite*, Cunningham's fleet also consisted of the battleships *Barham* and *Valiant*, the recently arrived aircraft carrier *Formidable* and nine destroyers. Regarding *Formidable*, the new aircraft carrier (second in the *Illustrious*-class) possessed an air group of ten Albacore and four Swordfish strike aircraft and 13 Fulmar fighters.

At daybreak the next morning reconnaissance aircraft from both fleets sighted elements of their opposing numbers in the waters south of Crete. By this time Iachino's fleet was split into three parts. *Vittorio Veneto* and four destroyers were on the starboard station; the cruisers *Trieste*, *Trento* and *Bolzano* and three destroyers were ten miles to port; and the cruisers *Zara*, *Fiume*, *Pola*, *Guiseppe Garibaldi* and *Duca degli Abruzzi* and six destroyers were a further 20 miles away. By comparison, Cunningham's forces were also split with Force B located about 100 miles forward of the oncoming main fleet. At 0800 hours the centre Italian squadron sighted Force B and commenced firing 12 minutes later at a range of about 23,000 yards. Outgunned by the Italian heavy cruisers, Pridham-Wippell turned his ships away and attempted to draw the Italians towards Cunningham's oncoming capital ships. However, at 0855 hours the Italians broke off their pursuit and retired westward. Pridham-Wippell followed suit to maintain long-range contact with the retiring Italian squadron. At 1056 hours Force B again came under hostile fire, but in this case the offending source was the battleship *Vittorio Veneto*. Pridham-Wippell immediately turned his ships away under the cover of smoke. Now both he and Admiral Cunningham realised that Force B was in danger of being caught between two superior forces.

Fortunately, a timely but unsuccessful air strike by *Formidable*'s Albacores along with a lack of promised air support from Fliegerkorps X quickly prompted Iachino to abandon his sortie and turn back towards Italy. At 1230 hours Admiral Cunningham's main force rendezvoused with Force B and continued its pursuit of the withdrawing enemy fleet. In the afternoon *Formidable* launched a second air strike in an attempt to immobilise or slow down the retreating Italian force. A handful of aircraft from Crete augmented this raid as the British targeted the powerful *Vittorio Veneto*. At 1519 hours one of *Formidable*'s Albacores scored a torpedo hit that temporarily stopped and then reduced *Vittorio Veneto*'s speed. Despite this development, Cunningham realised that he was unlikely to catch the fleeing Italians before nightfall, and instead braced himself for a nocturnal engagement as he sent Force B forward to regain contact with the enemy. While this was underway, a combined force of six Albacores and four Swordfish from both *Formidable* and Crete carried out a final dusk attack against the Italian fleet. Flying through intense anti-aircraft fire, these aircraft failed to hit the heavily defended *Vittorio Veneto*, but did score a single torpedo hit on the heavy cruiser *Pola*, which caused it to lose all power.

At 2018 hours Admiral Iachino, who was unaware of the close proximity of the Mediterranean Fleet, ordered the heavy cruisers *Zara* and *Fiume*, with four destroyers, to turn back and render assistance to the crippled *Pola*. At the same time, Cunningham's surface forces were continuing forward into the darkening night. Already, at 2015 hours the cruisers *Ajax* and *Orion* had detected a stationary ship about six miles to port on their radars. Upon receipt of this information, Cunningham altered course to investigate the contact, which he surmised might be the damaged *Vittorio Veneto*. In the meantime, Force B along with several destroyers continued to search for the remaining Italian fleet. At 2210 hours *Valiant*'s radar located the stationary vessel, which was in fact *Pola*. Then as Cunningham's ships closed on the crippled cruiser, the British detected six additional vessels, which were visually identified as Italian cruisers and destroyers, approaching from the west. Cunningham immediately ordered his battleships to alter course and form line ahead to bring their broadsides to bear on the unsuspecting Italian warships, which were the hapless *Zara*, *Fiume* and their attending destroyers.

At 2227 hours the destroyer *Greyhound* switched on its searchlights and illuminated the second ship in the Italian line, the cruiser *Fiume*, while *Warspite* opened fire on the exposed Italian warship at the relative point-blank range of 3,800 yards. Of the six 15-inch shells fired in this initial salvo, five were seen to hit the unlucky *Fiume* with devastating effect. Immediately thereafter, *Valiant* and *Barham* also opened fire on the two lead cruisers. This onslaught caught the Italians completely by surprise as incoming shells deluged their helpless warships. In a one-sided battle lasting just four and a half minutes, the three British battleships fired a series of salvoes that reduced *Fiume* and *Zara* to blazing, shattered wrecks. While this was underway, and in the minutes following, the British destroyers *Greyhound*, *Griffin*, *Havock* and *Stuart* engaged their opposite numbers in a chaotic melee that sank the Italian destroyers *Vittorio Alfieri* and *Giosue Carducci*. Meanwhile, the shattered *Fiume* sank at 2315 hours while the British destroyer *Jervis* torpedoed and finished off the devastated *Zara* some three hours later. At about the same time British destroyers found the crippled and powerless *Pola*, and after taking off its crew, dispatched the stricken cruiser with torpedoes.

So ended what became known as the battle of Cape Matapan. With the coming dawn air reconnaissance from *Formidable* confirmed that *Vittorio Veneto* was now beyond reach, and the threat of Luftwaffe reprisals prompted Cunningham to turn his ships for home. As he performed this manoeuvre, Cunningham signalled the Italian Admiralty and provided it with survivor locations so it could dispatch rescue vessels. That afternoon the expected Luftwaffe attack materialised, but all the British ships emerged unscathed, and *Formidable*'s fighters claimed two of the attacking aircraft destroyed. The next evening the fleet arrived safely back in Alexandria, thus completing a very satisfying sortie. Concurrently, Iachino's remaining ships also successfully completed their passages home, but they did so absent five of their number. In all, the battle cost the Italians three heavy cruisers and two destroyers sunk, along with 2,303 officers and men killed and another 1,015 taken prisoner.[21] Likewise, the damaged *Vittorio Veneto* would be under repairs until August. By comparison, no British ships suffered appreciable damage, and the only British loss for the battle was a single Albacore and its crew. In psychological terms, the battle had an understandably negative impact upon Italian morale and resolve. Never again

The most decorated ship in Royal Navy history, the battleship *Warspite* saw service in a number of theatres throughout the war. Of particular distinction, *Warspite* served as the flagship for the early Mediterranean Fleet and played a key role in destroying three Italian heavy cruisers during the battle of Cape Matapan in March 1941. (Oulds, D. C. (Lt), Royal Navy official photographer, public domain)

would the Regia Marina send major warships into the Eastern Mediterranean or openly attempt to engage the British Mediterranean Fleet on anything approaching equal terms. As such, the Italian surface fleet would be a non-factor during the upcoming Greek operations.

Unfortunately, the battle also signalled a high point during a period of increasing difficulty for the British. On the night of 25/26 March Italian special units attacked the heavy cruiser *York* with explosive-laden motor boats in Suda Bay and damaged it so severely that it had to be beached. Five days later the Italian submarine *Ambra* sank the British light cruiser *Bonaventure* 90 miles south of Crete. Of far greater consequence, on 24 March General Erwin Rommel, the commander of the newly formed German Afrika Korps, defied British estimates and the limited directives of his superiors by launching an offensive against the British in Cyrenaica. Advancing with a reinforced German division and three Italian divisions, this offensive caught the British in a precarious position as their under-strength and inexperienced units were hard pressed to mount a coherent defence. In a stark reversal of fortunes, the British began giving up ground they had so recently captured. On the 31st German assaults forced the British out of Marsa Brega, and Benghazi fell four days later. Thankfully, this loss of territory was not matched by correspondingly high casualty rates, as the majority of British units were able to avoid destruction or entrapment. Still, the British faced an alarming situation, as most of their territorial gains from the previous month and a half were lost.

In an attempt to stem this tide, the British finally opted to make a stand at Tobruk. Building a garrison out of the largely intact 9th Australian Division and several lesser formations, the British resolved to hold Tobruk until sufficient forces could be mustered in Egypt to restore the situation. Utilising the defensive perimeter recently held by the Italians, this garrison, commanded by Major-General L. J. Morshead, settled in to meet the Axis onslaught. They did not have long to wait. On 11 April German units made contact with the Tobruk defenders, and by the next day elements of four divisions encircled the perimeter. On the 13th Rommel launched a hasty and ill-prepared attack with some of his German units. Coming up against fortified Australian positions, the attack was a complete failure costing the Germans some 150 dead, 250 prisoners and 17 tanks. On the 15th and 16th, it was the turn of the Italians as infantry and armour units from the Trento and Ariete Divisions assaulted the western side of the perimeter. In a series of attacks and counter-attacks, the Australians defeated these efforts and took 1,063 prisoners, including an entire Italian infantry battalion. These failures convinced Rommel to pause and build up his forces for a prepared attack. Meanwhile, the skirmishing continued for the next several days as the Tobruk defenders held firm and added a further 650 prisoners to their growing bag.[22]

Throughout this period and during the succeeding weeks, the navy made vital contributions to the land battle. In most direct terms, this included the provision of essential logistical support for the Tobruk garrison. With Axis forces now encircling Tobruk and pushing on to the Egyptian border, the only viable means by which the British could re-supply the besieged stronghold was through maritime transport. This was no simple task given the requirement to provide food, water, ammunition, supplies and equipment to an initial garrison numbering some 35,700 men.[23] To facilitate this, the British employed the Inshore Squadron consisting of various old destroyers, minor warships and selected merchant vessels to conduct regular supply runs to Tobruk. During its first full month of operations in May the squadron delivered 1,688 reinforcements and 2,593 tons of supplies to Tobruk while evacu-ating 5,918 prisoners, casualties and non-essential personnel from the beleaguered fortress.[24] The squadron also carried out numerous bombardments and raids against Axis coastal positions, including at Bomba, Gazala, Sollum, Fort Capuzzo, Bardia and Bu Amud. However, these operations came at a cost as Luftwaffe aircraft sank the minesweeper *Stoke*, the gunboat *Ladybird* and the sloop *Grimsby* on 7, 12 and 25 May respectively.

A second major facet in the navy's support for the land battle was its interdiction efforts against Rommel's seaborne lines of communication. This was particularly important given the ongoing flow of Axis reinforcements and supplies en route to Libya, including a second division (15th Panzer) for the German Afrika Korps. Despite increased Luftwaffe bombing, Malta remained a primary base from which the British could launch their interdiction efforts. In April, a small contingent of destroyers from the 14th Destroyer Flotilla arrived at Malta to bolster the colony's offensive arsenal. Commanded by Captain P. J. Mack and under the designation Force K, this detachment consisted of the destroyers *Jervis*, *Janus*, *Mohawk* and *Nubian*. Although far from a substantial force, these destroyers added a new dimension to the threats arrayed against the transiting Axis convoys. In particular, with three of the four destroyers possessing radar, Force K appeared well suited for nocturnal operations.

As it was, it did not take long to test this hypothesis. On the night of 15/16 April Force K intercepted a five-ship German convoy off Kerkenah Bank that was transporting elements of the 15th Panzer Division to Tripoli. Approaching the convoy's rear, as it was silhouetted against the newly rising moon, the British opened fire at 0220 hours at a range of 2,400 yards. Initially caught by surprise and unsure where the fire was coming from, the three attending Italian destroyers were unable to mount a coordinated defence. As such, the British neutralised each of these destroyers in a piecemeal fashion while concurrently engaging the convoy's merchant ships. This was not an entirely one-sided affair as the Italian destroyer *Luca Tarigo* scored two torpedo hits on *Mohawk*. Still, this proved to be the only British misfortune for the engagement, and Force K was able to destroy all five merchant ships worth 14,398 tons as well as the attending destroyers *Luca Tarigo* and *Baleno*. The third Italian destroyer, *Lampo*, was heavily damaged and had to be beached, thus putting it out of service for 13 months. With the destruction of this convoy, some 1,700 men, 300 vehicles and 3,500 tons of stores destined for the Afrika Korps were lost.[25] The only British casualty for the engagement was the destroyer *Mohawk*, which had to be scuttled due to its torpedo damage.

While this action represented the navy's most complete victory during this period, it was by no means their only success. On the morning of 21 April elements of the Mediterranean Fleet, including the battleships *Warspite*, *Barham* and *Valiant*, penetrated deep into enemy-controlled waters and conducted a bombardment of Tripoli, Italy's principal port in Libya. Firing 478 15-inch and 1,500 6-inch and 4.7-inch shells, the bombarding warships sank the merchant ships *Assiria* and *Marocchino* (2,704 and 1,524 tons respectively) along with a minor auxiliary, damaged at least four other vessels, and caused varying degrees of damage to port facilities, depots and barracks for no loss to themselves.[26] Three days later the destroyers of Force K were once again at sea, and although they missed their intended convoy target, they still managed to sink the 3,311-ton Italian merchant ship *Egeo* near Kerkenah Bank. Meanwhile, during the month British submarines sank the Italian merchant ships *Persiano* and *Antonietta Lauro* and a patrol craft worth a combined 8,181 tons.[27] Finally, in April *Ark Royal* and Force H conducted two ferrying missions during which they successfully delivered a total of 35 Hurricane fighters to Malta.

Sadly, while these various successes provided the British a modicum of good news, the situation in Greece and the Balkans deteriorated at an alarming rate. On 6 April Germany declared war on Yugoslavia and Greece and launched large-scale invasions into both countries. Supported by Italy as well as the lesser recent Axis additions of Hungry and Bulgaria, the Germans committed substantial ground and air forces to this onslaught. After a mere two days of fighting, the ethnically fragmented Yugoslav army crumbled under German, Italian and Hungarian pressure. At the same time the powerful German Twelfth Army, supported by some 1,000 Luftwaffe aircraft, advanced into Greece through Bulgaria. These forces were soon joined by the German XL Corps, which crossed the Yugoslav–Greek border south of Monastir and assaulted the thinly defended Aliakhmon Line. Confronted by these incursions as well as their continued struggle along the Albanian frontier, the brave, but outmatched, Greek army was incapable of offering meaningful resistance and begrudgingly gave ground. Under these circumstances, the recently arrived British forces were also compelled to execute a series of withdrawals in the face of strong German thrusts.

On 21 April British authorities realised that the situation was beyond salvation and ordered a full evacuation of Greece. With the main port of Piraeus unusable due to damage from earlier air raids, the British opted to withdraw the bulk of their forces over open beaches at Raphti, Nauplia, Megara, Raphina, Tolon, Kalamata, Monemvasia, Kithera and Milos in southern Greece. Operating at night to mitigate Luftwaffe interference, the Royal Navy utilised seven cruisers, 20 destroyers, three sloops, two corvettes, two infantry assault ships, 19 transports and many smaller vessels under the command of Vice-Admiral Pridham-Wippell to enact the evacuation. Beginning on the night of 24/25 April and continuing for six consecutive nights, the British successfully withdrew 50,732 men from the Greek mainland, including a number of Greek and Yugoslav troops.[28] This evacuation saved about 80 percent of the British expeditionary force, but 13,958 men were still left behind to become prisoners.[29] Likewise, large quantities of supplies and equipment were lost, including 209 aircraft and some 8,000 lorries.[30]

The campaign also exacted a heavy toll on maritime assets. During the period covering the deployment, operation and subsequent evacuation of the British expeditionary force, a total of 32 Allied merchant ships and auxiliaries totalling 128,418 tons were destroyed or abandoned in various Greek and Cretan ports while a further 12 vessels of 94,406 tons were lost at sea.[31] The majority of these losses came from Greek or Allied sources, but a number of British merchant ships were also included in this tally. Britain's naval contribution to this butcher's bill included the destroyer *Diamond* and the escort destroyer *Wryneck*, which were sunk by Luftwaffe bombers south of Nauplia on the 27th. Meanwhile, the small Greek navy lost the pre-dreadnought battleships *Kilkis* and *Lemnos*, four destroyers and several lesser vessels to German air attacks. A fifth destroyer, *Vasilevs Georgios I*, was damaged and captured at Salamis. The Germans would later repair and put this ship into Kriegsmarine service under the new name *Hermes*. Likewise, German and Italian forces seized a number of Yugoslav naval vessels, including an old cruiser, three destroyers, a seaplane tender and six minesweepers, that were all subsequently incorporated into the Regia Marina or Kriegsmarine.

As bad as this was, ongoing events gave the British little time to lament their misfortunes. With the fall of Greece, British authorities surmised that the Germans would next strike at Crete. Realising this likelihood posed a threat to their position in the Eastern Mediterranean, the British resolved to defend the large Greek island. Therefore, even as the evacuation of Greece was still underway, the British diverted large numbers of troops to Crete. In the days and weeks that followed, these forces made feverish preparations to meet the expected German attack. Meanwhile, the situation in North Africa continued to demand attention. On 1 May Rommel launched a new attempt to capture Tobruk with a large-scale assault against the fortress' western perimeter. In four days of fighting the garrison's defenders blunted this effort and inflicted 954 casualties on the attacking formations for a cost of 797 casualties to themselves.[32] While this success continued to frustrate Rommel's ambitions, a limited British offensive in the Sollum-Capuzzo area 11 days later, Operation *Brevity*, attained equally disappointing results for the British, thus facilitating a stalemate in Cyrenaica.

To improve this general situation, the Royal Navy undertook Operation *Tiger* to pass five fast merchant ships loaded with 295 tanks and 53 crated Hurricane fighters directly through the Mediterranean to the British forces in Egypt. Concurrent objectives of the operation were to transfer warship reinforcements, consisting of the battleship *Queen Elizabeth*, the cruisers *Naiad* and *Fiji* and four destroyers, to the Mediterranean Fleet, while two tankers and four cargo ships delivered vital provisions to Malta. As was the case in earlier such undertakings, most of the Mediterranean Fleet, along with Force H, provided cover and support for these movements. Beginning on 5 May and concluding seven days later, Operation *Tiger* was remarkably successful given the potential threats arrayed against it. This result was partially facilitated by unseasonably bad weather that helped shield the British forces from enemy aerial reconnaissance and attack. As such, the only British loss for the operation was the 9,228-ton merchant ship *Empire Song* (carrying 57 tanks and ten Hurricanes), which sank after striking mines. The remaining British ships all arrived safely at their various destinations, thus delivering 238 tanks and 43 Hurricanes to Egypt as well as needed provisions to Malta and powerful naval reinforcements to the Mediterranean Fleet. As an added bonus, during the course of these movements British cruisers and destroyers carried out two bombardments of Benghazi and intercepted and sank the Italian merchant ships *Tenace* and *Capitano A Cecchi*, worth 1,142 and 2,321 tons respectively.

The period also saw other events that caused attrition to both sides. On 2 May the British destroyer *Jersey* struck a mine and sank at the entrance of Malta's Grand Harbour. Two days later Axis bombers destroyed the minesweeper *Fermoy* in a Maltese dry-dock. Against this, the Italian torpedo boat *Simone Schiaffino* was accidentally lost in an Italian minefield off Cape Bon on 24 April. Then on 3 May RAF bombers sank the Italian torpedo boat *Canopo* during a raid against Tripoli. The next day the Italian torpedo boat *Giuseppe La Farina* was mined and sunk off Kerkenah Bank. As for the submarine campaign, in May British submarines had their most profitable month to date in the young Mediterranean war as they sank at least seven merchant ships and a small sailing vessel worth a combined 34,711 tons.[33] This included the 17,879-ton troopship *Conte Rosso*, which was sunk by the submarine *Upholder* ten miles east of Syracuse on the 24th. Some 1,300 Italian fatalities accompanied this sinking, which earned *Upholder*'s commander, Lieutenant-Commander M. D. Wanklyn, a Victoria Cross.[34] Unfortunately, these successes came at a cost, as the submarines *Usk* and *Undaunted* were both lost during this period to presumed mine strikes.

Meanwhile, on 20 May all attention reverted back to Crete as the long-expected German invasion began. Supported by a massive preliminary aerial bombardment that lasted several days, German airborne forces began landing at key locations across the island. At the time Crete was defended by 32,000 British troops, but these forces were hamstrung by a number of factors. First, as previously indicated, the Germans enjoyed overwhelming air superiority that they effectively used as airborne artillery. Second, the island's poor transportation infrastructure and a lack of mobility assets prevented the British from easily moving their forces from one area to another. As such, the British were compelled to disperse their forces throughout the island with little chance of mutual support. This problem was exacerbated by a lack of reliable communication equipment and insufficient armour and artillery support. Yet, despite these shortcomings, the British initially offered effective resistance against German parachute troops that often landed directly over their defended positions. Throughout the first day of fighting these forces inflicted heavy losses on the attacking Germans, but on the 21st the situation slowly changed as the Germans secured Maleme airfield and began flying in supplies and reinforcements.

While this was underway, the Royal Navy did its part to try to stem the German onslaught. A component of the German invasion plan called for seaborne landings to supplement their airborne forces. To counter this, the British operated three squadrons of cruisers and destroyers north of Crete at night, while a battleship squadron remained west of Crete to deter intervention by the Italian battle fleet. On the night of 20/21 May these forces failed to find any invasion vessels, but British destroyers did carry out a bombardment of Scarpanto airfield. The next night British forces again entered the Aegean and this time encountered an invasion convoy 18 nautical miles north of Caneá, consisting of some 20 motor sailing vessels and the Italian torpedo boat *Lupo*. In a brisk action, the cruisers *Dido*, *Orion* and *Ajax*, along with four destroyers sank ten motor vessels, scattered the rest and heavily damaged *Lupo*. Despite this slaughter, prompt rescue efforts saved all but 297 of the 2,331 men embarked.[35] The next morning the cruisers *Naiad*, *Perth*, *Calcutta* and *Carlisle* and three destroyers encountered a second invasion convoy consisting of 30 odd coastal vessels and the Italian torpedo boat *Sagittario*. At the time these vessels were already en route back to Piraeus having been recalled due to the first convoy's fate, and the British only succeeded in sinking two stragglers before the threat of German air attacks forced them to break off their pursuit.

Through these actions, the British prevented the Germans from executing their seaborne invasion plans, but they paid a heavy price for this meagre victory. Although British ships could operate with reasonable impunity at night, daytime operations were severely restricted by the Luftwaffe. This point was demonstrated early in the campaign when Axis bombers sank the minesweeper *Widnes* on the 20th and the destroyer *Juno* on the 21st.[36] Then on the 22nd the situation became much worse as wave after wave of Luftwaffe and, to a lesser extent, Italian bombers attacked the British fleet and sank the cruisers *Gloucester* and *Fiji* and the destroyer *Greyhound* and damaged the battleships *Warspite* and *Valiant* and the cruisers *Carlisle* and *Naiad*. At the same time, the cruiser *York*, which was already immobilised due to damage from Italian special units, had to be scuttled in Suda Bay following further damage by German air attacks. On the night of 22/23 May British destroyers bombarded Maleme airfield, but this action facilitated a Luftwaffe response the next day that resulted in the destruction of the destroyers *Kashmir* and *Kelly*. Three days later the aircraft carrier *Formidable* joined the fray by launching air attacks against a key

Luftwaffe airfield at Scarpanto. While these attacks and subsequent aerial combat destroyed at least two enemy aircraft and damaged others, retaliating German bombers heavily damaged *Formidable* and the destroyer *Nubian*. Then, on the 27th German aircraft damaged the battleship *Barham*.

Despite these efforts and sacrifices, the situation on Crete continued to deteriorate as German airborne reinforcements increasingly tipped the scales against the British. On 26 May the island commander, Major-General Bernard Freyberg, informed his superiors that Crete's retention was no longer tenable. This position was endorsed by the theatre commander, General Archibald Wavell, and the next day the Chiefs of Staff in London authorised an evacuation. Some minor withdrawals had already occurred, but with this decision, the Royal Navy went forward to carry out yet another full-scale evacuation in the face of overwhelming enemy air superiority. Unable to use Suda Bay due to German advances, the British ordered the bulk of their forces to proceed to the tiny fishing port of Sphakia on Crete's rugged southern coast. However, between 4,000 and 4,500 men remained trapped at Heraklion on Crete's northern coast. Therefore, the British dispatched three cruisers and six destroyers under the command of Rear-Admiral Bernard Rawlings to enact an extraction. While en route, damage from air attacks caused the cruiser *Ajax* to turn back, but the remaining ships proceeded to Heraklion where they rescued 3,486 men on the night of 28/29 May. In a concurrent operation four destroyers delivered provisions to the gathering forces at Sphakia and successfully evacuated 680 men. Sadly, these operations exacted a heavy retribution the next day when Luftwaffe bombers sank or forced the scuttling of the destroyers *Hereward* and *Imperial* and severely damaged the cruisers *Dido* and *Orion*.

For the next three nights the focus of the evacuation reverted to Sphakia. Even before this began, the Admiralty queried Admiral Cunningham as to whether further evacuations were justified given his heavy warship losses. To this, Cunningham responded, 'It takes the Navy three years to build a ship. It would take three hundred years to build a new reputation. The evacuation will continue.'[37] Fortunately for those involved, this defiant declaration proved justified as the worst was already over. On the night of 29/30 May the navy successfully evacuated 6,029 men from Sphakia for little damage to itself other than a single bomb hit on the cruiser *Perth*. The next night two British destroyers evacuated another 1,510 men from the small Greek fishing port for no loss to themselves. Finally, on the night of 31 May/1 June the British concluded their evacuation efforts with a lift of 3,710 men from Sphakia. Sadly, this operation was marred on the 1st when German bombers hit and sank the cruiser *Calcutta*, which was acting in a supporting role. Despite this final calamity, the troop-laden ships all successfully completed their journeys. This, in turn, concluded the formal evacuation which resulted in the successful delivery of 16,511 men from Crete to Egypt.[38] During the next week a few hundred additional soldiers made good their escapes in minor vessels, thus adding to this total.

While this constituted a meaningful achievement, it could not alter the undeniable fact that the struggle for Crete had been a costly fiasco. When the final tally was counted, British military casualties for the short campaign numbered 1,742 dead, 1,737 wounded and 11,835 prisoners. Added to this were another 1,828 naval personnel killed and 183 wounded.[39] As for shipping casualties, the British lost three cruisers (excluding the previously damaged *York*), six destroyers and a minesweeper sunk and three battleships, one aircraft carrier, six cruisers and seven destroyers damaged to varying degrees. In terms of the latter, the British were compelled to withdraw *Warspite* and *Formidable* from the theatre to undergo extensive repairs lasting 22 and 20 weeks respectively.[40] Likewise, many of the other damaged warships would take several weeks to repair. As such, by the beginning of June the Mediterranean Fleet was dangerously weak and only a shadow of its former self. However, as bad as this was, it might have been much worse had the Regia Marina taken the opportunity to intervene in the Crete operation. In this regard, Italy's failure to take action demonstrated the value of the naval ascendancy the British had established at Taranto and Cape Matapan. Now with the Mediterranean Fleet so severely weakened, the British could only hope that the Italians continued their self-imposed inactivity.

On the other hand, the losses at Crete were not entirely one-sided. During the campaign German casualties consisted of 1,990 dead, 2,131 wounded and 1,995

Germany's intervention into the Mediterranean theatre proved to be an ominous development that changed the scope and complexion of the entire campaign. Pictured here is the British destroyer *Kelly*, which was sunk by Luftwaffe aircraft off Crete in May 1941. (Tomlin, H. W. (Lt) Royal Navy official photographer, public domain)

missing (mostly presumed dead), of which almost three-quarters came from their airborne and assault formations. Likewise, the operation cost the Luftwaffe 220 aircraft destroyed and another 148 damaged.[41] When combined together, these heavy losses reduced Germany's elite airborne arm into a spent force. As such, the struggle for Crete was arguably a Pyrrhic victory in that Germany's vaunted airborne formations were now unavailable for further, and potentially more important, operations such as an assault against Malta. In regards to maritime losses, on 20 May the Italian torpedo boat *Curtatone* was lost in a Greek minefield off Piraeus. The next night the British minelayer *Abdiel* laid 150 mines off Cape Dukato that claimed the destruction of the Italian destroyer *Carlo Mirabello*, the Italian gunboat *Matteucci* and the German transports *Marburg* and *Kybfels* (7,564 and 7,764 tons respectively). Finally, at the end of the month the 3,821-ton Bulgarian ammunition ship *Knyaguinya Marie Louisa* caught fire in Piraeus as the result of an accident or sabotage and blew up, destroying itself and the nearby merchant ships *Alicante* and *Jiul* (German and Romanian, worth 2,140 and 3,127 tons respectively).

Nor was this the full extent of Axis shipping losses in the Mediterranean during May. Already mentioned were Axis shipping losses to British submarines and warships. Further Axis losses included at least three merchant ships worth 11,188 tons that were sunk by British aircraft while engaging in support operations to North Africa. Mines also enjoyed considerable success claiming at least seven Axis merchant vessels worth 4,372 tons in addition to the aforementioned *Marburg* and *Kybfels*. Likewise, the 5,165-ton Italian merchant ship *Zeffiro* was either sunk by the British submarine *Urge* or by an accidental mine strike during this period. Finally, accidental, operational and unknown causes accounted for six further vessels worth 13,588 tons. When combined together, at least 32 Axis merchant ships worth 96,541 tons were sunk or otherwise rendered unusable in the Mediterranean during May.[42] This made May the costliest month for Mediterranean-based Axis merchant shipping thus far in the war. Thus, when viewing the maritime conflict as a whole, the losses sustained during this period were far more balanced than the debacles off Greece and Crete might have indicated.

Beyond this, the British could also take solace in their recent spectacular successes attained in East Africa. In terms of the maritime struggle, this was particularly pertinent in Eritrea, where on 27 March the British finally broke through the Italian defences at Keren, thus concluding an eight-week battle that had cost them 536 dead and 3,229 wounded.[43] During the same struggle the Italians lost at least 3,000 killed, 4,500 wounded and over 3,000 taken prisoner.[44] Now with their main defensive line broken and many of their best units severely depleted from the recent heavy fighting, the Italians were thoroughly demoralised and hard pressed to offer further coordinated resistance against the advancing British units. As such, the British made good progress and in less than a month completed their conquest of Eritrea, taking many thousands of prisoners in the process for minimal loss to themselves. The key prize in this victory was the port city of Massawa, which served as the main Italian naval base in the Red Sea. At the time the Italians still maintained a large naval contingent at this base, including six destroyers and two torpedo boats. Likewise, more than two dozen Italian and German merchant ships sheltered at Massawa and the surrounding area.

Now with the British pressing in on them, these naval assets came under attack. On 1 April the Italian destroyer *Leone* accidentally ran aground 15 miles north of Awali Hutub and was subsequently scuttled by its crew. The next day the five remaining Italian destroyers departed Massawa in a desperate one-way sortie to attack Port Sudan. In anticipation of this action, the British had already deployed two squadrons of Swordfish to the area. These aircraft came from the aircraft carrier *Eagle*, which was awaiting outbound passage through the Suez Canal. The next morning these Swordfish, along with Blenheim bombers, carried out a series of attacks that sank the destroyers *Nazario Sauro* and *Daniele Manin* and drove off *Pantera* and *Tigre* in damaged conditions. That afternoon the British found the latter two vessels aground and abandoned off the Arabian coast where they were finished off by British aircraft and gunfire from the destroyer *Kingston*. The fifth Italian destroyer, *Cesare Battisti*, suffered early engine trouble and was scuttled off the Arabian coast to avoid action with British forces.

Over the next few days, the British conducted a series of attacks and bombardments against Massawa culminating in a major assault on the night of 7/8 April. During these attacks British aircraft destroyed the Italian torpedo boat *Giovanni Acerbi*, while artillery hit and damaged the torpedo boat *Vincenzo Giordano Orsini*. For their part, the Italians scored a notable success on the 6th when a MAS motor torpedo boat hit and damaged the British light cruiser *Capetown* outside of the harbour. However, this proved to be a fleeting accomplishment as all Italian resistance collapsed two days later. Prior to this the Italians scuttled the damaged *Vincenzo Giordano Orsini*, the minelayer *Ostia* and five MAS boats. They further scuttled 11 Italian and six German merchant ships worth 89,870 tons, several minor vessels and a floating dock in Massawa. Meanwhile, five additional Italian merchant ships worth 38,125 tons were scuttled near the Island of Dalac, while three others worth 23,765 tons were scuttled at Assab on 10 April.[45] Of these merchant ships, many were later recovered and put into British service. Likewise, the British seized large quantities of rolling stock and stores, and they were able to put the port back into working order before month's end.

Through these events and other similar successes in the south, the British accomplished their key strategic objective for the campaign. By gaining mastery over the Horn of Africa and eliminating Italian naval and air forces from the region, the British secured their vital seaborne lines of communication to the Middle East. Additionally, since the area was no longer considered a war zone, the United States lifted restrictions prohibiting its merchant ships from entering the Red Sea. As such,

American merchant ships would soon join the ranks of British and Allied vessels delivering supplies and stores to the British forces throughout the region. The British also enjoyed considerable materiel success against the Italians. In addition to the maritime losses already described, the British destroyed five Italian divisions and several independent battalions and captured over 40,000 prisoners and 300 guns during their conquest of Eritrea.[46] Meanwhile, British forces to the south and west enjoyed similar success as they completed their conquest of Italian Somaliland, recaptured British Somaliland and advanced into the heart of Abyssinia seizing the capital of Addis Ababa on 6 April. When these successes were added together (including Eritrea), the British had thus far collected over 105,000 prisoners within the region.[47] Although sizable Italian forces still remained in the interior of Abyssinia, they were isolated and severely weakened and could do little more than tie down British units engaged in mopping-up operations.

The successful prosecution of the East Africa campaign provided an important counterbalance to the recent British defeats in Cyrenaica, Greece and Crete. Indeed, Italian personnel losses in East Africa far exceeded the concurrent British casualties suffered throughout the entire theatre during this period. Likewise, this campaign once again demonstrated that the British were more than capable of handling the Italians. Still, this was not good enough. In order to be successful going forward, the British also had to find a way to defeat the Germans. Thus far they had consistently failed to do this, with results ranging from disappointing to disastrous. The only success the British could point to in this regard was their dogged defence of Tobruk. The situation was much the same at sea. Time and again, the British had prevailed over the Regia Marina and successfully operated despite the best efforts of the Regia Aeronautica. However, the arrival of the Luftwaffe had significantly altered this situation. Now the British routinely found themselves severely challenged by German bombers, and it was this threat that facilitated the overwhelming majority of their recent maritime losses. As such, the Luftwaffe was now the Mediterranean Fleet's chief adversary, and as the carnage off Crete had clearly demonstrated, the British were dangerously vulnerable to this threat.

Table 3.1 Characteristics of German Aircraft Utilised in Anti-Shipping Operations

	Roles	Top speed (mph)	Range (miles)	Maximum ordnance load (lbs)
Junkers Ju. 87	Dive-bomber	238	490	1,100
Heinkel He. 111	Medium bomber, maritime strike	252	1,280	5,501
Junkers Ju. 88	Medium bomber, maritime strike	280	1,056	3,960
Dorner Do. 217	Medium bomber, maritime strike	320	1,430	4,410

This is not to say that victory was unattainable. Despite the loss of Greece and Crete and various other challenges throughout the region, Britain's position in North Africa was at least no worse off than it had been six months prior, and the situation in East Africa had clearly improved to the point of decisive victory. Concurrently, while maritime conditions were more complex and dangerous, the British were actually in a stronger position regarding their incoming lines of communication through the Red Sea. Likewise, despite months of Luftwaffe bombing, Malta continued to hold out, thus posing an ongoing threat to Axis supply traffic. Finally, despite the Mediterranean Fleet's weakened state due to its recent heavy losses, the Regia Marina showed little inclination to exploit the situation or assume a more aggressive posture. Even more important, Luftwaffe strength in the Mediterranean was actually poised to decline as steady attrition and competing priorities cut into their resources. As such, the situation in the theatre was dangerous, but not insurmountable. If the British could recover from their setbacks and build upon their successes, the prospect for victory was well within their grasp.

Table 3.2 Warship Losses in the Mediterranean and Red Sea from 10 June 1940 through 1 June 1941

	Capital ships	Cruisers	Destroyers	Torpedo boats/escorts/ mine vessels	Submarines
British	-	8	15	7	11
Italian	1	6	19	16	21

Note: Only includes warships that were a total loss and not those that were subsequently raised and put back into service by their respective navies. Of the 30 British surface warships listed above, 20 were lost due to Luftwaffe air attacks while one was shared between Luftwaffe aircraft and Italian special units. Included in the cruiser category are the Italian armoured cruiser *San Giorgio* and the British monitor *Terror*.

CHAPTER 4

Stabilising the Middle East

Early on the morning of 15 June 1941 the sound of gunfire and vehicle engines broke the silence on Egypt's western frontier as British forces attacked Axis positions in the Halfaya Pass. This was the beginning of Operation *Battleaxe*, Britain's latest attempt to assume the offensive in North Africa and relieve Tobruk. Conducting this operation was XIII Corps under the command of Lieutenant-General Noel Beresford-Peirse. At his disposal were the 7th Armoured Division, 4th Indian Division (recently returned from service in East Africa) and 4th Armoured Brigade. Together, this force possessed some 29,000 men and 190 tanks, of which the majority of the latter were recent arrivals from the *Tiger* convoy in May. Opposing this force according to British estimates were 13,000 men and 100 tanks along the frontier with another 25,000 men and 130 tanks encircling Tobruk 80 miles to the west. As such, the British hoped to defeat the Axis forces along the frontier before enemy reinforcements arrived, and then destroy those reinforcements in an armour battle of their own choosing. To carry this out, the 4th Indian Division and 4th Armoured Brigade were tasked to seize Fort Capuzzo and the Halfaya Pass while the 7th Armoured Division established itself on the Hafid Ridge.

Sadly, as is often the case in battle, things did not go according to plan. Warned of British intentions through signal intercepts, the Axis forces were well entrenched when the British arrived on the scene. Despite this, the British actually succeeded in capturing Fort Capuzzo and fought off an enemy counter-attack, but this was their only success for the day. At the Halfaya Pass and the Hafid Ridge Axis defences blunted British advances. Of particular distress to the British were enemy anti-tank guns that took a heavy toll on their armour formations. This unsatisfactory situation continued on the 16th as the British were unable to make any significant headway against their objectives. Then on the 17th a German counter-attack forced the British back, thus signalling an end to the failed battle. During the three days of fighting the British suffered 122 killed, 588 wounded and 259 missing, along with 91 tanks lost through enemy action or breakdowns and 36 aircraft destroyed. Meanwhile, German losses amounted to 93 killed, 350 wounded and 235 missing with materiel losses including 12 tanks destroyed, 50 more temporarily disabled and ten aircraft lost. Italian casualties are unknown, but included a number of prisoners taken.[1] In a hallmark of armour combat, since the Axis held the field, they were able to recover and repair most of their disabled tanks while a far larger percentage of British tank casualties were a total loss.

The outcome of Operation *Battleaxe* was profoundly disappointing to the British. This was particularly true for Winston Churchill, who had been the offense's chief proponent. After enduring so much risk and expending time and effort to transport the *Tiger* convoy tanks to the Middle East, he found it galling to see them so quickly squandered in such an unprofitable undertaking. Moving beyond this disappointment, the operation's failure brought about a number of tangible consequences. Amongst these, the stalemate in North Africa was now destined to carry on with no prospect for early victory in sight. Accordingly, the siege of Tobruk would continue, and the navy would have to maintain its often-costly logistical transport service in support of the fortress. In June, this requirement manifested itself in the passage of 1,900 reinforcements, the evacuation of 5,148 non-essential personnel and an average delivery rate of 97 tons of supplies per day.[2] Unfortunately, these operations cost the navy the sloop *Auckland* and the destroyer *Waterhen*, which were both sunk by Luftwaffe bombers during the final days of the month. Likewise, on the 30th Luftwaffe bombers severely damaged the river gunboat *Cricket* off Mersa Matruh, thus ending its seagoing career and reducing the vessel to a floating anti-aircraft platform in Alexandria harbour.

Another casualty of Operation *Battleaxe* was General Archibald Wavell, the Commander-in-Chief of British Forces in the Middle East. Alarmed by the growing number of recent setbacks and other perceived shortcomings, Churchill had become increasingly dissatisfied with Wavell's performance. Now with the failure of Operation *Battleaxe*, Churchill felt justified to remove the veteran warrior. Accordingly, on 21 June he relieved Wavell and replaced him with General Claude Auchinleck. In taking command, Auchinleck inherited a diverse theatre that was larger than the territorial size of Europe. Within this theatre, there were several varied campaigns underway. Of these, the conflict in North Africa was paramount. On a secondary note, East Africa still required considerable attention as the British mopped up sizable Italian forces in the interior of Abyssinia. Likewise, there was the continuing struggle in the Mediterranean where the British sought to retain Malta, support their forces in North Africa and interdict Axis supply traffic. This was no easy task and was made more difficult by the fleet's recent heavy losses off Crete. Finally, in addition to these major campaigns, the British had to wage secondary operations to secure areas not directly involved in the conflict.

Fortunately for Auchinleck, one of these secondary operations was already decided by the time he assumed command. This operation was related to the Kingdom of Iraq, which was created after World War I with the breakup of the Ottoman

Empire. In 1920 Iraq became a British mandate. Ten years later the two parties signed a treaty granting Iraq independence in 1932. As part of this treaty, Britain retained the right to transit troops through the newly independent nation. Likewise, Iraq was required to maintain internal security for its vital oil infrastructure and to provide the British with all aid, including the use of railways, rivers, ports and airfields, in the event of war. Finally, the British were allowed to maintain two RAF bases within the country. One of these was at Shaibah near Basra, while the other was at Habbaniya about 55 miles west of Baghdad on the Euphrates. In 1941 both bases were used as communication and training centres and thus lacked front-line aircraft. Yet, despite their limited resources, both bases were considered important staging posts on the route between Egypt and India.

In April 1941 a pro-Axis government under the leadership of Prime Minister Rashid Ali al Gailani came to power in Iraq as the result of a military coup. Alarmed by the threat this action posed to their vital oil supplies within the theatre as well as other logistical and political consequences, the British landed the 20th Indian Infantry Brigade, a Royal Artillery field regiment and the headquarters of the 10th Indian Division at Basra on 18 April. Eight merchant ships under the protection of the sloops *Yarra*, *Falmouth* and *Lawrence* facilitated this move. Further warships, including the aircraft carrier *Hermes* and the cruisers *Emerald*, *Leander* and *Enterprise*, also proceeded into the area to strengthen the British position. In the days and weeks that followed the British landed additional forces at Basra and flew military and aircraft reinforcements into their base at Habbaniya. While these actions were arguably permissible under Britain's treaty rights, the new Iraqi government responded by sending strong military forces to envelop the British base at Habbaniya. By 1 May these encircling forces numbered some 9,000 men and 50 guns. The British responded to this provocation by seizing control of the airport, docks and power station at Basra and demanding the withdrawal of Iraqi forces from Basra and the areas surrounding Habbaniya.

When the Iraqis refused to withdraw their forces, the British launched a pre-emptive campaign on 2 May to remedy the situation. Utilising various training and support aircraft that had been converted for offensive use, as well as a handful of recently arrived Wellington and Blenheim bombers, the British launched a series of strikes against their besiegers. This began a period of general hostilities. In this, the British were able to use their relative superiority in the air to keep the Iraqis at bay around Habbaniya while their ground forces consolidated control over Basra. FAA Swordfish from *Hermes* supported these operations, and within a week the British had largely neutralised the small Iraqi air force having destroyed some 30 aircraft with many more damaged.[3] The Iraqis responded to this onslaught by issuing urgent requests for Axis assistance. These requests prompted the Germans and, to a lesser extent, the Italians to send a few dozen aircraft to support their new Iraqi allies. Using Vichy-controlled Syria as a staging base, German aircraft first appeared over Iraq on 11 May, but these aircraft were too few in numbers and too poorly supported to have much of an impact on the campaign. Likewise, these appearances quickly incited the RAF to carry out a number of bombing raids against the main Syrian airfields at Aleppo, Damascus, Rayak and Palmyra, thus further disrupting the effectiveness of the small Luftwaffe contingent.

Meanwhile, on 11 May a 5,800-strong British relief column, designated 'Habforce', departed Palestine and proceeded eastward into Iraq. On the 18th the spearhead of this force, designated 'Kingcol', reached Habbaniya, thus formally lifting the siege. From there, the British pressed forward towards the Iraqi capital of Baghdad. During the next 12 days the British fought a series of intermediate actions before finally reaching the capital outskirts on the 30th. On the same day, Rashid Ali al Gailani and his close supporters fled Baghdad and sought refuge in neighbouring Iran. A few hours later the Lord Mayor of Baghdad petitioned the British for an armistice, which was agreed upon, going into effect on the 31st. With this, the fighting in Iraq ceased, and the situation was restored to Britain's satisfaction. British military casualties for the brief campaign numbered about 100, while the RAF lost 34 killed, 64 wounded and 28 aircraft destroyed.[4] Iraqi personnel casualties amounted to 497 dead, 686 wounded, 548 missing and over 1,000 prisoners taken.[5] Likewise, the small Iraqi air force, which numbered over 50 aircraft, was all but destroyed, while the Luftwaffe lost five bombers and 14 fighters and the Regia Aeronautica another three fighters in operations related to Iraq.[6]

Yet, even as the fighting in Iraq subsided, a new conflict arose within the region. As previously mentioned, Vichy complicity in allowing the Germans access to their Syrian airfields had already provoked a violent British response against those locations. In this, the Vichy government had instructed their local forces to cooperate with the Germans and Italians and to attack British aircraft with all possible means. This situation was made worse when the British learned that Vichy authorities in Syria had also succumbed to German pressure and authorised the shipment of arms and ammunition to the combatant Iraqi forces. During the short campaign, Vichy sources dispatched four railway trucks with arms and ammunition and two trains loaded with aviation fuel and an artillery battery to Iraq.[7] While these actions failed to impact the campaign's outcome, it gave the British reasonable cause for concern. Wary of continued Vichy collaboration and/or the prospect that Germany might use Syria or neighbouring Lebanon as a springboard for further offensive action, the British resolved to eliminate this threat from the region.

Therefore, on 8 June a force initially consisting of the 7th Australian Division, the 5th Indian Brigade Group, a Free French contingent and other minor units invaded Syria and Lebanon from Palestine. The expressed purpose for this action was to remove Axis influence from these areas. To carry this out, the British advanced on three fronts with the objective of capturing Beirut, Rayak and Damascus and then proceeding on to take Palmyra, Homs and Tripoli. Contesting this offensive was a Vichy force of 35,000 men, 120 guns, 90 tanks and 90 combat aircraft. Unlike recent events in Iraq, this defending force put up strong resistance, and the British quickly found themselves embroiled in heavy fighting. By the 13th, all three British advances had stalled after making initial inroads into Vichy territory. In the days that followed, Vichy forces launched a series of counter-attacks that failed to decisively dislodge the British, but generally continued to impede their forward progress. The British did make some headway in their advance towards Damascus, but even this success came at a laborious pace.

While this was underway, a number of British and Vichy warships participated in the fighting. For the French, this included the destroyers *Guépard* and *Valmy*, the sloop *Elan* and submarines *Caïman*, *Marsouin* and *Souffleur*, which were all stationed in Beirut at the time of the British invasion. Initial British naval units assigned to the operation included the 15th Cruiser Squadron consisting of *Phoebe*, *Ajax* and *Coventry*, the landing ship *Glengyle* and eight destroyers. Over a period of several days, commencing on 8 June, these varied naval units conducted a series of operations to support their competing ground forces. For the British, this included the landing of commando parties, the shelling of French positions, the defence of their own coastal advance and a blockade to prevent the arrival of Vichy reinforcements and supplies. No British ships were sunk during these operations, although a handful of vessels sustained damage. On the 9th the British destroyer *Janus* clashed with *Guépard* and *Valmy* off Sidon. During this fight *Janus* suffered heavy damage before the arrival of additional British destroyers forced the Vichy warships back to Beirut. Then on the 15th German and Vichy bombers (the former operating from Crete) attacked British ships off Sidon and damaged the destroyers *Isis* and *Ilex*.

For its part, the small French naval contingent initially fared well, but quickly suffered waning fortunes as the conflict progressed. A matter of primary importance for the Vichy forces was their desperate need to receive supplies and reinforcements. To help fulfil this requirement, the French navy dispatched two destroyers from Toulon to bring ammunition to Beirut. On 16 June British Swordfish torpedo-bombers from the Cypress-based No. 815 Squadron attacked and sank one of these destroyers, *Chevalier Paul*, west of Latakia on Syria's northern coast. The second Vichy destroyer, *Vauquelin*, safely arrived in Beirut, but was then damaged there by British bombers on the 17th. In the days that followed the British continued to tighten their blockade with the arrival of additional British warships, and the French found it increasingly difficult to transit the waters around Syria and Lebanon. On 23 June *Guépard* tried to break the British blockade, but was driven off by British warships. Two days later the British submarine *Parthian* sank the French submarine *Souffleur* as the latter was recharging its batteries in the Bay of Djounieh. Then on 4 July Albacore torpedo-bombers from No. 829 squadron sank the 2,778-ton French supply ship *Saint Didier* off the coast of Anatolia. With this, French authorities recalled a second supply ship that was en route to Syria, and a subsequent attempt to run troop-laden destroyers through to Tripoli was abandoned when British reconnaissance aircraft located the force.

As Vichy fortunes deteriorated at sea, so too did they decline on land. On 21 June Damascus fell to the advancing British forces. On the same day the British expanded their offensive by launching Habforce into Syria from Iraq with the objective of capturing Palmyra. This was later followed by elements of the 10th Indian Division, which also advanced out of Iraq to threaten the Vichy flank and rear. As this was happening, Vichy strength declined as losses, desertions and the effects of the British blockade increasingly took their toll. On 9 July the British captured Damour, thus compromising the main French defensive position before Beirut. With this, the Vichy commander, General Henri Dentz, realised the situation was beyond salvation, and he requested a ceasefire on the 11th. Three days later an armistice was signed in which the Free French assumed territorial command over Syria and Lebanon while Britain retained overall strategic control. The cost in obtaining this outcome amounted to 3,300 British and 1,300 Free French casualties as well as 27 RAF aircraft.[8] Vichy casualties were originally announced as 521 killed, 1,037 missing, 1,790 wounded and 3,004 prisoners, but after the war General Dentz raised the fatality number to 1,092.[9] Finally, total Vichy aircraft losses amounted to 169 of which 42 were lost in aerial combat or to anti-aircraft fire, 45 were destroyed on the ground and the bulk of the remainder were abandoned or lost due to accidental causes.[10]

Sadly, this bloodshed and materiel loss did not signal an end to British diversions within the region. In August the British fought their third peripheral campaign in almost as many months. With the German invasion of the Soviet Union, which commenced on 22 June, the British considered it a matter of utmost importance to dispatch supplies and materiel to their new Soviet allies. It immediately became apparent that an ideal route to do this was through Iran. Unfortunately, in the summer of 1941 large numbers of German nationals were located in Iran, including many who held key positions in railway operations, communications and government services. This German influence offered the potential to destabilise the very assets and routes the Allies hoped to use for their own supply operation. As such, on 17 August Britain and the Soviet Union issued a joint note to the Iranian government demanding the immediate expulsion of Axis personnel from the country. When the Iranian government failed to satisfactorily respond to this demand, Britain and the Soviet Union opted to take military action to secure their objectives.

This operation commenced on 25 August when British and Soviet forces moved in to seize key locations within Iran. For the British, this centred upon naval landings at Abadan, Khorramshahr and Bandar Shapur. Supporting these operations were a number of minor British warships, including the auxiliary cruiser *Kanimbla*, the sloops *Falmouth*, *Shoreham* and *Yarra*, the corvette *Snapdragon* and the river gunboat *Cockchafer*. Iranian resistance was nominal, and the campaign only lasted four days. Nevertheless, there was some naval action. At Abadan and Khorramshahr British warships sank the Iranian sloops *Palang* and *Babr* (both 950 tons, 3 × 4-inch guns) as the small Iranian navy attempted to put up resistance. The British also captured four *Charogh*-class patrol vessels (331 tons, 2 × 3-inch guns) that were later incorporated into the Indian navy. Meanwhile, at Bandar Shapur and Bandar Abbas the British captured four German and four Italian merchant ships worth 45,909 tons and forced the scuttling of a fifth German merchant ship worth 7,861 tons.[11] Total British losses during the short, successful campaign amounted to 22 killed and 42 wounded.[12] For this cost, the British secured a vital route to the Soviet Union that accommodated the shipment of some 4,160,000 tons of supplies and materiel by war's end, of which 96 percent arrived.[13] Included in this were 564 tanks, 53 guns, 3,941 vehicles, 823 aircraft, 50 locomotives, 16 tenders, 31 wagons, 12 marine craft and 160,965 tons of general stores that were sent directly from the United Kingdom to the Soviet Union via this route.[14]

Closing out Britain's peripheral action within the theatre was the completion of mopping-up operations in Abyssinia. With the fall of Addis Ababa in April 1941, the Italian Viceroy and Commander-in-Chief in East Africa, the Duke of Aosta, split his remaining forces into three portions and dispatched them throughout the interior of the country. In the area around Jimma and the lakes region he positioned seven under-strength colonial divisions consisting of some 38,000 men, 200 guns and 30 tanks. To the northwest in the large fertile area around Gondar he dispatched a further 41,000 men and 70 guns. This constituted a highly defensible area that was only approachable through the formidable 4,000-foot Wolchefit Pass. Finally, in the Dessie-Amba Alagi area north of the capital, he personally deployed the remainder of his army, including those forces salvaged from Eritrea. From there, he possessed highly defensible terrain that was ideally positioned to impede communications between Addis Ababa and Massawa.

The British conducted their mopping-up operations in three stages, corresponding with this disposition of Italian forces. The first of these focused upon the most critical threat in the Dessie-Amba Alagi area. Converging upon this area from both north and south, the 5th Indian and 1st South African divisions progressively squeezed the Italians into an ever-shrinking perimeter. On 26 April the South Africans captured Dessie, and on 19 May the Duke of Aosta formally surrendered at Amba Alagi, thus ceding this important territory to the British. During these and other related area operations, over 35,000 Italian soldiers were killed, captured or went missing. While this was underway and proceeding into July, elements from the 11th and 12th African Divisions conducted operations to pacify the territory around Jimma and the lakes region. In a series of progressive actions, these British colonial forces accounted for the entirety of the defending Italian formations, of which the vast majority were taken prisoner. The British concluded their mopping-up operations with an assault against the Italian forces in the Gondar area. On 27 September and 21 November, the Italian strongholds at Wolchefit and Kulkaber fell, and on 27 November the final bulk of Italian forces, numbering some 23,500 men, surrendered at Gondar.

With this, the East Africa campaign ended, and the British celebrated their first truly complete victory of the war. In a period of little more than ten months the British had eliminated Italy's East African Empire, conquered some 700,000 square miles of territory, secured vital lines of communication and removed a force of almost 300,000 men from Italy's military order of battle. In terms of the latter, Italian personnel casualties amounted to 5,211 European and approximately 10,000 African soldiers killed and 6,947 European and 16,000 African soldiers wounded.[15] Likewise, in excess of 200,000 Italian prisoners were taken while tens of thousands more deserted or simply disappeared into the countryside. Italian materiel losses included some 450 varied artillery pieces, 400 aircraft, 126 armoured cars and 60 tanks.[16] Meanwhile, related Italian maritime losses included seven destroyers, two torpedo boats, four submarines, a minelayer, five MAS motor torpedo boats and 43 assorted ocean-going merchant ships (both Italian and German) worth 255,239 tons.[17] The cost for this great victory was less than 6,000 combat casualties for the participating British forces.[18]

Beyond these various peripheral campaigns, a final area worth touching upon involved the occasional diversion of Mediterranean-based naval forces to support

In 1941 the British scored their first complete victory of the war with the conquest of Italian East Africa. This triumph secured vital maritime lines of communication through the Red Sea and cost the Axis over 60 assorted vessels either destroyed or captured. Pictured here is the cruiser *Leander* (foreground), which accounted for three of these Axis ships. (Naval History & Heritage Command, public domain)

operations in the Atlantic. The most dramatic of these occurred in late May when Force H temporarily vacated its normal function of securing the Western Mediterranean and proceeded into the eastern Atlantic to participate in the hunt for the German battleship *Bismarck*. Although a late participant in the operation, Force H played a critical role in bringing about the demise of this powerful adversary, as a last-minute strike by *Ark Royal*'s Swordfish aircraft scored two torpedo hits on *Bismarck* that crippled its steering gear and rendered it incapable of manoeuvring. At the time, *Bismarck* was heading for St. Nazaire on the French Atlantic coast and had almost reached the safety of German air cover, but this damage ensured that the great battleship would never arrive. Instead, elements of the British Home Fleet, which included the battleships *Rodney* and *King George V*, were able to catch up with *Bismarck* and destroy it in a classic surface engagement.

In the two months following the demise of *Bismarck*, the British conducted a series of interdiction operations to seek out and destroy the German tankers and supply ships that had been pre-positioned in the Atlantic to support its sortie as well as various blockade-runners that were attempting to transit through the area. Aided by SIGINT (Signal Intelligence), British forces captured, sank or forced the scuttling of 13 of these ships worth a combined 93,320 tons from 28 May through 25 July.[19] Once again, Force H and other warships stationed at Gibraltar participated in some of these operations. On 12 June the cruiser *Sheffield* from Force H intercepted and forced the scuttling of the 10,397-ton German tanker *Friedrich Breme* off Cape Finisterre. Eleven days later five British destroyers from Gibraltar forced a similar outcome upon the 3,039-ton German supply ship *Alstertor* in the same area. Meanwhile, on 6 June Swordfish from *Eagle*, which was operating out of Sierra Leone, sank the 9,179-ton blockade-runner *Elba* near the Azores. Nine days later *Eagle* joined up with the cruiser *Dunedin* to capture the 10,746-ton supply ship *Lothringen* about 1,000 miles west of the Cape Verde Islands. By inflicting these losses, the British markedly reduced Germany's ability to logistically support further surface raider or long-range U-boat operations throughout these areas.

For their part, the Italians continued to have their own Atlantic diversion as sizable numbers of Italian submarines continued to operate under German control from the French port of Bordeaux. This relationship would endure through the remainder of Italy's participation as an Axis partner, and eventually 32 Italian submarines saw service in the Atlantic. Of these, the majority fulfilled conventional attack roles, but some were also used as long-range blockade runners to transport cargos of scarce commodities into Europe from the Far East. During the roughly three-year period in which these Italian submarines operated in the Atlantic, they sank 106 Allied and neutral merchant ships worth 564,473 tons.[20] Against this, 16 of these submarines were lost, of which 12 were destroyed by British means. In terms of the latter, already mentioned were the four submarines sunk in 1940 and early 1941 (see Chapter 2). After that, British warships accounted for *Glauco*,

Maggiori Baracca, *Alessandro Malaspina*, *Galileo Ferraris*, *Pietro Calvi* and *Leonardo da Vinci*, while the British submarine *Severn* sank *Michele Bianchi* and RAF aircraft destroyed *Enrico Tazzoli*.

When viewing these results, Italy's activities in the Atlantic represented the Regia Marina's most successful interdiction effort of the war, but it was also arguably a strategic mistake. When compared to the totality of the Atlantic campaign, which lasted almost six years and was fought predominantly between British and German forces, this effort and these results were of little consequence to the overall impact of the battle. Perhaps more important from the Italian point of view, this diversion of effort failed to provide any positive impact to their position in the Mediterranean. As such, it is reasonable to surmise that the Axis war effort might have benefited had the Regia Marina retained its entire submarine force in the Mediterranean. Although ill-suited for Mediterranean operations, the presence of additional Italian submarines might have made a difference during close-run phases in the conflict, such as the Malta convoy battles that will be discussed in the upcoming chapters. Even more important, the presence of these submarines might have dissuaded the Germans from sending their own U-boats into the Mediterranean, as discussed later in this chapter, which proved to be a wasteful diversion of critical assets. From the overall Axis perspective, the presence of Italian submarines in the Atlantic proved to be a poor substitute for the substantial numbers of German U-boats that were eventually diverted into the Mediterranean, thus undermining Germany's greater global interdiction effort.

Returning now to the main campaign underway in the Mediterranean and Middle East, despite their many successes in peripheral operations, there was no sign of similar British victory in North Africa. Instead, both the British and Axis combatants found themselves locked in a period of stalemate in which neither side was strong enough to decisively prevail over the other. Yet, on at least a near-term basis, the British could expect their strength position to improve. At the time the Middle East was Britain's only active theatre for ground operations, and as such, the British were capable and willing to commit additional men and resources to the area. During the first seven months of 1941, the British transported 239,000 men and over a million tons of supplies and equipment to Egypt, and this trend was expected to continue for the remainder of the year.[21] This was no simple task given the arduous route the British were compelled to take around the Cape of Good Hope, but they possessed sufficient maritime resources and infrastructure to fulfil this requirement. As such, the British were able to increase their forces within the theatre and amass adequate (and often abundant) stocks of supplies and materiel to support their operations.

By comparison, Rommel's short-term strength projections were far less positive. By this time, Germany was fully engaged in its invasion of the Soviet Union, and the struggle in North Africa was given low strategic priority. As such, the German

High Command informed Rommel that he could expect no additional forces other than those already at his disposal. In the latter half of 1941 this consisted of two panzer divisions (the 15th and the 21st) and one motorised infantry division (the 90th Light). There were also seven Italian divisions in North Africa at this time, but only five of these fell directly under Rommel's control. Of the latter, all were infantry divisions, while the independent XX Italian Armoured Corps retained one armoured and one motorised division. From Rommel's perspective, these Italian formations were of dubious quality requiring him to infuse German detachments within their ranks to bolster their strength and resolve. In doing so, he was forced to weaken his more formidable German formations.

A second major factor constraining Rommel's force structure and freedom of action was his precarious supply situation. The Axis forces in North Africa ostensibly required 96,000 tons of supplies per month just to maintain themselves, with a further 20,000 tons required for offensive operations. When added to the 20,000 tons required to support the Libyan civilian population, this represented a monthly logistical burden of upwards of 140,000 tons. In fairness, there was probably some padding in these requirement numbers, but even if cut in half, this still represented some 60,000 to 70,000 tons of materiel that had to be delivered to North Africa on a monthly basis. Nearly all of this tonnage had to be transported across the Mediterranean in ships. In June the Axis successfully delivered 125,076 tons of supplies and materiel to North Africa out of 133,331 tons dispatched, but this was an exceptional result. In the five months prior, the average monthly arrival had been just 74,366 tons out of 79,324 tons dispatched.[22] Making matters worse, given the limited harbour capacity at Benghazi, the Italians were forced to direct much of their supply traffic to Tripoli in western Libya. From there, the Axis had to truck their supplies over 1,000 miles to reach the Tobruk perimeter or 1,100 miles to reach the Egyptian frontier. This inefficient system caused significant time delays, consumed prohibitive amounts of precious fuel and severely strained Rommel's limited transportation assets. Under these conditions, the Axis were incapable of significantly increasing the size of their committed forces, assuming reinforcements were available, and the units they did have often lacked adequate supplies with fuel being a particularly scarce commodity.

The British took various actions to perpetuate Rommel's supply difficulties and his freedom of action paralysis. Paramount amongst these was their continued defence of Tobruk. Britain's retention of Tobruk forced Rommel to split his forces, denied him a valuable forward port, added a 35-mile bypass to his already over-stretched supply lines and provided the British with a base from which they could attack his exposed lines of communication. When combined together, these factors forced Rommel to focus his attention on Tobruk and precluded further offensive operations until the fortress was eliminated. While this constituted obvious benefits for the British, it also continued to put a heavy strain upon the Royal Navy. In addition to its normal replenishment activities, which in September included the delivery of 3,330 tons of ammunition and supplies, 750 tons of fuel and 29 tanks to Tobruk, the navy undertook a new mission at the behest of the Australian government.[23] From August through October the navy withdrew 18,865 men from the 9th Australian division and replaced them with 19,568 fresh troops from the British 70th Division and the Polish Carpathian Brigade.[24] The navy successfully carried out these replenishment and reinforcement tasks, but continued to pay a price for their efforts. This included the destroyer *Defender* and the minelayer *Latona*, which were sunk by Luftwaffe aircraft off the Libyan coast on 11 July and 25 October respectively.

The British also intensified their interdiction efforts against the Italian merchant fleet and the convoys plying between Italy and North Africa. A key factor in this was a resurgent Malta, which became increasingly viable as the year progressed. Part of this was due to a marked reduction in German air activity over the island group as the Luftwaffe diverted resources to Russia, the Balkans and North Africa. With this departure, the Regia Aeronautica assumed the sole responsibility for the air assault against Malta, a task it was far less adept at performing. Adding to Italian difficulties, this development came at a time when Malta's own defensive capabilities were on the rise. In May and June, the British conducted four operations utilising Force H and the aircraft carriers *Ark Royal*, *Victorious* and *Furious* to ferry Hurricane fighters to Malta. During this period the British successfully delivered 183 Hurricanes to the holdout colony.[25] While many of these aircraft subsequently continued on to Egypt, Malta's operational fighter strength still stood at 75 in early August.[26]

Malta also benefited from an increased arrival of seaborne supplies and reinforcements. In July the British conducted Operation *Substance*, a sortie by Force H to deliver the troop transport *Leinster* and six freighters to Malta. Early during this operation *Leinster* went aground and had to return to Gibraltar, but the remaining merchant ships completed their journeys despite attempted interference from Italian submarines, motor torpedo boats and the Regia Aeronautica. In doing so, these vessels delivered some 65,000 tons of assorted stores and materiel to Malta. Likewise, the British also used the operation to successfully transfer seven empty merchant ships from Malta to Gibraltar. The only British loss for the entire undertaking was the destroyer *Fearless*, which was sunk by Italian aircraft south of Sardinia, and one cruiser, one destroyer and two merchant ships damaged. As an adjunct to *Substance*, at the end of July the British conducted Operation *Style* to transport the men and materiel stranded by the grounded *Leinster*. Conducted by the cruisers *Hermione* and *Arethusa*, the fast minelayer *Manxman* and two destroyers and supported by Force H, the British successfully delivered 1,750 army and RAF personnel and 130 tons of supplies to Malta for no loss to themselves. During this operation British aircraft and warships also bombarded the Sardinian harbour of Alghero, and the cruiser *Hermione* sank the Italian submarine *Tembien* off Tunis.

When combined together, these reinforcement and replenishment operations significantly improved Malta's ability to survive and serve as a base for offensive action. By August, Malta's growing fighter force was bolstered by a combatant garrison of 22,000 men with 112 heavy and 118 light anti-aircraft guns and 104 field guns of various calibres.[27] Together, these defences proved an effective counter to the Regia Aeronautica, and the Italian air assault failed to seriously impede Malta's growth and development as an offensive base. Likewise, these defences quickly proved capable of handling more than just the Regia Aeronautica. On the night of 25/26 July the Italian sloop *Diana* and two motor torpedo boats approached Malta and launched nine explosive motor boats, two motor launches and two human torpedoes from the 10th MAS Flotilla to attack shipping in Valletta Harbour. Unfortunately for the Italians, British radar observed these movements, and shore defences frustrated the Italian attack with the entire raiding force being destroyed. The next morning British fighter-bombers attacked and dispatched the two Italian motor torpedo boats and one of the motor launches while *Diana* made good its escape.[28]

Meanwhile, the British continued their replenishment and reinforcement operations. In September the British conducted Operation *Halberd*, their largest Malta re-supply mission to date. Supported by the battleships *Rodney*, *Nelson* and *Prince of Wales*, the aircraft carrier *Ark Royal*, five cruisers and 18 destroyers, the British successfully delivered eight merchant ships carrying 85,000 tons of supplies to Malta. This brought it to a total of 30 merchant ships that had successfully reached the isolated colony since the beginning of the year.[29] However, this accomplishment came at a cost as Italian torpedo-bombers sank a ninth merchant ship, the 12,427-ton *Imperial Star*, while other aircraft hit and damaged the battleship *Nelson*. Against this, the British exacted some retribution when the destroyers *Gurkha* and *Legion* sank the Italian submarine *Adua* in the Western Mediterranean. Meanwhile, during the same month Force H conducted two operations using *Ark Royal* and *Furious* to fly off 59 Hurricanes to Malta. Finally, throughout this period individual submarines and fast minelayers conducted a number of sorties to deliver critical materiel to Malta, including aviation fuel, anti-aircraft ammunition and torpedoes.

Of course, all of these efforts were only worthwhile to the extent in which they contributed to Britain's ability to interdict the flow of Axis supplies to North Africa. With the departure of Force K to support the evacuation of Crete in May, Malta's sole offensive power rested with its limited, but growing, number of submarines and strike aircraft. Fortunately, the British were able to enhance the effectiveness of this modest force through the use of timely and consequential SIGINT. Of particular importance was the output from the Government Code and Cypher School (GC and CS) at Bletchley Park, which enjoyed considerable success in breaking the various German and Italian encryption codes used by their naval, air and ground forces. From June 1941 on, this included regular access to the Regia

For the first year and a half of the Mediterranean conflict, the aircraft carrier *Ark Royal* saw extensive service with Force H during which it helped sink the German battleship *Bismarck*, participated in the bombardments of Mers-el Kébir and Genoa and helped facilitate numerous supply and aircraft ferrying missions to Malta. (United Kingdom Government, public domain)

Marina's C38m cypher. The British became very adept at not only reading, but also turning this vital intelligence around quickly so it was actionable. Utilising Special Liaison Unit links in Cairo, Alexandria and eventually Malta, GC and CS regularly had decrypted messages back to the naval commands in the Mediterranean within four to 12 hours of their initial transmissions.[30] This invaluable intelligence, which the British referred to as Ultra, often gave them forewarning and details regarding Axis shipping movements and other related activities. In turn, this allowed the British to launch targeted strikes against these operations while minimising their own expenditure of time and resources in unproductive patrolling. As such, Ultra intelligence economised the British effort and proved to be a key factor in many British interdiction successes.

In terms of results, from June through October 1941 British and affiliated Allied submarines operating from Malta, as well as Gibraltar and Alexandria, sank a total of 39 Axis and Axis-affiliated merchant ships worth 162,385 tons and 32 minor vessels worth an additional 5,000 tons in the Mediterranean.[31] Included in this number were three large troopships. The first of these was the 11,398-ton *Esperia*, which was sunk by the British submarine *Unique* on 20 August. Four weeks later the British submarine *Upholder* sank the troopships *Neptunia* and *Oceania* (19,475 and 19,507 tons respectively) while en route to Tripoli. None of these successes resulted in a significant loss of life, but they still constituted severe blows to Italy's irreplaceable merchant fleet. Adding to this toll, during the same five-month period British submarines also accounted for the Italian torpedo boats *Altair* and *Aldebaran*, the corvette *Albatros* and the submarines *Salpa* and *Jantina*.[32] Concurrent British submarine losses during this time consisted of *Union*, *Cachalot* and *P33*, sunk by Italian warships and *P32* and *Tetrach* lost to mines.

Malta's strike aircraft scored a close second to these submarine successes. In early August Malta's offensive air strength included a contingent of 20 serviceable Blenheim light bombers, 12 Wellington medium bombers, ten Maryland reconnaissance bombers and 20 FAA Swordfish.[33] These aircraft performed differing functions that afforded the Italians little respite in their seaborne supply operations. Assisted by intelligence from Ultra and other sources, the Marylands and certain designated Wellingtons performed reconnaissance duties to find and fix the Italian convoys. Once located, the Blenheims conducted low-level bombing attacks during the day while the Swordfish attacked at night using torpedoes. When not engaging these convoys, the Swordfish also conducted minor nocturnal raids and mining operations against Tripoli and other critical port locations. In this, they were joined by the Wellingtons, which carried out regular bombing raids against the key Italian harbours. A primary target was Tripoli, which was attacked 72 times between mid-June and mid-October. Meanwhile, during the same period Egyptian-based Wellingtons attacked Benghazi 102 times.[34] These attacks caused destruction and damage to moored Italian vessels as well as harbour installations, docks and warehouses.

When combined together, these various operations exacted a steady toll on Axis shipping. From June through October 1941 British aircraft accounted for the destruction of 49 Axis and Axis-affiliated merchant ships worth 133,579 tons in the Mediterranean. Of these, 29 ships worth 120,535 tons were sunk at sea or in open waters, while 20 vessels worth 13,044 tons were sunk during raids on ports.[35] Aircraft from Malta accounted for well over three-quarters of this total. When broken down by aircraft type, FAA Swordfish sank or participated in the destruction of at least 15 merchant ships worth 79,848 tons, while Blenheims accounted for another six merchant ships worth 29,324 tons plus three additional ships sunk in conjunction with the above-mentioned Swordfish. Finally, Wellington bombers sank three sizable merchant ships worth 15,150 tons, while the remaining losses were predominantly vessels of minor tonnage. British bombers also accounted for the Italian torpedo boat *Pleiadi*, which was damaged beyond repair during an October raid against Tripoli. Finally, mines, laid predominantly by British aircraft, added a further 11 ships sunk worth 16,369 tons to the toll exacted by conventional air attacks.[36]

These results had a debilitating effect upon the Axis supply situation. Of the Axis merchant ships sunk during this period, 32 vessels worth 167,280 tons were lost while engaging in North Africa supply operations.[37] These outcomes were the most profitable for the British in that they also resulted in the loss of much valuable cargo. However, even those ships that were sunk outside of this application still contributed to the overall interdiction effort by degrading and putting additional strain upon Italy's limited seaborne lift capability. The same held true for merchant ships that sustained damage and were thus forced to turn back and/or cease operational use to enact repairs. An example of such damage occurred in July when a Swordfish torpedoed the 6,212-ton Italian tanker *Panuco* off Tripoli. The impacted tanker did not sink, but was so badly damaged that it was unable to discharge its cargo and had to carry 6,000 tons of fuel back to Italy to undergo repairs. Finally, the mere presence or threat of British submarines and aircraft caused the Italians to recall or delay many of their convoys, thus further disrupting their supply operations. The net result of all of this was an Axis supply delivery to North Africa of 62,276 tons in July, 83,956 tons in August, 67,513 tons in September and 73,614 tons in October. This was a far cry from the minimum monthly requirement of 96,000 tons deemed necessary to sustain Axis forces in North Africa and represented an 80 percent delivery rate, with 20 percent of the dispatched supply tonnage failing to arrive during the four-month period.[38]

November intensified this trend to a significant degree. Much of this was attributable to the return of Force K to Malta. Consisting of the cruisers *Aurora* and *Penelope* and the destroyers *Lance* and *Lively*, this new Force K quickly made its presence felt to the detriment of Rommel's already precarious supply situation. On 7 November the Italians dispatched a large convoy, designated convoy Beta and consisting of seven merchant ships worth 39,787 tons, to North Africa. Carrying 34,473 tons of stores including 389 vehicles and 17,281 tons of fuel, the convoy maintained a direct escort of six destroyers with a further two cruisers and four destroyers serving as a distant escort. Assisted by Ultra and Maryland reconnaissance aircraft, Force K, under the command of Captain W. G. Agnew, located the convoy on the night of 8/9 November and commenced a devastating attack. Utilising radar and superior night fighting capabilities, *Aurora* and *Penelope* quickly scored a series of hits on the Italian destroyers *Grecale*, *Maestrale*, *Fulmine* and *Euro*, while *Lance* and *Lively* split their fire between the merchant ships and escorts. At first, the Italians thought they were under air attack, and as their defences fell into confused disarray, the British vessels increasingly switched their fire to the merchant ships, which they engaged with methodical precision. In less than 45 minutes, the attacking British squadron executed a complete circle around the convoy destroying all seven merchant ships along with the escorting destroyer *Fulmine*, while three other Italian destroyers sustained damage. The Italian distant escort, which was only six miles away, failed to effectively intervene in the action, and the British escaped the battle with no losses to themselves.

The destruction of convoy Beta came as a severe shock to the Axis, but it was by no means their only calamity for the month. The next day the British submarine

Upholder torpedoed and sank the Italian destroyer *Libeccio* as the latter was conducting rescue operations in the area. Other British and Allied submarine successes for the month included five merchant ships, a tug and three minor vessels worth a combined 17,080 tons sunk with other ships, including the cruiser *Trieste* and destroyer *Aviere*, damaged.[39] Meanwhile, on 24 November Force K scored another success when it intercepted and destroyed two German merchant ships worth 4,752 tons that were en route from Piraeus to Benghazi. Likewise, RAF aircraft added another nine merchant ships worth 8,910 tons and the Italian minelayer *Zirona* to this total, while a Malta-based Swordfish hit and damaged the Italian cruiser *Duca degli Abruzzi*.[40] As a result of these losses and other affiliated disruptions, the Axis only succeeded in delivering a paltry 29,813 tons out of 79,208 tons of supplies dispatched to North Africa in November.[41] This constituted a delivery rate of just 37.6 percent. Making matters worse, the portion of this delivery that was gasoline amounted to just 2,471 tons.[42] At this rate, the Axis leadership quickly realised that a continuation of this trend would render their position in North Africa untenable.

Fortunately for them, help was already on the way and making its presence felt. On 13 September Hitler ordered the transfer of U-boats to the Mediterranean to help reverse the growing British resurgence there. These U-boats began operations in October during which they enjoyed a handful of minor successes, including the crippling of the gunboat *Gnat* and the destruction of two small merchant ships worth 1,966 tons.[43] Then in November German U-boats scored two substantial successes against the British. The first occurred on the 13th when *U81* torpedoed the aircraft carrier *Ark Royal* as the latter was returning to Gibraltar from a ferry mission that successfully delivered 34 Hurricanes to Malta. Although only hit by a single torpedo, the carrier suffered extensive damage that included the loss of all power and internal communications. These factors complicated damage control operations, and the carrier slowly flooded until foundering on the 14th. Fortunately, there was only one fatality associated with this loss. The same was not true on the 25th when *U331* torpedoed the battleship *Barham* off the Libyan coast. Hit by three torpedoes, *Barham* capsized and exploded in less than five minutes, leaving only 451 survivors out of a crew of 1,313. Included with the survivors was the commander of the 1st Battle Squadron, Vice-Admiral Pridham-Wippel, but the ship's commander, Captain G. C. Cooke, perished.

While the loss of two capital ships certainly constituted a serious blow to the Royal Navy, it remained to be seen what impact this development would have on the overall situation in the Middle East. In this regard, in November the struggle reached a new level of urgency as the British launched Operation *Crusader*, their most recent offensive and largest attempt yet to relieve Tobruk. The instrument of this offensive was the newly formed Eighth Army, which, after months of unceasing seaborne reinforcements, consisted of 118,000 men, 860 assorted tanks and 849 field and anti-tank guns. This army was organised into two corps (XIII and XXX

Corps) with five divisions and three independent brigades.[44] The British also utilised the Tobruk garrison, which consisted of the 70th Division, the Polish Carpathian Brigade and the 32nd Army Tank Brigade, to launch a synchronised breakout attack from the west. Finally, the British supported their offensive with the recently formed Western Desert Air Force consisting of some 550 operational aircraft organised into 27 British and Commonwealth squadrons. Confronting this considerable effort was an equally formidable Axis force consisting of 119,000 men (65,000 Germans and 54,000 Italians), 390 tanks, 1,140 guns and 342 operational aircraft.

The British commenced Operation *Crusader* on 18 November. Initially the offensive went well, as XIII Corps enveloped Axis garrisons along the frontier while XXX Corps pushed deeper into Cyrenaica to provoke a response from the German panzer divisions. Unfortunately, as the offensive developed the British forces became increasingly dispersed, making synchronised mass and control more difficult. What followed next was a series of confused and extremely fluid attacks and counter-attacks during which the initiative repeatedly flowed from one side to the other. During this time both sides suffered heavy losses, but this was particularly true for XXX Corps' exposed tank brigades. By the evening of the 23rd British tank losses had reached such a state that the Eighth Army commander, Lieutenant-General Alan Cunningham of East Africa fame, advocated a cessation of the offensive, but General Auchinleck overruled him. Surmising that Rommel could not sustain a protracted battle given his precarious supply situation and lack of reserves, Auchinleck ordered the offensive to continue. Thus, for the remainder of the month and into December, the British army remained locked in a fluid battle of attrition with its Axis counterpart.

As this seesaw struggle continued in Cyrenaica, so too did it continue in the Mediterranean. The period started out on a high note for the British when a reinforced Force K departed Malta in two groups, along with aerial assets to seek out and destroy a series of one and two-ship Italian convoys en route to Benghazi. Early on, one of these convoys turned back after Blenheim bombers sank the 3,476-ton *Capo Faro* on 30 November.[45] Early the next morning the cruisers *Aurora* and *Penelope* and the destroyer *Lively* encountered the lone 1,976-ton auxiliary *Adriatico* and sank it. Later in the day British aircraft sighting reports vectored these same warships in on the 10,540-ton Italian tanker *Iridio Mantovani*, which had been immobilised due to an earlier Blenheim bomber strike. The British also encountered the Italian destroyer *Alvise da Mosto*, which was rendering aid to the stricken tanker. Despite a spirited defence, the British quickly dispatched *Alvise da Mosto* when a 6-inch shell from one of the British cruisers detonated the destroyer's aft magazine and blew off its stern. Thereafter, *Lively* finished off the crippled *Iridio Mantovani* with a torpedo, and the British ships safely returned to Malta having suffered no loss to themselves.

Twelve days later the British scored an even greater victory. To help counter their growing inability to pass merchant shipping through the Mediterranean, the Italians increasingly utilised warships to carry men and materiel to North Africa. On the night of 12/13 December the British destroyers *Sikh*, *Maori* and *Legion* and the Dutch destroyer *Isaac Sweers* intercepted two such warships, the Italian light cruisers *Alberico da Barbiano* and *Alberto di Giussano*, east of Cape Bon. Utilising radar and hugging the Tunisian coast to mask their approach, these destroyers surprised the Italian cruisers and engaged both with torpedoes and gunfire. This attack caught the Italians in a highly vulnerable state given their volatile cargoes of cased aviation fuel. At the onset the British scored at least three torpedo and multiple gunfire hits on *Alberico da Barbiano*, which sank almost immediately. *Alberto di Giussano* survived a little longer, but gunfire and a torpedo hit from *Legion* quickly transformed the unlucky cruiser into a blazing pyre that led to its demise. In all, over 900 Italian seamen perished in a battle that cost the British no appreciable damage or loss.

While these two events represented high points for the Royal Navy in December, other results during the month were far more varied. Continuing on the positive side, during December British submarines sank six Italian merchant ships worth 30,614 tons, along with six minor vessels and the torpedo boat *Alcione*.[46] The British submarine *Urge* also torpedoed and damaged the Italian battleship *Vittorio Veneto* thus putting it out of action for several months. Other Axis losses in December

Throughout much of the war the British used aircraft, submarines, warships and mines to wage a relentless interdiction campaign against Axis supply traffic to North Africa. Pictured here is an Italian merchant ship under attack by British Blenheim bombers. (Royal Air Force official photographer, public domain)

included three merchant ships worth 2,148 tons that were sunk by British aircraft and two merchant ships worth 2,835 tons that accidentally sank in a newly laid Italian minefield.[47] Meanwhile, in mid-December a squadron of British cruisers and destroyers successfully escorted the transport *Breconshire* to Malta despite an indecisive engagement with superior Italian warships in what became known as the first battle of Sirte.

Against these successes, the British suffered some significant losses themselves. On 6 December a mine strike claimed the British submarine *Perseus* off Zante. Eight days later *U557* sank the British light cruiser *Galatea* 30 miles west of Alexandria. Then on 19 December Force K strayed into an Italian minefield off Tripoli and lost the light cruiser *Neptune* and the destroyer *Kandahar* to mines while two other cruisers sustained damage, thus putting an effective end to the current reiteration of Force K. Although a diminished Force K would continue to operate out of Malta for some time, it would score no further interdiction successes. Five days later *U568* sank the British corvette *Salvia* 100 miles west of Alexandria. Finally, beyond these warship successes, U-boats also sank five merchant ships worth 17,891 tons during the month.[48] By comparison, the Germans lost three Mediterranean-based U-boats in December with two more having been sunk in November. Of these, British surface warships sank *U433*, *U79* and *U75*, while the Dutch submarine *O21* sank *U95*. Finally, an accidental collision with the Italian torpedo boat *Orione* claimed the loss of *U557*.

Returning now to the local British misfortunes, in mid-December the Italians launched a daring human torpedo raid against the Mediterranean Fleet in Alexandria. The human torpedo was a man-operated torpedo, crewed by two men in shallow water diving suits, that had a detachable warhead for placement and delayed detonation against a ship's hull. The first successful use of this weapon had occurred on the night of 19/20 September when three Italian human torpedo teams sank the 2,444-ton merchant ship *Fiona Shell* and severely damaged the 10,893-ton freighter *Durham* and the 8,145-ton naval tanker *Denbydale* in Gibraltar. Now on the night of 18/19 December the Italians carried out a similar attack against Alexandria. Utilising the specially modified submarine *Scirè* as a transport, three human torpedo teams penetrated into Alexandria harbour and planted their explosive charges under the battleships *Queen Elizabeth* and *Valiant* and the 7,554-ton Norwegian tanker *Sagona*. The next morning these charges detonated, and all three ships sustained sufficient damage to cause their grounding in the shallow water. While all three vessels were subsequently raised and repaired, *Valiant* would be out of service until August 1942 while *Queen Elizabeth* would require a staggering 20 months to fully repair and refit.[49] In the meantime, the attack rendered the Mediterranean Fleet devoid of operational capital ships.

Fortunately for the British, neither this event nor other recent misfortunes were sufficient to alter the near-term impetus underway in the theatre. In December total

Axis supply deliveries to North Africa once again fell far short of requirements at only 39,092 tons.[50] This shortfall added additional strain upon the already hard-pressed Axis formations in Cyrenaica, and on 7 December Rommel finally conceded the growing deterioration of his present situation and ordered his forces to disengage and retreat. In doing so, he was forced to abandon isolated German and Italian garrisons along the frontier that were subsequently overwhelmed by the British. On 8 December the British re-established land communications with Tobruk thus ending a gruelling siege that had lasted almost eight months. During the course of this siege British naval and merchant units had delivered 34,113 troops, 72 tanks, 92 guns and 34,000 tons of supplies to the garrison and evacuated 32,667 troops, 7,516 wounded and 7,097 prisoners.[51] This cost the British two destroyers, three sloops, seven submarine chasers and minesweepers, one gunboat, one minelayer, seven supply ships and six lighters sunk and seven destroyers, one sloop, 11 submarine chasers and minesweepers, three gunboats, one troop transport, six merchant ships, three lighters and one schooner damaged.[52]

Meanwhile, the British victory continued to manifest itself in Cyrenaica. On 25 December, after experiencing a temporary delay in the Gazala area, British forces re-captured Benghazi. Once again, the navy was at the forefront supporting this effort as the Inshore Squadron delivered 17,708 tons of stores to Tobruk from 18 November through 25 December while Mersa Matruh received another 13,600 tons.[53] The British then continued their advance, and by the middle of January all of Cyrenaica was once again under British control. During the course of the *Crusader* battle and subsequent re-conquest of Cyrenaica, the British inflicted over 38,000 casualties upon their Axis adversaries. This included some 1,100 Germans and 1,200 Italians killed, 3,400 Germans and 2,700 Italians wounded and 10,100 Germans and 19,800 Italians taken prisoner.[54] Likewise, Axis equipment losses were estimated at 216 German and 120 Italian medium tanks, 299 German and 481 Italian guns and 259 German and 204 Italian aircraft.[55] These latter figures included 458 Axis aircraft that were captured by the British in various states of disrepair during the battle.[56] British casualties for the offensive were 17,700 including 2,900 dead, 7,300 wounded and 7,500 taken prisoner.[57] The British also lost several hundred tanks, guns and aircraft that were disabled, but given their retention of the battlefield, a large number of these were recovered and repaired.

Therefore, as 1941 came to an end, the British army finally enjoyed its first significant victory over a sizable German force (or to be more precise, a mixed German/Italian army). It had been a hard-fought and incomplete victory, but it was victory nevertheless. Yet, the British also recognised that much difficult fighting remained ahead. Although Rommel's army had suffered a costly reverse, it emerged from Cyrenaica largely intact and still capable of both offensive and defensive action. Likewise, certain aspects of the struggle increasingly favoured the Axis. By abandoning Cyrenaica, Rommel had reduced his lines of communication and thus improved his supply situation. By comparison, Eighth Army's advance took it progressively farther from its logistical bases in Egypt, and the British supply situation was becoming increasingly precarious. Adding to this logistical dynamic was the recent intervention of German U-boats and a new, burgeoning expansion of Luftwaffe activity within the Mediterranean. Already the Royal Navy had suffered some serious losses, and it remained to be seen if the British could sustain their current level of attrition against Rommel's seaborne lines of communication.

Beyond these local considerations, December also saw momentous events occurring outside of the Mediterranean that promised to have major repercussions on the local fighting. In particular, during the month Japan came into the war on the side of the Axis, spurring the United States to do the same on the side of the Allies. While these events had both positive and negative consequences from the British perspective, it was clear that the long-term implications were overwhelmingly positive. This was true because the United States was an immensely more powerful ally than Japan was an adversary. Nevertheless, it would take time for America to bring its vast power to bear. In the meantime, the Japanese benefited from the effective use of surprise and decisive action and the fact that they were able to employ all of their military power to attain their regional objectives. By comparison, Southeast Asia was at best a secondary theatre for the British, who naturally maintained their most numerous and capable forces to confront the European Axis. Given these realities,

Table 4.1 Monthly Axis Materiel Deliveries to North Africa and Merchant Shipping Losses in 1941

	Tons dispatched	Tons arrived	Percent arrived	Axis merchant shipping lost*	Axis merchant tonnage lost*
January	50,505	49,089	97.2	37	40,283
February	80,352	79,183	98.5	25	24,217
March	101,800	92,753	91.1	13	31,578
April	88,597	81,472	92.0	16	40,080
May	75,367	69,331	92.0	32	96,541
June	133,331	125,076	93.8	32	65,244
July	77,012	62,276	80.9	23	54,802
August	96,021	83,956	87.4	27	57,925
September	94,115	67,513	71.7	31	102,881
October	92,449	73,614	79.6	29	60,958
November	79,208	29,813	37.6	30	66,569
December	47,680	39,092	82.0	29	50,580

Note: The table only covers materiel that was dispatched/delivered by sea.
* Comprises all Axis merchant shipping lost in the Mediterranean, including minor vessels and those vessels lost through accidental, unknown or other causes not directly related to Allied action. It also contains some minor vessels of unknown, but presumably minimal tonnage.

the Japanese were able to score a number of early victories, including the crippling of the American Pacific Fleet at Pearl Harbor, the destruction of two British capital ships off Malaya, the capture of British Hong Kong and the ongoing invasions of both British Malaya and the American Philippines.

For the British forces engaged in the Mediterranean and Middle East, the most likely impact this would have on their immediate future was a diversion of resources away from the theatre to provide assistance to the Far East. Already, the British considered themselves overstretched, and this added a new burden to further complicate the situation. Muddling this further was the fact that their adversaries were poised to gain in strength at the same time they were looking to decrease their own. Given these realities, the best hope for the local British forces to maintain the initiative centred upon their ability to finish off Rommel quickly. Under the circumstances, this seemed a difficult task. Therefore, while British fortunes in the theatre had clearly improved, the prospect for complete victory remained elusive. The only thing certain was that the fighting would continue and that control over the Middle East remained an open question.

CHAPTER 5

Malta under Siege

As the Middle East theatre entered its third calendar year of conflict in January 1942, a number of factors existed that resembled the situation of 12 months before. Whereas in January 1941 the British had been in the midst's of their first great desert offensive (Operation *Compass*), the beginning of 1942 found them in the closing stages of their second major offensive (Operation *Crusader*). In terms of the latter, during the last week in December and first week in January the British completed their occupation of western Cyrenaica as the bulk of the combined German/Italian Panzerarmee Afrika made good its withdrawal to El Agheila. Meanwhile, during the first 17 days of the new year the British, aided by naval gunfire support, successfully reduced the stranded Axis garrisons at Bardia, Sollum and Halfaya. In doing so, they collected some 14,000 prisoners and established themselves as the uncontested masters over Cyrenaica.[1] This outcome represented a noteworthy victory that mirrored results from the previous year when British forces had first conquered the impoverished Italian North African colony.

And like that earlier time, Britain's success quickly spurred newfound challenges. In January 1942, as had been the case a year earlier, the British faced the reality of an increased German intervention within the theatre. This intervention had already manifested itself with the arrival of German U-boats into the Mediterranean during the closing months of 1941, and now with the onset of the new year the Luftwaffe also reasserted itself in a new and powerful aerial offensive against Malta. The instrument of this new offensive was Fliegerkorps II, which had recently arrived in Sicily from operations in Russia. Armed with a mixture of Junkers Ju 87 and Ju 88 bombers and Messerschmitt Bf 109F and Bf 110 fighters, Fliegerkorps II represented a powerful adjunct to Axis air power in the central Mediterranean. By comparison, British strength within the theatre stagnated. For in a final repeat of history, just as the British had diverted forces to Greece with the culmination of Operation *Compass*, the beginning of 1942 saw a major diversion of reinforcements away from the Middle East to address the growing calamity that was unfolding in the Far East. As such, for the next several weeks the British would redirect troops, equipment, aircraft and ships to the Far East to the detriment of operations in North Africa and the Mediterranean.

While these similarities were quite striking, other factors existed that were contrary to the situation of the previous year. Unfortunately for the British, these factors generally favoured the Axis. First, after sustaining heavy losses during the ill-fated Greek/Crete campaigns and then during subsequent operations in November and December, the Mediterranean Fleet entered the new year in a significantly reduced state compared to that of 12 months earlier. This plight included a complete absence of capital ships, as all of the fleet's battleships and aircraft carriers had been sunk, temporarily disabled or withdrawn from the theatre during the previous year. As such, the British could only muster a handful of cruisers and destroyers for operations in the Eastern Mediterranean. The situation in the Western Mediterranean was only slightly better as Force H could call upon a single battleship, the aged *Malaya*, and the obsolete aircraft carrier *Argus* to bolster its meagre ranks. Against this, the Regia Marina possessed four modern or modernised battleships, over 60 assorted cruisers, destroyers and torpedo boats and some 70 submarines (including German U-boats) for immediate or short-notice use within the Mediterranean. Backing up this formidable force was a strong air contingent that included the aforementioned Fliegerkorps II.

A second major factor contrasting with the conditions of the previous year was the status of the Axis forces in North Africa. Whereas Operation *Compass* had resulted in the destruction of an entire Italian army, the results from Operation *Crusader* were far less absolute. Even though Panzerarmee Afrika had suffered heavy losses during its expulsion from Cyrenaica, it still possessed a coherent force structure with several units that were capable of both offensive and defensive action. As such, Panzerarmee Afrika was far from a defeated force, but rather had the potential to be quite formidable if given proper logistical support. To this end, by retreating to El Agheila, the army commander, General Erwin Rommel, had significantly shortened his supply lines thus improving his overall logistical situation. Likewise, on 5 January Axis fortunes received a further boost when a heavily escorted convoy of six merchant ships arrived safely at Tripoli with 56 German and 52 Italian tanks and other vital stores. The importance of this accomplishment was demonstrated by the large investment the Regia Marina had put into it, including an escort and covering force consisting of four battleships, six cruisers, 24 destroyers/torpedo boats and 11 pre-positioned submarines.

This, of course, only represented a single event in the ongoing supply struggle at the heart of the Mediterranean conflict. In this, the Italians, like the British, faced their own set of challenges. According to Regia Marina statistics, on 1 January 1941 Italy maintained control over 608 merchant ships of 500 tons or greater, worth a combined 2,205,980 tons in the Mediterranean.[2] Over the next year, they lost from all causes 156 of these vessels worth 603,299 tons, but gained from all sources, including new construction and seizures, 77 ships of 241,435 tons.[3] Thus, by the beginning of 1942 Axis merchant strength in the Mediterranean had fallen to 529 ocean-going vessels worth 1,844,116 tons. In tonnage terms, this constituted a decline of 16.4 percent since the beginning of 1941 and a 20 percent decline since the beginning of the Mediterranean conflict. When adding in damaged vessels and shipping awaiting repairs, this number declined further. Adding to this problem, many of the ships lost in 1941 were larger and more capable vessels, leaving the Italians with a dwindling merchant fleet increasingly ill-suited for the task at hand. Finally, the Italians suffered from a severely deteriorating fuel oil situation. At the beginning of the war the Regia Marina possessed 1,666,674 tons of oil in its fuel stockpile. Over the next 19 months it consumed a little over 1.7 million tons of oil against a limited replenishment that left it with just 108,000 tons remaining at the beginning of 1942.[4] This rapidly diminishing fuel reserve threatened to limit Italy's ability to mount sizable convoy escorts like that utilised during the 5 January convoy.

Despite these challenges and limitations, the Italians persevered in their ongoing logistical effort. Utilising aircraft, merchant ships and selected warships, the Italians (with German support) successfully delivered 7,120 personnel and 65,570 tons of materiel and supplies to North Africa in January 1942. This latter figure included 219 tanks and armoured vehicles, 768 other vehicles, 30,227 tons of general supplies and 21,844 tons of fuel.[5] While this constituted a significant improvement over the performance of the previous two months, the Italians continued to pay a heavy price for this success. In January British submarines sank eight Italian merchant ships worth 22,131 tons.[6] They also sank the Italian submarines *Ammiraglio St. Bon* and *Medusa*, the first of which was on a supply mission at the time of its demise. Meanwhile, British aircraft added three large merchant ships to January's toll. Malta-based Swordfish sank the first, the 5,741-ton *Perla*, on the 7th. Then on the 23rd Malta-based Beauforts and Benghazi-based Albacores shared in the destruction of the 13,098-ton troopship *Victoria*.[7] Finally, at the end of January, a Malta-based Swordfish hit and severely damaged the 5,628-ton *San Giovanni Battista*. Although eventually towed to Tripoli, this latter merchant ship was never put back into service and was essentially a total loss. When combined together, these results eliminated another 11 vessels worth 46,598 tons from Italy's slowly withering merchant fleet.

Fortunately for the Axis, these losses were not in vain. Although still far short of their theoretical requirements, January's influx of supplies and reinforcements provided Rommel with the minimum resources he needed to revitalise his flagging Panzerarmee Afrika. Not one to sit on the defensive for very long, on 21 January Rommel struck back at the British in western Cyrenaica. This bold action caught the British, who were struggling with their own logistical and structural difficulties at the time, completely by surprise, and in a final, tragic repeat of history, quickly sent them reeling back. Within a matter of days, all of western Cyrenaica, including Benghazi, came back under Axis control. The only solace the British could take from this abrupt reversal of fortunes was that in yielding ground, they had once again successfully extricated the vast bulk of their forces with losses numbering just 1,390 men, 72 tanks and 40 field guns.[8] Still, by early February better than half of the territorial gains attained during Operation *Crusader* were now lost as logistical exhaustion finally forced the two armies to settle on a line running between Gazala (some 30 miles west of Tobruk) in the north to Bir Hacheim in the south. Here, the two armies would remain for the next three months as each side toiled to bring in reinforcements and build up supplies.

During this lull in ground operations, attention on both sides shifted to Malta. In January the British successfully delivered five merchant ships with some 35,000 tons of supplies to Malta while concurrently evacuating three empties. However, these movements came at a cost as the British destroyer *Gurkha* and the 6,655-ton merchant ship *Thermopylae* were sunk by *U133* and Luftwaffe aircraft on 17 and 19 January respectively.[9] Unfortunately, these results represented a temporary pinnacle for British supply operations. In February the hazards of running additional ships through to Malta markedly increased when Axis forces once again regained use of airfields in western Cyrenaica. From there, as well as Crete and Sicily, swarms of German and Italian bombers were now positioned to attack any British shipping movements in the Eastern Mediterranean. As if to dramatise this point, in mid-February the British attempted to run a convoy of three fast merchant ships through to Malta from Alexandria. Despite an escort consisting of four cruisers and 16 destroyers, the convoy was deluged by repeated air attacks that eventually sank two of the merchant ships, the 7,262-ton *Clan Chattan* and the 7,798-ton *Rowallan Castle*, and forced the third, the 7,255-ton *Clan Campbell*, to turn back and put into Tobruk.

Undaunted by this result, in March the British attempted a similar operation to run four merchant ships with 37,249 tons of vitally needed supplies through to Malta, including 10,033 tons of military stores and ammunition, 22,216 tons of civil and government stores and 5,000 tons of fuel.[10] Under the designation of Convoy MW.10, these ships consisted of the aforementioned 7,255-ton *Clan Campbell*, 5415-ton *Pampas*, 6,798-ton *Talabot* (Norwegian) and the 9,776-ton naval auxiliary *Breconshire*. The anti-aircraft cruiser *Carlisle* and six destroyers provided a direct escort for this convoy while the light cruisers *Cleopatra*, *Dido* and *Euryalus* and four destroyers provided distant cover. Likewise, on the 19th the British dispatched seven Hunt-class escort destroyers to sweep the convoy route for Axis submarines prior to the convoy's departure. The 'Hunts' were then to proceed to Tobruk for refuelling before rendezvousing with the convoy on the 21st. However, before this occurred one of these escort destroyers, *Heythrop*, was sunk by *U652* east of Tobruk on the 20th. Finally, the British pre-positioned five submarines in the Gulf of Taranto and off Messina to detect and interdict movements of the Italian fleet.

On the morning of 20 March the convoy departed Alexandria, followed that evening by the distant covering force under the overall command of Rear-Admiral

Philip Vian. Things progressed well for the first day and a half as the convoy proceeded undetected towards Malta. However, at 1705 hours on the 21st the Italian submarine *Platino* encountered the British ships south of Crete and made a sighting report to the Italian Admiralty. This was followed by a second sighting report from the Italian submarine *Onice* at 1830 hours. Italian authorities responded to these reports by dispatching a powerful force consisting of the battleship *Littorio*, two heavy cruisers, a light cruiser and ten destroyers to intercept the convoy. Fortunately for the British, this movement was promptly detected by the submarine *P36*, which was patrolling the Gulf of Taranto, and Admiral Vian received timely warning of the pending danger proceeding towards him. Correctly surmising that the Italian ships would be in position to attack the convoy on the afternoon of the 22nd, Vian divided his force to meet the oncoming threat. Leaving five Hunt-class escort destroyers to accompany the merchant ships, Vian earmarked the anti-aircraft cruiser *Carlisle* and the sixth 'Hunt' to lay a continuous smoke screen while his remaining ships, now reinforced by the cruiser *Penelope* and the destroyer *Legion* from Malta, manoeuvred to confront the enemy.

After enduring several ineffective air attacks during the morning, Admiral Vian's brave little force finally came into contact with the Italian squadron at 1427 hours on the 22nd. For the next four and a half hours Vian's collection of cruisers and destroyers fought a series of masterful engagements with the superior Italian force. Aided by deteriorating weather conditions, the British effectively utilised smoke and aggressive tactics, including multiple torpedo attacks, to hold off *Littorio* and the other Italian warships. During this fight a number of British vessels sustained damage, but none were fatally struck. By comparison, British fire caused negligible damage to the Italian warships, but this was not the point of their resistance. Throughout the afternoon the British held the superior Italian force at bay and prevented it from getting through to the convoy. The scope of this accomplishment was demonstrated by the fact that the Italians held a four to one advantage in firepower with a combined broadside of some 24,000 pounds compared to just 5,900 pounds for the British. Finally, with the onset of dusk at 1858 hours, the Italian battle squadron broke off the engagement and retired back towards Italy. In doing so, it ceded a moral victory to Admiral Vian and his stout British defenders in what later became known as the second battle of Sirte, or as Admiral Cunningham referred to it, 'one of the most brilliant naval actions of the war.'[11]

Notwithstanding this laudatory praise or the exemplary nature of the accomplishment, the battle did have one consequence that benefited the Axis cause. Originally scheduled to arrive at Malta during the hours of darkness, the prolonged surface engagement delayed the convoy's arrival until the morning of the 23rd. With the coming of daybreak, waves of German bombers from Fliegerkorps II descended upon the hapless convoy. By midmorning these bombers sank *Clan Campbell* some 20 miles from Malta, while *Breconshire* was immobilised off the small Maltese harbour of

Marsa Scirocco. The two remaining merchant ships safely arrived at Grand Harbour, but were then subjected to continuous, heavy bombing as Fliegerkorps II launched an all-out effort to destroy these berthed vessels before they could discharge their valuable cargoes. On 26 March both ships were destroyed while the immobilised *Breconshire* was sunk on the 27th. In the end, only 5,022 tons of supplies were unloaded from these vessels, including a sizable portion salvaged from the wrecks through 13 April.[12] While there would be further minor salvage, this initial retrieval represented a mere 13.5 percent of the 37,249 tons originally dispatched.

Yet, these meagre results exacted a heavy toll. In addition to the four merchant ships sunk during the operation or its immediate aftermath, the British also lost three warships. The first of these was the aforementioned escort destroyer *Heythrop*. The second was the escort destroyer *Southwold*, which was mined off Malta on the 24th. Finally, German bombers accounted for the destroyer *Legion*, which was damaged on the 23rd and subsequently finished off on the 26th. For their part, the Italians also suffered some losses relating to the encounter. While returning to Italy on the

In 1942 the process of supplying Malta became extensively more difficult. Pictured here are British warships during the second battle of Sirte. (Zimmerman, E. A. (Lt), Royal Navy official photographer, public domain)

23rd, a severe storm battered the Italian squadron, and the destroyers *Scirocco* and *Lanciere* both foundered in the heavy seas with a loss of 453 men. The remaining Italian ships all suffered varying degrees of storm damage, including the light cruiser *Giovanni delle Bande Nere*, which was subsequently sunk by the British submarine *Urge* on 1 April as it was en route to La Spezia to enact repairs. Thus, in terms of warship losses, the Italians actually fared worse than the British, but this was of little consolation given the overall failure of the operation.

Making matters worse, the plight of Convoy MW.10 was only one of many misfortunes to assail Malta and its indomitable inhabitants during the first half of 1942. In January Fliegerkorps II and the Regia Aeronautica conducted 1,521 sorties against Malta. In February this assault intensified as Axis aircraft flew 1,970 sorties against the beleaguered island group. Then in March and April the Axis doubled and redoubled their efforts by launching 4,342 and 9,017 sorties respectively.[13] In doing so, they transformed the small British colony into the most heavily bombed place on Earth (at least up to this point in the war). In April alone the Axis dropped 6,728 tons of bombs on Malta.[14] Considering the colony's small size and the limited areas that were actually targeted during these attacks, Malta suffered a far higher concentration of bombing than did London during the height of the Battle of Britain or the subsequent bombing blitz. An example of this was the fact that in April the air raid sirens in Valletta sounded 275 times, which averaged out to nine times per day or about once every two and a half hours.[15]

The focus of this onslaught was Malta's three primary airfields as well as port installations, naval targets and general infrastructure. In terms of the former, in April alone the British lost 126 aircraft destroyed or disabled on the ground while a further 20 were shot down in aerial combat.[16] Meanwhile, on 12 February German bombers sank the destroyer *Maori* in Valletta Harbour. Then in the latter half of March and first half of April the Axis shifted a larger percentage of their attacks to raids against ports and naval targets. This had a devastating effect upon Malta's naval presence. In addition to those vessels sunk in the aftermath of Convoy MW.10, this assault brought about the destruction of the destroyers *Lance*, *Kingston* and *Gallant* (the latter being a derelict wreck from an earlier mine strike); the minesweeper *Abingdon*; the submarines *P39*, *P36*, *Glavkos* (Greek) and *Pandora*; the 5,916-ton naval tanker *Plumleaf* and several minor vessels. Meanwhile, during the same period the cruiser *Penelope* suffered heavy damage while trapped in dry dock due to a bomb-damaged caisson. Day after day Axis aircraft attacked the stationary cruiser, but failed to deliver a fatal blow against the valiant warship. Nevertheless, *Penelope's* sides and hull became so pockmarked from splinter damage that the vessel earned the nickname 'HMS Pepperpot.'

This constant bombing, plus the many privations caused by the quickly deteriorating supply situation, took a heavy toll upon Malta's inhabitants and severely restrained the island's effectiveness as a base for defensive and offensive action. Amongst other things, Malta's small air contingent suffered declining operational rates as well as heavy aircraft wastage. As a result, throughout much of February and March the British were only able to maintain about a dozen serviceable Hurricane fighters out of more than 60 available. Even with the arrival of Spitfires in early March, the British were hard pressed to maintain a viable fighter defence against their Axis antagonists. The situation was much the same for Malta's dwindling reconnaissance and strike squadrons, and by the middle of March Malta's operational air strength was down to just 14 Hurricanes, nine Spitfires, three Wellingtons, two Marylands, two Beaufighters and a few Albacores and Swordfish.[17] Meanwhile, Malta's port and naval facilities suffered similar deprivations as maintenance, repair and support activities steadily declined and personnel became worn down by the unrelenting strain and inadequate rations. Particularly hard hit was the 10th Submarine Flotilla, which was forced to keep its boats submerged on the harbour bottom during the hours of daylight to avoid German attack. Finally, the incessant pounding diminished Malta's ability to keep its coastal waters free from mines, which were laid by Axis aircraft and vessels with regular frequency.

Prompted by this deteriorating situation, all surviving warships that were capable of doing so evacuated Malta at the end of March and the first half of April. This included the bomb-scarred *Penelope*, which despite its damaged condition, successfully made it to Gibraltar after being released from dry dock. The cruisers *Carlisle* and *Aurora* and five escort destroyers made similar treks to either Alexandria or Gibraltar, but the destroyer *Havock* was not so fortunate. Hugging the Tunisian coastline to avoid Italian minefields, *Havock* ran aground on a sandbank off Kelibia and became a total loss. Then at the end of April and first part of May the British evacuated the remaining six submarines of the 10th Submarine Flotilla to Alexandria. In the process of doing so, one of these submarines, *Urge*, went missing and was presumably lost on a mine. By the second week in May, Malta's offensive striking power was reduced to a negligible state. At about the same time, Field Marshal Albert Kesselring, the German commander in the Mediterranean theatre, reported to Berlin that the neutralisation of Malta was complete.

Yet, even as he made this proclamation, changes were underway in the Mediterranean that promised to provide some relief to Malta. The first of these was the aforementioned arrival of Spitfire fighters to bolster the colony's hard-pressed Hurricane force. In March Force H, now under the command of Rear-Admiral E. N. Syfret, conducted three ferry missions using the aircraft carriers *Eagle* and *Argus* to successfully deliver 31 Spitfires to Malta. In April the British employed the American aircraft carrier *Wasp* to fly off 47 Spitfires to Malta (Operation *Calendar*) of which 46 arrived. Unfortunately, the Luftwaffe caught many of these fighters on the ground immediately upon their arrival, and after four days of heavy fighting, a mere six remained operational. Undaunted by this outcome, on 9 May *Wasp* and *Eagle* delivered another 61 Spitfires (out of 64 dispatched) during Operation *Bowery*.

This time, improved ground support quickly turned these fighters around, and a significantly larger portion survived into the coming days. Later in May and early June *Eagle* and *Argus* conducted three more ferry missions delivering 76 additional fighters to the besieged colony.[18] Malta's limited support facilities and the strain of continuous combat took a heavy toll on these aircraft, but by June these repeated ferrying missions provided Malta with an operational fighter strength of 95 Spitfires.[19] Given this result, after months of severe privation, Malta finally again possessed a viable defence to confront the Luftwaffe and the Regia Aeronautica.

Coinciding with this event was a corresponding reduction in the threat posed against the colony. In May the Luftwaffe began shifting assets away from Sicily for re-deployment to the Eastern Mediterranean, North Africa and Soviet Union. As such, the scale of attacks against Malta declined sharply. In May the Axis flew 3,221 sorties against Malta, which was only about a third of the number conducted the previous month. In June this number dropped again by better than 50 percent to just 1,571 sorties.[20] Added to this, a larger portion of these sorties were flown by the Regia Aeronautica, which still proved to be less effective in inflicting damage than the Luftwaffe. Meanwhile, during a conference in April Hitler and Mussolini formally agreed to defer a proposed invasion of Malta until July or August, pending events in North Africa. Planning and preparations for this proposed invasion, designated Operation *Hercules*, had been underway since 1941 and called for the use of a joint German/Italian force of 96,000 men to conduct both airborne and seaborne landings. Fortunately for the British, Hitler had little enthusiasm for the undertaking, and this deferment essentially signalled the demise of any serious intention to invade. As such, despite Malta's severely weakened state, the unwavering colony still possessed the capacity to make a recovery if given adequate time and support.

Of course, all of this depended upon Britain's ability to keep the island group effectively supplied. By the spring of 1942 Malta faced the prospect of slow starvation as foodstuffs ran dangerously low. To counter this, local authorities imposed strict rationing for both military and civilian personnel, but this could only delay the coming calamity and not prevent it without the benefit of substantial re-supply. Likewise, Malta suffered worsening shortages of other commodities that were critical to military operations including fuel, ammunition and spare parts. To help ease this growing crisis, the British used submarines and the fast minelayers *Manxman* and *Welshman* to deliver limited quantities of essential items such as medical supplies, aviation fuel, powdered milk, anti-aircraft ammunition, smoke canisters (which were used to obscure key assets from enemy observation) and mail. In 1942 these submarines conducted 20 such missions while the fast minelayers conducted six more.[21] For the loss of the submarine *Olympus*, which was sunk on a mine, these missions provided a degree of relief that extended Malta's limited endurance. Still, without substantial re-supply, Malta's days were numbered. Given Britain's worldwide naval commitments at the time, British authorities determined that the earliest they could attempt another convoy was June. Until then, Malta would just have to hold out.

In the meantime, British leaders had other logistical concerns to contend with. While Malta was enduring its aerial onslaught, the situation in the Far East had deteriorated to a disastrous level. By the end of April, the British were in the process of abandoning Burma and preparing to defend eastern India from Japanese assault, while a hastily assembled and understrength British fleet was making similar preparations to defend the Indian Ocean. In the five months prior, the British had lost much of their Southeast Asian Empire and suffered the worst series of defeats ever to befall their armed forces. In terms of ground losses, these disasters cost the British 166,867 casualties (including those from Commonwealth and imperial sources) of which nearly 94 percent were taken prisoner.[22] Meanwhile, the British and Commonwealth navies lost a battleship, a battlecruiser, a light carrier, four cruisers, eight destroyers, two sloops, a corvette, an armed merchant cruiser, several minor warships and auxiliaries and dozens of merchant ships. Against this, the British had only inflicted negligible losses upon the Japanese. In particular, Japanese ground casualties during the related campaigns were only about an eighth of those sustained by the British, while their naval losses consisted of just two submarines and a handful of merchant ships sunk solely or partially as a result of British or Commonwealth action.

Adding to Britain's many woes was the potential threat that the Vichy French-controlled island of Madagascar posed to its regional lines of communication. Located some 250 miles off the coast of Mozambique, Madagascar was perfectly positioned to menace Allied maritime traffic in the western Indian Ocean. In the hands of the Germans or Japanese, Madagascar would constitute an ideal base to launch submarine and air attacks against Allied shipping travelling to and from the Middle East, East Africa, the Persian Gulf and India, jeopardising Allied access to these critical areas. Taking into account the Vichy government's recent history of collaboration and appeasement in France, Syria and Indochina, the Allies believed that Madagascar was vulnerable to Axis encroachment.[23] At best, they feared the Vichy French would only offer token resistance against a Japanese invasion; at worst, they feared outright French cooperation with the Germans or Japanese. In either case, the Allies agreed that the threat associated with continued Vichy control over Madagascar was unacceptable. Thus, despite their many commitments, the British War Cabinet, with agreement from the American government, decided on 12 March 1942 to seize the naval base of Diego Suarez on the northern tip of Madagascar.

With this decision made, the British underwent the arduous process of collecting the ships and resources necessary to carry out the invasion. Given their other commitments and recent heavy losses, this was no easy task, but the British still managed to assemble a powerful force for the undertaking. Drawing upon ships from the United Kingdom, Ceylon, the Mediterranean and the West Indies, this included a sizable fleet consisting of the battleship *Ramillies*, the aircraft carriers *Illustrious* and *Indomitable* (with 42 fighters and 44 strike aircraft embarked between them), two cruisers, 11 destroyers, six corvettes, six minesweepers and 18 assorted transports and support vessels for the assault against Madagascar.[24] Beyond this, elements of the Eastern Fleet, including the battleship *Warspite* and the aircraft carrier *Formidable*, would provide distant cover in the east to screen against potential Japanese interference. Meanwhile, the military ground forces assigned to the undertaking consisted of three British army brigades and a Royal Marine Commando. Rear-Admiral E. N. Syfret commanded this fleet and served as the combined commander for the operation while Major-General R. G. Sturges, Royal Marines, was his second-in-command and served as the military commander for the ground assault. On 25 and 28 April the bulk of the invasion fleet departed Durban, South Africa and proceeded to Madagascar in two separate convoys, one slow and one fast. On 3 May this fleet rendezvoused with warships from Ceylon and then positioned itself to the east and west of Diego Suarez in final preparation for the assault.

The invasion, designated Operation *Ironclad*, commenced at 0439 hours on 5 May when British commando and army assault forces landed unopposed on three beaches in Ambararata and Courrier Bays to the west of Diego Suarez. The British launched these assaults after traversing a route through reefs, channels and minefields considered impassable by the French. Accordingly, the landings caught the French completely by surprise, and the British were able to easily seize their objectives. In less than an hour and at virtually no loss to themselves, the British captured a battery of 6.1-inch coastal defence guns along with some 300 French prisoners. By daybreak, the British had firm control over all the beaches and were landing follow-up forces and equipment, resulting in the arrival of at least 13,650 personnel as well as 339 assorted vehicles and guns and 590 tons of stores through the following day.[25] The only significant misfortune to occur during this process was the loss of the corvette *Auricula*, which struck a mine and sank. Meanwhile, sunrise brought an expansion to the operation as British carrier aircraft launched a series of attacks to neutralise French air and naval units within the area. Early on, this included a strike from *Indomitable* against Antsirane airfield, while *Illustrious* carried out attacks against French warships in Diego Suarez harbour that sank the armed merchant cruiser *Bougainville*, the submarine *Bévéziers* and the sloop *D'Entrecasteaux*.

The struggle continued over the next couple of days as British ground forces pushed inland towards the main French bases at Diego Suarez and Antsirane. With these advances, the British encountered increased French resistance and some hard fighting ensued. Fortunately for the British, the Royal Navy provided valuable fire support and other timely interventions that helped turn the tide of battle in their favour. In terms of the former, the navy fired a total of 515 shells ranging in size from 3-inch to 15-inch against shore targets during the course of the short operation.[26] In terms of the latter, the most important example of this occurred at 2050 hours on the 6th when the destroyer *Anthony* successfully landed 50 Royal Marines behind the French defences at Antsirane. This daring manoeuvre, carried out under difficult conditions at night, proved to be a turning point in the battle, and the French garrison at Diego Suarez surrendered shortly thereafter. While this was underway, the naval fighting continued as aircraft from *Illustrious* sank the French submarine *Le Héros* on the 7th, while the destroyer *Active* sank the submarine *Monge* on the morning of the 8th as the latter was attempting to attack *Indomitable*. This final action signalled an end to French resistance, and the battle ended with the British in firm control over their territorial objectives.

The successful conclusion of Operation *Ironclad* provided the British with a well-deserved and necessary victory during a period of otherwise bleak events throughout the world. With the seizure of Diego Suarez, the British removed a potential threat to their convoy routes in the Indian Ocean and helped secure essential lines of communication to the Middle East, Persian Gulf and India. In doing so, they achieved their overall strategic objective for the operation, the importance of which was demonstrated by the 3,250,700 tons of military cargo shipped into the region from the United Kingdom and North America in 1942 alone.[27] This success did not come at a high price. Altogether, *Ironclad* cost the British the corvette *Auricula*, 105 men killed, 283 wounded and four missing. By comparison, the Vichy French lost three submarines, a sloop, and an armed merchant cruiser sunk as well as 171 men killed, 343 wounded and several hundred men taken prisoner.[28] Finally, the British seized the 4,669-ton Vichy-controlled merchant ship *General Duquesne* and forced the scuttling of three Axis merchant ships (the 2,315-ton Italian *Duca Degli Abruzzi*, the 2,699-ton Italian *Somalia* and the 6,181-ton German *Wartenfels*) that had taken refuge in Diego Suarez earlier in the war.[29]

While *Ironclad* represented a peripheral triumph, the British still faced a difficult situation in the Mediterranean. Taking advantage of Britain's many misfortunes, the Axis enjoyed considerable success supplying their forces in North Africa during this period. From February through May 1942 the Axis successfully delivered 343,791 tons of supplies out of 361,775 tons dispatched.[30] When averaged out, this equated to an arrival of 85,948 tons per month and represented a 95.03 percent delivery rate. Included in these shipments were 561 tanks, 115 armoured cars, many thousands of other vehicles and guns and 106,500 tons of fuel.[31] Meanwhile, from January through June Italian naval and merchant shipping transported 9,009 personnel to Libya.[32] This represented a mere fraction of the Axis reinforcements sent to North Africa since aircraft were the primary means used to transport troops. As an example, in April and May alone Axis aircraft delivered 24,300 German and 16,700 Italian personnel to Libya.[33] When combined together, this inflow of personnel and materiel more than made up for the Axis losses from the *Crusader* battle and provided Rommel with an adequate, if slim, supply reserve for offensive operations.

Notwithstanding this logistical accomplishment, Italy's available merchant fleet continued to suffer a steady level of attrition. While British offensive fortunes clearly

To help secure vital supply routes through the Indian Ocean, the British embarked upon Operation *Ironclad* in May 1942 to seize Diego-Suarez in Vichy-controlled Madagascar. Pictured here are the aircraft carrier *Formidable* and the battleship *Warspite* (top right), which provided distant cover for the operation. (Oulds, D. C. (Lt), Royal Navy official photographer, public domain)

declined during this period, they did not altogether cease. In fact, some British forces performed surprisingly well given the adverse conditions they were operating under. This was particularly true regarding Britain's local submarine force, which from February through May sank or effectively neutralised 23 ocean-going merchant ships worth 91,020 tons in the Mediterranean.[34] This number included the Italian merchant ships *Napoli* and *Ariosto* (6,142 and 4,116 tons respectively), which were sunk by the submarines *Umbra* and *P38* in conjunction with FAA Albacores operating out of Malta. It also included the 5,417-ton Vichy tanker *PLM20*, which was operating in the service of the Germans, and three Axis vessels that were damaged beyond repair, or at least through the duration of the conflict. Finally, in addition to their merchant successes, British and British-affiliated submarines also sank the aforementioned light cruiser *Giovanni delle Bande Nere*, the Italian destroyer *Emanuele Pessagno*, the Italian submarines *Ammiraglio Millo*, *Guglielmotti* and *Tricheco* and 17 assorted minor vessels.[35]

Utilising other means, the British added to these interdiction successes. In addition to the aforementioned *Napoli* and *Ariosto*, British aircraft sank or participated in the destruction of five other ocean-going merchant ships and two minor vessels worth 21,951 tons during this period.[36] This included the results of a devastating raid carried out by Wellington bombers against Palermo harbour on the night of 2/3 March. During this attack the German merchant ship *Cuma* was hit and set ablaze. Over the next two days the ammunition-laden *Cuma* continued to burn until it exploded on the 4th, destroying itself and the adjacent merchant ships *Securitas* and *Le Tre Marie*. In addition to the loss of these three vessels worth 13,104 tons, the raid and *Cuma*'s subsequent explosion caused varying degrees of damage to at least 32 other merchant ships and auxiliary vessels worth 39,021 tons that were present in the harbour.[37] Likewise, the Italian destroyer *Freccia* was heavily damaged while four other destroyers/torpedo boats were damaged to a lesser extent. In other interdiction successes, a Swordfish aircraft combined with a mine strike to sink the 1,778-ton German merchant ship *Achaia* on 17/18 March, while Wellington bombers sank the 6,836-ton Italian *Gino Allegri* at the end of May. Meanwhile, mines claimed five vessels worth 7,759 tons while British destroyer sank two coasters worth 810 tons during this period.[38] When added together and including minor vessels, some 125,000 tons of shipping was sunk or rendered useless to the Axis cause from February through May 1942.

Of course, not all of these losses were one-sided as the British paid a heavy price for their interdiction efforts. In addition to the toll already noted in and around Malta, the British lost the submarines *Triumph*, *Tempest*, *P38* and *Upholder* from January through May.[39] The first was presumed lost to mines while Italian warships sank the latter three. Meanwhile, on 11 March at the conclusion of an unsuccessful anti-shipping sweep, the British light cruiser *Naiad* was sunk by *U565* off Mersa Matruh. Fifteen days later *U652* sank the British destroyer *Jaguar* off Sidi Barrani. Then on 10 May the British dispatched the destroyers *Jervis*, *Jackal*, *Kipling* and *Lively* from Alexandria to proceed into the central Mediterranean and intercept a Benghazi-bound Axis convoy. On 11 May German reconnaissance aircraft located the British force south of Crete thus prompting the British to abandon their sortie and turn back towards Alexandria. Despite their hasty retreat, the British destroyers were soon subjected to a heavy series of air attacks from German dive-bombers that sank *Lively*, *Kipling* and *Jackal* in quick secession. Only *Jervis* withstood this onslaught to arrive back in Alexandria on the 12th with 630 survivors from the sunken warships.

Returning now to the standoff in North Africa, at the end of May General Rommel realised that his balance of forces situation had achieved an optimum state that was only likely to decrease with the passage of time. He therefore ordered a resumed offensive against the Eighth Army along the Gazala line. Attacking with three German and six Italian divisions of his Panzerarmee Afrika, Rommel possessed some 90,000 men with 560 tanks and 704 assorted aircraft (of which 497 were serviceable). Opposing this offensive was the British Eighth Army, which possessed two armoured and three infantry divisions and two independent tank brigades broken down into two corps (XIII and XXX Corps) along with a sixth division held in army reserve.[40] When combined together, the British possessed about 100,000 men, 849 tanks and 320 aircraft (of which 190 were serviceable).[41] Although occupied with preparations for their own proposed June offensive, the British deployed a sizable portion of this force along the Gazala line in a series of brigade-sized defensive boxes. The British further augmented this line with the extensive use of minefields and a substantial mobile reserve built around the two armoured divisions.

On 26 May Rommel began his offensive. Utilising his Italian infantry to stage a diversionary attack against the northern end of the Gazala line, Rommel launched his main assault, consisting of the three German and two Italian mobile divisions, in an encircling movement around the Eighth Army's desert flank at Bir Hacheim. Over the next few days this force fought a series of engagements against dispersed British units, inflicting heavy losses upon the latter. Nevertheless, things did not go entirely Rommel's way as his advancing units encountered stiff resistance. This was particularly true at Bir Hacheim and the Knightsbridge Box (located east of the Gazala line) where the 1st Free French Brigade Group and the 201st Guards Brigade steadfastly refused to give ground. By the 28th Rommel's spearhead units had become dangerously dispersed, his tank strength was down by a third and his logistical situation bordered on critical as supply columns lagged behind the advancing units. In response to this, Rommel consolidated his German divisions between the Gazala line and the Knightsbridge Box in an area that became known as the Cauldron and assumed a defensive posture. Had the British decisively counter-attacked at this time, they would have likely destroyed Rommel's dangerously exposed units, which were essentially surrounded, but this was not to be. Instead, the British vacillated, and when their counter-attacks finally came in, they did so in a piecemeal and poorly coordinated manner that had little impact on the German defences.

Over the next two and a half weeks the fighting continued as the tide of battle slowly shifted in Rommel's favour. Even as the Deutsches Afrika Korps assumed the defensive, German engineers cleared two routes through the British minefields north and south of the 150th Brigade Box located along the Gazala line on the western edge of the Cauldron. This provided the Germans with direct lines of re-supply. To consolidate this position, Rommel launched an intense assault against the 150th Brigade Box beginning on 29 May. After three days of heavy fighting, the box finally fell on 1 June with most of the British defenders successfully breaking out to the east. Rommel now possessed a solid lodgement in the British line. Throughout this period and into the succeeding days the British launched a series of disjointed counter-attacks against this lodgement, but each ended in costly failure. Meanwhile, Rommel now turned his attention to reducing the Free French position at Bir Hacheim, which finally fell on the 11th after the garrison was ordered to breakout.

The next day the German 15th Panzer and 90th Light Divisions, along with the Italian Trieste Division, resumed the offensive out of the Cauldron. In two days of heavy fighting this Axis force badly mauled defending British armoured units, reducing the Eighth Army's tank strength to a dangerous level and prompting the evacuation of the Knightsbridge Box on the evening of the 13th.

A time of decision was now clearly at hand. With two British infantry divisions in imminent danger of encirclement on the northern portion of the Gazala line, Lieutenant-General Neil Ritchie, the Eighth Army commander, ordered a general withdrawal towards the Egyptian frontier. Over the next several days Eighth Army executed this retreat. The exception to this was at Tobruk, where bowing to political pressure, the British made a last-minute decision to defend the port. Sadly, in the time since its relief some six months earlier, Tobruk's defences had been allowed to deteriorate. Many of the minefields that had encircled the perimeter were now gone, while large stretches of anti-tank ditches had filled in with sand. Likewise, the hastily assembled garrison, built around the 2nd South African Division, was sizable in numbers but limited in tanks and modern anti-tank guns. As such, when Rommel unleashed his Panzerarmee Afrika against the fortress' south-eastern perimeter on 20 June, it only took a matter of hours for the assaulting forces to breach the British defences. By the evening German tanks were rolling through the streets of Tobruk proper, and the garrison surrendered the next morning.

The fall of Tobruk represented a low ebb for British fortunes in the Middle East. In personnel and materiel terms, the calamity netted Rommel some 32,220 British prisoners as well as over 2,000 vehicles, 5,000 tons of supplies and 1,400 tons of fuel. By comparison, German casualties from the beginning of the Gazala offensive numbered just 3,360.[42] Of similar consequence, the defeat also inflicted a significant psychological blow to British morale and confidence. In 1941 the British had touted their defence of Tobruk as a symbol of defiant determination in the face of unrelenting Axis aggression. Now, with the fortress' seemingly easy demise, especially coming so soon after other recent disasters in the Far East, many British openly questioned the competence of their leaders. For his part, Churchill, who was in Washington at the time meeting with President Roosevelt, took the news of Tobruk's capture particularly hard. In later years he wrote:

> This was one of the heaviest blows I can recall during the war. Not only were its military effects grievous, but it affected the reputation of the British armies…I did not attempt to hide from the President the shock I had received. It was a bitter moment. Defeat is one thing; disgrace is another.[43]

On the other hand, the loss of Tobruk spawned at least three positive consequences for the British. First, given their overstretched resources, Tobruk's fall removed any prospect of the Royal Navy having to support another long and costly siege, as had been the case in 1941. This was particularly beneficial since the Royal Navy was already embroiled in the increasingly difficult task of trying to sustain Malta. Second, it prompted the United States to intensify efforts to materially support the Eighth Army. This included the immediate dispatch of 300 new Sherman tanks, which was the best Allied tank available at the time, and 100 self-propelled 105mm guns to Egypt. It also included the deployment of six groups of American bombers and fighters from the United States Army Air Force (USAAF) to join the group of B-24 Liberator heavy bombers that had been in the theatre since May. Finally, Tobruk's easy capture signalled the end to any serious consideration for an Axis invasion of Malta. Instead, Rommel, who was flush with victory and newly promoted to the rank of field marshal, actively lobbied for a continuation of his offensive into Egypt. Hitler, who had never been keen on the idea of invading Malta, readily agreed, and soon the men and materiel that had been earmarked for the invasion were instead dispatched to North Africa to support Rommel's proposed drive to the Nile Delta.

Of course, Malta's reprieve from invasion was only meaningful as long as the British could keep the isolated colony adequately supplied. This was no trivial matter since by the late spring of 1942, Malta was on the verge of starvation. In June, British authorities estimated that Malta would be forced to surrender if meaningful supplies did not arrive soon. Therefore, despite the many dangers arrayed against them, the British decided to undertake a massive re-supply effort with two simultaneous convoys proceeding to Malta from both ends of the Mediterranean. The first of these, designated Operation *Harpoon*, consisted of six merchant ships with 43,000 tons of supplies sent from Britain via Gibraltar. Covering this convoy was a close escort consisting of the anti-aircraft cruiser *Cairo*, five destroyers and four Hunt-class escort destroyers with the battleship *Malaya*, the aircraft carriers *Eagle* and *Argus*, three cruisers and eight destroyers serving as distant escort. The British also sent four fleet minesweepers and six motor launches to perform minesweeping duties on the approach to Grand Harbour, while a Royal Fleet Auxiliary (RFA) tanker would provide refuelling for the escorts as needed. Finally, the fast minelayer *Welshman* was to proceed to Malta ahead of the main body with a vital load of ammunition and then return in time to support the convoy's final approach to the besieged colony.

The *Harpoon* convoy entered the Mediterranean on the night of 11/12 June. In the five days preceding this event, RAF Catalina aircraft operating from Gibraltar sank the Italian submarines *Veniero* and *Zaffiro* in the adjacent waters thus underscoring the dangers confronting the undertaking. Indeed, forewarned of the operation through signal intercepts of American diplomatic communiqués from Egypt, the Axis mustered 21 Italian and six German submarines, two light cruisers and two squadrons of destroyers to confront the re-supply effort. Despite this considerable force, the convoy did not encounter serious opposition until the 14th when it experienced a series of air attacks that destroyed the 8,619-ton Dutch merchant ship *Tanimbar* and damaged the cruiser *Liverpool*. On the other hand, British carrier-borne fighters and anti-aircraft fire shot down at least 13 attacking aircraft during the day's fighting. That night the covering force turned back for Gibraltar leaving the convoy to proceed through the Central Narrows with just the close escort as protection.

At 0520 hours on the morning of the 15th British aircraft from Malta warned Captain C. C. Hardy, the escort commander, that a force of Italian cruisers and destroyers was approaching the convoy from the north. A few minutes later this force, consisting of the Italian light cruisers *Eugenio di Savoia* and *Montecuccoli* and five destroyers, came into view. Directing his five fleet destroyers to engage the superior Italian squadron, Hardy, in *Cairo*, along with the four Hunt-class escort destroyers and the assorted mine craft stayed with the merchant ships to make smoke and provide anti-aircraft protection. In a fight that resembled the second battle of Sirte some three months earlier, the British warships, which at times included *Cairo* and the escort destroyers, successfully held off the superior Italian force and prevented it from inflicting serious loss to the convoy. However, this success came at a cost as the British destroyer *Bedouin* was sunk and the destroyer *Partridge* sustained heavy damage. Against this, the Italian destroyer *Ugolino Vivaldi* also sustained serious damage and had to be towed to Pantellaria for repairs.

Meanwhile, the convoy continued to soldier on towards Malta. Unfortunately, in another similarity with the second battle of Sirte, the surface action delayed the convoy and split the British defences, making the merchant ships more vulnerable to air attack. Taking advantage of this, Axis bombers conducted a series of raids throughout the day that eventually resulted in the destruction of the freighters *Burdwan* and *Chant* and the tanker *Kentucky*, worth a combined 20,510 tons. Things improved markedly on the 16th when the British ships finally came under the protection of Malta's Spitfires. Still, one final tragedy was yet to unfold when a timing error prevented the minesweepers from first clearing a channel as originally planned. As such, four destroyers and the merchant ship *Orari* struck mines on their approach to Grand Harbour. This resulted in the loss of the Polish-manned escort destroyer *Kujawiak*, but the remaining ships all successfully made port. Thus, out of an original force of six merchant ships dispatched in the convoy, only two successfully arrived in Malta to deliver 15,000 tons of desperately needed supplies.

While this struggle was underway in the Western Mediterranean, the second convoy, code-named Operation *Vigorous*, proceeded towards Malta from the east. Consisting of 11 merchant ships assembled from Alexandria, Port Said, Beirut and Haifa, the *Vigorous* convoy possessed a sizable escort consisting of the light cruisers *Cleopatra, Dido, Hermione, Euryalus, Arethusa, Coventry, Birmingham* and *Newcastle*, 17 fleet destroyers, nine Hunt-class escort destroyers, four Flower-class corvettes, two minesweepers and four towed motor torpedo boats. Also present was the old demilitarised battleship *Centurion*, which was disguised to resemble a *King George V-* class battleship, but was only armed with light anti-aircraft guns. Likewise, the British stationed 13 submarines off Taranto and the Strait of Messina to detect and interdict Italian fleet movements. Finally, the British made elaborate preparations, including a commando raid against Maleme airfield, to mitigate Axis air superiority and maximise their own limited strike and defensive air coverage.

On 13 June the various elements of *Vigorous* rendezvoused off Tobruk and began their run to Malta. Already, the transport *City of Calcutta* had dropped out due to bomb damage, and the Dutch *Aagtekerk* was soon to follow with engine trouble. On the 14th the convoy passed beyond the range of British fighter cover from Africa, and Axis air attacks sank the 6,104-ton freighter *Bhutan* and damaged a second merchant ship. Meanwhile, German bombers in Libya sank the detached *Aagtekerk* (6,811 tons) near Tobruk. Making matters worse, a British reconnaissance aircraft from Malta reported a force of two Italian battleships (*Vittorio Veneto* and *Littorio*), four cruisers and 12 destroyers proceeding south from Taranto. Realising that this Italian battle squadron heavily outgunned his own force, Admiral Vian, the convoy commander, queried Alexandria for instructions. At this time Vice-Admiral Henry Harwood, the new Commander-in-Chief of the Mediterranean Fleet (having replaced Admiral Cunningham, who went to Washington to head the British naval staff mission), ordered Vian to proceed on course until 0200 hours and then turn back.

At 0145 hours on the 15th Vian executed this order and began the process of turning the convoy around. It was during this cumbersome manoeuvre that six German E-boats (motor torpedo boats), which had recently arrived in the Mediterranean, carried out torpedo attacks that sank the destroyer *Hasty* and damaged the cruiser *Newcastle*. Meanwhile, during the night and morning, Wellington and Beaufort bombers from Malta and long-range American B-24 Liberator bombers from Suez carried out their own series of attacks to fend off the approaching Italian battle squadron. Pending the results of these attacks, Admiral Harwood sent Vian a number of contradictory orders regarding course changes before finally ceding the matter to Vian's discretion. With this, Vian ordered the convoy to steam for home, thus abandoning the re-supply effort. As it was, the Allied air attacks failed to seriously impede the Italian battle squadron, although a Beaufort did succeed in torpedoing the Italian heavy cruiser *Trento*, while a B-24 scored a 500-pound bomb hit on *Littorio*.

Despite this lack of overall Allied aerial success, at 1445 hours Admiral Iachino, the Italian commander, concluded that the convoy had passed beyond his reach and abandoned the pursuit on his own accord. A short time later, a British reconnaissance aircraft reported that the Italian ships were heading back towards Taranto. This development prompted Admiral Harwood to consider one final attempt to pass the convoy through to Malta, but he soon abandoned this notion with Vian's strong concurrence. At 2053 hours he signalled the convoy to return to Alexandria. While this ended the re-supply effort or any prospect of a surface engagement, both sides continued to suffer losses as their respective forces disengaged. Throughout the 15th and 16th Axis aircraft and submarines relentlessly harried the withdrawing British convoy sinking the escort destroyer *Airedale*, the Australian destroyer *Nestor* and the light cruiser *Hermione* (the latter being sunk by *U205*). At the same time the British submarine *Umbra* finished off the crippled *Trento* while a torpedo-carrying Wellington from Malta scored a torpedo hit on *Littorio* that put the Italian battleship out of service for three months.

So ended the combined re-supply effort that constituted Operations *Harpoon* and *Vigorous*. For the British, the struggle had been hard fought and generally unsatisfactory in its outcome. Of the 17 merchant ships dispatched in the two convoys, a mere two actually made it through to Malta. This meagre result came at a heavy price as the British lost a light cruiser, five assorted destroyers and six merchant ships sunk with several other vessels damaged. For their part, the Italians lost the heavy cruiser *Trento*, while the battleship *Littorio* and a handful of other warships suffered varying degrees of damage. Added to this were the two Italian submarines sunk immediately prior to the dispatch of the *Harpoon* convoy. Finally, the Germans and Italians lost 14 and 29 aircraft respectively in aerial operations relating to the dual convoy battles.[44] Yet, despite these seemingly disappointing results, the entire undertaking actually constituted a strategic victory for the Allies. Even though the British only succeeded in delivering a scant 15,000 tons of supplies to Malta, this was enough to keep the beleaguered colony going for another two months. Thus, the British had secured Malta's continued survival, albeit at a heavy cost, for at least the time being.

Still, if this was victory, it was a sad victory. And it came at a time when Britain's fortunes around the world were at a low ebb. The previous six months had constituted a period of almost uninterrupted defeat, and the British now seemed to be on the defensive everywhere. Nor was this a uniquely British affliction as all of the major Allied powers had suffered similar defeats within their own theatres of operation and were struggling against various Axis onslaughts. Given these realities, British defence planners even contemplated a nightmare scenario in which the various Axis powers launched coordinated offenses from both west and east to seize Egypt, the Arabian Peninsula, Iran and India. If successful, this would put the entire length of North Africa and southern Asia under Axis control and deprive the Allies of substantial resources, as well as an important communication link to the Soviet Union. It would also sever direct British access to Australia and New Zealand. Through the benefit of hindsight, we now know that no such plan for a coordinated offensive actually existed, and it is highly unlikely that the Axis could have mustered the immense logistical resources necessary to carry it out if it had. Still, given Japan's recent string of astonishing victories in the Far East as well as the deteriorating situation in the Mediterranean and North Africa, one can certainly understand the origins of this fear.

As such, for the struggling British forces in the Middle East, it was imperative to stop these waning fortunes before things became intolerable. Once this occurred, the British would then need to regain the initiative and reverse the setbacks they had endured. This would be no easy task given the conditions arrayed against them.

Even in the contested areas where they still managed to hold on, such as Malta, this result had only come at an exceedingly heavy cost, and it remained to be seen what the final outcome for the besieged colony would be. Still, despite the terrible aerial bombardment, tenuous supply situation and ever-present threat of invasion, the proud little colony refused to submit, and the British refused to let it go. Malta survived, and with it survived the prospect that it might yet turn the tables on its Axis assailants. If that happened, the British stood to prevail across the entire theatre. First, they needed to halt the Axis advance into Egypt. Britain's entire position in the Eastern Mediterranean depended upon it.

CHAPTER 6

Turning Point

With Malta's lease on life now extended through Britain's most recent resupply effort, all eyes turned to Egypt as the British girded themselves to meet Rommel's oncoming offensive. On 24 June Axis forces penetrated into Egyptian territory driving back British rear guards. The next day General Claude Auchinleck assumed direct command of the Eighth Army. Initially, the British had intended to make a stand against Rommel at Mersa Matruh, but at the last minute Auchinleck decided to pull his forces back to a defensive line located in the vicinity of El Alamein. In the confusion of this precipitous withdrawal, a number of British formations were encircled by Rommel's hard driving spearheads, and the British gave up another 6,000 prisoners. By this time the Eighth Army was in a precarious state having lost roughly half of its original personnel strength, a similar percentage of its artillery and nearly 1,200 tanks (lost or disabled). Nevertheless, the army soldiered on as its remaining, depleted units fell back to the El Alamein line where they met reinforcements hastily brought forward from other parts of the Middle East.

With time quickly running out, the army prepared to fight the final battle that would likely decide the fate of British fortunes in Egypt. In this, the British benefited from the terrain they had selected to make their final stand. With the Mediterranean Sea located in the north and the virtually impassable Qattara Depression located in the south, the 38-mile long El Alamein line provided the British with a relatively condensed defensive position that could not be outflanked. When Rommel assaulted this line, he would have to do so in a direct attack against the British defences. On the other hand, being located a mere 60 miles from Alexandria, the El Alamein line brought the Axis dangerously close to many of Britain's key logistical and support centres in the theatre. Amongst these was the main fleet anchorage at Alexandria. Based upon this danger and the close proximity of newly acquired Axis airfields, at the end of June the Mediterranean Fleet abandoned Alexandria and dispersed its ships to Haifa, Port Said and Beirut. In the process of doing so, the submarine depot ship *Medway* was sunk by *U372* off Port Said. The demise of this ship cost the British 90 valuable torpedoes, although 47 of these were later salvaged.[1] Of course, this loss was trivial compared to the potential calamity facing the fleet. If the Eighth Army failed to hold Rommel at El Alamein, Britain's whole position in the Eastern Mediterranean would likely become untenable.

On 30 June the leading formations of Rommel's Panzerarmee Afrika arrived on the El Alamein line where they quickly launched their assault the next day. The main Axis blow fell upon the 18th Indian Brigade, which held out for several hours before finally succumbing to the German assault in the early evening. Yet, this heroic sacrifice was not in vain as it gained the British valuable time to solidify their defences while costing Rommel 18 of his precious tanks. Moreover, other Axis thrusts throughout the day faltered in the face of strong British resistance. The same held true for the next two days as British aircraft, artillery and ground forces blunted each Axis attempt to advance. Meanwhile, on 3 July Auchinleck launched a local attack of his own when elements of the 2nd New Zealand Division severely mauled the Italian Ariete Division, seizing 44 guns and 350 prisoners.[2] The results of these initial actions, as well as logistical exhaustion, compelled Rommel to pause his offensive and regroup his tired and depleted units. Of utmost importance was the need to bring up supplies and reinforcements, but this process was hindered by the Panzerarmee's severely overextended lines of communication and the constant interference of the British Desert Air Force, which conducted 5,458 sorties during the first week of the battle.[3]

For their part, the British used this pause to strengthen their positions and launch a number of local counter-attacks targeting Rommel's less reliable Italian formations. On 10 July the newly arrived 9th Australian and 1st South African Divisions launched coordinated attacks towards Tel el Eisa and Tel el Makh Khan along the northern portion of the battlefield. Over a period of a week and with British armour and artillery support, both divisions attained their objectives and repelled a number of Axis counter-attacks. In this, the Australians were particularly effective inflicting an estimated 2,000 casualties on the Axis and collecting 3,708 prisoners during the fighting. A victim of much of this was the Italian Sabratha Division, which was largely destroyed during the action. Meanwhile, on 14–16 July the 2nd New Zealand Division and 5th Indian Brigade severely mauled the Italian Pavia and Brescia Divisions on the Ruweisat Ridge and then blunted a number of heavy counter-attacks by the German 15th and 21st Panzer Divisions. During this fighting the New Zealanders took another 2,000 prisoners, but suffered 1,405 casualties themselves. Keeping pressure on different portions of the line, on the 17th the 9th Australian Division with British armour support launched a new attack against the Miteirya Ridge where they inflicted heavy losses on the Italian Trento and Trieste Divisions, including the seizure of another 736 prisoners.[4] This action prompted Rommel to call off his own proposed attack in the centre and once again send German reinforcements to rectify this situation.

While these various actions were underway, the British continued their interdiction efforts against the Axis lines of communication. Much of this focused on attacking

Axis supply depots and ground transportation assets, but the British also targeted maritime commerce to the extent possible. At the time, British offensive strength in the central Mediterranean was still quite limited, thus restraining their ability to cause widespread disruption to the ongoing flow of Axis convoys to Libya. As such, during July the British only succeeded in sinking two Italian merchant ships, *Città di Agrigento* and *Vettor Pisani*, worth a combined 8,819 tons that were directly involved in these activities. Still, if the vast majority of Axis supply ships arrived safely in Tripoli or Benghazi, this provided little immediate relief to Rommel's forces at El Alamein. Accordingly, the Axis endeavoured to push as many merchant ships to Tobruk and Mersa Matruh as possible, but this was restrained by the limited unload capacities of these forward ports. Likewise, the anchorage at Mersa Matruh was too shallow to handle major ocean-going vessels. As such, the Axis also employed a small fleet of coasters, lighters and auxiliary craft to help address these problems. To counter this, the British conducted regular bombing raids against the Axis ports and used aircraft and destroyers to attack coastal shipping. Through early August these actions destroyed numerous Axis vessels, including three sizable merchant ships worth a combined 5,311 tons, a tug, 16 self-propelled lighters and a coastal sailing ship.[5] In turn, these various operations helped perpetuate Rommel's ongoing logistical crisis.

To this end, hampered by inadequate supplies, dwindling tank strength and the ongoing disintegration of his Italian formations, it became increasingly clear that Rommel had failed in his bid to attain a quick victory and that the initiative now rested with the British. To this end, Rommel contemplated withdrawing his forces from El Alamein to Sollum to ease his supply situation, but this was overruled by Field Marshal Kesselring in Rome. For his part, Auchinleck now sought to deliver a knockout blow that would destroy the Axis army or at least send it reeling back. In this, he was hampered by the ad hoc nature of his own army, which had suffered some 65,000 casualties during the previous two months of fighting and was still in the process of reconstituting itself.[6] Under these conditions, effective combined arms operations, which had never been Eighth Army's strong suit, were made even more difficult, as demonstrated in the last ten days of July when the British launched a series of attacks to break through the Axis line. On the 21st and 22nd various Indian, New Zealand, Australian and British units attacked along a number of points in and around the Ruweisat Ridge and coastal area where they made some initial progress, but then quickly bogged down or were thrown back due to poor follow-up by their supporting arms. Similar results occurred four days later when the Australian 24th and British 69th Brigades launched attacks along the Miteirya Ridge and towards Deir el Dhib. Once again, the assaulting units attained their initial objectives, but were subsequently pushed back by German counter-attacks when their supporting arms failed to arrive.

At the end of July, the fighting finally subsided as exhaustion forced both armies to pause and regroup. With this, what became known as the first battle of

El Alamein came to an end. In an overriding sense, both armies had fought each other to a stalemate, but for the British, stalemate equalled victory. Paramount above everything else, the Eighth Army had succeeded in blunting Rommel's drive to the Delta, thus securing Britain's continued presence in Egypt and the Eastern Mediterranean. In doing so, it had inflicted heavy losses upon Panzerarmee Afrika, including the seizure of 7,287 prisoners during the period of 1–30 July (of which 6,122 were Italians).[7] Added to this were thousands of additional Axis soldiers that were killed or wounded during the month-long struggle. Likewise, the battle's outcome put the British in an advantageous position to seize the strategic initiative. Unable to advance and unwilling to pull back, Rommel now found himself at the end of a long and tenuous supply line. By comparison, Eighth Army was literally only a few dozen miles from its key logistical bases. Thus, the British were far better situated to build-up and replenish their forces than was Rommel. Yet, for all of its advantages, the cost of this victory had been high as British casualties for the battle numbered roughly 13,250.[8]

If the pendulum in North Africa had reached its apex and was now poised to swing back in favour of the British, so too was the situation in the Mediterranean. With the formal demise of Operation *Hercules*, the Axis once again tried to intensify their bombing campaign to keep Malta fully neutralised. Unfortunately for them, attrition and re-deployments had sapped much of their air strength, and the Luftwaffe and Regia Aeronautica were only able to mount 3,066 sorties against Malta in July. While this constituted a significant increase over the previous month, it was nowhere near the level of intensity attained in March and April. Making matters worse from an Axis point of view, these attacks encountered significantly improved British defences that further degraded their effectiveness and eroded away their strength. Finally, the Axis air forces were unable to maintain this tempo, and sorties against Malta dropped to 1,245 and 574 in August and September respectively.[9]

Under these conditions, the effort to neutralise Malta failed, and the colony rapidly reconstituted its offensive striking power. Highlighting this re-generation was the return of the 10th Submarine Flotilla to Malta at the end of July. Malta's offensive air contingent enjoyed a similar renaissance as Beaufort torpedo-bombers and Wellington medium bombers became available in greater numbers to assume the primary strike role from the handful of surviving FAA Swordfish and Albacores that still remained on the island. In terms of the Wellingtons, this included a new anti-shipping variant that was capable of carrying two torpedoes. With their increased range and load capability, these torpedo-bearing Wellingtons could strike out much farther than their FAA counterparts and deliver twice the payload. Still, their lumbering speed and performance at low altitudes prompted these Wellingtons to operate primarily at night while the faster and nimbler Beauforts conducted most of their operations during the day using mass attack tactics.

It did not take long before these reconstituted assets began making their presence felt. In June and July British successes against Axis shipping had reached a low ebb as Malta still laid prostate in the aftermath of its earlier aerial ordeal. During this time British assets only succeeded in sinking 13 sizable Axis merchant ships worth 35,604 tons. This consisted of five vessels worth 7,234 tons sunk by British submarines and surface ships, seven vessels worth 27,620 tons sunk by aircraft and one vessel of 750 tons lost to a mine.[10] In August British successes against Axis merchant shipping increased significantly as British submarines sank seven vessels worth 40,036 tons, aircraft sank three more worth 12,020 tons, mines claimed one worth 4,894 tons and combined air and naval action shared in the destruction of a final vessel worth 8,326 tons.[11] When added together, this destruction of 12 sizable merchant ships worth 65,276 tons represented a near doubling of the combined tonnage sunk in the two previous months and was the largest monthly sinking total attained since November of the previous year. In addition to these merchant losses, British and British-affiliated Allied submarines sank the sloop *Diana*, the destroyer *Strale*, the torpedo boat *Generale Antonio Cantore* (sunk on a submarine-laid mine) and at least 12 minor vessels during the period of June through August.[12] British submarine losses during this time amounted to a single boat, *Thorn*, which was sunk by an Italian escort destroyer in August.

These elevated losses quickly made a discernible impact upon Axis supply operations. Whereas Axis supply deliveries to North Africa in June and July amounted to 123,818 tons out of 139,313 tons dispatched (an 88.88 percent delivery rate), in August this number dropped to 51,655 tons out of 77,224 tons dispatched, or a 66.89 percent delivery rate.[13] Making matters worse, 41 percent of the fuel shipped to North Africa in August was lost en route.[14] Of course, this was only the beginning of Rommel's supply problems. With his forces now positioned many hundreds of miles from their main logistical centres, the Axis had to truck most of their supplies over long distances to bring them to the front. In doing so, they consumed much of the fuel that did make it across the Mediterranean thus reducing the amount available for combat operations to a relative trickle. Even under the best conditions, Rommel's logistical situation had always been tentative. Now with his long and exposed lines of communication, this situation bordered upon intolerable as Panzerarmee Afrika consistently received reinforcements and supplies at an unsatisfactory rate.

By comparison, the summer of 1942 saw a significant inflow of men and materiel to the Eighth Army and other British formations in the Middle East. Utilising the long and arduous route around the Cape of Good Hope, this was no easy task. Yet, if this route was long, it was also relatively safe. With German U-boats predominantly operating against shipping off the Americas and in the North Atlantic, the W.S. series of military convoys (United Kingdom to Suez) were largely left unscathed. Meanwhile, the threat of a large-scale Japanese incursion into the Indian Ocean never materialised as the Japanese instead focused their attentions on the Pacific.

Table 6.1 Monthly Axis Materiel Deliveries to North Africa and Merchant Shipping Losses from January 1942 through August 1942

	Tons dispatched	Tons arrived	Percent arrived	Axis merchant shipping lost	Axis merchant tonnage lost
January	65,614	65,570	99.9	11	40,899
February	59,468	58,965	99.2	15	35,483
March	57,541	47,588	82.7	20	33,840
April	151,578	150,389	99.2	14	20,820
May	93,188	86,849	93.2	11	15,904
June	41,519	32,327	77.9	14	21,498
July	97,794	91,491	93.6	16	16,945
August	77,224	51,655	66.9	17	66,533

Note: See Note from Table 4.1.

As such, only one ship from a W.S. convoy was lost during passage. This ship, the 6,677-ton British merchant ship *Soudan*, was sunk on 15 May 1942 after striking a German mine (laid by the auxiliary minelayer *Doggerbank*) off South Africa. Given this substantial lack of interference, the British used the W.S. convoys to successfully transport the vast majority of troops dispatched to the Middle East. During the first eight months of 1942 this included 149,800 army, 32,400 RAF and 9,800 naval personnel. A further 32,400 men arrived from India. In terms of major units, the period saw the arrival of the 8th Armoured and the 44th and 51st Infantry Divisions from the United Kingdom. Meanwhile, from June through September British forces in the Middle East received 581 tanks, 1,711 assorted guns, 13,184 vehicles and 249,515 tons of ammunition and general stores sent from the United Kingdom, while a further 575 tanks and 18,699 vehicles arrived from North America.[15] During the same four-month period 2,173 Allied aircraft arrived in the Middle East from a variety of sources and means.[16]

While British maritime power continued to demonstrate its tremendous value in keeping the Middle East abundantly supplied, the situation in the Mediterranean remained far more precarious. With Axis aircraft and submarines abound, any British shipping movements, be they coastal or deeper sea, faced the potential for attack. This former threat was amply demonstrated by the numerous Allied merchant ships lost to Axis aircraft during recent supply missions to Malta. Losses to German U-boats were far less substantial, amounting to just 12 merchant ships worth a combined 27,828 tons sunk in the Mediterranean during the first seven months of 1942. Meanwhile, local Italian submarines failed to score a single success against Allied merchant shipping during this period.[17] When compared against the worldwide tonnage and shipping contest that was underway at the time, these trifling results were grossly insignificant and failed to justify the diversion of German U-boats from the Atlantic. Nevertheless, at the local theatre level, these losses were capable of exerting some influence, and in the case of Malta, could prove to be quite debilitating.

On the other side of the ledger, the British exacted a steady toll against both the local Italian and German submarine arms. Excluding the seven Italian submarines already noted as sunk during this period, British forces sank a further three Italian and seven German submarines in the Mediterranean from January 1942 through the first ten days of August. Breaking this down, British surface ships accounted for *U568*, *Perla* (captured) and *Scirè*, while shore-based aircraft accounted for *U577*, *U573* and *U652*. Of these, *U573* met an unusual demise being badly damaged by British aircraft off Algiers, thus prompting it to seek refuge in the Spanish port of Cartagena where it was interned. Meanwhile, air and naval units combined to sink *U74*, *Ondina* and *U372*, while the British submarine *Unbeaten* sank *U374*. An eighth U-boat, *U133*, was accidentally lost in a German minefield off Greece in March. Finally, in a related example of accidental fratricide, in June the Italian submarine *Alagi* attacked what it thought was a British warship, but instead sank the Italian destroyer *Antoniotto Usodimare* off Cape Bon.

Of course, the overriding focus of the Mediterranean struggle remained Malta. In July the navy conducted Operations *Pinpoint* and *Insect* using the aircraft carrier *Eagle* to successfully deliver another 59 Spitfires to the holdout colony.[18] While these deliveries further bolstered Malta's defence, what the colony truly needed was a major influx of supplies. Therefore, in August the British resolved to mount a major re-supply effort from Gibraltar designated Operation *Pedestal*. Consisting of 14 fast merchant ships of which the most critical was the American tanker *Ohio*, the British hoped to deliver 85,000 tons of food, fuel and other stores to the besieged colony. Supporting this effort was the strongest escort yet provided for such an undertaking. Utilising vessels on loan from the Home and Eastern Fleets, the main strength of this escort was Force Z, consisting of the battleships *Nelson* (flagship) and *Rodney*; the aircraft carriers *Indomitable*, *Eagle* and *Victorious*; the cruisers *Phoebe*, *Sirius* and *Charybdis* and 13 destroyers. Embarked upon these carriers were 72 fighters (Sea Hurricanes, Fulmars and Martlets) and 28 Albacore torpedo-bombers. While Force Z would only progress as far as the Central Narrows, a close escort, designated Force X, would bring the convoy all the way into Malta. This latter force, commanded by Rear-Admiral Harold Burrough, consisted of the cruisers *Nigeria*, *Kenya*, *Manchester* and *Cairo* and 11 destroyers.

The British augmented *Pedestal* with a number of concurrent operations and additional resources. The most prominent of these was Operation *Bellows*, in which the aircraft carrier *Furious* was to proceed with Force Z to a point south of the Balearic Islands and then fly off another 38 Spitfires for Malta. Accompanying *Furious* were eight additional destroyers that would escort the carrier back to Gibraltar upon the

The British employed numerous fleet carriers during various stages of the Mediterranean conflict. Pictured here is *Indomitable* as seen from the flight deck of *Victorious* during a Malta convoy operation. (Priest, L. C. (Lt), Royal Navy official photographer, public domain)

completion of its ferry mission. These destroyers would also be available to replace any casualties that the main forces might have. Likewise, two fleet oilers and a tug with four escorting corvettes were to provide refuelling and general support for the entire operation, while a second tug was assigned directly to Force X. Meanwhile, from Malta the two merchant ships that had arrived during Operation *Harpoon*, along with two destroyers, would break out for Gibraltar. For its part, the Mediterranean Fleet would conduct a dummy convoy in the eastern basin to draw attention away from the real convoy proceeding from the west. Finally, nine British submarines were deployed to screen against Italian naval interference, conduct a commando raid and provide further diversions.

Despite British efforts for secrecy and misdirection, Axis leaders were well aware that another British supply mission was likely, and they fully understood the critical nature of this undertaking. Accordingly, they had sizable forces on hand to destroy or otherwise prevent this mission from getting through. Included in these forces were more than 600 aircraft, of which some 200 were German, stationed in Sardinia and Sicily. If necessary, further aircraft from Greece, Crete and North Africa could be brought in to bolster this aerial armada. Likewise, at the time of the convoy's passage, five Italian and two German submarines were stationed between the Balearics and the Algerian coast, 11 were in the approaches to the Skerki Channel and one was positioned off Malta. Meanwhile, 19 Italian MAS motor torpedo boats and four German E-boats patrolled the waters south of Cape Bon. Finally, the Italians had a number of cruisers and destroyers that were available for dispatch if called upon to do so, but no battleships would likely be deployed due to limited fuel supplies.

On 10 August, the *Pedestal* convoy passed through the Strait of Gibraltar and began its trek towards Malta. Under the overall command of Vice-Admiral Syfret in Force Z, the convoy's first day in the Mediterranean was uneventful. However, this tranquillity was soon challenged as Axis reconnaissance aircraft persistently appeared over the convoy, beginning early on the 11th. By midday *Furious* was in position to launch its Spitfires, and 38 aircraft promptly departed the veteran aircraft carrier's flight deck. Of these, 37 successfully made it to Malta while the 38th made an emergency landing on *Indomitable* due to mechanical problems. With its task complete, *Furious* and its accompanying escorts departed the convoy to return to Gibraltar. While this was underway, tragedy struck the convoy at 1315 hours when four torpedoes fired from the German submarine *U73* slammed into *Eagle*. Fatally damaged, the venerable aircraft carrier, a veteran of numerous Mediterranean operations, sank in only eight minutes. In doing so, 231 men out of a crew of 1,160 perished and 12 Sea Hurricane fighters went down with the ship. Thus, in one quick blow, the convoy lost 17 percent of its fighter protection. Four other Hurricanes that were in the air at the time of *Eagle*'s demise diverted to the other carriers.

Sadly, this was only the beginning of the convoy's struggle. For the remainder of the day the British experienced additional submarine attacks while an air attack occurred in the evening, but no further damage was inflicted. Shortly after midnight on the morning of the 12th the British destroyer *Wolverine*, which was serving as one of *Furious*' escorts, exacted a degree of revenge for *Eagle*'s loss when it detected and sank the Italian submarine *Dagabur*. Later that day the British destroyer *Ithuriel* from Force Z sank a second Italian submarine, *Cobalto*, as the convoy battled a number of Italian submarines near Galita Island off the North African coast. Yet, it was the aerial threat that caused the greatest anxiety for the British as the Axis launched a series of heavy air attacks against the convoy throughout the day. British carrier-borne fighters and naval anti-aircraft fire successfully countered most of these attacks, but the 7,740-ton merchant ship *Deucalion* and the destroyer *Foresight* were both hit and subsequently sunk as a result of a follow-up attack and scuttling. Likewise, during an early evening attack *Indomitable* took three direct hits and three near-misses that rendered its flight deck unusable and caused serious flooding within the ship. Although *Indomitable* could still steam and would ultimately make port, it was unable to handle aircraft for the remainder of the operation, and those aircraft that were airborne at the time of its damage had to divert to *Victorious*.

At 1900 hours the convoy reached a position just northeast of Bizerte. This prompted Force Z to turn back for Gibraltar while the merchant ships continued on towards Malta with Force X as their sole protection. Less than an hour later as the convoy was changing formation to transit the Skerki Channel, the Italian submarine *Axum* fired a salvo of torpedoes that scored hits on no fewer than three ships, the cruisers *Nigeria* and *Cairo* and the tanker *Ohio*. Badly damaged, the British were forced to scuttle *Cairo* while *Nigeria* turned back towards Gibraltar with three destroyers in escort. This latter action prompted Admiral Burrough to transfer his flag to the destroyer *Ashanti*. Meanwhile, the damaged *Ohio* was able to extinguish its fires and carry on at a reduced speed with a gaping hole in its side. A short while later the British encountered more misfortune when the convoy came under an unexpected dusk air attack. Catching the convoy in a chaotic state following *Axum*'s attack, the German bombers were able to sink the 12,688-ton merchant ship *Empire Hope* and damage *Clan Ferguson* and *Brisbane Star*. Shortly thereafter, Italian submarines finished off the 7,347-ton *Clan Ferguson* and damaged the cruiser *Kenya*.

At midnight the convoy passed Cape Bon where it encountered a new menace in the form of enemy motor torpedo boats. For the next five and a quarter hours these motor torpedo boats (four German E-boats and 13 Italian MAS boats) carried out a series of attacks against the hapless convoy. Impaired by their limited ability to manoeuvre in the narrow passage around Cape Bon and the reduced and disorganised state of Force X, the British were hard pressed to defend the increasingly scattered convoy. Even with the arrival of reinforcements from Force Z, consisting of the cruiser *Charybdis* and two destroyers, the British were unable to beat off all of these attacks, and five merchant ships received torpedo hits. Of these, *Glenorchy*, *Santa Elisa*, *Almeria Lykes* and *Wairangi* (37,570 tons total) were eventually sunk while *Rochester Castle* was damaged. Meanwhile, two Italian MAS boats attacked the cruiser *Manchester* at close range and damaged it so severely with torpedo hits that it had to be scuttled later in the morning.

The convoy's plight did not abate with the rising sun. Instead, the onset of dawn signalled a resumption of Axis air attacks. By this time the convoy was hopelessly dispersed with various merchant ships and escorts spread over a wide area. On the other hand, the convoy had advanced to a point where fighters from Malta were able to provide a degree of aerial protection. Under these circumstances Axis bombers were able to sink the merchant ships *Waimarama* and *Dorset* (12,843 and 10,624 tons respectively) while the remaining vessels soldiered on. In the late afternoon *Melbourne Star*, *Port Chalmers* and *Rochester Castle* all safely arrived in Grand Harbour, while *Brisbane Star* arrived the following day. This left the damaged *Ohio* as the only merchant ship still unaccounted for. The disposition of this final vessel proved to be a struggle of epic proportions as *Ohio* was singled out as a target of primary importance. Repeatedly attacked by Axis aircraft on the 13th and 14th, *Ohio* suffered multiple bomb hits and near misses that caused extensive damage.

Included in this carnage was the loss of its boilers, engines and rudder, several buckled plates and a partially broken back. Immobile and in a sinking condition, *Ohio* was twice abandoned only to be re-boarded again. Eventually, a gaggle of British escorts managed to take *Ohio* under tow, and in an example of extraordinary perseverance and seamanship from everyone involved, safely shepherded the crippled giant into Grand Harbour on the morning of the 15th.

With this and the subsequent safe return of the escorting warships, Operation *Pedestal* came to an end. In many respects, the undertaking had been a tactical victory for the Axis but a strategic victory for the British. In terms of the former, Axis air and naval units succeeded in sinking nine out of the 14 merchant ships dispatched to Malta. Of the five vessels that arrived, *Ohio* would never again go to sea while *Rochester Castle* and *Brisbane Star* had both sustained significant damage. Likewise, the aircraft carrier *Eagle*, two cruisers and a destroyer were sunk, while *Indomitable* and two other cruisers suffered heavy damage. Yet, despite these extensive losses, the British succeeded in delivering 32,000 tons of general stores, 12,000 tons of fuel oil and 3,600 tons of diesel oil to Malta. In doing so, they attained their overriding objective by gaining Malta another lease on life that would last until December. Likewise, concurrent British actions to reinforce Malta's all-important Spitfire force and evacuate merchant ships left over from Operation *Harpoon* were completely successful. Meanwhile, in addition to the previously described destruction of the Italian submarines *Dagabur and Cobalto*, the British submarine *Unbroken* torpedoed and severely damaged the Italian cruisers *Muzio Attendolo* and *Bolzano* during this period. While both of these hapless vessels would eventually make it to port, neither would ever again be made seaworthy. Finally, a total of 62 Axis aircraft were lost during operations directly or indirectly relating to the convoy battle.[19]

The successful, if costly, conclusion of Operation *Pedestal* signalled the culmination of a change in direction for British fortunes in the Mediterranean and Middle East that had begun with the dispatch of Spitfires to Malta and continued with the Eighth Army's successful rebuff of Panzerarmee Afrika at El Alamein. Only a few short months earlier, the Axis had seemed poised to pummel Malta into submission, drive the British out of Egypt and make Britain's position in the Eastern Mediterranean untenable. Fortunately for the Allied cause, these dire predictions were avoided as British tenacity and resolve coincided with an Axis inability to sustain the full measure of their efforts. The result of this was an extraordinary turn of events that resurrected Malta and Egypt from the brink of disaster. In terms of the former, Malta was already re-emerging as an effective base for offensive operations, and with the successful conclusion of Operation *Pedestal*, the British now ensured the colony's survival for at least another four months. Thus, by failing to decisively interdict the *Pedestal* convoy, the Axis had lost their last, best opportunity to permanently neutralise the troublesome colony and secure their seaborne lines of communication to North Africa.

The badly damaged tanker *Ohio* entering Malta's Grand Harbour at the conclusion of Operation *Pedestal*. During the first two and a half years of the Mediterranean conflict the British conducted 35 major supply operations to maintain the besieged colony. (Cook, H. E. (Lt), War Office official photographer, public domain)

These developments held great potential for the British in the Middle East. With Panzerarmee Afrika now firmly stalled in front of the Eighth Army at El Alamein, the British were positioned to make the Axis pay for their recent failures and over extension. No one was more aware of this than Field Marshal Rommel, who found himself ensnared in a logistical trap of largely his own making. Each week British forces within the theatre became stronger as men and materiel flowed in from Britain, North America and the Commonwealth. By comparison, the Axis forces in Egypt found themselves at the end of a long and tenuous supply line that made reinforcement and logistical support exceedingly difficult. With Malta now on the rebound and the growing strain experienced by the Italian merchant fleet and Regia Marina, this difficulty was only likely to increase. In terms of this latter consideration, after more than two years of wartime attrition, the Italian merchant fleet found it increasingly difficult to maintain the tempo of supply runs to North Africa. The same held true for the Regia Marina, which continued to suffer steady losses to its all-important cruiser, destroyer and escort forces. This manifested itself in both vessels sunk and those awaiting repair. Likewise, the navy was increasingly hampered by dwindling fuel stocks. In August this fuel deficiency resulted in a

Table 6.2 Warship Losses in the Mediterranean from 2 June 1941 through 31 August 1942

	Capital ships	Cruisers	Destroyers	Torpedo boats/ escorts/mine vessels	Submarines
British	3	6	18	10	17
Italian/German	-	4	8	8	32

Note: Only includes warships that were a total loss. British Hunt-class escort destroyers are listed in the Torpedo boats/escort/mine vessel category. Axis submarine losses consisted of 19 Italian and 13 German boats.

21,000-ton shortfall from allocations to projected consumption, prompting Italian authorities to take drastic measures, including the draining of 7,000 tons of fuel oil from selected cruisers to transfer to convoy usage.[20]

Unfortunately for the Axis, this was just the beginning of their logistical challenge. Once arrived in North Africa, incoming supplies and materiel had to be unloaded at various ports and then reloaded onto trucks for transport to the front. Of the ports available, Tripoli and Benghazi were the largest and most capable, but these were located some 1,350 and 700 miles respectively from the El Alamein position. Tobruk was much closer (350 miles), but could only handle a limited portion of the Panzerarmee's needs, while the ports at Bardia, Derna and Mersa Matruh were too small to have any significant impact. Added to this, by 24 August the Axis were down to just 27 serviceable lighters available to support inshore operations while 51 more were either unserviceable or under repair.[21] As such, the vast majority of supplies had to be trucked long distances consuming large quantities of fuel and causing great wear on the vehicles involved. This was significant since petrol was a commodity of utmost importance but limited supply, while some 25 percent of Axis motor transport was generally unserviceable at any given time. Likewise, this arrangement exposed the Axis to Allied interdiction efforts as RAF and USAAF aircraft attacked Axis motor transport and the forward ports of arrival on almost a daily basis.

When combined together, these logistical difficulties had a constraining effect upon the Panzerarmee's combat power and freedom of action. In terms of manpower, the army was able to attain replacements and reinforcements without undue difficulty. This was because the Axis used aircraft to transport the vast majority of their military personnel to North Africa. By mid-summer this included the dispatch of several new units, including the German 164th Division, the Italian Folgore Parachute Division and the German Ramcke Parachute Brigade to Rommel's command. However, while aircraft could transport men, almost everything else had to come in by sea. In terms of heavy equipment, the army received reasonable allocations of tanks and guns, but motor transport was often in short supply. As such, many of Rommel's Italian formations were effectively immobile, while his logistical network suffered from inadequate ground transportation capacity. Meanwhile, stocks of ammunition and spare parts were often deficient against the requirement. Finally, of all the shortfalls plaguing Panzerarmee Afrika, none was more critical than its chronic shortage of adequate fuel supplies. In the desert, petrol was the lifeblood of mobile combat operations, and limitations of this essential commodity severely restricted Rommel's ability to manoeuvre and conduct large-scale movements.

Compounding Rommel's predicament was the rapidly shrinking window of opportunity he had to regain the initiative due to the growing strength of his British adversaries. Despite significantly longer and more complex lines of communication, the British were able to provide the Eighth Army and other Middle East commands with a continuous and lavish flow of men, units, equipment and supplies. In September, several large British convoys were due to arrive in the Middle East that promised to irreversibly alter the balance of forces in Egypt to Britain's favour. Accordingly, Rommel realised that his best opportunity to regain the initiative was to strike before these additional resources arrived and made their presence felt. Therefore, despite his many logistical difficulties, Rommel began preparations for a renewed offensive to tentatively begin on 26 August. Through luck and audacity, Rommel hoped to breach the British army's southern flank, roll up its line and continue his offensive towards Alexandria and the Nile Delta.

As a prerequisite for this undertaking, on 18 August Rommel informed his superiors that he would need an additional 6,000 tons of fuel and two issues of ammunition before he could launch his attack. Four days later he modified this requirement to include the delivery of 7,600 tons of fuel and 2,500 tons of ammunition to Tobruk and Benghazi by specified dates between 25 and 30 August.[22] Italian authorities promised to do their utmost to meet these requirements. They already had ships en route and devised an ambitious plan to send a further 20 supply ships to arrive in North Africa between 25 August and 5 September.[23] Yet, despite this maximum effort, the Italian plan quickly fell behind schedule as losses and delays took their toll. In terms of the former, during the last 11 days in August British aircraft, submarines and mines sank or otherwise disabled six merchant ships involved in this supply effort. As a result, during the period of 23–30 August a mere 2,322 tons of fuel arrived in Tobruk for army usage while ammunition deliveries amounted to about 1,200 tons.[24] As such, Rommel was forced to delay the start of his offensive and then scale back its scope to that of a local operation designed to destroy the British forces in the El Alamein area.

With time running out due to the waning moon, Rommel finally launched his attack on the evening of 30 August. Even then, he only possessed enough fuel to sustain four and a half days of combat with ammunition stocks at a similar level.[25] Confronting him was a new British leadership team as General Harold Alexander had replaced Auchinleck as Commander-in-Chief Middle East while Lieutenant-General Bernard Montgomery had assumed command of the Eighth Army. Forewarned of the pending offensive through Ultra and other intelligence sources, Montgomery had prepared a formidable defence in depth to meet Rommel's oncoming onslaught.

Almost from the start, RAF bombers attacked the Axis columns as they advanced through minefields and largely empty desert. It wasn't until late the next day that the Axis formations finally came upon the main British defensive position at Alam Halfa. Once there, the offensive ground to a halt as well-entrenched tanks, artillery and infantry blunted the Axis advance. After another night of unrelenting bombing and shelling, the Axis again tried to move forward on 1 September, but their efforts came to naught against the strong British defences.

By this time, the Axis offensive was in real jeopardy as the limited stocks of fuel and ammunition they had started out with were rapidly depleting for no appreciable gain. Adding to this problem, the British continued to score interdiction successes against Axis shipping at sea. On 2 September British aircraft attacked a convoy off Derna sinking the tanker *Picci Fassio*, which was carrying 1,150 tons of gasoline and 990 tons of diesel fuel. A second vessel, *Abruzzi*, was hit and damaged so severely that it was unable to continue to Tobruk, but rather diverted under tow to Ras Hilal. Then on the night of 3/4 September a torpedo-carrying Wellington bomber hit and sank the Italian merchant ship *Davide Bianchi* while the British submarine *Thrasher* sank the merchant ship *Padenna*. The loss of these two vessels deprived the Axis forces in North Africa of another 2,766 tons of much needed fuel.[26] Finally, on the morning of the 4th an Egyptian-based RAF Liberator bomber hit and sank the Italian torpedo boat *Polluce* some 50 miles north of Tobruk.

By 2 September the situation on the ground, plus news of recent shipping losses and other logistical delays, convinced Rommel to halt his offensive. Over the next few days, the Panzerarmee conducted a phased withdrawal back towards its own lines. By 5 September Rommel's forces were back in the vicinity of their starting position, and what later became known as the battle of Alam Halfa was over. In materiel terms, the battle was not one of significant consequence. Axis losses for the six-day action included 2,910 personnel casualties, 49 tanks destroyed with a further 76 damaged but subsequently recovered, 55 guns, 41 aircraft and 395 wheeled vehicles.[27] Against this, the British suffered 1,750 casualties and lost 67 tanks (some of which were repairable), 15 guns and 68 aircraft.[28] Yet, despite its modest materiel impact given the size of the forces involved, the battle was significant in giving the Eighth Army an important confidence boost under the leadership of its new commander. Of far greater importance, the battle represented a definitive tipping point that passed the initiative from Panzerarmee Afrika to Eighth Army. From this point forward, Rommel could do little more than solidify his defences and wait for the inevitable British counter-offensive, which would come at a time and place of their choosing.

As both sides feverishly prepared for this next anticipated battle, the British continued their interdiction efforts against Rommel's exposed supply lines. On the night of 13/14 September this included a bold series of raids against Tobruk, Benghazi and selected airfields by land and naval forces under the overall designation of Operation *Agreement*. Utilising raiding parties from the Long Range Desert Group (LRDG) that travelled overland and a seaborne landing force of some 500 men, the British hoped to destroy port installations, supply stockpiles and transportation assets, further degrading Rommel's already overstretched logistical infrastructure. Naval support for the operation consisted of the anti-aircraft cruiser *Coventry*, the destroyers *Sikh* and *Zulu*, four Hunt-class escort destroyers and 21 assorted coastal craft. Of the various targets attacked, the British considered Tobruk to be the most important, thus making it the sole focus of the seaborne portion of the operation.

Tragically, despite ambitious objectives, the various forays generally proved to be costly failures. At Tobruk, LRDG raiding parties successfully entered the port, but only succeeded in securing one of two shore batteries commanding the approach. This caused delays with the seaborne landings, and when they finally went in, confusion and heavy seas proved to be a major disruption. As it was, only two coastal craft actually succeeded in landing their troops. To assist this troubled process the destroyers *Sikh* and *Zulu* went close inshore, but found themselves engaged by Axis shore batteries. At 0510 hours Axis artillery targeted and disabled *Sikh*, which subsequently sank after attempts to tow it out of the area failed. As the British then withdrew, they came under heavy and persistent Axis air attacks that sank the cruiser *Coventry* and destroyer *Zulu*. Other British losses included three motor torpedo boats and two motor launches sunk, a fourth motor torpedo boat captured and 576 prisoners taken as a result of the Tobruk operation.[29] Raids against the other targets were also generally unsuccessful, although the British did succeed in destroying 16 Axis aircraft at Barce, with a further seven aircraft damaged.[30]

With the failure of Operation *Agreement*, the British had to settle for more conventional means to carry out their interdiction efforts. In this, they attained significantly better results. From 5 September through 23 October British and British-affiliated submarines in the Mediterranean sank or participated in the destruction of 18 Axis and Axis-affiliated merchant ships worth a combined 48,227 tons. During the same period these submarines also destroyed at least seven minor vessels worth an additional 1,511 tons and the Italian destroyer *Giovanni da Verazzano*. Meanwhile, British aircraft sank three ocean-going merchant ships worth 14,225 tons and participated in the destruction of three more that were included in the submarine tally listed above. Likewise, USAAF aircraft scored their first major success in the Mediterranean conflict by sinking the 7,949-ton Italian merchant ship *Apuania* during a September bombing raid against Benghazi.[31] Finally, a British Sunderland sank the Italian submarine *Alabastro* off Algiers on 14 September.

A key factor in many of these interdiction successes, as well as the overall effectiveness of Britain's anti-shipping campaign, was the use of Ultra intelligence. By monitoring German and Italian radio traffic, the British were able to learn valuable information regarding Axis shipping movements, including ports of departure

The RAF was an active participant in the maritime conflict accounting for, or sharing in, the destruction of roughly 15 percent of the total Axis vessels sunk in the Mediterranean theatre. Pictured here are Bristol Beauforts of No. 39 squadron in flight over the Mediterranean during the summer of 1942. (Royal Air Force official photographer, public domain)

and arrival, timing, routing and details of cargoes carried. Timely receipt of this intelligence enabled the British to plan and carry out precise attacks against high priority targets such as tankers and other fuel-carrying vessels, thus enhancing the efficiency of their limited anti-shipping resources. This was particularly important for operations out of Malta where limited fuel and torpedo stocks constrained widespread offensive action. To protect the security of this invaluable resource, the British often dispatched reconnaissance assets to first visually locate ships or convoys targeted through Ultra intelligence before attacks could go in. The point of this was to make it appear that the reconnaissance assets were the instruments behind the vessels' detection. While this precaution constrained some freedom of action and warned the Axis of pending trouble, the overall impact of Ultra intelligence was highly favourable. Of 48 Axis ships sunk in the Mediterranean during the period of 2 June through 6 November 1942, no fewer than 47 were first identified by GC and CS. Of these, GC and CS provided relevant information such as location, timing, routing and/or cargoes on all but two of these vessels.[32]

In October the Axis responded to Britain's growing anti-shipping renaissance by intensifying their bombing campaign against Malta. Referred to as the mini-blitz, the Axis deployed additional assets to Sicily, thus increasing their available air strength to 377 serviceable aircraft, of which 223 were bombers. Facing them on the eve of the blitz was a serviceable fighter force on Malta consisting of 113 Spitfires and 11 Beaufighters. Over a nine-day period beginning on 11 October Axis aircraft flew almost 2,400 sorties against Malta during which they dropped some 440 tons of bombs. Unfortunately for them, this was a mere shadow of the onslaught the Axis had been able to deliver against Malta during March and April, and their attacking formations were heavily challenged by Malta's fighter force, which flew 1,115 sorties during the same period. On the 19th the mini-blitz came to an end having caused little appreciable damage. British fighter losses during the nine-day battle consisted of 31 Spitfires and one Beaufighter, while the Germans lost nine fighters and 35 bombers and the Italians lost an undisclosed, but presumably similar number of aircraft.[33] From this point forward, the Axis would refrain from any further large-scale attempts to neutralise Malta, although nuisance raids would continue through the remainder of the year.

An essential factor in helping bring about this favourable outcome was the continuous receipt of fighter reinforcements to bolster Malta's hard-pressed defences. At the end of October Force H conducted Operation *Train*, resulting in the delivery of 29 Spitfires to Malta from the aircraft carrier *Furious*. In accomplishing this feat, the British essentially made good their fighter losses from the recent mini-blitz. Of perhaps greater notoriety, this operation proved to be the Royal Navy's last aircraft ferry mission to Malta. During a two-year period culminating with Operation *Train*, the Royal Navy conducted 28 such runs (including two carried out in conjunction with the American aircraft carrier *Wasp*) during which they delivered 719 fighters to Malta.[34] Together, these fighters formed the core of Malta's defence, which in turn, challenged and eventually defeated Axis attempts to bomb the colony into submission. In attaining this outcome, the British exacted a heavy toll upon their attackers, including 352 German and 241 Italian aircraft lost in operations over Malta during 1942 alone.[35]

Strategically, the main beneficiary of these successes in the Mediterranean was the Eighth Army in Egypt. During September and the first three weeks of October, Eighth Army made feverish preparations for its proposed offensive that was scheduled to begin on the 23rd. Included in these proceedings was the absorption of new men and materiel, the deployment and stockpiling of resources and a thorough training programme designed to ensure that every unit was fully prepared for its role in the upcoming offensive. At the conclusion of this period, Eighth Army boasted a front-line strength of 220,476 men, 1,029 tanks, 892 artillery pieces and 1,451 anti-tank guns organised into three corps with 11 divisions. Against this, Panzerarmee Afrika possessed four German and eight Italian divisions mustering

108,000 men (of which 53,736 were Germans), 548 tanks (including light tanks), 552 artillery pieces and 1,063 anti-tank guns. The situation was much the same in the air as the British possessed 530 serviceable aircraft ready for immediate use as compared to 350 for the Axis.[36]

Yet despite this numerical advantage, the British faced a formidable task that in no way guaranteed an assured success. Confronted by a well-entrenched enemy and constraining terrain that prevented flanking movements, the British would have to fight their way through an elaborate and extensive defensive system that included a lavish use of mines. In many respects, the battle promised to be a head-to-head slogging match reminiscent of the trench-style combat so prevalent during World War I, and General Montgomery privately predicted a 12-day struggle that would cost his army 13,000 casualties. For their part, the Axis, who were now without a sick Rommel, hoped to attain a defensive victory similar to that attained by the British during the battles of First El Alamein and Alam Halfa. If accomplished, General Georg Stumme, the acting Panzerarmee commander, even held open the prospect of renewing the offensive to destroy Eighth Army and proceed on to the Delta. Thus, on the eve of the British offensive, both sides faced a struggle of potentially great consequence.[37]

At 2140 hours on the evening of 23 October, a deluge of flashes and noise shattered the serenity of the Egyptian landscape as 456 British guns opened an intense bombardment against Axis positions along the northern portion of the El Alamein line. This was the beginning of Operation *Lightfoot*, the long expected British offensive to drive the Axis out of Egypt. The main component of this opening onslaught was an assault by four infantry divisions to breach the Axis defences and establish two corridors for the passage of British armour. Throughout the night British infantry and engineers advanced forward seizing ground and clearing passages through the extensive minefields. By morning the British had made substantial progress, but still found themselves entangled in the Axis minefields with no breakthrough achieved. During the next 48 hours Eighth Army consolidated and expanded its positions but was unable to make appreciable headway forward. By comparison, local German counter-attacks were equally unsuccessful in making an impression against the British incursions.

The fighting continued over the next week as Montgomery conducted 'crumbling' operations to systematically reduce and wear down the Axis formations. During this time the British launched a series of local attacks along differing lines of advance, thus compelling Rommel, who had returned to Africa from sick leave in Germany, to respond in kind.[38] In doing so, Rommel consumed large amounts of precious fuel and other resources as he shifted his forces to meet the various British thrusts. Worse yet from his perspective, Axis counter-attacks repeatedly failed to stem the British tide, and his forces suffered heavy losses from the continuous fighting. Particularly hard hit was his tank strength, which declined precipitously. British losses were also high, but they were in a much better position to weather these losses, whereas Rommel could ill afford the level of attrition he was suffering. Thus, despite the failure of the original *Lightfoot* plan, Montgomery was steadily achieving his objective of wearing down the German/Italian Panzerarmee while Rommel seemed powerless to reverse this trend.

A major factor contributing to Rommel's growing predicament was his ever-deteriorating supply situation. As the Eighth Army engaged the German/Italian Panzerarmee along the El Alamein line, Allied air units scored timely successes against Axis shipping that further exacerbated this situation and had a direct influence on the battlefield. On 26 October Egyptian-based Beauforts and Wellingtons sank the 4,869-ton tanker *Proserpina* and the 5,890-ton cargo ship *Tergestea*, which were carrying 4,553 tons of fuel and 2,000 tons of mixed fuels and ammunition respectively. On the night of 28/29 October Malta-based Wellingtons sank the 2,557-ton tanker *Luisiano*, thus depriving Rommel of a further 1,459 tons of fuel. During the same evening, a second Italian merchant ship, the 2,143-ton *Etiopia*, was hit and forced to turn back to Greece. Three nights later Wellingtons and Beauforts sank the 1,464-ton Italian *Tripolino* and the 359-ton German *Ostia*, which were shuttling a combined 867 tons of rations and ammunition from Benghazi to Tobruk. Finally, on the morning of 2 November Egyptian-based Beauforts sank the 1,976-ton naval auxiliary *Zara* some 50 miles north of Tobruk. Its companion ship, the 1,987-ton *Brioni*, continued on and actually arrived in Tobruk, but was subsequently sunk there a few hours later by USAAF Liberator bombers.

The loss of these merchant ships and their valuable cargoes caused Rommel great angst as he struggled to hold back the powerful British tide assailing his army. Upon learning of *Luisiano*'s destruction on the 29th, Rommel seriously considered a general withdrawal, but decided against this due to fuel and transportation shortages. Instead, realising that such a move would force him to abandon many of his Italian formations, Rommel opted to make one final attempt to stem the next British assault. In this, he did not have long to wait. On the night of 1/2 November Eighth Army launched Operation *Supercharge*, its follow-up attempt to breach the Axis line. Under the cover of a tremendous artillery bombardment, a reinforced 2nd New Zealand Division opened a new corridor through the minefields, allowing the 9th Armoured Brigade to pass through and establish a bridgehead deep within the Axis defences. The next day the British expanded their salient and successfully defeated several desperate Axis counter-attacks that cost the latter 70 German and nearly 50 Italian tanks.

On 3 November Rommel realised that the situation was beyond salvation and began disengaging portions of his army. The next day the British broke through the final remnants of the Axis line and advanced through open desert in pursuit of the fleeing Panzerarmee. On this day and over the next week the British fought a number of engagements resulting in the destruction or seizure of large quantities of equipment and the collection of many thousands of prisoners. Thousands more simply gave themselves up as they were left behind without hope of escape or support. By the 11th the aggregate of prisoners taken since the beginning of the British offensive numbered 7,802 Germans and 22,071 Italians.[39] Other Axis casualties were more difficult to determine, but estimates ranged from 2,120 dead and 4,819 wounded to 10,000 dead and 15,000 wounded.[40] Axis equipment losses included some 450 tanks, over 1,000 guns and 84 aircraft. In terms of units, the Italian Trento, Trieste and Littorio Divisions were all but destroyed, while several other Axis divisions were severely mauled. British casualties for the battle amounted to 2,350 dead, 8,950 wounded and 2,260 missing (a total of 13,560), along with some 500 tanks disabled (most of which were repairable), 111 guns and 97 aircraft (including 20 that were American).[41]

Complementing this great triumph, the period also saw the Royal Navy score a small, but impactful victory in the region. On the morning of 30 October, a Sunderland of No. 201 Group located the German submarine *U559* some 70 miles north-northeast of Port Said. In response to the aircraft's sighting report, a total of five British destroyers along with additional aircraft converged upon the area to search for the elusive U-boat. In the early afternoon contact was finally attained, and for the next nine and a half hours the destroyers *Pakenham*, *Petard*, *Dulverton* and *Hurworth* subjected *U559* to a series of depth charge attacks. Finally, at 2240 hours *U559* broke the surface and was immediately engaged by gunfire from *Petard*. Realising that escape was impossible, the German crew took action to scuttle their vessel and abandoned ship. However, *U559* did not immediately sink, and a boarding party from *Petard* entered the submarine and secured numerous classified documents, including the current editions of the short-signal codebook and the weather cipher. Sadly, this success came at a cost as Lieutenant Anthony Fusson and Able Seaman Colin Grazier both lost their lives when the U-boat abruptly foundered with them still inside.

Fortunately, this sacrifice was not in vain as the British immediately sent the captured documents to Bletchley Park to assist the codebreakers at GC and CS. Nine months earlier the Kriegsmarine had added a fourth rotor to its Enigma encryption machines for radio communications with Atlantic and Mediterranean-deployed U-boats. This action significantly multiplied the possible number of combinations the Germans could use to encrypt and decrypt their messages. The result was an immediate breakdown in GC and CS' ability to decipher and read radio transmissions using this enhanced key, known as Triton by the Germans. With the documents garnered from *U559*, the codebreakers at GC and CS were finally able to make significant progress in accessing this formidable code. It would still take several months before Triton was fully mastered, but once this occurred, the British would have a near complete ability to read this valuable radio traffic with normal time delays of less than 24 hours. Beyond that, this ability prompted the British to tighten their own signal security, which deprived the Germans of a similar intelligence capability. Thus, the seizure of materiel from *U559* and the breaking of the Triton key played a major role in winning the cryptic intelligence war and helped turn the tide against the German U-boat threat. In recognition of this, the aforementioned Lieutenant Fusson and Able Seaman Grazier both posthumously received the George Cross for their sacrifice and contribution to the war effort.

Of course, it would take time for the scope of this success to fully materialise, and in the meantime, the fighting in Africa continued. On 5 November Eighth Army set off in pursuit of the defeated German/Italian Panzerarmee as it hoped to deliver a decisive blow that would lead to the total destruction of Axis forces in Africa. In doing so, the British pursued a goal that had eluded them for almost two and a half years. In the period following Italy's declaration of war, the struggle in both North Africa and the Mediterranean had generally mirrored a pendulum in which the initiative had swung back and forth between the two competing sides. In the two previous years at almost the same time of the year, the British had won similar victories, and their fortunes had been on the ascendency. In both cases, these gains were short lived. Now in the opening days of November 1942, the British enjoyed victory once again, and Churchill ordered the church bells in Britain to be rung in celebration of this fact. Egypt had been saved, and with it, control over the Suez Canal and the vital Persian Gulf oil region had been assured. Perhaps equally important, the battle went a long way in restoring British prestige and confidence following the disastrous series of defeats that had befallen their forces during the first half of the year.

Still, the question remained if this victory represented a true turning point or just another temporary phase in an ongoing conflict that had already seen numerous changes of fortune. While history would serve as the ultimate arbiter on this matter, there were a number of immediate factors that seemed to indicate that the tide had in fact turned in Britain's favour. Unbeknown to the vast majority of participants currently engaged in the Middle East, events were already underway that proposed to change the entire course of the campaign. In this, the British were bolstered by the fact that they were no longer fighting alone. The United States, which had already provided substantial logistical and air support to the British forces in the Middle East, was now poised to become a full-fledged partner in the conflict. Beyond that, Britain's own mobilisation efforts had largely come to fruition, allowing it to substantially expand its own force projection into the region. Given the substantial might that was about to be unleashed into the theatre, the prospect of attaining Britain's longstanding goal of destroying all Axis forces in North Africa now seemed fully attainable if not inevitable. Only time would tell if this came to pass, but the pendulum that had swung back and forth during the previous two and a half years now seemed irrevocably locked on a path favouring the British.

The entry of the United States into the war constituted a pivotal development in the Mediterranean conflict and a major boon to the British, who had confronted the Axis for almost two and a half years alone. Pictured here are the American battleships *Nevada* and *Texas*, which both saw service within the theatre. (National Museum of the U.S. Navy, public domain)

CHAPTER 7

Masters of the North African Shores

In the spring and summer of 1942, the senior leadership of the United Kingdom and the United States held a series of meetings to formulate the future strategy for the war. A major concern at the time was the need to relieve pressure off the Soviet Union, which was under great strain from ongoing German assaults. The result of these deliberations was an agreement to launch an Anglo-American invasion of Vichy French North Africa. This decision only came after considerable internal debate, in which the Americans initially advocated for a cross-channel invasion of northern France (Operation *Sledgehammer*). Arguing that such an undertaking was impractical at this stage in the war, the British vehemently opposed this option. Eventually, the American leadership, led by President Roosevelt, acquiesced to Britain's point of view and agreed to the less ambitious alternative of an invasion of French North Africa. By doing this, Allied strategists surmised that they would draw some German attention away from the Soviet Union while ultimately making the Axis position in North Africa untenable. This had the added benefit of easing inexperienced American and British forces into the conflict under less trying conditions and against a less potent adversary. Finally, the Allies hoped that their occupation of French North Africa might entice France to re-join the Allied cause.

With this decision made, the Allies undertook the extensive task of making plans and preparations for their upcoming invasion, which they code-named Operation *Torch*. Although less dangerous than the proposed invasion of northern France, Operation *Torch* was nevertheless a highly complex and large-scale undertaking. At its core, the Allies proposed to conduct simultaneous landings at three disparate locations on both the Atlantic and Mediterranean sides of French North Africa. Matching these objectives were three separate Allied forces. The first, the Western Force, was an all-American effort staged out of the United States that would land 34,305 troops on the Moroccan coast near Casablanca. The second was the Central Force, which consisted of British naval and maritime assets staged out of the United Kingdom that would land some 39,000 American troops at Oran. Finally, the Eastern Force was also a British undertaking from the United Kingdom that would land 23,000 British and 10,000 American troops in the vicinity of Algiers. Once ashore, the Allies would rapidly reinforce and expand their bridgeheads, linking the Moroccan and Oran forces to form the American Fifth Army while the Eastern Force became the British First Army.[1] In turn, this latter army, under the command of Lieutenant-General K. A. N. Anderson, would race eastward to seize Tunisia and threaten the Axis rear in Tripolitania.

Under the overall command of American Lieutenant-General Dwight Eisenhower and the naval command of Britain's Admiral Andrew Cunningham (recently returned from his posting to the United States), the Allies assembled sizable naval and maritime assets to carry out and support their landings. Of these, the all-American Western Task Force, under the command of Rear-Admiral Henry Hewitt, possessed 105 vessels for the immediate assault, including the battleships *Massachusetts, Texas* and *New York*, the aircraft carrier *Ranger*, four escort carriers, seven cruisers and 38 destroyers.[2] The British Central and Eastern Task Forces, under the commands of Commodore Thomas Troubridge and Vice-Admiral Harold Burrough respectively, possessed a combined 193 vessels, including the headquarters ships *Largs* and *Bulolo*, the monitor *Roberts*, the aircraft carrier *Argus*, three escort carriers, six cruisers (including an anti-aircraft cruiser) and 26 destroyers. Covering the Mediterranean landings was Force H under the command of Vice-Admiral Syfret and consisting of the battleships *Duke of York* and *Rodney*, the battlecruiser *Renown*, the fleet carriers *Victorious, Formidable* and *Furious*, three cruisers, 17 destroyers and seven support vessels.[3] Naval aircraft embarked on the Allied carriers totalled 183 for the British and 172 for the Americans.[4]

Beyond these naval assets, the Allies also earmarked large contingents of ground-based aircraft to support the landings and exploit the situation once the ground forces were firmly ashore. The initial force available for this undertaking consisted of 1,041 aircraft broken down into 722 fighters, 243 bombers, 64 maritime patrol and 12 photo-reconnaissance. Some of these aircraft would operate from Gibraltar while others would fly in as soon as the local airfields were secured. In this regard, Allied planners hoped to have 410 fighters amassed in the Casablanca, Oran and Algiers areas by the third day of the invasion. Thereafter, the build-up would continue with reinforcements coming from Britain and the United States eventually reaching a projected strength of nearly 1,700 aircraft by the end of a seven-week period.[5] This force would be split between two commands, Eastern and Western, with the British in charge of the former and the Americans making up the latter.

Arrayed against these powerful forces were a number of potential threats. The most obvious of these was the prospect of Vichy opposition to the Allied landings. At both Casablanca and Oran, the French maintained sizable naval units. Paramount amongst these was the unfinished battleship *Jean Bart* located at Casablanca. Although immobile and only possessing one operational main gun turret, this turret contained four 15-inch guns, which made *Jean Bart* a potentially formidable adversary in a static defence role. Other naval forces in and around the proposed landing areas included the cruiser *Primauguet* (also at Casablanca) and nearly 30 destroyers and submarines. The French also possessed a number of powerful shore batteries and 486 aircraft, including 218 fighters and 185 bombers that were in position to oppose the Allied invasion.[6] Likewise, the main French fleet at Toulon or the battleship *Richelieu* at Dakar might choose to intervene. Although of dubious readiness given their general inactivity over the previous two and a half years, these distant forces still possessed a combined strength of four capital ships and over 70 other warships that could pose a potential danger if even a handful of these vessels sortied to confront the Allies.

Beyond potential French opposition, the Allies also anticipated a degree of interference from Axis sources. At a minimum, the Allies expected Axis submarines and bombers to attack their forces with their easternmost elements being particularly susceptible to these assaults. In this regard, on the eve of the invasion the Germans had 25 U-boats in or en route to the Mediterranean, while further U-boats were likely to be sent once Allied intentions became known. For their part, the Italians had 21 submarines located in the Western Mediterranean. Meanwhile, the Germans had 940 combat aircraft in the theatre, including some 400 that were stationed in Sicily and Sardinia along with 515 Italian aircraft.[7] Considered far less likely, but still plausible, was a sortie by the Italian fleet. The Allies also considered the possibility that Spain might intervene on behalf of the Axis and/or allow Axis forces access to Spanish territory. If this occurred, the Allies surmised that they would likely lose retention of Gibraltar thus potentially entrapping the Central and Eastern Task Forces within the Mediterranean. It was for this reason that the Allies opted to land part of their invasion force on the Atlantic side of Morocco.

A second factor complicating Allied planning efforts was the need to rapidly occupy Tunisia. This requirement was predicated on the knowledge that Tunisia was the ultimate prize in French North Africa and the belief that the Axis would make their own attempt to occupy Tunisia once Allied intentions became clear. To this end, the British had originally advocated landings as far east as possible with Bône, Bizerte and Tunis all considered potential targets, but American fears of possible Spanish intervention and inadequate air support ultimately prompted the Allies to adopt more limited objectives. As such, the British realised that once firmly ashore, they would be in a race to build-up and reach Tunisia before the Axis had time to dispatch adequate forces to block their advance. A major factor impacting this race would be the degree to which the French opposed the Allied landings. To preclude or at least minimise the intensity of this opposition, the Allies engaged in clandestine negotiations with General Henri Giraud, a high-ranking Vichy official. Likewise, prompted by the hope that the French would be less likely to oppose the Americans than they would the British given recent British actions at Mers-el-Kébir, Dakar, Syria and Madagascar, the Allies attempted to put an American face on the invasion. It was for this reason that American forces were so prevalent in the initial landings.

Other related actions included the painting of American markings on British aircraft and the flying of American flags on selected British warships.

D-day for Operation *Torch* was set for the morning of 8 November. As a prerequisite to this, in October and early November the British sailed six advanced convoys to Gibraltar, consisting of 84 ships and 42 escorts.[8] In addition to personnel and equipment, these convoys brought the colliers, tankers, ammunition ships, tugs and auxiliary ships that were required to support the invasion. Then between 22 October and 1 November four assault convoys departed Britain with the troops and specialised landing ships designated for the Oran and Algiers landings. Routed west of Ireland and travelling well into the Atlantic before turning east to pass through the Strait of Gibraltar, these convoys were able to avoid loss despite being sighted by numerous U-boats. Once inside the Mediterranean, these assault convoys divided into various components and proceeded to their designated landing areas, which were marked by pre-positioned submarines. During the same time frame American convoys of the Western Task Force departed the United States and made similar treks to the Moroccan coast.

By the night of 7/8 November everything was in place, and shortly after midnight the Allies proceeded with their invasion. Allied hopes for nominal French resistance were quickly dashed as Vichy authorities initially opted to defend their territory. This was particularly true in the Casablanca area where numerous Vichy warships, shore batteries and the unfinished battleship *Jean Bart* engaged the attacking American task force. Despite spirited opposition, the American warships, led by the battleship *Massachusetts* and supported by aircraft from the carrier *Ranger*, had little difficulty in prevailing over their French counterparts. In a one-sided battle the American naval forces silenced *Jean Bart*, disabled the cruiser *Primauguet*, sank four destroyers and disabled two more and sank or forced the scuttling of eight Vichy submarines.[9] By comparison, although a number of American warships received hits, none were sunk or severely damaged. Meanwhile, American assault forces made successful landings despite the loss of several landing craft that were wrecked by the heavy surf and harsh conditions on the beaches.

The situation off Algeria was much the same with deadlier consequences paid out to the assaulting Allied forces. A bold attempt by the British sloops *Walney* and *Hartland* (ex-American Coast Guard cutters) to land an American ranger detachment within Oran harbour failed when Vichy shore batteries and warships heavily engaged the British vessels. Despite great heroism in the face of the unrelenting fire, both British warships were sunk with the loss of 189 American soldiers, five American naval personnel and 113 British seamen killed and 164 Americans and 86 British wounded.[10] A similar situation occurred at Algiers when the elderly destroyers *Broke* and *Malcolm* attempted an identical landing to seize vital port installations and to prevent the French from scuttling their ships. Once again, this assaulting force came under heavy fire from Vichy shore batteries, and *Malcolm* was forced to abandon the operation after sustaining damage to its boiler spaces. *Broke* continued on and eventually succeeded in landing some 250 men from the American 135th Regimental Combat Team. Sadly, heavy fire forced *Broke* to withdraw shortly thereafter, and the bulk of the American soldiers were eventually forced to surrender having failed in their mission. For its part, the badly damaged *Broke* was taken in tow by the destroyer *Zetland*, but subsequently succumbed to slow flooding and had to be scuttled.

Fortunately for the Allies, these actions proved to be the only real successes that Vichy forces achieved in their defence of Algeria. In other fighting around Oran, the British were able to easily cope with attempted interference by Vichy warships and inflict heavy losses upon their antagonists. Part of this was due to the disjointed nature of the French response as individual or small groups of Vichy warships attempted to contest the British invasion. The first of these was the sloop *La Surprise*, which tried to engage British destroyers off Oran on the morning of the 8th and was quickly sunk by the destroyer *Brilliant*. Minutes later, the French destroyers *Tramontane*, *Typhon* and *Tornade* sequentially sortied out of Oran and fought a series of separate engagements with the British light cruiser *Aurora* in which the venerable British warship sank *Tramontane* and *Tornade* and drove *Typhon* back into the harbour. The next day, *Typhon* again sortied out of Oran accompanied by the destroyer *Epervier*, but once again encountered *Aurora* and the cruiser *Jamaica*. In the battle that followed, the British cruisers sank *Epervier* and drove *Typhon* back to Oran where it scuttled itself. In other actions, the British destroyers *Westcott* and *Achates* combined to sink the Vichy submarines *Actéon* and *Argonaute*, while British warships sank a French patrol vessel off Fidalah. Meanwhile, other Vichy losses included the submarines *Ariane*, *Danae*, *Diane*, *Cérès* and *Pallas*, six auxiliary patrol and minesweeping vessels and 13 merchant ships that were scuttled at Oran and the surrounding area.

While this was underway, the British carriers were also active in the battle. In this, the larger fleet carriers primarily focused on countering external threats, while the smaller carriers directly supported the landings and launched strikes to neutralise the French air threat. In terms of the latter, on the morning of the invasion the British launched 42 aircraft to attack the main French airfields at La Senia, Maison Blanche and Tafaroui. Of these, the strike against La Senia was particularly effective as eight Albacores and 12 Sea Hurricanes from the carriers *Furious*, *Biter* and *Dasher* destroyed 47 Vichy aircraft on the ground and five more in aerial combat. British losses for this raid amounted to four Albacores. Meanwhile, ground haze hampered the foray against Maison Blanche, but the attack against Tafaroui destroyed at least three French aircraft on the ground with a fourth subsequently destroyed in the air. For the remainder of the day and into the next, the British conducted further strikes as well as regular patrols over the assault areas that solidified their dominance in the air. On the 9th French aerial resistance largely ceased, but the Luftwaffe and Regia Aeronautica began launching sporadic sorties against the conglomeration of

Allied ships. Fortunately, these initial efforts failed to cause appreciable damage, and fighters from *Formidable* destroyed one of the attacking German bombers.

Of course, the point of these activities was the successful landing of the assault forces, which occurred around Oran and Algiers without undue difficulty. Once ashore, these Allied formations encountered some opposition, but with the help of naval air and gunfire support, were generally able to make steady progress in attaining their objectives. Included in this assistance was the battleship *Rodney*, which engaged Fort du Santon near Mers-el-Kébir to silence a troublesome coastal battery. Within three days all Vichy opposition ceased as an agreement was reached with Admiral Jean-François Darlan, the Commander-in-Chief of French military forces, who happened to be in North Africa at the time of the Allied invasion. By this agreement, all French territory in Africa, excluding Tunisia but including the strategically important French naval base at Dakar, became aligned with the Allied cause. With this, the Allies gained territory that vastly improved their strategic position in both the Western Mediterranean and central Atlantic. In return, the

In November 1942 the Allies used maritime power to open a second front in the theatre by launching Operation *Torch*, the invasion of French North Africa. This action brought the United States directly into the conflict and eventually ensnared two Axis armies in a powerful Allied pincer in Tunisia. (Hudson, F. A. (Lt), Royal Navy official photographer, public domain)

Allies recognised Admiral Darlan as the High Commissioner for North Africa, while General Giraud became Commander-in-Chief of the local French armed forces. The human cost in attaining this outcome amounted to 2,342 Allied casualties, including 1,181 fatalities.[11] Meanwhile, French losses in the short battle probably approached 3,000.

With the cessation of hostilities in Morocco and Algeria, the Allies turned their attention to Tunisia. Since most of the Allied formations were located in the western and central portions of French North Africa at the time, only a small number of units were actually available to advance on Tunisia. Despite this imbalance, the Allies began their advance in earnest. On 11 November three fast troopships, with an escort led by the cruiser *Sheffield*, landed the British 36th Infantry Brigade at Bougie. Located some 110 miles east of Algiers, the British occupied the small port without opposition. The next day British airborne troops seized Djidjelli airfield while commandos from the escort destroyers *Wheatland* and *Lamerton* took possession of Bône. In doing so, the British gained a useful staging base that was another 125 miles closer to the Tunisian border. Within two days Spitfire fighters were operating from Bône while Allied forces renewed their push into Tunisia. Moving overland in two lines of advance towards Bizerte and Tunis, the Allies made slow progress as logistical constraints and difficult terrain hampered their efforts.

The Axis responded to these developments in a swift and decisive manner. Immediately upon learning of the Allied invasion, Hitler ordered forces into Tunisia, Corsica and the unoccupied portions of southern France. On 9 November the first contingents of German aircraft and ground personnel arrived in Tunisia. Encountering no resistance from local Vichy forces, the Axis followed this up with a continuous flow of men and materiel during the ensuing days. By the end of the month total Axis deliveries to Tunisia included 15,273 men and 581 tons of supplies brought in by air and 1,867 men, 159 tanks and armoured cars, 127 guns, 1,097 vehicles and 12,549 tons of supplies brought in by sea.[12] The Axis also deployed forces overland from Libya thus bringing their total troop strength in Tunisia during this period to 15,575 Germans and some 9,000 Italians. Meanwhile, by 25 November Axis air strength in Tunisia had grown to five fighter groups, a bomber group and a unit of short-range reconnaissance aircraft.[13]

The Axis took little time in putting these forces to effective use. By 10 November German aircraft were operating from Tunisian airfields, while the first clash of ground forces occurred on the 17th. Then during the latter half of November and the better part of December these newly arrived Axis forces fought a series of engagements with the advancing British and American spearheads. In this, the Axis enjoyed a number of short-term advantages that aided their efforts. By seizing Tunis and Bizerte ahead of the Allies, the Axis commanded a centralised position that maintained a compact logistical centre of gravity. By comparison, the Allies were forced to operate hundreds of miles from their primary port of entry at Algiers over a ground-based logistical infrastructure that was generally inadequate to the task. The Axis were also able to attain local air superiority over Tunisia due to their access to better all-weather airfields compared to the improvised dirt airstrips generally available to the Allies. Likewise, despite their growing numerical strength in North Africa, the Allies were only able to initially dispatch a fraction of their forces to Tunisia, thus meeting the Axis on roughly equal terms. Finally, with the onset of winter, the Allies encountered cold and wet conditions that only served to exacerbate their difficulties.

While this build-up and subsequent combat was underway in Tunisia, the Axis also endeavoured to engage the large mass of shipping present in the waters off Morocco and Algeria. True to Allied predictions, the Italian surface fleet did not attempt an intervention, but Axis aircraft and submarines did carry out numerous attacks against the invasion fleet and follow-up convoys. In this, the Axis gained a fair degree of success sinking a total of 16 merchant ships worth 181,732 tons during the assault and build-up phases of Operation *Torch*.[14] Additionally, several British warships were sunk in and around the invasion area during November and December. This included the escort carrier *Avenger*; the destroyers *Martin, Isaac Sweers* (Dutch), *Ithuriel, Porcupine* and *Partridge*; the escort destroyer *Blean*; the sloop *Ibis*; the corvettes *Gardenia* and *Marigold*; the minesweeper *Algerine* and the anti-aircraft ship *Tynwald*.[15] Unfortunately for the Axis, heavy though these losses were, they failed to seriously impede the Allied build-up, which saw the arrival of 13 British and four American follow-up convoys to the region as well as the execution of 17 local replenishment convoys from 8 November through the end of the year.[16] Likewise, the Axis paid a heavy price for their achievements with 14 Axis submarines sunk in the Mediterranean or its approaches from 7 November through 15 December 1942. Of these, British escort vessels and submarines sank *Granito, Emo, U660, U98, Dessie, Porfido, Corallo* and *Uarsciek*, while British aircraft accounted for *U411, U605, U595, U259* and *U331* and American bombers sank *Antonio Sciesa*.

Turning now to the other major Axis reaction to Operation *Torch*, on 11 November German forces began their move into southern France to take possession of the Vichy-controlled portion of the country. Once again, Vichy authorities offered no resistance to this incursion, and the Germans were able to complete their task with little difficulty. The sole exception to this was at Toulon where the French fleet refused to surrender to German forces surrounding the harbour. A standoff ensued that lasted over two weeks as both the Allies and Axis vied to gain control over these valuable warships. This was no minor issue given the potential prizes at stake, which included the battleship *Provence*, the battlecruisers *Dunkerque* and *Strasbourg*, the seaplane carrier *Commandant Teste*, four heavy cruisers, three light cruisers and over 60 assorted destroyers, submarines, sloops, torpedo boats, minesweepers and other minor vessels. On 27 November the Germans finally attempted to seize the fleet by force. Fortunately for the Allies, the French, who had pledged to never let their fleet fall into German hands, made good on their promise and scuttled their warships before the Germans could capture them. So thorough was this job, that the Axis were only able to ultimately raise and fully repair four destroyers and a handful of lesser vessels.

These events in North Africa and southern France, along with the concurrent Italian occupation of Corsica, signalled an inglorious end to the puppet Vichy regime. From this point on, the French ceased their state-sponsored collaboration with Germany and increasingly aligned themselves to the Allied cause. Of course, with all of France now under German control, it primarily fell upon their colonial forces to carry on the war. As such, French contingents would soon join the British First Army in combating the Axis in Tunisia. Likewise, a number of North African-based French warships, including the battleship *Richelieu*, three cruisers, six destroyers, 17 submarines, a submarine depot ship and 35 minor and miscellaneous vessels would eventually find service in the Allied fleets, while 51 merchant ships worth 169,954 tons from Dakar and the nearby French ports came under Allied control.[17] The fall of the Vichy regime also signalled an end to the quasi conflict that had existed between Britain and France since the summer of 1940. During this time the British had engaged Vichy forces in five major operations and several minor engagements involving naval combat. In most cases the British had prevailed over their French opponents with the great preponderance of casualties suffered by the latter. Now this conflict was over, and an adversary, both real and potential, had been eliminated.

While the demise of the Vichy regime represented a small victory for the British, Britain's primary enemies were far from defeated. Returning now to the Mediterranean war, November saw another major British push to get supplies through

Table 7.1 Comparative Vichy and British Warship Losses 1940–1942

	Battleships	Cruisers	Destroyers	Torpedo boats/sloops/ escorts/ minesweepers	Submarines
Vichy losses					
Sunk through British action	1	-	5	3	14
Sunk through American or Free French action	-	-	4	1	8
Seized or voluntarily demilitarized in July 1940	3	4	7	18	8
Total Vichy losses	4	4	16	22	30
British losses					
Sunk through Vichy means	-	-	1	3	-

to Malta. The impetus behind this was a report from the Maltese governor stating that foodstuffs brought in by the *Pedestal* convoy were quickly depleting and would be exhausted by mid-December. Accordingly, in early November the British used submarines and the minelayers *Manxman* and *Welshman* to deliver small quantities of key provisions to the island. Then on the 16th the British dispatched a four-ship convoy from Suez to Malta under the designation Operation *Stoneage*. Escorted by the cruisers *Cleopatra*, *Orion*, *Arethusa*, *Dido* and *Euryalus* and 17 destroyers, the convoy successfully arrived at Malta on the 20th despite enduring bad weather and heavy air attacks. The only British casualty for the operation was the cruiser *Arethusa*, which suffered heavy damage from a torpedo hit. A fortnight later the British conducted Operation *Portcullis* that successfully passed a second convoy consisting of four merchant ships and a tanker through to Malta. Together, these two convoys delivered 56,000 tons of supplies, apart from heavy oils, that effectively lifted the siege that had plagued Malta for the past ten months. Thereafter, the British would deliver additional supplies without loss to Malta using a succession of two-ship convoys thus solidifying this success.

In other operations during this period, the British continued their interdiction efforts against Axis seaborne traffic running between Europe and North Africa. In this, the British faced new challenges as the Axis diverted much of their shipping to Tunisia instead of Libya. This move significantly shortened the transit times of many ships proceeding to Africa, reducing their exposure to attack. The distance between Sicily and Tunis is a mere 130 miles, which is roughly only a third of the distance to Libya. If timed correctly during the lengthening winter nights, faster ships could make most of this journey shielded in darkness. The British also had to contend with extensive minefields that impeded submarine and surface warship operations in the area. The Italians had long laid mines in the Strait of Sicily, and by late 1942 they had a continuous mine barrier running from Cape Bon on the northeast tip of Tunisia to the Aegadian Islands off Sicily. Then in November they started laying a parallel mine barrier to the west running from Bizerte to the Skerki Bank. In doing so, they established a safe corridor 50 miles wide that protected their ships most of the way to Tunisia.

Under these conditions, it took until December before the British finally attained success against the Axis Tunisian-bound traffic. However, when this success occurred, it proved to be spectacular. At the end of November the British deployed a squadron of cruisers and destroyers to Bône under the designation of Force Q. On the night of 1/2 December this force, consisting of the cruisers *Aurora*, *Argonaut* and *Sirius* and the destroyers *Quiberon* and *Quentin*, entered into the Strait of Sicily in search of Axis shipping. Circumventing the Italian minefields, which were still incomplete at the time, the British squadron encountered an Axis convoy, designated Convoy H, consisting of three merchant ships and a military transport some 60 miles northeast of Bizerte. Attacking with great vigour, the British destroyed all four of these ships worth a combined 8,042 tons, along with the escorting Italian destroyer *Folgore*. Two other Italian escorts, the destroyer *Da Recco* and the torpedo boat *Procione*, sustained heavy damage. Accompanying these shipping casualties was a heavy loss of life as some 2,200 men out of 3,300 naval and military personnel embarked upon the convoy perished, while cargo losses included four tanks, 32 vehicles, 12 anti-tank guns and 698 tons of supplies.[18] The British escaped the battle unscathed, but the next morning a German torpedo-bomber sank the destroyer *Quentin* as it was retiring towards Bône.

The Allies scored a number of other interdiction successes during this period, although most of these occurred outside of the newly established Tunisian route. On the night following the destruction of Convoy H, British Albacores from Malta torpedoed and sank the 5,464-ton Italian merchant ship *Veloce* off Kerkenah Bank as the latter was en route to Tripoli. Minutes later British destroyers from a recently reconstituted Malta-based Force K arrived on the scene and sank the Italian torpedo boat *Lupo*, which was rescuing survivors from the demised merchant ship. Amongst other things, this event highlighted a renaissance of fortunes for the Fleet Air Arm operating out of Malta. For most of 1942, Malta's FAA contingent had struggled to attain meaningful results against transiting Axis shipping, but with the cessation of the aerial blitz and the easing of supply constraints, this abruptly changed in the last two months of the year. Including the aforementioned *Veloce*, FAA Albacores sank or shared in the destruction of ten Axis merchant ships worth 34,699 tons in November and December. During the same period the USAAF increasingly came into its own as American bombers sank 16 merchant ships worth 19,438 tons. Meanwhile, RAF aircraft accounted for a further 22 merchant ships worth 31,276 tons sunk during the closing two months of the year.[19] In addition to these anti-shipping efforts, RAF aircraft operating out of Malta carried out numerous raids against airfields in Sicily and Tunisia, as well as air intercept missions along the Axis transport routes to North Africa. During the course of these missions the RAF destroyed at least 97 German aircraft, including 32 transports and an unspecified number of Italian aircraft from 8 November through 31 December. This cost Malta 43 aircraft in return.[20]

During the same period the British also scored numerous successes with both submarines and mines. In terms of the former, from 24 October through 31 December British submarines sank 15 Axis merchant ships and 12 minor vessels worth a combined 47,739 tons in the Mediterranean. Added to this were three merchant ships worth 16,985 tons that were sunk in conjunction with British aircraft (also counted above).[21] Meanwhile, the British were increasingly effective in their use of mines during this period. Of particular consequence were the minelayer *Manxman* and the submarine *Rorqual*, which used SIGINT intelligence to exploit gaps in the Axis mine belts and plant their own mines within the Italian safe corridors. Together these mines, along with those laid by other sources, accounted for seven merchant ships plus two minor naval vessels worth a combined 14,371 tons sunk during November and December.[22] Included in this number were the 5,418-ton *Citta di Napoli* and the 2,467-ton *Citta di Trapani*.

In addition to merchant losses, the period also witnessed the demise of several Italian surface warships. On 4 and 6 November USAAF bombers attacked Benghazi, sinking the torpedo boat *Centauro* and the minesweeper *Selve* (ex-Yugoslav *Galeb*). Three weeks later the Italian torpedo boat *Circe* sank in an accidental collision with the merchant ship *Citta di Tunisi*. Then on 4 December the newly activated US Ninth Air Force carried out its first attack against the Italian mainland by bombing naval targets in the port of Naples. During this raid American B-24 Liberator bombers hit and damaged the Italian light cruiser *Muzio Attendolo* so severely that it capsized and sank, becoming a total loss. Two other cruisers and four destroyers were damaged to lesser degrees. Thirteen days later the British submarine *Splendid* torpedoed and sank the Italian destroyer *Aviere* north of Bizerte. Finally, on 3 January the British submarines *Thunderbolt* and *Trooper* arrived off Palermo and launched Chariot human torpedoes to attack shipping within the harbour. The Chariot was an improved British version of the man-operated human torpedo first developed by the Italians and used by them to such great success against the British fleet at Alexandria in December 1941. Now it was Britain's turn to use these unconventional weapons as two human torpedo teams penetrated into the harbour and successfully placed their detachable warheads to sink the new Italian light cruiser *Ulpio Traiano* and severely damage the 8,657-ton transport *Viminale*.

When combined together, these interdiction successes took a heavy toll upon the Axis. During the last four months of 1942 Axis merchant shipping losses in the Mediterranean from all causes amounted to 304,782 tons, of which almost 100,000 tons were sunk in December alone.[23] This, in turn, had a significant impact upon Axis materiel deliveries to North Africa. From September through November the Axis successfully delivered 188,000 tons of supplies and equipment to Libya out of 268,630 tons dispatched. When averaged out, this equated to an arrival of 62,667 tons per month and represented a 69.98 percent delivery rate. In December this supply situation deteriorated to an unsustainable level as the Axis delivered a mere 6,151 tons out of 12,981 tons dispatched to Libya.[24] This paltry amount was wholly inadequate in meeting the needs of Rommel's German/Italian Panzerarmee as it reeled back from its defeat at El Alamein. Of course, a major factor in the near collapse of Rommel's supply situation was the overwhelming diversion of Axis merchant traffic to Tunisia. Yet, even here some 23 percent of the materiel shipped in December was lost in transit, representing a shortfall of about 17,550 tons.[25] Sadly, these successes came at a cost as no fewer than seven British or British-affiliated submarines were lost in the Mediterranean during the last four months of 1942. Of these, *Utmost*, *Triton* (Greek), *P222* and *P48* were lost to Axis surface escorts while *Talisman*, *Traveller* and *P311* presumably succumbed to mines.

Despite these interdiction successes and the near collapse of the supply situation in Libya, the vast bulk of reinforcements and materiel dispatched to Tunisia during this period arrived intact. By the end of December this included 41,768 men and 8,651 tons of supplies flown in by air with a further 89,072 tons of materiel and stores delivered by sea.[26] With this influx of men and materiel, the Axis were able to mount an effective defence of Tunisia and launch a series of local counter-attacks that forced the Allies to yield some of their earlier gains. By the end of December it was clear that the First Army's offensive had run out of steam, and General Eisenhower ordered a pause in the fighting to give his forces time to build-up, regroup and wait for better weather. With this, the campaign in Tunisia went into a period of relative calm and stalemate as both sides prepared for future operations. Thus, despite initial Allied hopes for a quick Tunisian victory, they now faced the prospect of a protracted struggle with much hard fighting ahead.

The same was not true in Libya where the German/Italian Panzerarmee found itself in a state of near perpetual retreat. Driven by events in Algeria and Tunisia, as well as the deteriorating supply situation, Rommel declined to make a prolonged stand against the advancing Eighth Army. One by one the key geographical prizes in Cyrenaica fell as the British captured Bardia, Tobruk, Derna and Benghazi on 11, 13, 15 and 20 November respectively. Of equal consequence, the British seized vital airfields in western Cyrenaica, thus significantly easing their ability to transit the Eastern Mediterranean and send supply convoys to Malta. On 23 November the first British units arrived in the vicinity of El Agheila, which constituted a highly defensible natural position. Twice before, the British had advanced to this point only to be thrown back by subsequent Axis counter-attacks. This would not be repeated a third time. When Eighth Army renewed its offensive on 14 December, they encountered little resistance as the bulk of the Panzerarmee had already abandoned the El Agheila position, leaving behind a rear guard that gave up 450 prisoners, 18 tanks and 25 guns.[27]

By the end of December Eighth Army was well inside of Tripolitania having advanced some 1,100 miles from its starting point at El Alamein. During this process Eighth Army had taken a total of 8,611 German and 23,594 Italian prisoners from the beginning of its El Alamein offensive through 31 December.[28] During roughly the same period it had also captured large quantities of equipment and military stores, including 408 German and 111 Italian aircraft left derelict on abandoned Axis airfields.[29] Yet, despite these accomplishments, the British faced an increasingly difficult supply situation as their units advanced progressively farther from their main logistical bases in Egypt. This situation would have been far worse if not for the quick reclamations made in putting the ports of Tobruk and Benghazi back into service. Despite extensive damage from Allied bombing and Axis demolition efforts, the British had both ports up and receiving cargo within days of their respective captures, and from the beginning of November 1942 through 23 January 1943 the British Inshore Squadron delivered 157,070 tons of supplies to bolster Eighth Army's advance.[30] While this helped, Montgomery was still compelled to pause at Buerat to build-up his logistical stockpiles and reorganise his forces. Finally, on 15 January

Eighth Army resumed its offensive with a proposed timetable to capture Tripoli in ten days. Encountering little resistance due to Rommel's earlier decision to withdraw to Tunisia, Eighth Army met its objective and took possession of Tripoli on the 23rd.

In the days leading up to this event, Tripoli saw considerable activity as the Italians continued to deliver supplies while simultaneously evacuating empty merchant ships and navel auxiliaries from the endangered port. To counter this traffic, the British employed Force K out of Malta. On a succession of nights in mid-January British destroyers from Force K proceeded into the central Mediterranean and sank the 4,537-ton Italian merchant ship *D'Annunzio*, the naval transports *Tanaro* and *Stromboli*, the small tanker *Irma*, the motor minesweepers *RD31*, *RD36*, *RD37* and *RD39*, three auxiliary minesweepers and two minor vessels for no loss to themselves. During this period British warships also sank two Italian submarines, *Narvalo* and *Santorre Santarosa*, which were engaged in or returning from supply operations to Tripoli. For their part, British submarines sank or participated in the destruction of seven merchant ships and seven minor vessels worth a combined 16,741 tons in the waters east of Tunisia and/or north of Tripoli during January.[31] Meanwhile, prior to abandoning Tripoli the Italians scuttled five immobilised merchant ships worth a combined 24,781 tons.[32] Finally, in another example of Axis materiel wastage, the British found 114 German and 327 Italian aircraft left abandoned on area airfields, bringing the total number of captured Axis aircraft since the beginning of the El Alamein offensive to nearly 1,000.[33]

The scuttling of these derelict merchant ships comprised just part of the extensive demolition the Italians had carried out prior to evacuating Tripoli. With Libya now firmly under British control, Eighth Army prepared to continue its advance into southern Tunisia. An essential condition in accomplishing this was the need to open the port of Tripoli for incoming supplies. This was no simple task given the degree of devastation inflicted upon the harbour and dock areas. Nevertheless, the British set about accomplishing this Herculean task, and on 2 February the first ship arrived in the partially restored port. A week later the first convoy arrived, and by the end of February the British were discharging over 3,000 tons of supplies per day in Tripoli. During the month as a whole the British Inshore Squadron delivered 115,137 tons of supplies in support of the Eighth Army, of which a sizable portion was off-loaded in Tripoli's reclaimed port.[34] This timely and essential sustenance allowed the Eighth Army to advance into Tunisia where it joined the British First Army in opposing the newly formed German Fifth Panzerarmee and the remnants of Rommel's ejected command; soon to be re-designated the Italian First Army.

The maintenance of these competing forces quickly impacted the corresponding maritime struggle. After two and a half years of general absence, vast numbers of Allied ships now routinely proceeded into the central Mediterranean from both east and west to support the Allied armies in Tunisia, along with their partnering air forces. This increase in traffic naturally invited unwanted attention from Axis submarines and aircraft, and during the first four months of 1943 Allied merchant losses within the Mediterranean numbered 50 vessels worth 200,426 tons.[35] Included in this were 27 merchant ships worth 99,466 tons that were sunk by German U-boats.[36] Still, given the scale of the undertaking and viewed within the context of the overall shipping situation, these losses were not prohibitive and failed to seriously disrupt Allied logistical operations. Against this, Allied forces sank seven German U-boats and four Italian submarines (excluding the aforementioned *Narvalo* and *Santorre Santarosa*) within the Mediterranean during the same four-month period. Of these, British forces accounted for *U224*, *Tritone*, *U301*, *Avorio*, *Asteria*, *U205*, *U562*, *U443*, *U83* and *U77*, while the Dutch submarine *Dolfijn* sank *Malachite*. Meanwhile, two additional Axis submarines, *Delfino* and *U602*, were lost to accidental and unknown causes.

For their part, Axis naval authorities faced a crisis of growing proportions that threatened to make their remaining position in North Africa untenable. In the two and a half years prior some 1,500,000 tons of Axis shipping had been lost in the Mediterranean, representing about 65 percent of their available capacity at the beginning of the war. Italian replacement construction during the same period amounted to just 218,405 tons or about 15 percent of this loss.[37] Seizures of Greek and Yugoslav vessels added some further shipping to the Axis pool, but losses had clearly surpassed replacements. Making matters worse, much of the tonnage that remained was un-seaworthy due to battle damage or normal wear and tear. Accordingly, a large number of ships, both military and commercial, languished in Italian shipyards awaiting repairs or refits. Likewise, the Italians had other requirements, including support for their forces in Greece and the Aegean islands and the maintenance of Sicily and Sardinia, that placed demands against their dwindling merchant fleet. To help compensate for this, the occupation of Vichy France allowed the Axis to take possession of some 535,000 tons of French shipping, but many of these vessels required repairs or maintenance that further strained the already overstretched Axis repair infrastructure. When combined together with dwindling fuel stocks and normal turnaround times, the Axis rarely had more than 50,000 tons of shipping available to support Tunisia at any given time.

Undaunted by this challenge, the Axis continued their reinforcement and supply activities. To help compensate for shortages of suitable merchant ships, the Axis employed a number of smaller vessels to support their Tunisian supply operations. Included in these were German military transports called *kriegstransporters* or KT ships. Displacing 834 tons, these coal-powered transports were capable of carrying 600 tons of cargo and had a top speed of 14.5 knots. Built in sections and assembled in various Italian and Yugoslav ports, the Germans had 30 of these useful vessels in service or under construction at the time of the Tunisian campaign. The Germans also employed smaller, slower landing craft called *ahrprahms* (MFPs) or F-boats by the Allies that displaced 200 or 280 tons and carried 80 to 100 tons of cargo at seven to ten knots. Finally, the Germans utilised a number of shallow-draft *Siebel* ferries that displaced 137 to 170 tons (depending upon the model) and were capable of carrying 45 tons of cargo at speeds approaching eight knots. In addition to these auxiliary vessels, the Italians used several of their destroyers and torpedo boats in a troop-carrying capacity. Likewise, the Germans continued to use airlift as a primary means to transport troops and small quantities of supplies to North Africa.

Arrayed against this supply effort was an ever-increasing assemblage of Allied forces. Paramount amongst these was a build-up of Allied air power. This was particularly true regarding the USAAF, which with the activation of the US Ninth and Twelfth Air Forces in North Africa, assumed the predominant role in the Allied aerial campaign against Axis shipping. Much of this American effort manifested itself in the form of heavy bombing raids against Italian ports and harbour installations. When combined with concurrent, although less sizable, RAF raids, the Allies subjected the Italian transportation infrastructure to a level of destruction and strain yet unseen during the Mediterranean war. The Allies also increased the number of sorties devoted to direct attacks at sea with the USAAF conducting regular daytime sweeps while the RAF and FAA concentrated their efforts at night. Together, these various activities resulted in the destruction of 38 merchant ships and 50 minor vessels worth a combined 154,814 tons during the first three months of 1943.[38] Of these, USAAF aircraft sank 70 vessels worth 95,061 tons, while RAF and FAA aircraft accounted for the remaining 18 vessels worth 59,753 tons.[39] During the same period USAAF aircraft sank a number of Italian warships, including the destroyers *Bersagliere* and *Geniere*, the escort destroyer *Monsone* and the minesweeper *Unie* while FAA and RAF aircraft sank the minesweeper *Eso* and the aforementioned *U83* and *U77*.

The navy's contribution to these interdiction successes was also substantial. This included British and British-affiliated Allied submarines that sank 43 Axis and Axis-affiliated merchant ships worth 118,537 tons from January through March 1943. During the same period these submarines accounted for the Italian destroyer *Bombardiere*, the previously mentioned submarines *U301* and *Malachite* and 46 minor vessels worth at least 4,851 tons.[40] Concurrent British losses consisted of the submarines *Tigris*, *Turbulent* and *Thunderbolt* which were sunk by Axis surface escorts or unknown causes. Meanwhile, the minelayers *Abdiel* and *Welshman* and the submarine *Rorqual* continued to lay mines within the Italian safe corridors to devastating effect. For the loss of *Welshman*, which was sunk by *U617* on 1 February, these mines claimed the destruction of the Italian destroyers *Corsaro*, *Saetta*, *Lanzerotto Malocello* and *Ascari*; the escort destroyers *Uragano* and *Ciclone*; the torpedo boat *Generale Marcello Prestinari*; the corvette *Procellaria* and at least two merchant ships worth 6,752 tons.[41] Mines laid in other areas and/or by other means accounted for seven additional commercial vessels worth 12,058 tons.[42] Finally, in addition to Force K's previously mentioned successes off Tripoli, destroyers from Force Q sank the 1,323-ton German merchant ship *Favor* on 18 January and a

The British submarines *Taku* (foreground) and *Unison* in Malta harbour. During the duration of the Mediterranean conflict, British and British-affiliated submarines sank 43 principal warships and 286 primary Axis merchant ships and naval auxiliaries within the theatre for the cost of 52 of their own number. (Roper, F. G. (Lt), Royal Navy official photographer, public domain)

ferry barge on 8 March, but these surface successes came at a cost as the destroyer *Lightning* was sunk by the German motor torpedo boat *S55* on 12 March.

Given these heavy losses, the Axis attained a degree of success in supporting their forces in North Africa that was both laudable and yet also inadequate. During the first three months of 1943 the Axis successfully delivered over 108,000 personnel and 188,700 tons of supplies and equipment to Tunisia.[43] Of this, about a third of the personnel and 8.8 percent of the materiel tonnage arrived by air while the remainder arrived by sea. When broken down on a monthly basis, materiel deliveries to North Africa amounted to 73,955 tons in January, 63,969 tons in February and 50,776 tons in March.[44] While this represented a reasonable result given the obstacles arrayed against them, it generally fell short of the 69,000-ton minimum monthly delivery requirement established by the Axis leadership. Likewise, it exposed a growing imbalance between the increasing number of soldiers on the ground and the amount of supplies getting through to support them. The totality of this shortfall was entirely attributable to Allied interdiction efforts as 23 percent of the Axis tonnage dispatched by sea in January and February and 41.5 percent of the tonnage dispatched in March failed to arrive.[45]

Notwithstanding this deteriorating supply situation, the Axis launched a series of limited counter-attacks against the Allied forces in Tunisia from the beginning of January through the first week in March. These were largely German affairs, although Italian forces did play minor roles in some of the undertakings. The first of these targeted French positions in the Fondouk Pass, resulting in a German consolidation of the Eastern Dorsals and the seizure of some 4,000 French prisoners.[46] The Germans next moved against the American II Corps on First Army's southern flank. During a ten-day battle culminating in the Kasserine Pass, the Germans sharply rebuked the largely untested American formation, which suffered over 6,000 casualties and lost 183 tanks, 104 half-tracks, over 200 guns and 500 vehicles.[47] Immediately following this the Germans switched their attentions to the north as nine battle groups from the German Fifth Panzerarmee launched a series of attacks against British V Corps. During these attacks the Germans made some territorial gains and took about 2,500 prisoners, but they ultimately failed to seize their primary objectives and suffered similar heavy losses for their efforts.[48] This included 2,200 German prisoners taken by V Corps from 26 February through 24 March.[49] Finally, on 6 March Rommel launched three panzer divisions in an attack against the Eighth Army at Medenine in southern Tunisia. Pre-warned by Ultra intelligence, the British handily repulsed this attack in a short, sharp battle that cost Rommel some 645 casualties and 52 tanks for a British loss of 130 casualties.[50]

By the middle of March it was the Allies turn to go onto the offensive. On the 19th Eighth Army launched a two-pronged assault against the strongly held Mareth line in southern Tunisia. The first of these forays was a direct assault made against the line by XXX Corps in which 50th Division breached the Axis defences, but was then bogged down due to heavy counter-attacks and poor weather/terrain conditions that prevented the arrival of adequate follow-on forces. With this assault stymied, Montgomery switched his main effort to a western flanking movement by an improvised New Zealand Corps with support from X Corps. Launching their attack through the Tebaga Gap on the 26th, the British made steady progress that compelled the Axis to abandon the Mareth line, and on 29 March 1st Armoured Division and 2nd New Zealand Division captured El Hamma and Gabes respectively. Eighth Army then advanced to a second strongly held line at Wadi Akarit. On the night of 5/6 April XXX Corps, consisting of 4th Indian, 50th and 51st Highland Divisions, conducted a brilliant assault that breached this line and forced the Axis to once again retreat. Continuing its advance, Eighth Army captured Sfax on the 10th, thus concluding a successful series of battles that netted the British some 20,000 prisoners taken since the start of the Mareth offensive.[51]

While this was underway, First Army also carried out a series of assaults that inflicted similar territorial and manpower losses upon the Axis. On 17 March US II Corps launched an attack that captured Gafsa and then pushed on towards the El Guettar mountain pass. During a three-week period these forces made additional territorial gains, repulsed two German counter-attacks and collected some 4,700 prisoners.[52] Meanwhile, during concurrent operations French forces took over 1,000 prisoners between Ousseltia and Kairouan while the British 6th Armoured Division accounted for 650 prisoners, 14 tanks and 15 guns in fighting around the Fondouk Gap.[53] Together, these various operations, combined with Eighth Army's advance along the coast, forced the Axis to abandon southern Tunisia thus reducing their holdings in the contested region by about half. Finally, in the north the British 46th and 78th Divisions launched attacks in the Sedjenane-Cap Serrat and Béja-Medjez road areas that more than recovered all the territory lost the month before and resulted in the capture of 850 and 1,080 prisoners respectively.[54]

By the middle of April the situation in Tunisia had turned decidedly against the Axis. Confronted by two powerful Allied armies containing 19 divisions (12 of which were British), the Axis mustered two armies of their own containing nine German and five Italian divisions.[55] Thus, in terms of major units, the Allies maintained a modest numerical advantage over their Axis opponents. However, this was only the beginning of the disparity that existed between the two competing sides. The Allies possessed a significant superiority in tanks and a growing ascendancy in air power. Likewise, the Allies were able to support their forces with lavish amounts of supplies. By comparison, the German Fifth Panzerarmee and the Italian First Army found themselves trapped in an ever-shrinking enclave in northeast Tunisia. This territorial contraction deprived the Axis of space and depth to disperse and defend critical assets, such as airfields and depots, from Allied air and ground intervention. Of even greater consequence, logistical constraints and Allied interdiction efforts increasingly reduced the amount of supplies getting through to the Axis forces, severely limiting their effective combat power. To many observers, the Axis seemed ensnared in a trap of largely their own making. Amongst them was Rommel, who returned to Germany and openly petitioned for an Axis evacuation from Tunisia. However, Hitler would hear none of this and instead ordered resistance to continue as he hoped to delay Allied action against Southern Europe.

To help hasten an outcome contrary to Hitler's design, the Allies continued their interdiction activities with successes scored against all facets of the Axis supply operation. Once again, aircraft proved to be the most potent adversary in this campaign accounting for 15 merchant ships and 39 minor vessels totalling 63,020 tons that were sunk in April as well as three additional merchant ships worth 11,904 tons that were sunk in conjunction with naval units.[56] USAAF aircraft claimed the majority of these losses sinking 46 vessels totalling 52,527 tons and sharing in the destruction of four more worth 9,757 tons. The vast majority of these were sunk in raids against ports, as were the Italian heavy cruiser *Trieste* and the torpedo boat *Giacomo Medici*. The RAF and FAA's contribution to April's toll consisted of five merchant ships worth 5,374 tons sunk directly, three ships of 5,119 tons shared with USAAF aircraft and two ships of 7,266 tons that were sunk in conjunction with naval units.[57] Likewise, RAF bombers sank the Italian destroyer *Alpino* during a raid against La Spezia. Finally, in April the Allies intensified their efforts to disrupt Axis aerial re-supply. Under the designation of Operation *Flax*, the Allies carried out a number of large-scale bombing raids against Axis airfields in Italy and Tunisia as well as regular fighter sweeps along the aerial transit routes to Africa. During these operations, which lasted from 5 to 27 April, the Allies destroyed at least 157 German transport aircraft and possibly as many as 432 aircraft of all types. This cost the Allies 35 aircraft in return.[58]

The navy also scored a number of interdiction successes during this period. In April British and British-affiliated submarines sank 14 merchant ships worth 38,200 tons, eight minor vessels worth 1,894 tons and the Italian torpedo boat *Climene*.[59] Against this, the British lost the submarines *Regent*, *Splendid* and *Sahib* to Axis surface escorts or unknown causes. Meanwhile, British destroyers and motor torpedo boats sank three merchant ships worth 7,487 tons, the military transport *KT7* and a *Siebel* ferry and participated in the destruction of a fourth merchant ship worth 5,324 tons.[60] Likewise, on the morning of 16 April the British destroyers *Pakenham* and *Paladin* from Force K engaged two Italian torpedo boats southwest of Marsala as the latter were escorting a convoy bound for Tunisia. In the fight that followed, the British destroyers sank the torpedo boat *Cigno* and heavily damaged the second (*Cassiopea*), but lost *Pakenham* in return. Finally, mines accounted for the destruction of six small vessels worth 1,729 tons during the month.[61]

Together, these various Allied interdiction efforts had a profound impact upon the Axis supply situation. In April the Axis only succeeded in delivering 29,233 tons of supplies and materiel by sea, with a further 4,327 tons delivered by air.[62] In terms of the former, this represented a delivery rate of just 58.5 percent and a result that was totally inadequate compared to the need. By the end of the month the Axis forces in Tunisia were suffering severe shortages of essential stores, with fuel being a particularly scarce commodity. Making matters worse, the delivery of just three tanks, 17 guns and 21 vehicles to German forces in April represented a mere fraction of their recent heavy losses.[63] The situation was so untenable that on 20 April the Germans began transferring their last air units out of Africa. By the beginning of May the besieged Axis armies in Tunisia were largely alone and without support as they faced the prospect of their own annihilation.

In this, they did not have long to wait. In late April and early May the Allies embarked upon their final series of operations to destroy the Axis forces in North Africa. To disrupt this, the Germans launched a spoiling attack on the night of 20/21 April between Medjez and Goubellat with elements from three divisions. The British easily repulsed this effort taking some 450 prisoners and destroying or damaging 25 tanks. On 4 May the Germans launched a follow-up attack south of Djebel Bou Aoukaz, but this too was repulsed, costing them a further 12 tanks.[64] For their part, on 22–27 April First Army launched Operation *Vulcan*, resulting in the seizure of several key positions on the approach to Tunis. Then on 6 May a reinforced First Army launched Operation *Strike* in which British IX Corps, consisting of the 4th Infantry, 4th Indian, 6th Armoured and 7th Armoured Divisions, attacked towards Tunis while US II Corps attacked towards Bizerte. Utilising overwhelming artillery, air and armour support, the twin Allied attacks blasted holes in the Axis defences with devastating efficiency. Once through the forward positions, the Allied spearheads made steady progress towards their respective objectives as fuel and ammunition shortages prevented the Axis from mounting an effective follow-up defence. At 1540 hours on 7 May the first British units entered Tunis, where they encountered little opposition and quickly took possession of the city along with several thousand prisoners. US forces entered Bizerte 35 minutes later attaining similar results.

In the days leading up to and following these events, the Allies and Axis fought the final naval actions of the Tunisian campaign. On 30 April American and South African fighter-bombers carried out a series of attacks against Axis warships en route to Tunisia, during which they sank the Italian destroyers *Leone Pancaldo* and *Lampo* and two motor torpedo boats and disabled the German destroyer *Hermes* (ex-*Greek Vasilevs Georgios I*). On the night of 3/4 May the British destroyers *Nubian*, *Petard* and *Paladin* encountered the 3,566-ton merchant ship *Campobasso* and the Italian torpedo boat *Perseo* off Kelibia and sank them both. Over the next few days American bombers sank the transports *Sant'Antonio*, *Belluno* and *Arlesiana* and the escort destroyer *Tifone* while en route to or in Tunisian waters. The final Axis ships to try to make it to Tunisia were the military transports *KT5*, *KT9* and *KT21*, which arrived on 8 May, but could find no place to unload their supplies and were sunk by British destroyers (in the case of *KT5* and *KT21*) and Allied fighter-bombers (in the case of *KT9*) the following day. Finally, with the capture of Tunis and Bizerte, the Allies found the German destroyer *Hermes*, the captured French destroyer *L'Audacieux*, the captured French submarines *Calypso*, *Nautilus*, *Turquoise* and *Circe*, 12 minesweepers, 25 freighters, nine tugs and 23 small craft sunk or scuttled in the various Tunisian harbours.[65]

Meanwhile, with Tunis and Bizerte in their hands, the Allies moved quickly to end the campaign in North Africa. The most important factor in accomplishing

Table 7.2 Warship Losses in the Mediterranean from 1 September 1942 through 13 May 1943

	Capital ships	Cruisers	Destroyers	Torpedo boats/ escorts/mine vessels	Submarines
British/Allied	1	1	9	13	13
Italian/German	-	3	15	18	32

Note: Only includes warships that were a total loss. Does not include Vichy losses or Allied ships sunk by Vichy forces but does include certain vessels sunk in Atlantic waters while supporting/opposing the Allied landings in French North Africa. The escort carrier *Avenger* is listed as a capital ship. Axis submarine losses consisted of 16 Italian and 16 German boats.

this was the prompt capture of the Cap Bon Peninsula. This peninsula formed a highly defensible position with limited port facilities from which the Axis could stage a last stand or even attempt a withdrawal. A key position to the peninsula was the heavily defended resort town of Hammam Lif, located on the northern coast between the sea and the Djebel el Rorouf. On 9 May the British 6th Armoured Division conducted an audacious attack that breached the Axis defences and captured the town. The Axis had considered Hammam Lif to be nearly impregnable, and its quick demise greatly demoralised their resolve and ability to resist. From this point, the 6th Armoured Division had little difficulty in cutting across the base of the peninsula and captured Hammamet on the 11th. Meanwhile, elements of the British 4th Division advanced up both sides of the peninsula and took possession of Cap Bon on the same day (11 May). In the process of doing so, 4th Division encountered minimal opposition and collected upwards of 50,000 prisoners.[66]

While this was underway, and in the days immediately thereafter, the Allies mopped up the remaining Axis forces languishing in Tunisia. In this, the Allies benefited from an enemy that had largely given up the will and/or lacked the means to resist. On the 9th the remnants of Axis forces in northern Tunisia surrendered to US II Corps, bringing the total number of prisoners taken by the Americans during the final offensive to almost 40,000.[67] At the same time the British 7th Armoured Division pacified the coastal area north of Tunis, collecting some 19,000 prisoners in and around Porto Farina in little more than a 24-hour period.[68] These prompt actions, and those at Cap Bon, eliminated the feasibility of a large-scale Axis evacuation. Nevertheless, small groups of Axis personnel did attempt to escape in a variety of minor craft. Of these, 653 men actually succeeded in making it to Europe, while British destroyers and motor torpedo boats took 879 prisoners at sea.[69] These British warships were patrolling the waters off Tunisia as a result of Operation *Retribution*, in which Admiral Cunningham ordered them to 'Sink, burn and destroy. Let nothing pass.'[70]

Meanwhile, in areas all over Tunisia Axis formations continued to capitulate. On 12 May the 21st Panzer Division and 90th Light Division surrendered to the French XIX Corps and British 6th Armoured Division respectively. At the same time, 4th Indian Division took the surrender of the Superga Division along with General Hans-Jürgen von Arnim, the commander of Axis forces in Tunisia, and his headquarters in the vicinity of Stainte Marie du Zit. Finally, on 13 May Italian Field Marshal Giovanni Messe and the remains of the Italian First Army, consisting of the Young Fascist, Trieste and 164th Divisions, surrendered to British X Corps. When combined together, the Allies collected a total of 238,243 prisoners during the final days of the Tunisia campaign, of which at least 101,784 were German.[71] The British were responsible for taking approximately 70 percent of these prisoners while American and French forces accounted for the rest. On 13 May General Alexander signalled Churchill stating: 'Sir, it is my duty to report that the Tunisian campaign is over. All enemy resistance has ceased. We are masters of the North African shores.'[72]

The successful application of maritime power facilitated corresponding victories on the battlefield. Pictured here are Axis prisoners following the fall of Tunis. (National Archives and Records Administration, public domain)

So ended the campaign in Africa. After nearly three years of struggle and hard-fought combat, the British and their allies had finally prevailed over the Axis to claim mastery over the African continent. In doing so, they achieved their overriding strategic objective for the campaign by securing the Suez Canal and the vital oil fields in the Persian Gulf. They also gained valuable territory and bases from which they could take the conflict to Southern Europe. Finally, they handed the Axis a significant defeat in materiel and psychological terms while gaining practical experience and confidence for themselves. In terms of the former, Axis losses associated with the fighting in both North and East Africa included some 950,000 personnel casualties, 2.4 million tons of shipping, 8,000 aircraft, 2,500 tanks, 6,200 guns and 70,000 trucks.[73] Over 70 percent of these personnel casualties were in the form of prisoners, but an estimated 21,994 Germans and 37,780 Italians were killed or went missing in Africa.[74] Many thousands more perished in the Mediterranean, including upwards of 28,000 Italian naval personnel and merchant seamen.[75] At a time when Britain lacked the means to directly challenge Germany and Italy on the European continent, this human and materiel drain represented a consequential impairment to the Axis war effort. This was particularly true in the case of Italy, which exited the campaign in a significantly diminished state. In fact, after three years of costly and demoralising defeats in both Africa and the Mediterranean area, Italy's ability and willingness to continue waging war had been significantly reduced.

A number of factors contributed to this immense victory. Paramount amongst these was the success of the British/Commonwealth ground forces and their American and French allies in prevailing over the Germans and Italians. The cost the British army paid for this success was 174,045 casualties suffered from June 1940 through May 1943.[76] Of course, this victory was only made possible through Allied efforts in the maritime war. This was true for two reasons. First, it was through seaborne transport that the British provided virtually all of the men, materiel and supplies that allowed them to conduct the campaign. Second, throughout this time the British, and later the Americans, waged a persistent and debilitating interdiction effort that limited the Axis' ability to do the same for their own forces in Africa. Without taking anything away from the many accomplishments attained by the British and Allied ground forces, Axis fortunes in North Africa clearly coincided with the ebb and flow of their supply situation. Allied interdiction successes played a key role in many important battles, including Operation *Crusader*, Alam Halfa and El Alamein, and eventually rendered the Axis situation in Tunisia so untenable that it led to its precipitous collapse.

Table 7.3 Monthly Axis Materiel Deliveries to North Africa and Merchant Shipping Losses from September 1942 through May 1943

	Tons dispatched	Tons arrived	Percent arrived	Axis merchant shipping lost	Axis merchant tonnage lost
September 1942	98,965	77,526	78.3	25	38,895
October 1942	83,695	46,738	55.8	30	59,693
November 1942	116,279	94,045	80.9	64	106,711
December 1942	est. 89,296	64,914	72.7	59	99,483
January 1943	est. 90,789	69,908	77.0	87	123,213
February 1943	est. 76,644	59,016	77.0	70	98,482
March 1943	est. 73,718	43,125	58.5	85	118,115
April 1943	est. 49,971	29,233	58.5	114	120,561
May 1943	est. 11,297	3,728	33.0	158	130,448

Note: See Note from Table 4.1. Tonnage dispatched to Tunisia from December through May is only shown as an estimate, based upon the tonnage and percentage that arrived. May's merchant losses include losses sustained throughout the entire month and not just the period culminating at the end of the North Africa campaign.

A final factor worth reviewing is the role that Malta played in the Mediterranean conflict. From the beginning of 1941 through the capture of Tunisia, Malta served as the primary base for British interdiction efforts against Axis supply traffic. For much of this period, Malta's aircraft, submarines and warships accounted for the majority of Axis shipping sunk and particularly those ships sunk while directly engaged in supply operations to Africa. Without Malta, Britain's interdiction campaign would have been severely hindered. Nor was Malta's value limited to the fighting in Africa. Instead, Malta was ideally positioned to serve as a base for future operations as the Allies prepared to carry the war into Southern Europe. Still, Malta's triumph did not come easy, but rather came at a heavy cost. This included an aircraft carrier, three cruisers, an anti-aircraft cruiser, 11 destroyers and 23 merchant ships that were sunk during supply operations to the besieged colony. It also included heavy privations suffered by the Maltese people as a result of bombing and blockade. In all, 1,436 civilians were killed and 3,415 wounded, as well as 37,000 buildings destroyed or damaged during the siege.[77] Now, with the cessation of fighting in Africa, Malta's civilian population and the Allies could take solace in the knowledge that their sacrifices and efforts had not been in vain, but had rather contributed to a decisive and overwhelming victory. Soon, the fruits of this victory would be unleashed against Italy and the entire Axis position in Southern Europe.

CHAPTER 8

Italy Subdued

Long before the cessation of hostilities in North Africa, the Allies considered their options regarding follow-up operations in the Mediterranean. This was a subject of considerable debate during the Casablanca Conference in January 1943, where American authorities argued for a strategy primarily focused on Northwest Europe. In this, they proposed a precipitous build-up in Britain followed by an invasion of France at the earliest possible date. The British countered that given the ongoing U-boat threat in the Atlantic and the pace of Allied mobilisation efforts; it would be the spring of 1944 before a successful invasion of France was feasible. As such, they argued for a continuation of operations in the Mediterranean until this could occur with the goal of knocking Italy out of the war and tying down German forces. They surmised that an Italian collapse would deprive Germany of its most significant European ally and compel it to shift sizable resources to Southern Europe to compensate for this loss. To this point, the Italians had upwards of 800,000 men stationed as occupiers in southern France and the Balkans that would have to be replaced if Italy departed the war.[1] Likewise, additional forces would be needed to seize Italy itself or defend Southern Europe from real or potential Allied gains within the region.

This British position enjoyed support from a number of quarters. Naval authorities wanted to secure the Mediterranean for the passage of merchant traffic, thus eliminating the 7,000 to 8,000-mile detour that Allied ships took when rounding the Cape of Good Hope. By routing convoys directly through the Mediterranean when travelling to and from the Middle East and Indian Ocean, the British estimated they would free-up some 2,000,000 tons of cargo space or the equivalent of about 225 merchant ships.[2] This was no small matter given the perceived shipping shortage that existed at the time. Likewise, the Admiralty saw the elimination of the Italian fleet as an opportunity to send sorely needed reinforcements to the Indian and Pacific Oceans for operations against the Japanese. For their part, the air staff advocated for the seizure of Italian territory as a means to gain valuable airfields for a strategic bombing campaign against southern Germany and the surrounding area. Finally, civilian and military leaders acknowledged that it was politically and practically unacceptable to let their armies sit idle for a year or more while the Soviet Union battled the vast bulk of German forces. Something needed to be done to reduce pressure upon the Russians, and a Mediterranean offensive offered a viable means to do this.

Given these considerations, the conference attendees eventually agreed to follow-up operations in Tunisia with an invasion of Sicily. They surmised that this action would go a long way in attaining many of the larger objectives already stated. In particular, the Allies hoped that capturing Sicily would convince an already teetering Italy to leave the war. Likewise, the seizure of this strategically positioned island would eliminate Axis airfields and naval facilities that threatened Allied merchant traffic while conversely providing the Allies with excellent bases to launch air attacks and stage further amphibious assaults against Italy and Southern Europe. Likewise, this action would force the Germans to remain focused on their southern flank. Finally, the capture of Sicily offered the prospect of a relatively cheap victory against acceptable risks. This, in turn, would keep the Allied armies active, continue their successful momentum and provide valuable combat experience to fledgling leaders and formations.

With this decision made, planning and preparation for the proposed undertaking progressively materialised. By the conclusion of the Tunisian campaign in mid-May, the plans and structure for the upcoming invasion, designated Operation *Husky*, were largely in place. Under the overall command of American General Dwight Eisenhower, with Britain's General Harold Alexander, Admiral Andrew Cunningham and Air Chief Marshal Arthur Tedder serving as service chiefs, the Allies intended to utilise two armies for their assault. The first of these, the veteran British Eighth Army under the command of General Bernard Montgomery, would land in the southeast corner of the island and seize the port of Syracuse and the airfield at Pachino. To their west, the American Seventh Army under the command of Lieutenant-General George Patton would land in the vicinity of Licata, Gela and Scoglitti to secure the British flank and seize local airfields. Once these initial objectives were secured, the British would push north to seize Augusta, Catania and the group of airfields at Gerbini, while the Americans continued to provide flank protection. Then when the logistical situation permitted, the Allied armies would complete their conquest of Sicily with the island's north-eastern corner along the Strait of Messina as their ultimate objective.

To achieve these tasks, the Allies earmarked substantial resources. Each of the Allied armies eventually utilised six divisions plus numerous lesser formations in the conduct of the campaign. For Eighth Army, this included the 5th, 50th, 78th, 51st Highland, 1st Airborne and 1st Canadian Divisions, the 4th Armoured, 23rd Armoured, 1st Canadian Tank and 231st Infantry Brigades and various army and Royal Marine commandos. Major American units assigned to the operation included the 1st, 3rd, 9th, 45th, 2nd Armoured and 82nd Airborne Divisions. Meanwhile,

Allied air strength for the operation amounted to some 3,680 aircraft broken down between 113½ British and 146 American squadrons.[3] Finally, the naval component for Operation *Husky* consisted of a staggering 2,590 assorted vessels, of which 1,614 (62.3 percent) were British or British-affiliated. The Royal Navy's contribution to this massive force included the battleships *King George V, Howe, Nelson, Rodney, Warspite* and *Valiant*, the aircraft carriers *Indomitable* and *Formidable*, 13 cruisers, three monitors, 71 destroyers, 35 escorts, 34 minesweepers and 23 submarines. The United States provided a further five cruisers, 48 destroyers and eight minesweepers. Finally, both nations added large numbers of merchant ships, troop transports, landing vessels, coastal craft and other assorted vessels to this endeavour.[4]

The organisation of these naval forces primarily broke down into two subordinate commands that coincided with the invading armies. Supporting Eighth Army was the predominantly British Eastern Naval Task Force commanded by Admiral

Table 8.1 Allied Maritime Forces Assigned to Operation *Husky*

	British and Commonwealth	American	Other	Total
Battleships	6	-	-	6
Fleet aircraft carriers	2	-	-	2
Cruisers	13	5	-	18
Monitors and gunboats	6	-	2	8
Destroyers	71	48	9	128
Escort vessels	35	-	1	36
Minesweepers	34	8	-	42
Minelayers	1	3	-	4
Submarines	23	-	3	26
Auxiliary anti-aircraft ships	1	-	-	1
Fighter direction ships	2	-	-	2
Headquarters ships	5	4	-	9
Landing ships infantry	8	-	-	8
Assorted landing craft	1,034	700	-	1,734
Coastal craft	160	83	-	243
Miscellaneous vessels	58	28	-	86
Merchant ships and transports	155	66	16	237
Total	1,614	945	31	2,590

Source: ADM 234/356, Battle Summaries, No. 35: Invasion of Sicily (Operation *Husky*). Condensed and organised for easier presentation.

Bertram Ramsay and tasked to carry out landings from Cape Murro di Porco on the southern side of Syracuse to the western side of Cape Passero. To do this, the British split their area into five landing sectors designated Acid North, Acid South, Bark East, Bark South and Bark West. The forces assigned to assault these sectors would come from the Middle East, Tunisia/Malta and Britain, and fall under the subordinate commands of Rear-Admirals T. H. Troubridge, R. R. McGrigor and Philip Vian respectively. Meanwhile, naval operations in the Seventh Army area fell under Vice-Admiral Henry Hewitt, USN, and his predominantly American Western Naval Task Force. The mission of this task force was to conduct landings on Sicily's southern coast adjacent to the most westerly British assault. Like their British counterparts, the Americans split this area into three sectors, designated Cent, Dime and Joss, and utilised forces coming from the United States and North Africa to carry out their assaults.

Beyond this general overview, the naval portion of Operation *Husky* involved the coordinated movement of multiple sub-units. This included 22 separate convoys that were established to conduct the initial invasion and follow-up. Coming from different locations and travelling at different speeds, Allied planners had to orchestrate these diverse elements so they would simultaneously converge to deliver 115,000 British and 66,000 American troops on the targeted beaches. In doing so, they had to maintain the security of the forces involved and strive to attain a degree of surprise as to the purpose and timing of these movements. Beyond the assault convoys, the British also planned to dispatch Vice-Admiral A. U. Willis's Force H into the Ionian Sea to screen the invasion from possible interference by the Italian battle fleet at Taranto. Included in Force H were the battleships *Nelson*, *Rodney*, *Warspite* and *Valiant* and the two British aircraft carriers. Meanwhile, Force Z, with the battleships *Howe* and *King George V*, would protect the invasion's western flank and serve as a reserve force.

As Allied authorities finalised their plans for Operation *Husky*, they determined that a valuable prerequisite to this undertaking was the seizure of the Italian island bases of Pantellaria and Lampedusa. Located in the waters between Sicily and the Tunisian coast, these small islands were ideally positioned to provide the Axis with early warning of the Allied invasion. To this end, both islands had airfields, radar installations and observation posts that increased the threat of detection for transiting Allied forces. Likewise, Pantellaria had a large underground hanger that was capable of accommodating up to 100 aircraft and numerous caves and grottoes that were used to refuel Axis submarines and motor torpedo boats. Because of these factors and its more westerly location, Pantellaria was considered the more valuable of the two islands since it would provide the Allies with excellent facilities to support the American landings while denying those same assets to the Axis.

That being the case, Pantellaria posed a potentially difficult target to seize. With an 11,000-man garrison, a large number of coastal guns and a generally inaccessible coastline due to cliffs, Pantellaria was reputed to be a fortress. To address these difficulties, the Allies launched a massive bombing and bombardment campaign to degrade Pantellaria's ability and willingness to resist. Beginning modestly on 8 May, the aerial campaign gradually intensified until by 11 June the Allies had conducted 5,285 sorties and dropped some 6,200 tons of bombs on the hapless island.[5] Meanwhile, from the night of 12/13 May through 5 June various combinations of British cruisers and destroyers shelled Pantellaria on six separate occasions. Then on 8 June a strong British force consisting of five cruisers, eight destroyers and three motor torpedo boats subjected Pantellaria to its harshest bombardment to date.

Despite this intense pounding, calls for Pantellaria to surrender went unheeded, and the Allies decided to take the island by force. On the morning of 11 June three assault convoys rendezvoused off Pantellaria, bringing with them a brigade group from the British 1st Infantry Division embarked upon the headquarters ship *Largs* and the troop transports *Queen Emma*, *Princess Beatrix* and *Royal Ulsterman*. At 1100 hours the British began landing operations as the covering force, commanded by Rear-Admiral R. R. McGrigor and consisting of the cruisers *Orion*, *Newfoundland*, *Aurora*, *Euryalus* and *Penelope* and eight destroyers, subjected the island to further preparatory bombardment. Given the sight of this transpiring assault, Pantelleria's governor, Vice-Admiral Gino Pavesi, decided to surrender the island. Nevertheless, the British still encountered sporadic artillery and small arms fire as their forces made their initial landings. This resistance was quickly subdued, and in the afternoon the British advanced inland against negligible opposition. By 1715 hours it was all over as Admiral Pavesi signed the official terms of surrender. With this, the British disarmed the remaining garrison and eventually took a total of 78 German and 11,121 Italian prisoners.[6] In turn, British losses for the assault, which was designated Operation *Corkscrew*, amounted to just three casualties.

With the capture of Pantelleria, the Allies moved quickly to seize Lampedusa and the nearby islands of Linosa and Lampione. On the afternoon of 11 June Allied bombers turned their attention to Lampedusa, and on the 12th they subjected the island to near continuous bombing. Lampedusa's discomfort was further intensified when the cruisers *Aurora*, *Orion*, *Penelope* and *Newfoundland* and six destroyers arrived offshore to bombard the island with naval gunfire. This pounding proved to be more than the Italians were willing to withstand, and on the evening of the 12th a British infantry company went ashore to accept the surrender of Lampedusa and its 4,600-man garrison. Over the next couple of days Linosa and its 240-man garrison surrendered to the British destroyer *Nubian*, while British forces found Lampione unoccupied. Thus, in a period of only four days the British seized all four islands and collected some 16,000 prisoners for almost no cost to themselves. Soon they would enjoy the fruits of these victories as British aircraft were operating from Lampedusa within a week, while an American fighter group began operations from Pantelleria on 26 June.

While Operation *Corkscrew* was an unmitigated success, Allied planners clearly recognised that the invasion of Sicily, which was scheduled to begin on 10 July, constituted an immensely more formidable task. First, the Axis had sizable forces stationed in Sicily including the 200,000-man Italian Sixth Army, which contained four mobile and the equivalent of six coastal divisions. Based upon the inconsistent performance exhibited by the Italian army thus far in the war, it was unclear how effective these Italian forces would be, but Allied planners had to consider the prospect that they might show increased resolve in the defence of their homeland. In addition to this, two German divisions were also present in Sicily. These units, the Hermann Göring and 15th Panzer Grenadier Divisions, were nearly at full strength and constituted highly capable formations. When combined with Luftwaffe and administrative personnel, the Germans had some 70,000 men in Sicily, with additional forces available in Italy should the Axis decide to send reinforcements.

Beyond these ground elements, the Allies also faced the prospect of formidable opposition at sea. Naval planners believed that their greatest threats would come from air attacks and submarines. In terms of the former, Allied intelligence estimated that the Luftwaffe and Regia Aeronautica possessed some 1,260 and 1,695 aircraft in the theatre, of which 990 and 880 were located in the central Mediterranean. These projections were fairly accurate as German and Italian air strength in the central Mediterranean actually stood at 960 and 700 aircraft respectively on the eve of the invasion. Of course, only a fraction of these aircraft were bombers, but Allied planners projected that as many as 300 Allied vessels might be lost to Axis air attacks off the beaches.[7] Meanwhile, Axis naval strength included 17 German and 48 Italian submarines located in the Mediterranean that posed a constant threat to the Allied invasion forces and supporting convoys. Likewise, the Axis might use E-boats and other fast attack craft to carry out hit and run raids and lay mines. Finally, the Allies had to contend with possible interference from the Italian battle fleet, which still possessed an operational strength of six battleships, seven cruisers and 48 destroyers/torpedo boats. Given its recent inactivity and lack of fuel oil, Allied planners thought it unlikely that the Italian fleet would attempt to intervene, but they had to be prepared for this contingency. After all, if the Italian battle fleet ever planned to fight again, this would seem an appropriate time to do so.

In response to these various threats, the Allies carried out a number of preliminary operations to weaken Axis defences and isolate Sicily. In terms of the former, during the month leading up to Operation *Husky*, Allied bombers conducted a widespread campaign to neutralise Axis airfields on Sicily and Sardinia, resulting in the destruction of 122 German and 105 Italian aircraft on the ground with 66 and 117 more damaged.[8] Beyond this, these attacks rendered most of Sicily's 30 airfields unusable, forcing the Axis to withdraw the bulk of their remaining aircraft to the mainland. Allied bombers also carried out a series of raids against key logistical targets such as ports, rail junctions and ferry crossings. As part of this, in

May and June Allied aircraft sank 115 commercial and 56 military vessels worth 132,504 and 17,704 tons respectively in the Mediterranean, of which more than 80 percent were sunk in port.[9] USAAF aircraft inflicted most of these losses, but British aircraft contributed 18 commercial and ten military vessels worth 25,376 and 5,515 tons respectively that were sunk solely or in conjunction with their American counterparts.[10] This included the 1,339-ton naval tanker *Velino*, which was sunk by FAA Albacores in May thus constituting the last major vessel sunk by shore-based FAA aircraft within the theatre.[11] Other Axis naval losses included the light cruiser *Bari*, the escort destroyer *Groppo*, the torpedo boats *Angelo Bassini* and *Antares* and the submarine *Mocenigo*, all sunk by USAAF aircraft, while British aircraft sank the German submarines *U755* and *U97*.[12] Meanwhile, in May and June local British and British-affiliated submarines sank 38 assorted vessels worth 60,460 tons and the German submarine *U303*.[13] Finally, on 25 May the British corvette *Vetch* sank *U414* in the Western Mediterranean, while on the night of 1/2 June the destroyers *Jervis* (British) and *Vasilissa Olga* (Greek) sank the Italian torpedo boat *Castore* off Cape Spartivento.

While these various actions and preparations were underway, the Allies also undertook numerous measures to maintain the element of surprise. Realising that it was impossible to fully shield this undertaking from Axis observation, the Allies hoped to misdirect Axis attention away from their true intentions and timing. Of the various deception measures adopted, none was more ingenious than Operation *Mincemeat*. In this, the British submarine *Seraph* set adrift the corpse of a recently deceased man dressed as a Royal Marine officer off the coast of Spain. Attached to the man's body was a briefcase containing falsified documents indicating that the build-up towards Sicily was a diversion for the real Allied objectives of Greece and Sardinia. The perpetrators of this ruse wanted the body to appear to be that of a courier who had died in a plane crash while en route to the Middle East. They speculated that the body would wash ashore and that Spanish authorities would share the documents with German agents. This is precisely what happened, and soon the highest levels of the German command were taken in by the deception. As such, the Germans sent substantial reinforcements to Greece and the Balkans, while Sicily received little more than what it already had.

For their part, the Allies finalised their planning and preparations, and on 4 July Admiral Cunningham gave the execution order for Operation *Husky*. Five days later various armadas of ships of all shapes and sizes converged in the waters around Malta and Lampedusa and proceeded north towards Sicily. The next morning the Allies announced their return to Europe with the sounds of naval gunfire and the whine of landing craft engines. As to be expected, there were some setbacks. In particular, a British airborne assault degenerated into a costly fiasco as navigational errors caused the carrying glider force to land over a wide area, including several into the sea. Yet despite this calamity, Britain's seaborne landings went remarkably well as assault forces attained their objectives against largely ineffective and disjointed Italian opposition. By the end of the day, Eighth Army was firmly ashore, and Syracuse was in British hands. The landings in the American sector experienced greater difficulties, including heavier opposition and their own airborne debacle, but here too Seventh Army was able to obtain a firm foothold in enemy territory.

Over the next several days the Allies consolidated and expanded their gains. To the east, British forces initially made steady progress against predominantly Italian formations to seize several key locations within their area of operation. Paramount amongst these was the port of Augusta, which fell to the British 5th Division on 13 July. With Syracuse and Augusta now under their control, the British moved quickly to reopen these ports for the logistical use of Eighth Army, and soon they had the capacity to discharge 5,000 and 1,600 tons of cargo per day respectively.[14] As the British forces advanced northward, they encountered increasingly stiff resistance from German units as the latter concentrated their forces on the eastern portion of the island. Soon the British were embroiled in heavy fighting, and their advance slowed to a crawl. Still, this provided an opportunity for the American Seventh Army, which had pushed out of the coastal plain after repulsing several counter-attacks during the first few days of fighting. Now with the Germans concentrated in the east, the Americans secured the western portion of the island against indifferent Italian opposition. The pinnacle of this success was the capture of Palermo on 22 July which gave the Americans their own major port for logistical support.

While this ground fighting was underway, the Allied navies played their part in supporting the operation. First and foremost, they conducted a continual series of reinforcement and replenishment convoys to expand the Allied armies and fulfil their logistical needs. In this, the Allies eventually landed a total of 407,175 men, 72,695 vehicles and 485,278 tons of stores in Sicily from the opening landings through 21 August.[15] Likewise, the navies provided valuable fire support to Allied forces operating in proximity to the coastline. The weight of these efforts was demonstrated by the fact that British warships alone answered roughly 200 calls for fire during the course of the campaign.[16] Participants in these naval bombardments ranged from battleships and monitors to destroyers and gunboats. Finally, at various times during the battle both the American and British navies conducted local amphibious operations to reduce or bypass enemy strong points.

Of course, these actions did not go unchallenged, and the Allies also had to contend with various threats arrayed against their maritime activities. As predicted, the Italian battle fleet declined to leave its protected anchorages, but there were a handful of skirmishes involving lesser warships and motor torpedo boats. These actions had no impact upon the overall operation, and losses were light on both sides. Enemy air attacks were far more troublesome, but these too failed to decisively impede *Husky's* naval component. In all, the Eastern Task Force lost nine assorted merchant ships and auxiliary vessels worth 41,509 tons to Axis air attacks while the

Operation *Husky*, the invasion of Sicily, constituted the war's largest seaborne assault in the Mediterranean theatre, ultimately encompassing 2,590 assorted ships, of which 1,614 (62.3 percent) came from British or Commonwealth sources. Pictured here is the British destroyer *Eskimo* patrolling off one of the landing areas. (Roper, F. G. (Lt), Royal Navy official photographer, public domain)

Western Task Force lost the American destroyer *Maddox*, the American minesweeper *Sentinel*, two landing ships and a 7,176-ton merchant ship. These attacks further damaged several additional ships, including the aircraft carrier *Indomitable*, the monitor *Erebus* and two destroyers.[17] While not insignificant, this tally was a far cry from the 300 vessels that Allied planners had feared might be lost to Axis aircraft. In return, the Axis paid a heavy cost for these limited successes. During the first week of Operation *Husky* Allied fighters from Malta claimed 151 Axis aircraft destroyed along with 28 probably destroyed and 74 damaged for the loss of 35 of their own number. Anti-aircraft fire and raids against airfields accounted for additional Axis losses, and on 15 July the Axis could only muster 161 aircraft to operate over Sicily compared to 481 aircraft available just four days earlier.[18] Thereafter, Axis aerial opposition fell off precipitously, and the threat largely diminished to periodic nocturnal raids.

In a similar outcome, the massive submarine assault anticipated by the Allies never materialised. At the time of the invasion, a number of German U-boats were operating off Algeria and were thus out of position to impede the initial landings. It would take several days to remedy this situation, and in the meantime, it fell upon a handful of Italian submarines to carry out the fight. Fortunately for the Allies, these Italian boats were poorly handled and/or lacked determination in their efforts. Moreover, when the U-boats finally arrived on the scene, they encountered stiff opposition from Allied countermeasures. As a result of these various factors, Axis submarines only succeeded in sinking four British merchant ships and two American landing ships out of the vast *Husky* force. Likewise, they further damaged three additional merchant ships and the British cruisers *Cleopatra* and *Newfoundland*.[19] Against this, the Allies sank or captured three German and nine Italian submarines. Of these, British warships and submarines accounted for *Flutto*, *Bronzo* (captured), *U409*, *U561*, *Nereide*, *Acciaio*, *Remo*, *Ascianghi* and *Pietro Micca* while RAF aircraft sank *Romolo* and American warships destroyed *U375* and *Argento*.

Beyond this defensive fighting, Allied forces also continued their assault against Italian and Italian-affiliated military and commercial shipping. In July and August Allied aircraft sank a total of 57 Axis merchant ships and 53 military vessels worth 74,617 and 9,626 tons respectively in the Mediterranean.[20] The RAF's portion of this total consisted of 27 vessels worth 28,800 tons sunk solely by British aircraft and 46 further vessels worth 10,061 tons sunk in conjunction with American aircraft.[21] Amongst these losses, RAF bombers sank the destroyer *Freccia* at Genoa, USAAF aircraft sank the corvette *Cicogna* and the torpedo boat *Pallade* at Messina and Naples respectively, and British and American aircraft combined to sink the German escort sloop *SG14* (ex-French *Matelot Leblanc*, 647 tons, 2 × 4.1-inch guns) off Capri. Beyond this, RAF bombers also sank the Italian submarine *H8* at Spezia. Meanwhile, during the same period British and British-affiliated submarines sank 15 merchant ships and 42 minor vessels worth a combined 53,256 tons, along with the Italian destroyer *Vincenzo Gioberti*, the torpedo boat *Lince*, the minelayer *Durazzo* and the German auxiliary escort *SG10*.[22] British losses against these successes amounted to the submarines *Parthian* and *Saracen*, which were sunk by a presumed mine strike and Italian escorts respectively.

Table 8.2 Warship Losses in the Mediterranean from 14 May 1943 through 8 September 1943

	Capital ships	Cruisers	Destroyers	Torpedo boats/ escorts/ mine vessels	Submarines
British/Allied	-	-	2	2	2
Italian/German	-	1	2	11	20

Note: Only includes warships that were a total loss. Axis submarine losses consisted of 12 Italian and eight German boats.

Returning now to the ground campaign, by the end of July the Allies controlled roughly two-thirds of Sicily while the Axis controlled the remaining third, consisting of the northeast portion of the island. By this time, Eighth Army was stalled on the Catania Plain against entrenched German positions while the Seventh Army's advance had also sputtered to a crawl once it had turned east and encountered similar stout resistance. Still, German authorities had already decided to abandon Sicily, and their current opposition was just a delaying tactic. The Germans intended to obstruct the Allies as long as possible as they executed a phased withdrawal from the island. To this end, they had already begun evacuating wounded and selected nonessential personnel. The Italians were unhappy about this decision, but given the progressive disintegration of their forces, they were in no position to overrule the strategy.

During the first week of August the Allies launched a series of hard-fought attacks that seized Regalbuto, Centuripe, Troina and Adrano, rendering the German defensive line untenable. Under pressure from both British and American forces, the Germans slowly contracted their lines, thus reducing the number of soldiers necessary to defend their condensed frontage and freeing units to withdraw to the Italian mainland. By this time an evacuation of Italian forces was already underway, and on 11 August the Germans commenced their own full-scale departure across the Strait of Messina using a small fleet of coastal steamers, ferries and barges. The Allies were slow to respond to this development and then limited their interdiction efforts to a half-hearted bombing campaign due to the large concentration of anti-aircraft and coastal guns that defended the straits. This included 40 heavy and 52 light anti-aircraft guns on the Sicilian side of the straits and 82 heavy and 60 light anti-aircraft guns defending the Italian side.[23] Against this formidable defence, the Allies eventually destroyed 15 evacuation vessels and damaged five more that were subsequently scuttled, but this failed to seriously impede the Axis withdrawal.[24] Meanwhile, unfavourable terrain, extensive demolitions and effective rear-guard actions continued to slow the oncoming Allied armies. When American and British forces finally converged on Messina on 16 and 17 August respectively, they found it empty as the remaining Axis defenders had successfully completed their evacuation.

With this, the battle for Sicily came to an end. This was a substantial victory for the Allies, but the totality of this victory was marred by the escape of sizable German and Italian forces. In all, the Germans evacuated 39,569 men, 9,605 vehicles, 47 tanks, 94 guns and some 17,000 tons of stores and ammunition during the period of 11–16 August while the Italians evacuated a further 62,000 men, 227 vehicles and 41 guns from 3 to 16 August.[25] Yet despite this feat, the Axis did not escape unscathed. German casualties for the campaign consisted of 4,325 dead, 6,663 taken prisoner and 17,944 wounded.[26] Italian losses were significantly higher with the Sixth Army giving up 137,488 prisoners as well as an estimated 2,000 dead and 5,000 wounded.[27] Of the massive number of prisoners taken, Eighth Army's portion consisted of 3,163 Germans, 40,988 Italians and 489 unclassified detainees.[28] In terms of materiel cost, the Germans lost 78 tanks and armoured cars, 287 guns and over 3,500 vehicles while the Luftwaffe and Regia Aeronautica lost 320 aircraft in fighting over Sicily with a further 1,110 left wrecked or abandoned on Sicilian airfields.[29] Against this, the Eighth and Seventh Armies suffered 11,843 and 8,781 casualties respectively while Allied naval losses for Operation *Husky* amounted to another 1,255 men.[30]

Of course, the true value of this victory went well beyond an accounting of the competing costs. To one extent or another, the Allies advanced all of their strategic objectives for the theatre. Amongst other things, Operation *Husky* prompted Hitler to halt a major offensive in Russia, Operation *Zitadelle*, so he could send reinforcements to the Mediterranean. The Germans would never again regain the initiative against the Soviets. Of even greater consequence, the invasion of Sicily set in motion events that would quickly drive Italy out of the war. Alarmed by the calamities that had befallen Italy, on the early morning of 25 July the Fascist Grand Council deposed Mussolini by a vote of 19 to seven, thus making the king the head of the armed forces. Later that day King Victor Emmanuel III had Mussolini arrested and replaced him with Marshal Pietro Badoglio. Despite public declarations that Italy would continue the war alongside its Axis partners, Badoglio immediately began covert negotiations with the Allies to enact an armistice. While the Allies welcomed this development, it presented them with a new challenge. Given the growing presence of German units in Italy, the Badoglio government was in no position to simply surrender. Allied forces would be needed to bolster Italy's break from the Axis.

Fortunately, the Allies already had several invasion plans under consideration, and they eventually decided upon two primary courses of action. First, the Eighth Army under General Montgomery would cross the Strait of Messina and land in Calabria on the toe of Italy (Operation *Baytown*). Shortly thereafter, the Anglo-American Fifth Army under the command of American Lieutenant-General Mark Clark would land some 180 miles north at Salerno (Operation *Avalanche*).[31] In terms of the former, the Strait of Messina is only about two miles wide at its narrowest point, and the Eighth Army's landing was little more than an extended river crossing. By comparison, the landings at Salerno represented a major maritime operation involving 663 vessels, including four battleships, two monitors, three aircraft carriers, four escort carriers, 16 cruisers, 76 assorted destroyers and escort destroyers, 23 fleet minesweepers, three headquarters ships, 148 landing ships and transports and 223 assorted landing craft. The Royal Navy's contribution to this force (including affiliated Allied craft) consisted of 354 vessels, including most of the heavy warships listed above.[32]

Under the overall command of Vice-Admiral Henry Hewitt, this armada was primarily divided into two assault forces. The first of these was the predominantly British Northern Attack Force under the command of Commodore G. N. Oliver, which would land the British X Corps in an area between Salerno and the River Sele. The second was the predominantly American Southern Attack Force under the command of Rear-Admiral J. L. Hall, USN, which would land the American VI Corps in the vicinity of Paestum. Force H, under the command of Vice-Admiral A. U. Willis, was tasked to provide overall cover for the operation with the battleships *Nelson*, *Rodney*, *Warspite* and *Valiant*, the fleet aircraft carriers *Illustrious* and *Formidable* and 20 destroyers. Beyond this, the British also provided the light carrier *Unicorn* and the escort carriers *Attacker*, *Battler*, *Hunter* and *Stalker* to provide fighter cover for the assault area.[33] Organised as Task Force 88 (also referred to as Force V) and under the command of Rear-Admiral Philip Vian, these light/escort carriers possessed 106 Seafire fighters, which were a naval version of the famous Spitfire land-based fighter.[34] Finally, the monitors *Roberts* and *Abercrombie*, along with several cruisers and destroyers, were earmarked to provide fire support for the landings.

Before these warships were called upon to perform these various duties, the British first had to conduct Operation *Baytown*. On 31 August the battleships *Nelson* and *Rodney* along with a cruiser and nine destroyers carried out a preparatory bombardment against targets between Reggio di Calabria and Pessaro. Two days later the British returned to conduct an even heavier bombardment with the battleships *Warspite* and *Valiant*, the monitors *Erebus*, *Roberts* and *Abercrombie* and several lesser vessels. The next morning (3 September) a force of some 300 assorted ships and craft proceeded across the Strait of Messina to land the British XIII Corps consisting of 1st Canadian and 5th British Divisions in the vicinity of Reggio and Villa San Giovanni. Supported by gunfire from the aforementioned monitors, two cruisers, two gunboats, six destroyers and army artillery firing from Sicily, the British forces seized their objectives against minimal opposition and took some 3,000 Italian prisoners.[35] In the days that followed the British feverishly brought in reinforcements as their forces advanced inland. In doing so, they encountered little enemy opposition, but struggled with logistical constraints, difficult terrain and extensive demolitions carried out by the retreating Axis forces. Despite these difficulties, the army advanced some 100 miles in five days, thus bringing it to the location where Italy's foot connected with the rest of the peninsula.

While this was underway, the strategic situation in Europe changed monumentally. Only hours after Eighth Army landed on Calabria on 3 September, General Giuseppe Castellano secretly signed an armistice agreement on behalf of the Badoglio government. Five days later while Eighth Army was advancing up the toe of Italy and Fifth Army was poised to land at Salerno, General Eisenhower made a radio broadcast from North Africa that publicly announced this armistice. The Germans had long anticipated this eventuality, and upon Eisenhower's message, they moved quickly to seize control over Italy. Unfortunately, the Italians were ill prepared to respond to this incursion. Despite the interval between the signing and announcement of the armistice, the Badoglio government had done little to disseminate this information to key military leaders or to formulate an organised response to the predictable German reaction. Making matters worse, as soon as the armistice became public,

Badoglio and King Emmanuel fled Rome to seek protection from the Allies. In doing so, they left the Italian armed forces in a state of leaderless confusion. Thus, caught by surprise and lacking definitive orders, the vast majority of Italian military units simply submitted to the Germans and allowed themselves to be disarmed without offering resistance.

The only major exception to this was the Regia Marina. A key provision in the armistice agreement was the surrender of the Italian fleet. Despite much internal dissension, most Italian naval commanders complied with this order, and within hours a steady stream of warships and other vessels departed La Spezia, Taranto and other Italian ports to rendezvous with the British. Not surprisingly, the Germans reacted violently to this mass exodus. Of particular consequence, on the afternoon of 9 September German aircraft armed with FX-1400 glider-bombs attacked an Italian battle squadron in the Gulf of Asinara. The FX-1400 was an early version of a smart bomb that could be dropped and guided to target using radio control from a parent aircraft. During this attack the Germans succeeded in hitting the battleship *Roma* with two of these recently acquired weapons. Possessing a 710-pound warhead, the second bomb hit abreast of *Roma*'s 'B' turret and detonated a main powder magazine. The resulting explosion ripped the modern battleship apart causing it to quickly sink, with the loss of 1,253 crewmen and some 200 naval staff who were also onboard.

While this was the most spectacular calamity relating to Italy's naval exodus, it was by no means the only mishap. Throughout this day and in the days that followed, German forces turned upon their former Italian partners with deadly efficiency. In a variety of actions German artillery, mines, aircraft and E-boats sank the destroyers *Antonio da Noli*, *Ugolino Vivaldi* and *Quintino Sella*; the torpedo boats *Giuseppe Sirtori*, *Francesco Stocco* and *Enrico Cosenz*; the minelayer *Pelagosa* and the corvette *Berenice*. Numerous other Italian warships that were unable to get away scuttled themselves to avoid German capture or proceeded to Spain to seek internment. In terms of the latter, the light cruiser *Attilo Regolo*, three destroyers and one torpedo boat eventually arrived at the Balearic Islands where they were interned by the Spanish, while two further torpedo boats scuttled themselves upon arriving in Spanish waters. Nor were these actions entirely one-sided as Italian motor torpedo boats and shore fire sank the German torpedo boat *TA11* (ex-French *L'Iphigénie*, 610 tons, 2 × 3.9-inch guns) off Piombino.

Yet despite these various calamities, most of the Italian battle fleet succeeded in making it to Malta or other Allied ports. By 21 September the Allies had taken possession of the battleships *Vittorio Veneto*, *Italia* (ex-*Littorio*), *Giulio Cesare*, *Andrea Doria* and *Caio Duilio*, eight cruisers, 33 destroyers/torpedo boats, 20 assorted escorts, 34 fleet submarines and 33 miscellaneous vessels.[36] Eventually, the five warships interned by Spain were also handed over to the Allies, thus completing the totality of the Regia Marina's dictated capitulation. Meanwhile, 101 Italian merchant ships worth 183,591 tons and 13 minor craft of unknown tonnage also surrendered to the Allies, while 168 commercial vessels worth 76,298 tons were scuttled.[37] These developments prompted Admiral Cunningham to send the following message to the Admiralty on 11 September: 'Be pleased to inform their Lordships that the Italian Battle Fleet now lies at anchor under the guns of the fortress of Malta.'[38]

With this, a major chapter in Britain's maritime war came to an end. After nearly 39 months of conflict, the Regia Marina, which had been the world's fifth largest navy at the beginning of the war, ceased to exist as a hostile combatant. This represented a triumph reminiscent of the surrender of the German High Seas Fleet in 1918. When viewed in a global context, the three major naval powers that had confronted Britain and the Allies were now reduced to two. A number of factors contributed to this victory, including actions taken on land, sea and in the air. Likewise, a number of nations participated in bringing about this outcome. Still, without diminishing the contributions of any other nation, Britain was clearly the main architect of this victory. For over two years the British had operated alone in the Mediterranean and Middle East against the Italians and Germans. During this time the British had repeatedly triumphed over all branches of the Italian military, and it was only the presence of the Germans that prolonged the conflict. In recent months American and French forces had joined the struggle in a meaningful way, but even then, Britain remained the dominant partner within the theatre. When

The Italian battleship *Andrea Doria* surrendering at Malta on 9 September 1943. With the acceptance of the armistice agreement, the Italians eventually surrendered 108 principal warships to the Allies, constituting a significant triumph for the Royal Navy. (U.S. Navy, public domain)

considering these factors and the fact that British forces accounted for 78 percent of the principal Italian naval losses sustained prior to the armistice (including the Italian submarine *Velella*, which was sunk by the British submarine *Shakespeare* on 7 September), it is reasonable to assign primary credit for this great accomplishment to the British.

Of course, this development was not an end in itself. On the morning of 9 September, the Allies launched Operation *Avalanche*. Omitting a preliminary bombardment in order to attain the element of surprise, the Northern Attack Force landed the British 46th and 56th Divisions along with five commando/ranger battalions, while the Southern Attack Force landed the American 36th Division in their designated areas. These forces immediately encountered stiff resistance from the German 16th Panzer Division, and heavy fighting ensued. With the assistance of naval gunfire, the Allies eventually prevailed, and by the evening the Allies had captured or advanced to the vicinity of most of their objectives. Nevertheless, the Allied beachhead was precariously held, and both sides spent the next few days trying to build-up and consolidate their positions. For the Allies, this included the landing of the American 45th Division, while the Germans rushed five divisions into the area.

On the 12th and 13th, the Germans launched a series of heavy counter-attacks against both the British and American sectors that threatened to destroy Fifth

Table 8.3 Italian Warship Losses from 10 June 1940 through 8 September 1943 in all Theatres

	Sunk through British action	Sunk partially through British action	Sunk by American or other Allied forces	Sunk by accidental or unknown causes	Total
Battleships	1	-	-	-	1
Heavy cruisers	5	-	1	-	6
Light cruisers	6	-	2	-	8
Destroyers	34	-	4	5	43
Torpedo boats/escort destroyers/sloops	27	1	9	4	41
Corvettes	3	-	1	-	4
Minelayers	2	-	-	-	2
Fleet minesweepers	2	1	2	-	5
Submarines	69	1	6	8	84
Total	149	3	25	17	194

Note: This includes Italian submarines and warships lost in the Atlantic and Red Sea.

Army's tentative hold on the Salerno beachhead. The Americans were particularly hard pressed as both of their divisions gave ground thus allowing the Germans to advance to within two miles of the beach. On the 14th General Clark considered re-embarking VI Corps, but upon advice from supporting naval authorities, instead opted to fight on. Fortunately for him, the tide of battle was already shifting in his favour as Allied reinforcements continued to arrive. In particular, elements of the American 82nd Airborne and British 7th Armoured Divisions arrived to bolster his hard-pressed defenders. Perhaps even more important, Allied aircraft and warships pounded German positions around Salerno in an unrelenting barrage of bombs and shellfire. On the 15th the battleships *Warspite* and *Valiant* arrived on the scene to add their massive guns to this effort. While German attacks continued through the 16th, they were unable to make meaningful progress against this immense weight of fire, and the crisis confronting Fifth Army gradually abated.

As already alluded to, the Allied navies played an indispensable role in bringing about this outcome. Not only did they deliver the vast majority of Allied reinforcements and supplies, but throughout the operation British and American warships provided essential fire support for the ground forces, eventually expending some 23,000 shells (4-inch or greater).[39] This naval gunfire was key in helping the Allies prevail during their initial landings and then was paramount in repulsing many of the subsequent counter-attacks that threatened the beachhead. During the latter part of this battle Allied warships were almost in continuous action as they engaged German positions and troop concentrations. Meanwhile, in the airspace above Salerno, Seafires from Admiral Vian's Task Force 88 joined fighters from Sicily to provide a continuous aerial umbrella over the landing area. During the course of four days these Seafires flew 713 sorties, during which they turned back numerous Luftwaffe attacks and shot down two enemy aircraft with four others damaged. Against this, no Seafires were lost in combat, but a staggering 42 were lost or written off due to deck landing and other operational accidents.[40]

Not surprisingly, these actions did not go without incident. Throughout this period the Luftwaffe launched a number of hit and run raids against Allied shipping, including some using FX-1400 glider-bombs. Most of these attacks were driven off or repulsed by Allied defences, but a handful of aircraft got through to inflict damage upon the assault forces. On 11 September a FX-1400 hit and damaged the American light cruiser *Savannah* so severely that it had to be withdrawn from the combat area. Two days later the British light cruiser *Uganda* sustained a similar hit and also had to withdraw. Then on the 16th German bombers scored their biggest success yet when a FX-1400 hit the veteran battleship *Warspite* and caused extensive damage, including the loss of all power and massive flooding. With the aid of numerous support vessels, the British towed the severely damaged battleship to Malta for emergency repairs. After additional repairs in Gibraltar and Britain, *Warspite* returned to service in early 1944, but did so without its 'X' turret, which remained inoperable for the rest of the war. In other actions around Salerno, German air and naval units along with ground fire sank the American destroyer *Rowan*, the American minesweeper *Skill*, the hospital ship *Newfoundland*, two American merchant ships, a tug and 20 assorted landing craft, while a further 18 vessels were damaged, excluding those mentioned above.[41]

While this fighting was underway, various related actions took place within the region. First, Eighth Army continued its advance through southern Italy against light German resistance. As part of this effort, the British conducted an improvised landing to seize the Italian port and naval base at Taranto. Under the designation of Operation *Slapstick*, a British squadron consisting of the cruisers *Aurora*, *Penelope*, *Sirius*, *Dido* and *Boise* (American) and the fast minelayer *Abdiel*, transported the British 1st Airborne Division from Bizerte to Taranto. Arriving there on the 9th, the British seized the valuable port and its vital facilities intact against negligible opposition. The only notable mishap occurred that evening when *Abdiel* struck a

A regular benefit to the Allied ground forces was the ample application of naval gunfire support. During the Mediterranean conflict British warships, such as *Warspite* pictured here, conducted hundreds of fire support missions that expended tens of thousands of shells against Axis shore targets. (Coote, R. G. G. (Lt), Royal Navy official photographer, public domain)

mine and sank with the loss of 48 naval and 120 army personnel aboard. From there, British forces proceeded eastward and northward to capture the lesser ports of Brindisi and Bari on the Adriatic coast. Then with the arrival of follow-up forces, Eighth Army conducted a two-pronged advance with V Corps pushing towards the Foggia Plain and the east coast of Italy while XIII Corps moved westward.

In terms of the latter, on 16 September Eighth Army units completed a 300-mile trek through difficult terrain to make contact with elements of the American 36th Division at Vallo, south of the embattled Salerno beachhead. By this time the Germans had already determined that their Salerno offensive had lost its momentum, and the arrival of Eighth Army units only served to reinforce this view. Accordingly, the next day the Germans began a deliberate withdrawal to the north, thus ceding the battlefield to Fifth Army. British losses at Salerno consisted of 725 dead, 1,800 missing and 2,734 wounded, while the Americans suffered a further 3,500 casualties. For their part, the Germans lost 840 dead, 630 missing and 2,002 wounded along with 70 tanks and 21 assault guns.[42] Over the next several days the Allies pushed steadily northward, and on 1 October British X Corps captured the major port city of Naples, thus gaining the ultimate prize associated with the Salerno landings. Despite extensive demolitions and the presence of hundreds of sunk and scuttled vessels, the Allies quickly restored Naples to a functioning port that was capable of discharging over 5,000 tons of cargo per day by 18 October. In turn, the Allies landed 155,134 tons of cargo and 37,013 vehicles in Naples during October alone.[43]

This turn of events and Eighth Army's continued advance, which included a well-executed amphibious assault that seized the Adriatic port of Termoli, gave the Allies control over the southern third of Italy. With this, they also seized several area airfields containing 574 German and 523 Italian aircraft left abandoned in various states of disrepair from 3 September through 15 October.[44] Meanwhile, the Germans also abandoned Sardinia and Corsica, thus ceding these strategically important islands to the Allies. In terms of the larger geopolitical situation, on 13 October the exiled Badoglio government declared war on Germany thus technically aligning Italy with the Allies. However, this was little more than a gesture since the Italian armed forces were largely disbanded and the Germans firmly controlled the northern two-thirds of the country. Complicating matters, in September the Germans rescued Mussolini from confinement at Gran Sasso in the Apennine Mountains and reinstated him as the leader of the newly formed Italian Social Republic in northern Italy. This puppet government was entirely subservient to the Germans, and few Italians joined the Fascist military forces operating under its authority. Thus, Italy became an occupied country with the Allies and Germans battling for its control, and small contingents of Italians aligned to both sides but doing very little actual fighting.

Meanwhile, given the surrender of the Italian fleet, one might reasonably surmise that the maritime war in the Mediterranean was over, but this was not the case. While the Regia Marina was now out of the picture, the Luftwaffe and

Kriegsmarine continued the struggle. The latter was able to do this using captured Italian, French and Yugoslav warships as well as the handful of U-boats stationed in the Mediterranean. Despite the exodus of the major units of the Italian fleet, the Germans were able to seize control over the heavy cruisers *Bolzano* and *Gorizia*, the light cruiser *Taranto*, seven destroyers, three escort destroyers, 15 torpedo boats, 11 submarines, seven corvettes and scores of other vessels. The vast majority of these were unserviceable, having been scuttled or under repair at the time of their capture. Beyond this, the Germans also seized large numbers of additional vessels at various stages of construction, including the battleship *Impero*, the aircraft carriers *Sparviero* and *Aquila*, six light cruisers and dozens of assorted destroyers, torpedo boats, submarines and corvettes.[45]

The Kriegsmarine immediately began efforts to salvage and restore these vessels to operational status. Ignoring the larger combatants and the bulk of the seized Italian submarines, the Germans focused their recovery efforts on the lesser surface warships. Of these, the Germans eventually pressed some three dozen destroyers, torpedo boats and corvettes, along with large numbers of minor and auxiliary craft, into active service. The Germans renamed these captured vessels with the destroyers and torpedo boats receiving a TA (torpedo boat) designation, the corvettes receiving a UJ (sub-chaser) designation and certain other vessels receiving a SG (fast escort) designation. Staffing these warships with German crews, the Kriegsmarine quickly established itself as a regional presence in the coastal waters off Southern Europe. This was critical since the Germans depended upon maritime commerce to support many of their operational and logistical needs along the coasts of Italy, southern France and within the Balkans. With the Regia Marina gone and the Allies pressing ever closer, the Germans now had to defend these vital areas on their own.

The Aegean was the first area where this was tested. With the collapse of Italy, the British sought to capitalise upon the many potential benefits that an incursion into the Aegean might present. Realising that Italian garrisons constituted the sole or primary occupation forces on most Aegean islands, the British hoped to exploit the void that would likely occur if and when these forces abandoned the Axis cause. Of particular interest to the British was the island of Rhodes, which possessed a good harbour and three airfields that would allow the Allies to dominate the rest of the Aegean and stage bombing raids against Greece, Romania and Bulgaria. Even more tantalising, the British hoped that a strong Allied presence in the area might prompt Turkey to enter the war against Germany. Unfortunately, given the operations already underway in Italy and the need to support demands in other theatres, the Allies had limited resources left to pursue this strategy. Adding to this problem, American authorities made it clear they would lend little support to this undertaking, thus forcing the British to go it alone. Finally, and perhaps most decisively, Rhodes possessed a 7,500-man German garrison that quickly subdued its larger Italian counterpart when news of the Italian armistice arrived. Considering these factors, the British reluctantly realised that an imminent seizure of Rhodes was impractical.

Despite this admission, the British were loath to abandon their overall strategic objective. Realising that Rhodes was temporarily unattainable, the British instead opted to seize a number of smaller islands in the Dodecanese chain, including Leros, Kos and Samos. As such, during September the British conducted a series of operations using destroyers and various coastal craft to land small contingents of commandos and other related troops on these islands. Once ashore, these forces contacted the local Italian garrisons to facilitate their support against the Germans. In most cases, they found the Italians willing to cooperate, but lacking in resolve and poorly equipped. While this was underway, British aircraft and destroyers carried out a number of anti-shipping sweeps in the adjacent waters. On 17 September British Beaufighters sank a 700-ton vessel south of Naxos. The next day the destroyers *Faulknor*, *Eclipse* and *Vasilissa Olga* (Greek) encountered a small German convoy off Stampalia and sank the merchant ships *Pluto* and *Paula* (3,830 and 3,754 tons respectively) and the escorting sub-chaser *UJ2104*. Then on the 23rd *Eclipse* intercepted and sank the 2,428-ton merchant ship *Donizetti* while driving the defending German torpedo boat *TA10* (ex-French *La Pomone*, 610 tons, 2 × 3.9-inch guns) aground off Rhodes where it was destroyed two days later by Beaufighters.

The Germans were quick to respond to these incursions. Citing the political repercussions that Allied control of the Aegean would likely bring to the Balkans, Hitler personally overruled the advice of his military commanders and ordered a counter-attack. A key to doing this was attaining sufficient Luftwaffe strength to neutralise Britain's naval superiority in the area. At the beginning of September, the Luftwaffe had 215 combat aircraft in the region, of which none were long-range bombers. By bringing in reinforcements from Russia, Vienna and France, the Germans were able to increase this strength to 362 aircraft by the end of the month. Included in this number were some 130 twin-engine bombers and 90 Stuka dive-bombers. By comparison, the British could only muster some 280 aircraft to counter this threat. Even more importantly, the Germans possessed two major airfields on Rhodes and two more on Crete that were only 70 and 150 miles from Kos, while the closest British airfields at Cypress and Libya were some 350–370 miles away. The British did possess a minor airfield on Kos itself, but this was too small to handle more than a handful of aircraft. Thus, despite the overall air superiority the Allies enjoyed within the theatre, the Germans were able to attain local air superiority in the Aegean.

It didn't take long for the Germans to put this advantage to good use. On 26 September German aircraft attacked and sank the British destroyer *Intrepid* and the Greek destroyer *Vasilissa Olga* in Leros harbour. During follow-up attacks over the next nine days these aircraft returned to Leros and sank two Italian warships, the destroyer *Euro* and the minelayer *Legnano*, which had gone over to the Allies.

Meanwhile, at the beginning of October the Germans dispatched four convoys from Crete, Piraeus and Naxos carrying invasion forces for the recapture of Kos. On 2 October British air reconnaissance located some of these vessels off Paros and Naxos, but British destroyers were out of position to intervene, while two submarines that were in the area failed to make contact. The next morning these convoys, consisting of a combined five merchant ships, two minelayers and several coastal and auxiliary vessels, converged upon Kos and began landing operations. Supported by aircraft and airborne paratroopers, the Germans eventually landed some 4,000 men along with artillery and armoured cars to confront the lightly armed British/Italian garrison defending Kos. Under these conditions, it only took two days before resistance collapsed, and 1,388 British and 3,145 Italian prisoners went into German captivity.[46]

With the fall of Kos, the British abandoned any thoughts of invading Rhodes, but they still resolved to retain Leros and Samos if possible. The British already had naval reinforcements coming into the area, and over the next few weeks they increased their presence within the Aegean. On 7 October the British light cruisers *Sirius* and *Penelope* and two destroyers intercepted a German troop convoy consisting of the 5,216-ton merchant ship *Olympos*, the sub-chaser *UJ2111* and six naval ferry barges off Levita, and sank every vessel except a single barge. Some 400 Germans perished in this encounter while 80 more were taken prisoner. The next day the British submarine *Unruly* sank the minelayer *Bulgaria*, resulting in the deaths of another 200 Germans. A week later the submarine *Torbay* and the destroyers *Jervis*, *Penn*, *Hursley* and *Miaoulis* (Greek) combined to sink another German convoy consisting of the merchant ships *Kari* and *Trapani* (1,925 and 1,855 tons respectively) and the corvette *UJ2109*.[47] In other encounters during this period British aircraft, submarines and warships sank several additional vessels in the area, including the merchant ships *Sinfra*, *Marguerite*, *Tarquinia* and *Ingeborg* worth 4,470, 747, 749 and 1,160 tons respectively. Finally, in related actions, Allied air and naval units destroyed or captured seven out of nine German merchant ships attempting to breakout from the Adriatic to support operations in the Aegean.

Yet, despite these many successes, the situation in the Aegean continued to deteriorate. Of particular consequence was the Luftwaffe's growing dominance in the area. On 9 October German aircraft attacked British warships in the Scarpanto Strait sinking the destroyer *Panther* and damaging the anti-aircraft cruiser *Carlisle* so badly that it became a total loss. In other attacks throughout this period German aircraft destroyed a number of minor vessels and damaged several warships, including the cruisers *Penelope*, *Sirus* and *Aurora*. Meanwhile, mines also took a toll on the hard-pressed British forces when the destroyers *Adrias* (Greek), *Hurworth* and *Eclipse* ran onto a recently laid field east of Kalymnos, resulting in the loss of the latter two vessels while the former was severely damaged. When combined together, these calamities reduced the Royal Navy's ability to support Leros and Samos. Although reinforcements and supplies continued to get through on a limited basis, the British garrisons found themselves increasingly isolated and under regular bombardment from Luftwaffe aircraft.

On 12 November German forces landed by sea and air on Leros thus beginning the final stage of the battle. Once again, British destroyers were out of position to impede this assault, and the Germans were able to seize key positions that cut the island in two. Over the next few days the British/Italian garrison doggedly resisted the German invaders while British warships made regular sweeps around the island to provide what assistance they could. In one case British destroyers brought in 500 reinforcements from Samos and destroyed three troop-laden landing craft, but this proved to be the highlight of their activities. In general, the navy was unable to seriously impede the German build-up on Leros, and it suffered the loss of the escort destroyer *Dulverton* to a Luftwaffe glider-bomb in return. On 16 November the garrison on Leros surrendered, giving up another 3,200 British and 5,350 Italian prisoners.[48] Following this, the British evacuated their remaining forces from Samos and Casteloriso, and the fighting in the Aegean came to an end.

Thus concluded another unsuccessful British adventure in these waters. The first had been in 1941 with the battle for Crete, and now the British suffered a similar reversal two and a half years later. British losses for this most recent struggle included the cruiser *Carlisle* damaged beyond repair, four destroyers (one Greek), two escort destroyers and 10 minor vessels sunk and three other cruisers and four destroyers damaged. Beyond this, army casualties amounted to some 4,800 men, mostly taken prisoner, while the RAF lost 115 aircraft in support of the undertaking.[49] If there was a silver lining in the debacle, it was that the Germans also suffered heavy losses during the three-month campaign. This included some 35,000 tons of shipping and 21 military vessels that were sunk. Most of the latter were minor craft, but this included a torpedo boat, a corvette and a minelayer. German personnel losses were much harder to calculate, but included 1,184 army casualties suffered on Kos and Leros and at least a similar number of men lost at sea. Finally, the Luftwaffe did not escape the fighting unscathed, losing 156 aircraft during the campaign.[50]

With the end of operations in the Aegean, all eyes returned to Italy, which was now the focal point of the theatre. After the capture of Naples, the Allies continued their northward push up the Italian peninsula with Eighth Army on the right and Fifth Army on the left. This advance quickly slowed as the Allies encountered harsh terrain, deteriorating weather and increasingly stiff resistance. In terms of the latter, the Allies were victims of their own success since a key tenet in their Mediterranean strategy was to attract and tie down German units, thus making them unavailable for service in Russia or France. By early October 1943 the Germans had 17 divisions stationed in Italy with another 13 located in the Balkans.[51] While this development satisfied an Allied strategic objective, it made progress in Italy very difficult. The onset of winter weather only served to make this problem worse, and by year's end the competing battle lines had largely stabilised along the Sangro and Garigliano Rivers, roughly a third of the way between Naples and Rome.

Meanwhile, the related maritime conflict continued unabated. Notwithstanding the substantial changes that had occurred within the theatre over the past few months, the fundamentals of this struggle remained the same as both sides sought to sustain their own maritime lines of communication while denying the same to the other. For the Allies, the demise of the Regia Marina and the occupation of Sicily, Sardinia, Corsica and the southern third of Italy secured a second major objective of the Allied strategy in that it opened the Mediterranean to large-scale convoy traffic. From September through December 1943 an average of 800 Allied ships traversed the Mediterranean in convoys each month, and in 1944 this number would increase to 1,100–1,200.[52] Some of these various convoys passed through the Mediterranean while others terminated in Italy and the surrounding area to support local operations. Despite the many geographical and situational factors now favouring the Allies, these endeavours still involved a degree of danger that could not be ignored. In particular, German aircraft operating out of southern France and Crete represented a constant threat that was made worse by the handful of U-boats still present within the theatre.

The result of these various dangers was the loss of 80 Allied and neutral merchant ships worth 397,710 tons within the Mediterranean during the last seven months of 1943 (including vessels already listed as sunk during operations off Sicily and Italy). Of these, aircraft accounted for the majority with 41 ships worth 225,448 tons sunk by this means. U-boats were the next deadliest antagonist accounting for 31 vessels worth 136,071 tons.[53] In addition to these merchant casualties and beyond the warship losses previously described, German aircraft and submarines also sank the American destroyers *Buck*, *Bristol* and *Beatty*, the British escort destroyers *Puckeridge*, *Tynedale* and *Holcombe* and the British minesweeper *Hythe* within the Mediterranean during this period. Meanwhile, local mines claimed the British destroyer *Quail* and the British minesweepers *Cromarty*, *Hebe*, *Felixstowe* and *Clacton*. While these losses were not insignificant, they were not prohibitive either considering the scale of Allied shipping movements within the region. For instance, in December no fewer than 1,012 Allied merchant ships passed through the Mediterranean, and by year's end convoy traffic in the Mediterranean exceeded that concurrently underway in the North Atlantic.[54]

Moreover, the Germans suffered some losses of their own in attaining these successes. In addition to the previously mentioned seven U-boats that were sunk during the run-up to and conduct of Operation *Husky*, the Germans lost a further six U-boats in the Mediterranean from August through December. Of these, British aircraft and warships sank *U458*, *U617*, *U431* and *U340*, while American warships sank *U73* and British and American assets combined to sink *U593*. These losses outstripped the trickle of new U-boats entering the Mediterranean, and by the end of December German strength within the theatre numbered just 13 U-boats. Adding to this, on 24 November USAAF bombers conducted a heavy bombing raid on Toulon that wrought havoc upon the local U-boat base and damaged five U-boats so severely that they would be out of service for several weeks. The raid further destroyed several non-operational French warships that were under German control, but this was of secondary importance.

While these defensive actions were underway, the Allies continued their own assault against German shipping in the waters off Southern Europe (including operations already discussed in the Aegean). In a departure from recent trends, naval assets attained the highest degree of success in this effort, accounting for 48 assorted commercial vessels worth 107,228 tons that were sunk from September through December.[55] Of these, British and Allied surface warships sank 15 vessels worth 25,967 tons, while British and British-affiliated submarines accounted for the rest.[56] Against the latter, the British lost the submarines *Katsonis* (Greek), *Usurper*, *Trooper* and *Simoon* to mines and German escort vessels. Meanwhile, during the same period Allied aircraft sank 32 merchant ships worth 49,522 tons within the Mediterranean. This tally included 11 vessels worth 14,237 tons that were sunk by British aircraft and two further vessels worth 12,113 tons that were sunk by British and American aircraft combined. Finally, during the last four months of the year mines sank an additional 13 merchant ships worth 12,139 tons within these waters.[57]

When expanding the period to the beginning of June and including losses attained from all causes, including vessels that were scuttled or surrendered to the Allies, the total number of Axis merchant ships lost within the Mediterranean during the last seven months of 1943 increased to a staggering 748 vessels worth 875,792 tons.[58] This represented a nearly tenfold increase in the number of vessels and more than twice the tonnage of the comparable Allied shipping losses sustained during the same seven-month period. Making matters worse from a German point of view, while the Allies were able to easily replace their losses due to an expanding shipping pool from new construction, the Germans could not. To this point, in 1943 American shipyards produced a staggering 1,949 merchant ships worth some 13 million tons, while British shipyards added a further 1.2 million tons to this total.[59] By comparison, shipbuilding activity in Southern Europe had virtually ground to a halt, and the Germans had minimal means to attain additional shipping beyond what they already possessed. As such, the local German merchant fleet was a wasting asset that could not be replaced. The Germans compensated for this by increasingly using ferry barges and other minor craft to fulfil their logistical needs, but these had limited capacity and were also susceptible to wasting attrition.

Returning now to the Allies' anti-shipping effort, during the last four months of 1943 the Allies also sank a total of 36 military vessels worth 16,917 tons plus 16 additional vessels of unknown tonnage.[60] The vast majority of these were minor craft or auxiliary vessels, but this included a handful of purpose-built warships. Already mentioned were *TA10* and *UJ2109* that were sunk by British warships in the Aegean in September and October. Then in November American bombers sank the torpedo boat *TA12* (ex-French *Baliste*, 610 tons, 2 × 3.9-inch guns) at Toulon. Finally, on 22 December the British motor torpedo boats *MTB276* and *MTB298* sank the old light cruiser *Niobe* off Silba Island in the Adriatic. *Niobe* had a long and varied history. Built as a German light cruiser before World War I, *Niobe* was sold to the Yugoslav navy in 1925 and renamed *Dalmacija*. With the invasion of Yugoslavia in 1941, *Dalmacija* came under Italian control and was renamed *Cattaro*. Then with the German occupation of Italy in September 1943, *Cattaro* reverted back to German control and was returned to its original name. Displacing 2,360 tons and armed with six 3.3-inch guns, *Niobe* lacked the size and armament of a modern light cruiser, but still constituted a formidable escort vessel within the confined waters of the Adriatic. As such, its demise constituted a blow to the local German forces.

Beyond that, the destruction of *Niobe* also reflected some of the changes that characterised the situation in the Mediterranean by the end of 1943. A year prior the Axis had controlled all of Southern Europe and a sizable portion of North Africa, with command of the central Mediterranean being a matter of open contention. During that time a substantial naval conflict was underway in which Italian maritime forces played the predominant role in the Axis order of battle. Likewise, German military officials considered the entire Mediterranean theatre to be a secondary concern. One year later, the Allies controlled all of North Africa, along with Pantellaria, Lampedusa, Sicily, Sardinia, Corsica and the southern third of the Italian peninsula. Italy was now out of the war, and the bulk of the Italian fleet rested under Allied custody. Meanwhile, the vast expanse of the Mediterranean Sea was largely under Allied control while the Germans were confined to the coastal waters of Southern Europe. To this end, the Mediterranean theatre had become a major German military front, but they had to depend upon captured Italian and Allied ships and other improvised vessels to carry out maritime operations. To be sure, the fighting would continue, but it would do so on a reduced scale. The prospect for large fleet actions was now over, and the two sides settled into a coastal conflict where lesser vessels, aircraft and submarines reigned supreme.

CHAPTER 9

Supporting the Southern Flank

In November 1943 the senior leadership of the principal Allied nations conducted two consecutive conferences to formalise their war strategy for the upcoming year. The first occurred from the 22nd through the 26th at Cairo, with Prime Minister Churchill, President Roosevelt, China's Generalissimo Chiang Kai-shek and their respective military chiefs and advisors in attendance. The second occurred two days later in Tehran where a Soviet contingent led by General Secretary Joseph Stalin joined the British and American delegations in a three-day conference. By the end of these proceedings the Allies had agreed upon a number of key issues. Paramount amongst these, they agreed that the long-awaited invasion of northern France, designated Operation *Overlord*, would take place in May and have priority over all other Allied undertakings. They further resolved that a follow-up invasion of southern France would occur sometime thereafter as soon as sufficient landing craft became available to do so. For their part, the Soviets consented to launch a spring offensive that would coincide with the timing of Operation *Overlord*. Finally, the Allies agreed to continue the offensive in the Mediterranean with the forces not allocated for service in France and Northwest Europe. In doing so, they set the capture of Rome as their immediate objective with subsequent operations to be determined based upon conditions and resources.

The securing of this latter objective represented a major advancement of Britain's strategic position, but it soon became clear that the capture of Rome would be no easy task. Following the capture of Naples in early October, the Allied advance had precipitously slowed until it ground to a halt along a line roughly corresponding with the Sangro and Garigliano Rivers. The reasons for this abrupt deceleration included harsh terrain, the onset of winter weather and increasingly stiff German opposition. In terms of the former, the Allies found their line of advance impeded by a continuous chain of mountains and intersecting rivers. This situation was only made worse by cold and rainy weather that swelled the rivers and turned much of the landscape into a muddy morass. Meanwhile, by December the Germans had 18 divisions present in Italy with a similar number located in the Balkans and southern

France. This disposition actually constituted more divisions than the Allies had within the theatre, and this disparity was only likely to get worse as the Allies had already earmarked seven divisions to deploy to Britain for use in Operation *Overlord*.[1]

Accompanying these departing divisions were many of the key leaders that had honed their skills and provided valuable service within the region. Some of these leaders had already departed while others would soon follow. One of the first to go was Admiral Andrew Cunningham, the long-serving commander of the Mediterranean Fleet, who relinquished this position in October to assume the role of First Sea Lord. Replacing him was Admiral John Cunningham. A couple of months later American General Dwight Eisenhower departed the theatre to become the Supreme Allied Commander for Operation *Overlord*, and British General Henry Maitland Wilson replaced him as the Supreme Allied Commander in the Mediterranean. Other senior Allied leaders that departed or would soon depart the theatre to assume postings for the upcoming invasion of France included American Generals George Patton and Omar Bradley, British General Bernard Montgomery, British Admirals Bertram Ramsay and Philip Vian, and British Air Marshals Arthur Tedder and Arthur Coningham.

Despite these departures and other adversities, the Allies were determined to retain the initiative. In this, they had some advantages of their own to exploit. Paramount amongst these were firepower, mechanisation and mobility. In terms of the former, the Allies enjoyed a significant supremacy in air power and lesser ascendancy in both artillery and armour support. The Allies also benefited from their substantial naval power that offered them the ability to bypass ground obstacles and prohibitive terrain and threaten the entire length of the Italian coastline. Striving to exploit these advantages, in November Allied authorities devised a plan to launch a coordinated offensive utilising both Allied armies in Italy. The first stage of this offensive called for the British Eighth Army to launch an attack across the Sangro River to draw German reserves to the Adriatic front. The Anglo-American-Franco Fifth Army would then attack to breach the German defences along the Bernhardt Line and advance into the Liri and Sacco valleys. Once this latter attack attained sufficient progress, the Allies would then launch a seaborne flanking movement by landing a division-sized force near the Tyrrhenian coastal town of Anzio some 35 miles south of Rome. In carrying out this seaborne assault, which was designated Operation *Shingle*, the Allies hoped to further hasten a German withdrawal that would lead to their abandonment of Rome.

On the night of 19/20 November Eighth Army made its crossing of the Sangro River. Unfortunately, heavy rain and flooding delayed the army's build-up for several days. Finally, on the 28th the 8th Indian Division seized Mozzagrogna, and the British were able to pass tanks along a track the Germans had thought impassable. Over the next few days, the British 78th and 2nd New Zealand Divisions launched attacks that rolled up the German defences and severely mauled the German 65th Infantry Division, which gave up over 1,000 prisoners during the fighting. However, when the British advanced against the next river line, the Moro, they encountered the German 90th Panzer Grenadier and 1st Parachute Divisions, and progress became more difficult. This was particularly true at Ortona where it took the 1st Canadian Division nearly three weeks of heavy fighting to secure the important port town. By the end of December, the British had advanced 14 miles, but mounting casualties, diminishing ammunition stocks and the resumption of rain compelled the British to halt their offensive. In terms of cost, Eighth Army suffered 6,453 casualties during the fighting in December. Against this, German casualties, including those suffered on the Fifth Army's front, numbered 13,362 for the month.[2] This included large numbers of prisoners, which brought the total tally of German prisoners taken in Italy from 3 September through 31 December 1943 to 7,790, of which 4,684 were taken by Eighth Army or the British contingent in Fifth Army.[3]

While this fighting was underway, Fifth Army launched its portion of the coordinated offensive. On 6 December the British 46th and 56th Divisions captured Monte Camino, although it took another four days to clear the mountain's western slope. Meanwhile, the American 36th Division and First Special Service Force, a joint American-Canadian commando unit, launched assaults to seize Monte Sammucro and Monte la Remetanea. These attacks made initial headway, but soon slowed against increased German resistance. Heavy fighting continued along the whole front for several days, but it wasn't until the 2nd (French) Moroccan Division joined the battle that the Allies finally made meaningful progress. However, by this time it was too late. Behind schedule and plagued by the same logistical and weather conditions impacting Eighth Army, the Allied timetable for implementing Operation *Shingle* was now hopelessly compromised, and on 18 December Lieutenant-General Mark Clark, the Fifth Army commander, recommended its cancellation. Four days later, General Eisenhower, who had yet to leave for Britain, concurred, and Fifth Army's offensive slowly ground to a halt.

The failure to break through the German defences came as an obvious disappointment to the Allies, but this was particularly true for Winston Churchill, who viewed the growing stalemate in Italy with great consternation. Unwilling to accept this static situation, on 25 December Churchill chaired a conference in Tunis to devise strategies to regain the initiative. Almost immediately, the attendees focused their energies on revising the plan for Operation *Shingle*. Realising that if Fifth Army could not reach Anzio quick enough to support the proposed division-sized landing force, the landing force would have to be substantially increased to give it greater capacity to operate independently. The goal for this increased force would be to seize the Alban Hills, which were located some 20 miles inland from Anzio. By seizing these hills, the Allies would put themselves in an excellent position to threaten Rome while simultaneously severing key logistical routes that the Germans used to support their forces confronting the Fifth Army. In doing so, the Allies hoped to compel the Germans to abandon their southern defences along what was now known as the Gustav Line. Short of that happening, the Allies hoped to at least draw sizable German forces away from the Gustav Line to counter the Anzio threat and therefore hasten a Fifth Army breakthrough.

The key to implementing this expanded *Shingle* option depended upon acquiring sufficient sealift capacity to move and support the forces involved. In particular, the Allies required adequate numbers of Landing Ship Tanks (LSTs), which were specialised assault vessels designed to deliver tanks and other vehicles onto unimproved beachheads. Displacing between 1,809 and 2,140 tons (depending upon the variant), LSTs were shallow-draught, ocean-going transports that could proceed right up to a gradually inclining shoreline and deposit their cargoes directly onto the beach using a bow ramp. Allied planners estimated they would need a minimum of 88 of these specialised landing ships to carry out Operation *Shingle*. At the time the Allies had 102 LSTs stationed in the Mediterranean, but 68 of these were scheduled to depart for Britain in mid-January as part of the build-up for Operation *Overlord*. The British gained approval to retain 56 of these landing ships in the Mediterranean for an additional three weeks, thus making them available for the proposed landing. They also gained additional shipping by cancelling planned amphibious operations in the Indian Ocean and Aegean. By attaining these resources, the navy determined that *Shingle* was feasible, and the landing was scheduled for 22 January.

With approval given, the Allies went about the process of gathering forces for the upcoming operation. The original *Shingle* plan had called for the landing of a reinforced division consisting of some 24,500 men and 2,700 vehicles with an estimated time of independent operation lasting no more than seven days. The new plan increased this effort by more than fourfold, with an estimated duration time of 15 days. American VI Corps under the command of Major-General John Lucas would carry out the landings with an initial assault force consisting of two divisions (the American 3rd and British 1st) augmented by three American ranger battalions, an American parachute regiment, an additional parachute battalion and two British commandos. Follow-up formations would include the American 1st Armoured Division (minus one of its combat commands), a regimental combat team from the American 45th Division and various other support and artillery units. In all, this represented a force of about 110,000 men, of which some 50,000 would land in the first few days of the assault.

As for the naval portion of the operation, the Allies assigned 379 assorted vessels to carry out the initial landings.[4] This constituted a mere fraction of the naval assets used during other recent amphibious operations such as *Torch*, *Husky* and *Avalanche*, but this reduced allocation reflected the vastly changed situation present in the Mediterranean since the surrender of the Italian battle fleet. Gone were the battleships, aircraft carriers and vast surface armadas that had characterised these earlier undertakings, and in their place the main combatant portion of the invasion fleet consisted of just four cruisers, two anti-aircraft ships, 24 destroyers, two gunboats and 39 minesweepers. These warships would provide security and fire support for the assault forces, which were split into two groups. The first was the predominantly British Northern Attack Force, which was earmarked to land the British 1st Division and the two commandos in an area designated Peter Beach, some six miles northwest of Anzio. To do this, the force, which was commanded by Rear-Admiral T. H. Troubridge (RN), contained the headquarters ship *Bulolo*, three infantry-landing ships, 33 LSTs, 56 assorted landing craft and a number of support vessels. The second was the Southern Attack Force, which was to land the American contingent on X-Ray Beach located four miles east of Anzio. Commanded by Rear-Admiral F. J. Lowry (USN), who also commanded the overall operation, this force consisted of the headquarters ship *Biscayne*, five infantry-landing ships, 51 LSTs, 104 assorted landing craft and various other vessels.[5]

To pave the way for the assault, Allied planners called for Fifth Army to launch an offensive a few days before the scheduled landings. The purpose of this was twofold. First and most immediate, the Allies hoped to draw German reserves away from the Anzio/Rome area thus minimising the initial opposition that VI Corps would likely encounter. Second, the Allies hoped to use the assault as a catalyst for further offensive operations that would help compromise the Gustav Line. This latter point was critical since VI Corps was not capable of attaining decisive success on its own. Despite its substantial increase in size and scope, Operation *Shingle* lacked the strength to do anything more than seize and hold the Alban Hills. Thus, *Shingle* could only be successful to the extent it facilitated or contributed to the collapse of German defences along the Gustav Line. Short of that happening, VI Corps would likely find itself dangerously exposed to a German build-up and counter-attack that could lead to its destruction. Still, given its potential to break the stalemate in southern Italy, the Allies considered *Shingle* a worthwhile risk.

Beyond Fifth Army's attack, the Allies took other actions to help bring about the operation's success. This included a three-phased air plan that sought to isolate the targeted combat areas from outside logistical support, deceive the Germans regarding Allied intentions and directly support ground forces once combat commenced. To carry this out, the Allies possessed some 2,700 aircraft that were readily available for the undertaking against an estimated 260 German aircraft in Italy and another 110 bombers in Greece and southern France.[6] Meanwhile, in order to attain surprise, the Allies devised an elaborate deception plan to convince the Germans that the Allies were planning to launch an amphibious assault against northern Italy or southern France. As part of this ruse, the Allies directed much of their aforementioned bombing effort against targets in these areas, assembled landing craft and men in Corsica and Sardinia and dispatched naval units to conduct a bombardment and dummy landing at Civitavecchia on the night of 21/22 January.

While these plans and preparations were underway, Fifth Army opened its offensive against the Gustav Line. On 12 January French forces launched a preliminary attack towards the Upper Rapido River. Five days later British X Corps, consisting of the British 5th and 56th Divisions, successfully crossed the Garigliano River and established strong bridgeheads in the vicinity of Minturno and Castelforte. This move prompted the Germans to commit their reserves, which included the 29th and 90th Panzer Grenadier Divisions and elements from the Herman Goring Division, to contain the British threat. On the 20th the Germans commenced a series of counter-attacks that brought the British advance to a standstill. On the same day the American 36th Division attempted to cross the Rapido River, but was sharply rebuked with the loss of 1,681 casualties.[7] Over the next few days British, American and French units continued their attacks, but none were able to make significant progress against the resolute German defenders. By the eve of Operation *Shingle*, Fifth Army had succeeded in straining the German line and drawing German reserves to its front, but it was clear that no early breakthrough would occur.

It was now VI Corps' turn to try to end the deadlock. On 21 January the various *Shingle* assault forces departed the Bay of Naples and began their 120-mile trek up the coastline. That night these forces arrived off Anzio where they rendezvoused with two British submarines that guided them to their respective landing areas. After dispatching minesweepers to clear channels through suspected German minefields, the first waves of landing craft made their run-ins on the targeted beaches at 0200 hours on the 22nd. Allied planners had anticipated heavy resistance to these incursions, but this did not materialise as the Germans were caught completely by surprise and possessed minimal forces in the area to contest the invasion. In both the Peter and X-Ray sectors British and American assault forces were able to land and seize their primary objectives against little or no opposition. Meanwhile, American rangers captured the port of Anzio where they took possession of a mole that was capable of berthing six landing ships at a time. Within a matter of hours the port was cleared for Allied use, and by the end of the day the Allies had a total of 36,034 men and 3,069 vehicles ashore in and around Anzio.[8] The only significant mishap to mar this accomplishment was the loss of the American minesweeper *Portent*, which sank on a mine.

The advent of Operation *Shingle* caused great consternation within the German hierarchy. This was no truer than in the case of Field Marshal Albert Kesselring, the commander of German forces in Italy. Kesselring had long anticipated an amphibious assault somewhere along the Italian coastline, but the recent heavy fighting in the south had compelled him to send reserves to shore up the Gustav Line. Now with VI Corps' arrival at Anzio, the Germans possessed minimal forces in central Italy to counter this threat. Within hours of the landings Kesselring began gathering forces from northern and southern Italy as well as France, Germany and the Balkans to confront VI Corps, but he realised that it would take at least two days before any of these units would arrive in meaningful strength. In the meantime, he recognised that if VI Corps launched a prompt and powerful attack, there was nothing he could do to prevent it from capturing the Alban Hills or even advancing upon Rome. As such, a number of German authorities, including the commanders of the Tenth Army and XIV Panzer Corps, called for an immediate withdrawal and shortening of their lines along the Garigliano-Rapido front.

Fortunately for Kesselring, he soon received assistance from an unlikely source. Despite the clear objectives of the *Shingle* plan, General Clark had purposely issued vague instructions to VI Corps regarding its mission. Even more important, on the day of the landings General Clark verbally cautioned General Lucas to act conservatively and avoid sticking his neck out. As such, General Lucas declined to take bold, prompt action, but rather contented himself with a gradual expansion of the beachhead while he built-up and fortified his forces. When Kesselring saw this happening, he surmised that VI Corps would give him time to assemble his blocking forces, and he ordered his units defending the Gustav Line to stand firm. Thus, by failing to act decisively, General Lucas allowed the initiative to slip away and lost his best opportunity to compromise the German position in southern Italy.

Over the next several days the Allies and Germans focused their efforts on building up their respective forces. The Allied logistical plan called for a series of staggered convoys to shuttle men and materiel from the Naples area to Anzio on a rotating three-day cycle. Despite a storm that significantly disrupted operations on the 26th, as many as 30 LSTs arrived at Anzio on a daily basis to unload their valuable cargoes. By 29 January the Allies had landed 68,886 men, 237 tanks, 508 guns and 27,250 tons of supplies.[9] Meanwhile, the Allied beachhead had expanded to a perimeter that was 16 miles wide and up to 10 miles deep, bringing it almost halfway to the outskirts of the Alban Hills. Against this, the Germans enjoyed considerable success in bringing in their own forces to contain the Allied perimeter. Under the command of the Fourteenth Army, which had moved into the area from northern Italy, the Germans assembled elements of eight divisions to confront VI Corps. At the same time, Tenth Army continued to defend the Gustav Line with seven divisions, while three additional divisions opposed the Eighth Army on the Adriatic front. Finally, six German divisions remained in northern Italy and the Ljubljana Gap to provide security and defend against the prospect of further Allied amphibious incursions.

While these competing build-ups were underway, the Luftwaffe joined the battle with deadly efficiency. Although the Allies enjoyed overwhelming air superiority within the theatre, they found themselves hard pressed to counter Luftwaffe hit and run raids against the Anzio beachhead and the supporting ships. On 23 January the Luftwaffe scored its first major success when German bombers hit and sank the British destroyer *Janus* in an early dusk attack using either a Hs 293 glider bomb or a conventional torpedo. A few minutes later a Hs 293 glider bomb hit and severely damaged a second British destroyer, *Jervis*. The Hs 293 was a similar weapon to the FX-1400, which had caused such injury off Salerno four months earlier. However, whereas the FX-1400 was designed for use against heavy warships, the Hs 293 was more suitably used against merchant ships and lightly armoured warships. The next day Luftwaffe aircraft sank the 2,702-ton hospital ship *St. David* and damaged the American destroyer *Plunkett*. Finally, on the 29th the Germans enjoyed their greatest success to date when Hs 293 glider bombs hit and sank the British light cruiser *Spartan* and the 7,181-ton American merchant ship *Samuel Huntington*.

For its part, on the 29th General Lucas finally felt strong enough to order VI Corps onto the offensive. That night the American 3rd Division, along with a ranger brigade, attacked towards Cisterna to cut Highway 7 while the British 1st Division attacked towards Campoleone. Not surprisingly given the expeditious German build-up, these attacks encountered heavy resistance and made little progress. This was particularly true in the Cisterna area where a German ambush destroyed two American ranger battalions with the loss of 761 men.[10] On the 31st the 3rd Division renewed its attack, but was thrown back with heavy losses by the Hermann Göring Division. Meanwhile, to the northwest the British 1st Division made initial good progress on the 29th but then encountered heavy resistance on the 30th that stalled its advance short of Campoleone and left it in a dangerously exposed salient stretching up the Albano Road.

It was now clear that the time for offensive action had passed, and on 2 February General Harold Alexander, the Allied ground forces commander, ordered VI Corps to go over onto the defensive. In doing so, he essentially acknowledged that Operation *Shingle* had failed in achieving its objective of compromising the Gustav Line. Instead of alleviating that stalemate, the operation had only created a second stalemate around the Anzio beachhead. Even more disturbing, the Allies faced the very real prospect that VI Corps might be overwhelmed and destroyed by the growing German army opposing it. Indeed, this was precisely what Kesselring intended to do. As if to emphasise this point, on 3 February the Germans launched a major counter-attack to reduce the British salient in the Campoleone area. After a week of heavy fighting that cost both sides dearly, the British were forced to abandon the contested area. The Allies now knew that it was only a matter of time before the Germans launched an all-out offensive to destroy the entire beachhead.

To prevent this from happening, the Allies poured men and materiel into Anzio to bolster VI Corps. This effort included the transfer of additional units such as the British 56th and American 34th Divisions into the contested area, eventually increasing VI Corps' strength to approximately 150,000 men. The task of transporting and supporting this force fell to an already overstretched naval contingent that had initially only agreed to conduct an operation lasting no more than 15 days in duration. Now the navy was charged to support a substantially larger ground force for an open-ended period of time. This mission was made all the more difficult by the loss of substantial naval assets that had to be released for service in Northwest Europe. Despite these adversities, the Allied navies did their utmost to fulfil the expanded mission. On almost a daily basis small convoys of merchant ships and support vessels departed the Bay of Naples to deliver men and supplies to Anzio. To facilitate this, the Allies established a dedicated inshore route that was regularly swept and patrolled to keep it free from German mines and naval interference. Meanwhile, a rotating contingent of cruisers and destroyers constantly remained on station off Anzio to provide fire support for the besieged defenders. Finally, the Allies maintained additional warships in Naples that could quickly reinforce this endeavour when needed.

While this build-up and support effort was clearly essential to VI Corps' survival, the Allies understood that the ultimate restoration of the situation now depended upon Fifth Army's ability to breach the Gustav Line and link up with the isolated garrison. By February the constant pressure applied by Fifth Army had made some progress in breaking into sections of the Gustav Line and straining the German defences. Now Fifth Army focused its efforts on capturing the hill mass immediately

At Tobruk in 1941 and Anzio in 1944, British sea power helped sustain Allied ground forces through long and debilitating sieges. In both cases, the British/Allies eventually prevailed despite great adversity. Pictured here is the British cruiser *Mauritius* and other Allied shipping operating off of Anzio. (Royal Navy official photographer, public domain)

north and west of the town of Cassino. By securing this commanding terrain, the Allies would gain access to the Liri Valley and Highway 6, which, in turn, would give them a direct route to the Alban Hills and Rome beyond. During the period of 1–20 February the Allies launched two major attacks to capture Cassino. A reinforced American 34th Division conducted the first (before it was transferred to Anzio), while an improvised New Zealand Corps, consisting of the 2nd New Zealand and 4th Indian Divisions, conducted the second. While each of these attacks succeeded in seizing key terrain features in and/or around Cassino, the Allies were unable to sustain their gains in the face of heavy German resistance and counter-attacks. Together, these actions cost the Americans some 2,200 casualties while the Commonwealth forces suffered a further 816.[11] Meanwhile, the defending German XIV Panzer Corps paid an even heavier price for this victory as it suffered 4,470 casualties during the same period.[12]

Fortunately for the Allies, the lack of progress they were experiencing was not unique to the Fifth Army. On 16 February the German Fourteenth Army launched its attack to destroy VI Corps. In doing so, the Germans hoped to win a significant materiel and moral victory that would help perpetuate their hold on central Italy and impact the attitude of the opposing forces set to confront each other in Northwest Europe. After a day of probing attacks along the Allied perimeter, the Germans launched their primary assault against the American 45th Division in the area of the Albano Road. By the 18th the Americans were forced back to their final defensive line, and it looked like the perimeter might collapse. Fortunately, the line held, and over the next two days British and American counter-attacks pushed the Germans back. Then on the 29th the Germans resumed their offensive with a series of attacks aimed at the American 3rd Division. In three days of heavy fighting these attacks failed to make any appreciable headway, and on the evening of 2 March the Germans suspended their offensive.

With this, the Germans recognised that their opportunity to destroy VI Corps had passed. In the previous two weeks Fourteenth Army had thrown its maximum strength at the Anzio lodgement area for a cost of 8,120 casualties, but had come up short in both attempts.[13] It was now clear that further offensive action would only induce more fruitless loss, and on the 3rd the Germans went over to the defensive. In doing so, they solidified their failure to capitalise on one of the last great opportunities they would ever have to inflict a crushing defeat upon the Allies. From this point on, the Germans contented themselves with containing the Anzio perimeter, and the crisis confronting VI Corps abated. Still, the Allies paid a heavy price for this success as VI Corps suffered 3,496 casualties during the critical period of 16–20 February and 20,943 casualties from the beginning of Operation *Shingle* through 3 March.[14] Nevertheless, this only represented a fraction of the losses that would have occurred had Fourteenth Army been successful in its offensive.

A major factor that contributed to this positive outcome was the impact of Allied naval power. In February the Allies delivered 62,048 tons of cargo to the Anzio beachhead, thus fulfilling VI Corps' extensive need for logistical replenishment.[15] During the same period the Allied navies provided invaluable fire support to the besieged defenders. At the height of the German offensive the British cruisers *Orion*, *Mauritius*, *Phoebe* and *Penelope*, the American cruiser *Brooklyn*, the Dutch gunboats *Soemba* and *Flores* and a number of destroyers were all present off Anzio where they conducted numerous engagements against German troop concentrations, vehicles and artillery positions. By the end of February Allied warships had fired 8,400 6-inch shells, 7,800 5.25-inch shells and 3,500 4.7-inch shells, and the Germans later cited this heavy gunfire as a primary factor in preventing them from attaining a breakthrough.[16] Sadly, like their army brethren fighting ashore, the navy paid a heavy price in providing this support. On 18 February the U-boat *U410* sank the British light cruiser *Penelope* as the latter was en route from Naples to Anzio. Seven days later a German glider bomb hit and sank the British destroyer *Inglefield* off the beachhead. Finally, in other attacks during this period German U-boats and aircraft sank two liberty ships worth 14,330 tons and three LSTs.

Notwithstanding these losses, March brought about a relative calm to the contested Italian peninsula. At Anzio both sides hunkered down in their respective defensive positions to recoup their strength from the recent heavy fighting. Meanwhile, along the Gustav Line the New Zealand Corps launched a third attempt to capture Cassino on 15 March. After a week and a half of heavy fighting that cost the Commonwealth forces 2,106 and the Germans some 2,321 casualties, the two sides disengaged with Cassino still under German control.[17] Thereafter, the Allied leadership realised it was time to pause and rebuild their tired and depleted formations before proceeding with further offensive action. As such, for the remainder of March and through April major combat operations ceased along the Gustav Line as the Allies prepared for their next major push, Operation *Diadem*, which was scheduled to commence in May.

This temporary cessation in major ground operations brought no concurrent reduction in maritime activities. To the contrary, certain aspects of the local maritime struggle intensified during this period. This was certainly true regarding the effort to maintain VI Corps as the Allied navies delivered 158,274 and 97,658 tons of stores to Anzio in March and April respectively.[18] Of course, this only represented a small portion of the Allies' seaborne logistical effort. Nearly everything the Allied armies and air forces used had to be brought in from outside the theatre, and the overwhelming majority of this was transported on ships. Likewise, the Mediterranean was a major transportation hub for men and materiel passing to and from the Indian Ocean. As such, various convoys, some containing up to 100 ships, traversed these waters on a daily basis to fulfil the vast logistical requirements within the theatre and those beyond.

The same was true for the Germans, although on a greatly reduced scale. German maritime commerce was limited to the coastal waters of the Ligurian, Tyrrhenian, Adriatic and Aegean Seas; the purpose of which was to support their military forces in these areas. In some cases, such as on the Aegean Islands and in remote portions of the Yugoslav coastline, seaborne re-supply was the only practical way to support isolated garrisons and occupation forces. In others, the Germans used maritime transport to augment limited road and rail lines of communication that were under constant pressure from Allied air attacks. This gave the Germans a degree of logistical flexibility that would have been otherwise lacking without the use of this seaborne lift. This effort was exemplified in April when the Germans transported 47,028 tons of cargo along the Italian coasts, 36,156 tons in the Adriatic and 21,315 tons in the Aegean.[19]

During the first five months of 1944 both sides expended considerable efforts to interdict these competing logistical activities. Starting first with the Germans, in January the Kriegsmarine possessed 13 U-boats and a number of largely non-operational Italian submarines in the Mediterranean. Over the next four months the Germans attempted to send additional U-boats to bolster this force. Of these, *U761*, *U392* and *U731* were located by American MAD-equipped aircraft while transiting through the Strait of Gibraltar and were subsequently sunk by British warships.[20] Despite these mishaps, the Germans succeeded in passing ten new U-boats into the Mediterranean by May. Unfortunately for them, this was negated by the loss of 12 U-boats during roughly the same period. Of the U-boats sunk, USAAF bombers sank *U81*, *U380*, *U410* and *U421* in port while British warships sank *U343*, *U223* and *U453*. Meanwhile, various combinations of British and Allied warships and aircraft accounted for *U450*, *U371*, *U616* and *U960* while *U455* was lost to unknown causes. In addition to this, three captured Italian submarines, *UIT19*, *UIT4* and *UIT5*, were also sunk due to USAAF bombing. Against these losses, Germany's Mediterranean U-boat force succeeded in sinking ten merchant ships worth 76,760 tons plus a number of warships and auxiliaries, including the aforementioned British cruiser *Penelope*, the British destroyer *Laforey* and the American destroyer escort *Fechteler*.[21]

Other German interdiction efforts attained similar results. Throughout this period the Luftwaffe employed between 100–125 medium-range bombers in southern France for anti-shipping purposes. In addition to their previously mentioned successes off Anzio, these bombers carried out regular attacks against Allied convoys traversing the Western Mediterranean. Despite this outlay of effort, these bombers only succeeded in sinking ten merchant ships worth 61,217 tons, plus the previously mentioned British warships sunk off Anzio and the American destroyer *Lansdale* from January through May.[22] Mines and E-boats took a further toll on the local Allied shipping with losses including a few merchant ships, two LSTs and the previously mentioned American minesweeper *Portent*. When everything was combined together, total Allied merchant losses in the Mediterranean from January through May amounted to 25 ships worth 152,532 tons.[23] Given the volume of Allied maritime traffic plying through the Mediterranean at the time, these results were hardly prohibitive.

For their part, the Allies sank significantly higher numbers of German-controlled vessels from January through May, but most of these were of limited tonnage, reflecting the composition of the local German shipping pool at this stage in the war. Of the various participants involved, air power was by far the most successful accounting for 131 commercial and 202 military vessels worth 121,640 and 17,885 tons respectively that were sunk within the theatre during this period. Approximately 75 percent of these losses were incurred during bombing raids against ports of which the USAAF played the predominant role. The RAF also carried out numerous attacks against German-controlled ports and was the primary force involved in attacking German ships at sea. As such, the RAF's portion of this tally came to 49 commercial and 113 military vessels worth 37,784 and 6,690 tons sunk, with another 22 assorted craft worth 13,238 tons destroyed in conjunction with USAAF aircraft.[24]

Allied naval units, mines and other causes accounted for the remaining German maritime losses. By this stage in the war, British and British-affiliated submarines encountered few ocean-going merchant ships within their patrol areas, but still managed to sink eight such vessels worth 25,732 tons, along with multiple minor craft

A Catalina of No. 202 squadron on anti-submarine patrol from Gibraltar. During the war Axis submarines accounted for 137 Allied vessels sunk within the theatre while the Allies destroyed 145 Axis submarines in the Mediterranean and approaches to Gibraltar thus attaining an exchange rate of roughly one-to-one. (Daventry, B. J. H. (Fg Off), Royal Air Force official photographer, public domain)

and the escort destroyer *SG15* (ex-French *Rageot de la Touche*) during this period.[25] Against this, the Allies lost two submarines, the Italian *Axum*, which was in active Allied service at the time of its demise, and the French *Protée*, which were sunk due to accidental and unknown causes respectively. Meanwhile, Allied warships ranging from motor torpedo boats to destroyers carried out numerous offensive sweeps that added to the German losses. When combined together, these submarines and warships sank 93 German vessels of various types worth 44,763 tons from January through May. During the same period mines added a further 14 vessels worth 6,419 tons to this tally. Finally, various other causes such as sabotage, seizures and scuttling rounded out this count bringing the total number of German-controlled maritime assets sunk in the Mediterranean from January through May to 263 commercial and 308 military vessels worth 208,784 and 31,480 tons respectively.[26] Included in these warship losses were the escort/torpedo boats *SG20* and *TA15* which were wrecked by British aircraft, the corvette *UJ201* which was sunk by French destroyers and the torpedo boats *TA36* and *TA23* which were lost to mines.[27]

Beyond these dedicated anti-shipping efforts, the Allies also carried out two related offensive campaigns. First, in January British commandos occupied the Yugoslav Island of Vis located on the Dalmatian coast some 30 miles southwest of Split. Once there, they established a small naval base and airfield to support the growing partisan uprising that was underway in Yugoslavia. In addition to launching numerous sorties by coastal forces and aircraft against the local German shipping, the British used Vis as a staging area to carry out commando raids against the surrounding islands. From March through May the British launched raids, sometimes up to 1,000-men strong, against Solta, Hvar, Mljet and Korcula, thus compelling the Germans to deploy the 118th Jäger Division to defend against these incursions. Meanwhile, during the same period the RAF began a systematic effort to mine the Danube River, which was a principal transportation artery in central and Eastern Europe. From 8 April through 1 June British Liberator and Wellington bombers laid 531 mines along various stretches of the river, causing immediate disruptions to the already strained German logistical system.[28] Amongst other things, in May this mining effort delayed the delivery of 10,000 tons of ammunition for the Dniester front and contributed to a halving of crucial oil exports from Romania.[29]

While these ancillary operations were underway, the Allies prepared for their next major offensive in central Italy. Designated Operation *Diadem*, the Allies planned to use overwhelming force and synchronisation to push through key portions of the Gustav Line. In order to accomplish this, the Allies moved most of the Eighth Army westward to assume responsibility for the Cassino/Liri Valley sector, which they planned to assault with nine divisions. To their left, Fifth Army would attack the area along the Garigliano River to the Tyrrhenian coast with four French and two American divisions. Thus, the Allies planned to use 15 divisions, along with some 1,600 artillery pieces, to assault a front that was only 30 miles wide and defended by seven German divisions. Once sufficient progress was made in this offensive, VI Corps would launch its own breakout attempt from the Anzio lodgement with seven and a half divisions, including the British 1st and 5th (the latter having relieved 56th Division), to enact a linkup with the oncoming Allied forces. Finally, to help facilitate *Diadem*, the Allies conducted a massive air campaign and deception plan to isolate the targeted areas and compel the Germans to hold back their mobile reserves.[30]

On 11 May the Allies launched their attack with four corps simultaneously assaulting key German positions along the Gustav Line. Despite this massive onslaught, the Allies failed to attain an immediate breakthrough. Instead, the battle resembled a 'crumbling' affair similar to El Alamein where the Allies applied constant pressure across a wide area that systematically wore down and pushed back the German defenders. The first major success came on the 13th when French forces fighting in the centre broke through the German 71st Division and captured Monte Majo. Over the next few days, the French continued their forward pressure and captured San Giorgio on the southern end of the Liri Valley. Similar success was soon attained on both flanks. Along the coast the American II Corps conducted a series of attacks that slowly pushed the German 94th Division back. Supporting this effort were the British cruiser *Dido* and the American cruisers *Brooklyn* and *Philadelphia*, which fired 1,865 5.25-inch and 1,735 6-inch shells against inshore German positions.[31] By the 16th II Corps had outflanked the Gustav Line and was advancing up Highway 7. Meanwhile, to the east British XIII Corps, consisting of 4th, 78th, 8th Indian and 6th Armoured Divisions, successfully fought its way across the Rapido River and slowly advanced into the Liri Valley. On the 17th a pincer attack by XIII Corps and the British-equipped Polish II Corps compelled the Germans to abandon Cassino and retreat towards their secondary line of defence, the Hitler Line.

The Allies maintained heavy pressure on the Germans as the battle continued into the second half of May. On the 22nd and 23rd French and Canadian forces broke through separate sections of the Hitler Line, compromising the entire Tenth Army position. On the same day (23 May) VI Corps launched its breakout offensive from Anzio and quickly breached the now thinly held defensive perimeter surrounding the beachhead. The Allied plan now called for VI Corps to advance to Valmonte and cut Highway 6. In doing this, the Allies hoped to block the main German line of retreat and destroy Tenth Army in a giant pincer. Unfortunately, General Clark had other intentions. Sending only token forces towards Valmonte, he ordered the bulk of VI Corps to attack directly towards Rome. This action allowed Tenth Army to escape encirclement while VI Corps' attack towards Rome quickly stalled against the final German defensive position, the Caesar Line. Despite this unhappy development, the German situation was already beyond salvation. Having committed all of their reserves to stem earlier Allied advances, the Germans had nothing left to plug the breaches caused when Fifth Army renewed its offensive at the end of the month.

On 2 June Kesselring ordered his forces to begin a fighting withdrawal, and two days later Fifth Army elements entered Rome.

With this accomplishment, the Allies attained a prize that had eluded them for over six months. Sadly, the realisation of this objective came at a very heavy cost. From 11 May through 4 June total Allied casualties for the ground forces involved in Operation *Diadem* numbered 43,746 men, of which 10,727 were killed or missing. Britain's portion of this butcher's bill, including Commonwealth and affiliated forces, amounted to 16,064 casualties, of which 4,240 were killed or missing. Against this, an analysis of German losses determined that they probably suffered at least 51,754 casualties during the same period, including 24,334 prisoners that were counted in Eighth and Fifth Army cages.[32] Meanwhile, the successful conclusion of Operation *Diadem* ended the navy's long and costly effort to maintain VI Corps at Anzio. During the last month of this endeavour (May) the navy delivered 131,424 tons of stores to Anzio, bringing the total amount of supplies and materiel delivered during the 19-week ordeal to 523,358 tons.[33]

Notwithstanding these heavy losses and unwavering efforts, the Allied forces in Italy soon found their hard-won victory overshadowed by events in Northwest Europe. On 6 June the Allies finally embarked upon their long-anticipated return to France with the commencement of Operation *Overlord*. This was a huge undertaking that encompassed some 7,000 assorted vessels, 11,590 aircraft, 3,500 gliders and more than two million men in the initial landings and follow-up. Having been delayed a month to accumulate additional landing craft, Operation *Overlord* was completely successful in breaching the German Atlantic defences and establishing elements of two (and ultimately five) Allied armies in strong positions along the Normandy coastline. Then, in the succeeding weeks the Allies built up their forces and slowly expanded the lodgement area against determined German resistance until finally attaining a substantial breakout at the end of July. Given these actions, the Mediterranean theatre, which up to this point had been the centre of the Allied ground effort against Germany, suddenly found itself consigned to a secondary status. Never again would the Allied forces in the Mediterranean garner the level of attention they had enjoyed in the previous four years of conflict.

Yet, despite this reduced notoriety, plenty of combat remained to be waged within the theatre. In this regard, the British scored a small but meaningful victory during the opening days of June. On the night of 31 May/1 June the Germans dispatched a small convoy from Piraeus to Crete consisting of the merchant ships *Gertrud*, *Sabine* and *Tanais* (1,960, 2,252 and 1,545 tons respectively), along with an escort of four torpedo boats, four sub-chasers and three motor minesweepers. The purpose of this convoy was to deliver 8,500 tons of much needed supplies to the Cretan garrison. Almost immediately, British reconnaissance aircraft began tracking the convoy, and the next evening the British launched a series of heavy air attacks that sank *Sabine* and the sub-chasers *UJ2101* and *UJ2105* and seriously damaged *Gertrud* and two other escorts. Early the next morning the surviving vessels entered Heraklion harbour, but a subsequent British bombing raid that evening destroyed *Gertrud* and the torpedo boat *TA16*. Finally, on its return trip to Piraeus, *Tanais* was sunk by the British submarine *Vivid*. Given the loss of all three merchant ships and three escorts, the Germans determined that further convoys to Crete were impractical, and thereafter only used minor vessels sailing independently to sustain the increasingly isolated garrison. British losses for the battle amounted to just six aircraft.

June saw a number of other notable naval successes for the Allies. First, during two separate engagements American patrol torpedo (PT) boats (the American equivalent to British motor torpedo boats) sank the German torpedo boats *TA26*, *TA30* and *TA25* in the Ligurian Sea. On the other side of Italy, British motor gunboats and a motor torpedo boat scored a similar success when they sank *TA34* off the island of Murter in the Adriatic.[34] Meanwhile, USAAF aircraft destroyed *TA27* and *TA22* at Elba and off Trieste respectively. Likewise, in the Aegean Royal Marine canoeists penetrated Porto Lago harbour in Leros and disabled *TA14* and *TA17* with limpet mines. Finally, during the latter part of June the Allies carried out two joint British/Italian commando raids to sink captured Italian warships located at La Spezia that the Germans intended to use as blockships. During the first operation on the 22nd British-manned Chariot human torpedoes successfully penetrated the harbour defences and sank the heavy cruiser *Bolzano*. Four days later British and Italian divers performed a similar feat and crippled the heavy cruiser *Gorizia* with explosive charges.

Of course, these exploits only constituted a small portion of the successes attained by the Allies during their ongoing anti-shipping campaign. In June and July Allied aircraft destroyed 32 German-controlled merchant ships and 89 military vessels worth 80,707 and 12,138 tons respectively in the Mediterranean. Once again, the USAAF carried out most of its attacks against German-controlled ports while the RAF predominantly attacked ships at sea. As such, the USAAF sank a larger portion of the German tonnage even though the RAF sank more vessels. Specifically, the RAF's share of this tally amounted to 16 merchant ships and 54 military vessels worth 13,807 and 4,567 tons respectively, while a further nine vessels worth 657 tons were sunk jointly with the USAAF. During the same two-month period Allied naval units and mines sank a further 16 commercial and 36 military vessels worth 28,453 and 11,522 tons respectively.[35] Included in this were nine sizable merchant ships worth 21,585 tons and the 2,588-ton auxiliary warship *SG11* (ex-*Alice Robert*) that were sunk by British submarines.[36] When combined together and including casualties from all causes such as sabotage and scuttling, the Germans lost a total of 101 commercial and 156 military vessels worth 202,116 and 45,506 tons respectively in the Mediterranean during June and July.[37]

Against this, local German interdiction efforts largely collapsed. Of the 11 U-boats present in the Mediterranean at the beginning of June, USAAF bombers accounted for *U586*, *U642*, *U471*, *U952* and *U969* during raids against Toulon on 5 July

With the conclusion of the Africa campaign and Italy's departure as an active Axis partner, Allied interdiction efforts switched to impeding German coastal traffic off Southern Europe. Pictured here is a RAF Beaufighter strike against German flak vessels south of Kalymnos in the Dodecanese. (Royal Air Force official photographer, public domain)

and 6 August. Meanwhile, given the situation in Northwest Europe, the Germans opted not to send further U-boat reinforcements into the Mediterranean. Thus, by the second week in August the local German U-boat force was reduced to just six boats, which were largely confined to port undergoing repairs or upgrades. The same held true for the Luftwaffe, which saw its strength siphoned away to confront the threat in Northwest Europe. The result of this progressive decline was a virtual cessation of German anti-shipping successes within the theatre. During June and July, the Germans only succeeded in sinking a single Allied merchant ship worth 2,037 tons in the Mediterranean.[38] Meanwhile, local Allied naval losses during this period amounted to just two principal warships, the British submarine *Sickle* and the American minesweeper *Swerve*, which were both sunk by mines.

Turning now back to mainland Italy, the Allies continued their northward push following the capture of Rome. During a two-month period (early June through early August) the Allied armies advanced some 150 miles up the Italian peninsula and captured a number of important locations, including the coastal cities/harbours of Civitavecchia, Ancona and Leghorn and the historic city of Florence located in central Italy. This advance was not a rout, but rather a series of local attacks and intermediate progressions as the Germans conducted an effective fighting withdrawal. The ferocity of this fighting was demonstrated by the fact that Eighth Army, which was advancing on the right flank, suffered 15,966 casualties during this pursuit period, while Fifth Army suffered even heavier losses with a total of 17,939 casualties.[39] By comparison, the Allies continued to take a steady flow of prisoners, and by 22 August the total number of prisoners taken since the beginning of the *Diadem* Offensive was 13,151 and 29,023 for the Eighth and Fifth Armies respectively.[40]

As always, the navy provided valuable service in supporting this advance. As the Allied armies progressed up both coasts of Italy, minesweepers kept pace clearing many miles of inshore routes, allowing the Allies to maintain forward units with seaborne re-supply and gunfire support. In keeping with this, naval authorities carried out Herculean efforts to open captured ports for the receipt of Allied supplies. This was no easy task given the degree of demolition the Germans usually inflicted, but the Allies typically had supplies flowing into these ports within a matter of days. In turn, this influx of seaborne supplies was critical in maintaining the advance since the Italian road and rail network was often inadequate in fulfilling this task. Finally, the navy provided direct support for the capture of Elba Island located between Italy and Corsica. On 17 June a force of some 270 British, American and French naval vessels under the command of Britain's Rear-Admiral T. H. Troubridge landed the French 9th Colonial Division on Elba. After two days of heavy fighting, the French, with support from British commandos, secured the island, giving the Allies unimpeded access to Italy's Ligurian coastline.

Meanwhile, in early August the Germans fell in upon their next major prepared position, the Gothic Line, which ran from just south of La Spezia on the Ligurian coast to Pesaro on the Adriatic. This ended the pursuit phase of the recent campaign as the Allies paused to prepare a deliberate attack against this new defensive feature. As such, this hiatus constitutes a good stopping point to evaluate recent events and the overall strategic situation. At the beginning of 1944 the Allies controlled the southern third of Italy. After eight months of heavy fighting, culminating in Operation *Diadem* and the post-*Diadem* advance, the Allies added the middle third of Italy to their sphere of control. In doing so, they gained valuable airfields that extended their ability to bomb targets throughout the region and into southern Germany. They also severely mauled the defending German forces inflicting some 170,000 casualties upon them from September 1943 through the third week in August 1944.[41] Included in these losses were a total of 58,212 German prisoners, of which 21,541 were taken by Eighth Army or the British units assigned to Fifth Army.[42] Added to this were a further 8,062 prisoners that were from nationalities other than German that were taken by Eighth Army during this period.[43]

Finally, and most important in a strategic sense, this unrelenting Allied offensive tied down valuable German forces that might have been better utilised in Northwest Europe or the Eastern Front. During the summer of 1944 when the Germans faced growing calamities in both northern France and Eastern Europe, they were still compelled to maintain 53 divisions in Italy, southern France and the Balkans.[44] Had the Allies not eliminated Italy from the war, thus forcing the Germans to occupy and defend this country and compensate for the loss of regional Italian garrison troops, the Germans would have been able to utilise the majority (and perhaps the vast majority) of these divisions in other theatres. This, in turn, would have likely impacted operations in Northwest Europe and/or the Eastern Front and might have altered the course or duration of the war. Instead, the Germans faced defeat everywhere as their forces strained to hold back the torrent of Allied power pushing in on them from all sides.

Clearly, the southern flank had played an important role in bringing about this reality. Both through its past contributions as well as its more immediate impacts, success in the Mediterranean had tangibly advanced Allied strategic fortunes against the Axis. Obviously, this had come at some great cost in terms of time, resources and effort, but these benefits were undeniable. Now as the European war entered its closing stages, local Allied commanders sought to continue this contribution and retain a degree of relevance within the overall Allied war effort. Much of this would depend upon a continuation of critical activities already underway within the theatre, but the Allies also hoped to capitalise upon additional opportunities for exploitation that had already presented themselves or might arise. Only time would tell how successful these efforts would be, but one thing was certain; this quest for relevance meant that the bloody fighting underway in the region would continue into the immediate future.

CHAPTER 10

Victory on the Peripheries

By the summer of 1944 the war in the Mediterranean was clearly waning in terms of its importance and notoriety. For more than four years the region had served as Britain's primary theatre of operations, but recent events in Normandy had abruptly overshadowed the area in terms of its strategic relevance. Suddenly, the path to victory found itself firmly established in the plains and cities of Northern Europe, and the Mediterranean theatre became little more than a sideshow. This reality did not negate the immense contributions the theatre had already made in propelling the Allies to this advantageous position. To the contrary, control over the Mediterranean had provided the Allies with numerous benefits, including possession of a direct transportation artery between Europe and the Indian Ocean, access to local airfields and a means to tie down German formations away from the more crucial theatres of Northwest and Eastern Europe. Still, with the firm establishment of Allied forces in Normandy and a massive Soviet offensive underway in the east, Allied efforts in the Mediterranean were relegated to playing a supporting role with the maintenance of these benefits as their primary function.

Given this reality, one might reasonably surmise that the local Allied forces would assume a passive posture, but this was not the case. Instead, the Allies maintained an offensive strategy with the goal of expanding their hold throughout the region. The main proponents of this offensive approach were the British, who advocated for the conquest of northern Italy followed by an advance into the Danube Valley and other possible moves into the Balkans depending upon the situation. By doing this, the British hoped to put themselves in a better position to shape the political landscape of central and Southern Europe once Germany collapsed. The Americans, who were predominantly focused on military efficiency over post-war considerations, countered that operations in the Mediterranean would have to support and be subservient to the main Allied effort in Northwest Europe. As such, the Americans insisted upon an invasion of southern France as previously agreed upon at the Cairo and Tehran conferences in order to gain needed ports to handle the flow of reinforcements and supplies coming from the United States. On a conciliatory point, the Americans agreed to continue operations in Italy with the forces already at hand, but stated that additional actions after that would largely depend upon British resources.

For the common fighting men, these high-level deliberations and strategic applications were overwhelmingly transparent and irrelevant. From their perspectives, the war continued on with changes in location and intensity, but always with the ever-present spectre of hardship, sacrifice and potential danger. In terms of the local maritime struggle, this reality manifested itself in four interrelated missions. First and foremost, the Allies had to maintain the extensive flow of logistical traffic travelling to destinations within the theatre as well as those passing to and from the Indian Ocean. The immense scale of this mission was demonstrated by the fact that from July to September 1944 a total of 14,898 ships used the local convoy and routing system within the theatre.[1] Second, they had to conduct operations in the Tyrrhenian and Ligurian Seas to support the American Fifth Army and interdict the local German maritime traffic. Third, they had to perform a similar function in the Adriatic Sea for the British Eighth Army while concurrently providing assistance to the growing partisan movement in Yugoslavia. Finally, they had to conduct interdiction operations in the Aegean Sea to further weaken isolated German garrisons and undermine Germany's hold over the entire area.

On the morning of 15 August, the Allies added a new major addition to these missions when they launched Operation *Dragoon*, the aforementioned invasion of southern France. Unlike similar previous undertakings, *Dragoon* constituted the first major amphibious assault in the European theatre that was not predominantly a British-run affair in terms of maritime operations, although British assets still played a significant role. Under the overall command of American Lieutenant-General Jacob Devers, the Allies proposed to land three American divisions (the 3rd, 45th and 36th) on a series of beaches along a 45-mile stretch of coastline east of Marseille ranging from the bays of Cavalaire and Pampelonne in the southwest to San Raphaël and Rade D'Agay in the northeast. French commandos would protect the flanks of these landings by seizing gun positions near Cap Négre and cutting the coastal road near Théoule, while American rangers and Canadian special forces seized the nearby islands of Levant and Port Cros to further neutralise local gun batteries. Likewise, the Allies would drop an airborne task force, which included a British brigade, in the area behind Fréjus-San Raphaël to isolate the assault beaches from potential German reinforcements. Finally, follow-up formations would include seven French divisions that would begin landing on D plus 1 and several American divisions that would eventually arrive from the United States.

To carry this out, the Allies assembled a powerful naval force under the command of Vice-Admiral Henry Hewitt, consisting of 881 assorted warships, assault craft and support vessels, plus a further 1,370 minor craft that were towed or transported to the assault areas.[2] Once the landings occurred, additional ships and craft would join the undertaking, eventually bringing the total force to 1,034 primary vessels

Operation *Dragoon* constituted the first and only time in the European conflict that the United States Navy played the dominant role in a major amphibious landing. Pictured here is the command ship USS *Catoctin*, which served as the flagship for the operation. (U.S. Navy, public domain)

of which 59.4 percent came from the United States. The British provided a further 35.6 percent of these vessels while the remaining five percent came from other Allied nations, most notably France. The combatant portion of this force included five battleships, nine escort carriers, 25 cruisers, 86 destroyers, 19 escort destroyers and sloops, two corvettes and 43 fleet minesweepers. Meanwhile, the assault portion contained three headquarters ships, 20 combat loaders, 32 assorted assault ships, 81 LSTs, 307 assorted landing craft and numerous support and auxiliary vessels. Finally, Britain's contribution to this enterprise included the battleship *Ramillies*; the escort carriers *Emperor, Pursuer, Searcher, Attacker, Khedive, Hunter* and *Stalker*; 11 cruisers; 29 destroyers and escorts; 18 minesweepers; two gunboats and 300 assorted support and landing vessels.[3]

The Allies split the vast majority of this naval force between four attack groups known as Alpha, Delta, Camel and Sitka. Of these, the first three attack groups were tasked to land the 3rd, 45th and 36th divisions respectively on the targeted

French coastline, while Force Sitka assaulted the offshore islands of Levant and Port Cros and also carried out commando landings in the vicinity of Cap Négre. Under the command of American naval officers, these attack groups were divided into various sub-elements to carry out their assigned tasks in a succession of waves. Likewise, each attack group possessed an attached bombardment force to provide gunfire support against German gun batteries, defensive positions and other targets of opportunity. In all, some 60 Allied warships were allocated to this task, including the aforementioned *Ramillies*, the American battleships *Nevada*, *Texas* and *Arkansas*, the French battleship *Lorraine* and numerous cruisers and destroyers. Finally, a contingent of minesweepers and dan-layers preceded each attack group to mitigate the threat of mines and establish a series of safe corridors to the assigned assault beaches.

To facilitate air support for the operation, Admiral Hewitt also possessed his own internal air element known as Task Force 88. Built around the seven previously mentioned British escort carriers as well as the American escort carriers *Tulagi* and *Kasaan Bay*, and under the command of British Rear-Admiral T. H. Troubridge, Task Force 88 embarked an initial strength of 224 fighter-bombers (Seafires, Hellcats

Table 10.1 Allied Maritime Forces Assigned to Operation *Dragoon*

	British and Commonwealth	American	Other	Total
Battleships	1	3	1	5
Escort carriers	7	2	-	9
Cruisers	11	8	6	25
Gunboats	2	-	-	2
Destroyers	27	47	12	86
Escorts	2	8	11	21
Fleet minesweepers	18	25	-	43
Headquarters ships	-	3	-	3
Combat loaders	-	20	-	20
Assorted assault ships	31	-	1	32
Landing ship tanks	3	75	3	81
Assorted landing craft	133	174	-	307
Coastal/minor craft	53	153	3	209
Merchant ships/auxiliaries	80	96	15	191
Total	368	614	52	1,034

Source: ADM 186/796, Battle Summaries, No. 43: Invasion of the South of France, Operation *Dragoon*, 15 August 1944. Condensed and organised for easier presentation.

and Wildcats) plus two additional aircraft for liaison duty.[4] Together, these aircraft had a threefold mission. First, they would provide fighter cover for protection of the fleet and landing areas against potential Luftwaffe interference. Second, they would provide spotter aircraft to assist the bombardment forces. In this regard, many of the pilots on both the British and American carriers were trained to carry out this specialised task. Finally, they would provide close air support for the ground forces and fulfil an offensive strike role when conditions allowed.

While Task Force 88 constituted the most accessible aerial component available to the naval commanders, it only represented a small portion of the Allied air assets assigned to support Operation *Dragoon*. The main effort would come from the Mediterranean Allied Air Force, with the XII Tactical Air Command being the primary subordinate formation assigned to support ground operations in southern France. Based in Corsica, the XII Tactical Air Command possessed 37 squadrons of tactical aircraft (including 12 from the RAF) plus a further six squadrons assigned on a temporary basis. Beyond this, the Allies earmarked two wings of American medium bombers and three reconnaissance squadrons (a total of 30 squadrons) from the Mediterranean Allied Tactical Air Force to operate against targets in southern France through 29 August.[5] Finally, the Allies made available the heavy bombers and long-range fighters of the Mediterranean Allied Strategic Air Force to further bolster this effort as needed. When combined with Task Force 88 and further squadrons earmarked for troop transport and convoy defence, this brought the total number of aircraft assigned or available to support the invasion to roughly 4,000.[6]

Beyond these vast numbers, the Allies also benefitted from the significantly improved aircraft designs filling out their front-line squadrons. For the Fleet Air Arm, long gone were the days when it depended upon Swordfish, Albacore and Fulmar aircraft that were clearly inferior to their shore-based counterparts. Instead, the British carriers were now equipped with robust and capable designs such as the American-built Grumman Wildcat and Hellcat fighter-bombers. They also possessed the renowned Seafire, which although prone to deck landing accidents as demonstrated off Salerno, would eventually prove itself to be an effective fighter-bomber both in the Mediterranean and later in the Pacific. Of the various air force aircraft on hand, none was more impactful on maritime operations than the Bristol Beaufighter. Originally designed as a night-fighter and still used as such, the twin-engine Beaufighter also saw extensive service as an anti-shipping strike aircraft. Capable of carrying bombs, torpedoes or rockets, the nimble Beaufighter proved to be the RAF's most prolific ship-killer in a direct attack role. A second twin-engine design that saw limited, but effective use by the South African Air Force was the American-built Lockheed Ventura. In terms of heavy bombers, the four-engine, American-built Consolidated B-24 Liberator was the primary bomber used in the Mediterranean Strategic Air Force, equipping both the American Fifteenth Air Force and a number of British squadrons in No. 205 Group. Finally, the Allies possessed a number of excellent single-engine fighters, including the British Supermarine Spitfire Mk IX and the North American P-51 Mustang that were often used as fighter-bombers when not employed in escort or air superiority roles.

Already the Allied air forces had conducted numerous operations to prepare the way for the invasion. Beginning on 29 April 1944 and proceeding through the morning of 15 August 1944, the Mediterranean Allied Strategic Air Force carried out a series of raids designed to isolate the landing areas from the rest of France. In doing so, it conducted 5,408 sorties and dropped 6,704 tons of bombs that succeeded in breaching all but one of the targeted bridges across the Rhone, Durance and Var Rivers, as well as inflicting considerable damage on the local road and rail networks.[7] Then, from 5 to 14 August, the Allies intensified their bombing effort with a new focus on neutralising German coastal defences and radar stations in the targeted area, as well as substantial diversionary attacks over a wide arch from Cette and Marseille in the west to Genoa in the east. These operations would culminate on the morning of the invasion when the Allies planned to dispatch some 1,300 aircraft to attack German gun batteries, defensive positions and military concentrations within the assault area itself.[8]

Against this massive array of resources, the Germans defended southern France with limited forces that were hardly adequate for the task. The main formation responsible for this defence was the German Nineteenth Army, which only possessed seven under-strength infantry divisions spread along France's Mediterranean coast. Of these, only two divisions (the 242nd and 148th) were actually in position to

Table 10.2 Characteristics of Selected Allied Aircraft used in the Final Stages of the Mediterranean Conflict

	Roles	Top speed (mph)	Range (miles)	Maximum ordnance load (lbs)
Carrier-borne				
Grumman Wildcat	Fighter, fighter-bomber	331	845	200
Grumman Hellcat	Fighter, fighter-bomber	376	1,090	2,000
Supermarine Seafire LIII	Fighter, fighter-bomber	358	725	500
Land-based				
Bristol Beaufighter	Maritime strike	330	1,470	2,127
Lockheed Ventura	Medium bomber	312	1,600	5,000
Consolidated B-24 Liberator	Heavy bomber	300	2,100	8,800
Supermarine Spitfire Mk IX	Fighter, fighter-bomber	408	434	1,000
North American P-51 Mustang	Fighter, fighter-bomber	437	950	2,000

oppose the Allied landings. The Germans held two further divisions (11th Panzer and 157th Mountain) in reserve, but it was questionable whether these would be able to mount a timely intervention given the poor state of the local German logistical network and the overwhelming air superiority enjoyed by the Allies. Nor could the German army expect any meaningful help from its sister services. By this stage in the war the Luftwaffe could only muster a serviceable strength of 45 torpedo-bombers, 15 bombers and five single-engine fighters to defend southern France.[9] Meanwhile, the Kriegsmarine possessed a mere six U-boats left in the Mediterranean, of which only one was immediately available to confront the Allied armada. The Germans also had two flotillas of surface vessels stationed at Marseille and Genoa, but most of these were minor or auxiliary types that were of little offensive value. Given these pronounced weaknesses and the growing calamity befalling their forces in Normandy, the Germans had little reason to believe they could mount a successful defence of southern France.

Unfortunately for them, this hypothesis was soon borne out by events. Shortly after midnight on 15 August the first Allied airborne and commando forces began arriving in the targeted areas. A few hours later at sunrise the Allies commenced an extensive naval and air bombardment followed by their main assault landings. As the Allied forces arrived ashore, they generally encountered sporadic or light resistance that was quickly overcome, often with the aid of naval gunfire. The one exception to this was at Camel Red Beach where persistent German artillery fire compelled the Allies to cancel their intended landing and move the impacted forces to an adjacent beach. Fortunately, this proved to be a minor setback as the Allies quickly captured Camel Red Beach by an overland approach. By nightfall the Allies were firmly ashore with most of their forward units positioned well beyond their assigned D-day objectives. The cost for this achievement amounted to just 95 dead and 385 wounded.[10] As a point of comparison, this represented less than a 20th of the Allied casualties suffered during the first day of the Normandy invasion.

Over the next few days, the Allies moved quickly to maintain the momentum and capitalise upon their initial success. A key component to this was the landing of follow-up French forces, which proceeded at an accelerated pace. By the evening of the 17th the Allies had 86,575 men, 12,250 vehicles and 46,140 tons of supplies ashore, and this number would increase to 190,565 men, 41,534 vehicles and 219,205 tons of supplies by 2 September.[11] Together, the American and French forces expanded outward from the initial lodgement area and proceeded inland against minimal German opposition. A major factor aiding this advance was a decision by Hitler on the 16th to heed the council of his military commanders and authorise a general withdrawal from southern France. In doing so, however, he stipulated that the ports of Toulon and Marseille must be held as long as possible to deny their use to the Allies. As such, some 31,000 troops remained behind to garrison these newly designated fortresses while the bulk of the German Army retreated northward.

For their part, the Luftwaffe and Kriegsmarine failed to have any appreciable impact upon the Allied invasion or its follow-up. In terms of the former, the Luftwaffe's response was so feeble that on 18 August the British Air Ministry described its efforts as 'too insignificant for comment'.[12] In fact, Luftwaffe aircraft did succeed in sinking *LST282* and two landing craft with glider bombs, but this proved to be the extent of their success. Meanwhile, the Kriegsmarine's performance was even less productive and only resulted in German losses. On the morning of D-day, the American destroyer *Somers* encountered the German corvette *UJ6081* (ex-Italian *Camoscio*) and the fast escort *SG21* (ex-French *Chamois*) off Port Cros and sank both in a spirited engagement. Shortly thereafter, a group of British minesweepers encountered five German patrol craft in Pampelonne Bay and sank them all. Then two days later the American destroyer *Endicott* teamed up with the British gunboats *Aphis* and *Scarab* to sink the German corvette *UJ6082* (ex-Italian *Antilope*) and an auxiliary sub-chaser in the Bay of La Ciotat. Also, on the 17th *U230* sortied out of Toulon to patrol the approaches to the harbour, but accomplished nothing and was eventually scuttled four days later after it accidentally grounded in shallow water. Likewise, on the 19th the Germans scuttled the unserviceable U-boats *U466* and *U967* in Toulon, thus ending the U-boat threat in the Western Mediterranean.

The impetus behind this final action was the approach of French forces advancing overland towards Toulon. Originally the French had intended to capture Toulon and Marseille in succession, but the accelerated pace of the Allied build-up allowed them to assault both ports simultaneously. By 20 August French forces had encircled Toulon and were advancing towards Marseille. Over the next few days, the French launched repeated assaults that progressively reduced the German defences at both ports. In this, they were supported by the heavy guns of numerous Allied warships, including the British battleship *Ramillies* and a British cruiser. They were also aided by the fact that a large portion of the defending German garrisons were comprised of Kriegsmarine, Luftwaffe and administrative personnel that were of dubious combat value. Given this reality, the German defences rapidly collapsed, and by 28 August both ports, along with some 28,000 prisoners, were in Allied hands. In return, the price for this achievement amounted to roughly 4,525 French casualties.[13]

With the fighting complete, the Allies began the arduous task of restoring their newly won prizes to an operating condition. In keeping with their usual practice, the Germans had extensively blocked and wrecked both ports before giving them up. Fortunately, the Allies had become very adept at rectifying this type of demolition, and by early September both ports were opened to receiving ships on a limited basis. This recovery process continued and by 25 September Marseille had 16 quayside berths available to handle Liberty ships, along with 23 holding berths and 45 bow-on berths for landing craft. Meanwhile, on the same date Toulon had nine quayside berths available plus 31 bow-on berths for landing craft.[14] This pattern repeated itself across the French Mediterranean coast as the Allies reclaimed increasingly more territory from the retreating German army. In the 40 days following the assault, this included the clearing of six ports and the elimination of 550 mines.[15] In turn, this increase in logistical capacity gave the Allies greater ability to build up and support their forces in southern France, which by 25 September included the arrival of 324,069 men, 68,419 vehicles, 490,237 tons of dry stores and 325,730 barrels of wet stores.[16]

Against this, the Germans were all but powerless to impede the torrent of Allied resources flowing into the area. With the local U-boat arm eliminated and the surface fleet and Luftwaffe rendered ineffective, the Germans turned to small battle units as a means to attack the Allied logistical effort. Already on 18 and 19 August the Germans had attempted to use Italian-built assault boats to attack Allied shipping, but these accomplished nothing and cost the Germans three boats in return. Then in September the Germans introduced *Marder* human torpedoes and *Molch* midget submarines into the struggle. The *Marder* was a three-ton, submersible manned torpedo that possessed a second 21-inch explosive torpedo slung below its carrier body. Operating out of the Italian port of San Remo, the Germans launched two *Marder* sorties on the nights of 4/5 and 9/10 September, but failed to attain any success for the loss of 14 of their number. Two weeks later the Germans attempted a similar undertaking using ten *Molch* midget submarines. The *Molch* was a one-man midget submarine that displaced 11 tons and was capable of carrying two 21-inch torpedoes or two mines. Unfortunately for the Germans, this attack too failed as Allied warships destroyed eight *Molch* for no loss to themselves. By the end of September these setbacks, plus a series of naval bombardments against their home bases, compelled the Germans to cease further small battle unit operations, and the short lived campaign ended in complete failure.

While these various actions were underway, the bulk of the German army continued its northward withdrawal from southern France. In this, pursuing American units, French partisans and Allied air attacks constantly harried the retreating German forces. Included in this aerial onslaught were the carrier aircraft of Task Force 88, which enjoyed considerable success during Operation *Dragoon*. Active from 15 to 28 August, Task Force 88 conducted over 2,300 combat sorties, of which 1,672 were flown by British aircraft.[17] A large part of this effort was dedicated to defensive air patrols, spotting for the bombardment forces or attacking fixed positions such as beach defences and gun emplacements, but it also included several hundred sorties that sought out and attacked German transportation assets throughout the region. In terms of the latter, aircraft from Task Force 88 destroyed or seriously damaged over 750 assorted vehicles, 21 locomotives and numerous rail cars, about 20 ferries and barges and 19 German aircraft.[18] Allied losses in return amounted to 43 aircraft destroyed during combat operations, plus several additional aircraft that were lost through deck landing accidents.[19]

A view from HMS *Pursuer*, part of the escort carrier force that took part in the invasion of southern France. Throughout much of the war Allied escort carriers provided valuable service within the theatre, including during Operations *Torch*, *Avalanche* and *Dragoon* and the re-conquest of the Aegean. (Hampton, J. A. (Lt), Royal Navy official photographer, public domain)

The conclusion of Task Force 88's activities coincided with the twin captures of Toulon and Marseille and the winding down of Operation *Dragoon*. A little more than two weeks later on 15 September, General Eisenhower assumed command over the *Dragoon* ground forces, which by this time had advanced well into central France. From this point on, all major combat operations in France proceeded under the dominion of the Northwest Europe campaign, and the Mediterranean theatre ceased to have any affiliation with these actions. In fact, the only major role left for the Allies in the Western Mediterranean was to provide logistical support for the armies in France. This was no simple task given the immense materiel requirements involved, but the Allies did a remarkable job fulfilling this mission. In October the Allies discharged 524,894 tons of materiel through the French Mediterranean ports, and this level of activity continued for the remainder of the war, with an average of 493,772 tons delivered per month.[20] Without this input, the Allied build-up and execution of operations in Western Europe would have been markedly restricted.

Beyond this vast logistical benefit, Operation *Dragoon* provided a number of other tangible results that were advantageous to the Allied cause. First and foremost, the landings in southern France helped facilitate the precipitous withdrawal of German forces from Normandy, Brittany and the French Atlantic region. In doing so, the Germans opted to retain control over the key Atlantic ports of Brest, Lorient, St. Nazaire, La Pallice, La Rochelle and parts of the Gironde in the Bay of Biscay to deny their use to the Allies. Designating these ports as fortresses, the Germans left behind sizable garrisons to defend these isolated outposts in what was otherwise a sea of Allied-controlled territory. In September American forces captured Brest after a long and difficult siege, but thereafter decided to forgo further attempts to capture the remaining Atlantic ports. Instead, they chose to let the sequestered German garrisons wither on the vine, thus making some 75,000 men little more than prisoners.[21] This misuse of valuable manpower had little impact upon the overall Allied war effort in Northwest Europe as British and Canadian forces were able to capture and put into service more-ideally positioned ports in northern France and Belgium that made access to the Biscay ports unnecessary.

Yet, this was only the beginning of Germany's misfortune within the area. Even though the Germans retained possession of the Biscay ports, these valuable assets were no longer capable of supporting naval operations, and the Germans were compelled to move their U-boat bases to Norway and Germany. These Norwegian bases could only handle about a third of the number of U-boats that the Biscay ports had handled. Moreover, they were located farther from the U-boat patrol areas. As such, these factors significantly impeded German U-boat operations for the remainder of the war. Added to this, during the process of evacuating the Biscay ports, the Germans suffered very heavy naval losses. In August and early September British and Allied warships, aircraft, mines and scuttling accounted for three German destroyers, two torpedo boats/escort destroyers, 22 U-boats, 23 fleet minesweepers and roughly 350,000 tons of merchant and auxiliary shipping lost within the area.[22] When combined together, this constituted a calamity of immense proportions. Although outside the direct realm of the Mediterranean theatre, Operation *Dragoon* clearly contributed to these many results.

Nor was this the extent of *Dragoon*'s success. During the month-long campaign the *Dragoon* forces inflicted heavy casualties upon the Germans, including the seizure of some 78,928 prisoners (including those taken at Toulon and Marseille).[23] German materiel losses were equally high, with maritime assets being particularly hard hit. In addition to the German naval losses already described, USAAF bombing and German scuttling destroyed large numbers of military vessels, including the torpedo boats *TA9* and *TA13*, the fast escorts *SG16*, *SG22*, *SG24* and *SG25* and the converted minelayers *M6062* and *M6063*.[24] Even more damaging, the Germans scuttled or surrendered 97 merchant ships and commercial vessels worth a combined 279,305 tons.[25] In keeping with this, the seizure of southern France permanently eliminated the threat of U-boat and Luftwaffe activity in the Western Mediterranean. Finally, the Allies attained these many benefits for the relatively small sum of just 12,911 ground casualties.[26] For their part, naval losses were inconsequential, amounting to just one LST, two auxiliary motor minesweepers, two PT boats and five landing craft for the Americans and one motor launch and two landing craft for the British.[27] This minor accounting compared quite favourably to the 209,672 personnel casualties and 60 military vessels, 45 supply ships/transports and 419 landing craft that were lost to the Allies during the three-month long Normandy campaign.[28]

Yet, even as the Allies savoured their many triumphs from Operation *Dragoon*, a new situation arose on the other side of the Mediterranean that offered additional opportunities for political and military exploitation. During the summer of 1944 the Soviets made great advances across the breadth of their front, and by the middle of August their forces were poised to enter Eastern Europe. Given this imminent threat, Germany's easternmost allies abruptly collapsed. While Italy had been Germany's primary and most powerful European ally, Finland, Romania, Hungry and Bulgaria had also joined the Axis cause.[29] Of these, the first to go was Romania, which deserted the Axis on 23 August and declared war on Germany two days later. Then in early September an armed uprising against the pro-German government in Bulgaria quickly prompted that country to follow suit. As this growing calamity unfolded, the Germans became increasingly aware that their forces in Greece were poised to be cut off, and on 26 August Hitler made the uncharacteristic decision to authorise a phased withdrawal. At first, the Germans hoped to limit this withdrawal to the Aegean and southern Greece, but as the situation deteriorated in Eastern Europe, it quickly became apparent that a full evacuation was required.

As the Allies became aware of these decisions through Ultra and other intelligence sources, they devised actions to capitalise upon the situation. In this, their goals were twofold. First, in a strictly military sense, they wanted to inflict as much attrition and delay to the retreating German forces as possible. Second and even more important, they wanted to ensure an orderly return of a friendly Greek government once the Germans departed. This latter desire was facilitated by the knowledge that the Communist-leaning ELAS partisan movement intended to seize control. Already, for almost a year ELAS fighters had launched attacks against their royalist EDES rivals, and by the summer of 1944 ELAS was poised to fill the void once the Germans withdrew. To prevent this from happening, the Allies planned to deploy significant naval forces into the Aegean and utilise aircraft from Italy and Africa to interdict German shipping movements, thus slowing the German withdrawal and attritting their forces. Then as conditions allowed, the Allies would land ground forces to occupy key territory culminating in a return to mainland Greece. Again, the purpose for this was not to facilitate a German withdrawal, but to rapidly follow it up as it occurred.

The beginning of September saw both sides gathering forces to carry out their respective missions. For the Germans, this included the acquisition of 52 merchant ships worth 27,230 tons plus numerous small warships and landing craft and upwards of 200 *caïques* (local Greek fishing vessels). To further bolster this force, the Germans transferred three torpedo boats from the Adriatic into the Aegean and assembled some 80 transport aircraft on the airfields around Athens to perform airlift duties. Against this, the Allies overwhelmingly depended upon British assets to impede the German evacuation. This was particularly true regarding the naval forces, which came exclusively from British or British-affiliated sources. The main element of this was Force 120, which came under the operational command of Rear-Admiral Troubridge and included seven escort carriers with 140 fighter-bomber strike aircraft, seven cruisers, eight destroyers and 11 escort destroyers. The British also dispatched submarines and coastal craft to participate in the interdiction effort. Likewise, the Allies called upon the long-range aircraft of the Mediterranean Allied Air Force and RAF Command, Middle East, to carry out raids and anti-shipping sweeps. Finally, the Allies assembled two British army brigades and various Royal Marine and Free Greek army units to carry out the initial landings when they occurred.

The first phase of the Allied offensive was designed to isolate and neutralise Crete, Rhodes and the outer Aegean islands by attacking German shipping and infrastructure targets. The British began this assault on 6 September when Beaufighter strike aircraft attacked the 1,348-ton merchant ship *Carola* off Piraeus and damaged it so severely that it was rendered a total loss. Over the next three weeks Beaufighters carried out similar attacks throughout the area that sank a number of vessels, including the minelayers *Drache* and *Pelikan* (1,870 and 834 tons respectively), the 707-ton merchant ship *Orion*, the 314-ton transport *Helly*, the 272-ton tanker *Elli*, the 260-ton minesweeper *Nordstern* and the sub-chaser *UJ2142*. Meanwhile, on 15 September USAAF bombers attacked Salamis and sank the German torpedo boat *TA14* (ex-Italian *Turbine*), the 834-ton military transport *Mannheim*, the sub-chaser *UJ2107* and two minor craft. Three days later British bombers attacked Piraeus and severely damaged the torpedo boat *TA17* (ex-Italian *San Martino*), leaving it a total wreck.

While this aerial assault was underway, elements of Force 120 joined the fray by launching Operation *Outing*, a series of sweeps and attacks against targets in the southern Aegean. On the night of 12/13 September the destroyers *Troubridge* and *Tuscan* attacked a small German convoy north of Crete and sank the 638-ton transport *Toni* and five minor vessels. Two nights later the cruiser *Royalist* and the destroyer *Teazer* encountered and sank the German war transports *KT4* and *KT26* worth a combined 1,668 tons off Cape Spatha. Then on the 16th and 17th aircraft from the escort carriers *Attacker*, *Pursuer*, *Khedive*, *Emperor* and *Searcher* attacked targets on Crete and Melos and destroyed or seriously damaged some 30 motor vehicles and about a dozen *caïques* and other minor craft. During that same time the cruiser *Aurora* bombarded Melos harbour and destroyed a beached merchant ship and three minor vessels, while the destroyers *Garland* (Polish), *Troubridge*, *Terpsichore*, *Brecon* and *Zetland* sank one of the last remaining German U-boats left in the Mediterranean, *U407*, in the same area. Finally, on 19 September the escort carriers *Attacker*, *Emperor*, *Khedive* and *Pursuer* launched a strike of 22 Seafires, ten Hellcats and ten Wildcats against Rhodes Harbour that sank the 639-ton merchant ship *Pomezia*, a naval ferry barge and two minor vessels and damaged three depot ships and a KT ship.

After a brief respite, Force 120 returned to the Aegean to further isolate the exterior islands and begin neutralising the interior region. From 24 September through 6 October British warships and carrier aircraft conducted a series of sweeps and strikes that destroyed at least 18 additional vessels of mostly minor tonnage. During the same period Allied aircraft and submarines continued their interdiction efforts. In terms of the former, on 24 September USAAF bombers attacked Skaramanga and sank the last two U-boats left in the Mediterranean, *U565* and *U596*, along with the sub-chaser *UJ2108*, a small commercial vessel and two patrol craft. At about the same time the fighter direction ship *Ulster Queen* moved into the area to guide RAF night-fighters to interdict the flow of German transport aircraft evacuating key personnel from the exterior islands. Over the course of several nights these British fighters destroyed 20 German Ju 52/3m transport aircraft and damaged 20 more. Meanwhile, strikes by long-range British and American fighter-bombers destroyed a further 25 German transport aircraft on the airfields around Athens.[30] Finally, British and British-affiliated Allied submarines carried out numerous attacks that sank four German merchant ships worth 8,309 tons and ten minor vessels in the contested area.[31]

By the second week in October British naval forces were operating off the Greek mainland, and the fighting intensified as the Germans moved to transfer shipping from Piraeus to Salonika. On the night of 6/7 October the British destroyers *Termagant* and *Tuscan* intercepted a small German convoy consisting of the minelayer *Zeus*, which had 1,125 evacuees onboard, along with an escort consisting of the torpedo boat *TA37* (ex-Italian *Gladio*), the sub-chaser *UJ2102* and the harbour patrol boat *GK32* in the Gulf of Salonika. In the battle that followed, *Zeus* was able to escape, but the British destroyers sank all three of the German escorts for no loss to themselves. Twelve days later these same two British destroyers enjoyed a similar success when they intercepted and sank the German torpedo boat *TA18* (ex-Italian *Solferino*) off Skiathos. During the same period, other British warships, including motor torpedo boats, sank an additional 12 German vessels of mostly minor tonnage within the region.

Beyond these surface actions, British carrier and shore-based aircraft continued to pummel the evacuating forces. In terms of the former, aircraft from the escort carriers *Stalker*, *Hunter*, *Emperor* and *Attacker* carried out a series of wide-ranging attacks that destroyed or severely damaged some 30 assorted vessels, 12 locomotives and over 100 railway cars and motor vehicles. Included in this were two small merchant ships worth 888 tons, a 120-ton *Dresden*-class tanker, a 600-ton concrete barge and

The last year and a half of the Mediterranean conflict featured numerous clashes between British forces and elements of the Kriegsmarine. Pictured here is the destroyer *Tuscan*, which in September and October 1944 participated in three engagements that destroyed two German torpedo boats and several other vessels in the Aegean. (Allan C. Green, public domain)

a *Siebel* ferry that were sunk by Seafire fighter-bombers from 7 through 9 October while several other craft were damaged. Amongst the latter was the German torpedo boat *TA38* (ex-Italian *Spada*), which was damaged by Seafires in the Peliti Channel on 9 October, thus forcing it to take shelter in Volos harbour. Meanwhile, on the 11th Hellcats from *Emperor* attacked three separate convoys in and around the Gulf of Salonika where they destroyed nine minor vessels and damaged nine more. Then on 12 October British shore-based bombers attacked Piraeus and destroyed the non-operational torpedo boats *TA15* (ex-Italian *Francesco Crispi*) and *TA17* (ex-Italian *San Martino*).[32] Finally, the next day British and South African aircraft carried out a devastating raid against Volos that resulted in the destruction of the previously damaged torpedo boat *TA38*, two merchant ships worth 9,352 tons and 25 auxiliaries and minor vessels.

Beyond these many interdiction successes, the British also conducted a number of minor landings to establish control over key portions of Greek and regional territory. This included the seizure of several islands, including Kithira, Levitha, Samos, Naxos, Lemnos, Scarpanto, Santorini and Corfu as well as the capture of the Albanian port of Sarande. In most cases, the British encountered small German or Fascist Italian garrisons still present in these areas, but these quickly surrendered after offering little or no resistance. During the same period British commandos landed at Araxos in northwest Peloponnese where they joined with EDES partisans to clear the northern portion of the peninsula and take the surrender of isolated Axis forces stranded in the Gulf of Corinth. When combined together, these various peripheral operations provided the British with an important foothold in southern Greece and netted them over 4,000 prisoners for minimal cost to themselves.[33]

On 13 October the British moved their ground incursion to the next level when elements of the British 2nd Parachute Brigade conducted airborne landings at Megara airfield near Athens. With the arrival of reinforcements, these paratroopers entered Athens unopposed on 15 October. That same day further British and Free Greek forces, including the British 23rd Armoured Brigade, disembarked by sea at Piraeus to occupy the port and solidify their hold over the capital and surrounding area. Warships directly supporting this undertaking, which was designated Operation *Manna*, consisted of the escort carriers *Attacker* and *Stalker*, the cruiser *Royalist* and six destroyers, while a detached *Emperor* carried out further interdiction strikes in the Gulf of Salonika. There was no opposition to the British landings, although fighters from *Stalker* did shoot down a German reconnaissance aircraft that strayed into the area and a floatplane caught taking off from Volos harbour. By 17 October the British had successfully disembarked some 5,000 men, 400 vehicles and 1,000 tons of stores in conjunction with the operation.[34] The ultimate payoff for this occurred the next day when Prime Minister Georgios Papandreou and the Greek government-in-exile arrived in Athens to set up a government for the newly liberated nation.

While this was underway, the Germans continued their northward withdrawal from mainland Greece. For the remainder of the month small contingents of British commandos and paratroopers harried the retreating German forces. During this time these elements fought a number of skirmishes with German rear guards that hastened the German retreat and compelled them in some cases to abandon equipment or cut short demolition efforts. Meanwhile, British naval and air units continued their interdiction campaign against the diminishing number of transportation targets still operating in the area. Some of Germany's final maritime losses in Greek waters included the torpedo boat *TA39* (ex-Italian *Daga*) and the 1,193-ton merchant ship *Lola* that sank on mines on 16 October, and the 13,870-ton hospital ship *Gradisca*, which was captured by the British destroyer *Kimberley* on 29 October. Then at the end of the month the Germans abandoned Salonika and scuttled the 2,423-ton minelayer *Zeus*, two sizable merchant ships worth 4,884 tons, four lesser commercial vessels worth 1,644 tons, an E-boat, three motor minesweepers and nine minor auxiliaries.[35]

This final action signalled the end to the short, but highly successful Greek liberation campaign. Twice before in 1941 and 1943 British forces had made attempts to control the Aegean only to be ejected with heavy losses. Now in the autumn of 1944 the British exacted revenge for these past failures and gave the Germans a dose of their own high losses. This was particularly true regarding maritime assets. Of the 52 German merchant ships assembled to conduct evacuation operations in the Aegean, 29 were sunk outright (worth 19,434 tons) while most of the remainder were scuttled as blockships.[36] Added to this, the Germans also lost seven torpedo boats, three U-boats, three minelayers, a large hospital ship and scores of auxiliaries and minor vessels. Beyond these materiel losses, the Germans abandoned 22,400 army and 4,095 naval personnel on Crete, Rhodes and some of the other Aegean islands. Added to this were 12,000 Fascist Italians that were also left behind.[37] Isolated and impotent, these men were all but lost to the Axis war effort and might as well have been prisoners of war given their limited combat value. Finally, by promptly filling the void left by the German evacuation, the British helped establish a pro-western government in Greece. Communist insurgents would soon challenge this outcome, but with British and later American help, Greece would remain in the western camp, thus providing the British with an important post-war triumph.

The victories attained in southern France and Greece were noteworthy in a number of regards and indicative of the overriding success the Allies were experiencing in the greater war effort. In terms of the former, both victories were attained relatively quickly and at little cost to the Allied forces involved. By comparison, the impacted German forces suffered substantially higher losses in terms of men captured or left behind and materiel resources destroyed or abandoned. Similarly, both victories garnered important strategic benefits beyond a mere accounting of the corresponding casualties and materiel costs attained. In executing these victories, the Allies employed multiple services, but sea power provided the essential foundation for each undertaking. Finally, in both cases, the Germans made little if any attempt to resist the Allied assaults, but rather focused most of their attention on trying to escape the growing tide enveloping them. Given this reality, Germany's cause was clearly doomed, and final victory now seemed right around the corner. The main question that remained was how long it would take to secure this inevitable victory and at what cost?

CHAPTER 11

Britannia's Sea, Victory in the Mediterranean

With their victories in southern France and Greece in the late summer and early autumn of 1944, the Allies concluded the realisation of an objective that had eluded them since the beginning of the conflict – unimpeded transit through the Mediterranean Sea. The Allies had opened the Mediterranean as a crucial transportation artery the year before, but during the intervening period, transiting ships had still faced a degree of opposition from German U-boats and aircraft. Now, other than the isolated and impotent German garrisons remaining on some of the Aegean Islands, this threat was entirely eliminated, and the Allies controlled the length and breadth of the Mediterranean passage. Corresponding with this was the almost complete eradication of Axis offensive air and naval capacity within the region. While these outcomes were clearly the result of joint Allied action, this victory was particularly gratifying for the British, who had done the bulk of the fighting through the duration of the campaign and had endured the greatest hardships during the dark periods of 1941 and 1942.

Of the various beneficiaries from these developments, none was more important than the burgeoning British war effort in the Far East against Japan. Over the previous year a constant stream of ships had passed through the Mediterranean bringing men and resources to India to painstakingly rebuild the British ground, air and naval forces stationed there. In February 1944 the recently created British Fourteenth Army won its first major victory over the Japanese during the battle of Ngakyedauk Pass in western Burma. Then during the next five months (March through July) Fourteenth Army won a substantially greater victory at Imphal and Kohima that handed the Japanese army the worst defeat in its history up to this point. Casualties for these combined battles numbered 58,840 for the Japanese compared to 20,173 for the British.[1] Bolstered by these successes, Fourteenth Army was now poised to launch a large-scale offensive to liberate Burma and destroy the Japanese forces located there.

Meanwhile, the British matched this success on the ground with a revitalised Eastern Fleet that reasserted British dominance in the Indian Ocean and increasingly assumed an offensive posture against the Japanese. As part of this, the British neutralised the small, but persistent U-boat threat that had existed in the Indian Ocean while concurrently expanding their own submarine operations against the local Japanese shipping. Then in the spring and summer of 1944 the British added the deployment of surface naval forces built around aircraft carriers that conducted a series of raids against regional targets. Eventually, a sizable portion of these surface forces would morph into the British Pacific Fleet, which would operate alongside the Americans against the Japanese home islands. Many of the warships that served (or would serve) in these fleets were veterans from the Mediterranean conflict, including the battleships *Queen Elizabeth, Valiant, King George V, Howe* and *Nelson*, the battlecruiser *Renown* and the aircraft carriers *Illustrious, Formidable, Victorious* and *Indomitable*. The fact that these vessels were available to serve in the Indian and Pacific Oceans was a testament to the ascendancy the British had attained in the Mediterranean over their Italian and German rivals, thus freeing them for use against the Japanese.

The successful application of British sea power in the Atlantic and Mediterranean helped bring France back into the Allied camp and released numerous ships to operate against the Japanese. Pictured here are the battlecruiser *Renown* (front), the battleship *Valiant* (right) and the French battleship *Richelieu* (left) during a 1944 sweep of the British Eastern Fleet in the Indian Ocean. (Pilot from USS *Saratoga* (CV-3), public domain)

Another major beneficiary of this Mediterranean success was the Soviet Union. As discussed in Chapter 4, one of the key access points used by the Allies to transfer war materiel to the Soviet Union was through the Persian Gulf region. During the first half of the war the Allies delivered this aid through a long and arduous trek around the Cape of Good Hope, but with the opening of the Mediterranean, the duration and difficulty of this process was significantly eased. This, in turn, helped facilitate a greater transfer of resources through the Persian Gulf, which eventually accounted for some 23.8 percent of all aid shipped to the Soviet Union.[2] This situation would improve even more in 1945 when the expulsion of German forces from the Balkans and Turkey's entry into the war allowed Allied ships to travel through the Mediterranean into the Black Sea, thus facilitating an even quicker delivery of resources much closer to their actual points of use. Again, the ability to do this was only made possible through the prevailing control the Allies had over the Mediterranean.

Still, even as the British and their Allied partners enjoyed the benefits of this maritime dominance, they were also acutely aware that their victory was incomplete. Despite Allied successes throughout the theatre, the Germans still occupied the northern third of Italy as well as much of Yugoslavia. While this presence was isolated from the flow of seaborne traffic transiting through the Mediterranean and had minimal impact upon the local Allied strategic bombing operations, the Allies still sought to eliminate these German enclaves, thus completing their conquest of the region. Likewise, German warships continued to operate in the adjacent waters. In fairness, none of these warships was larger than a destroyer, and other than local mine-laying and small battle unit sorties, German naval operations were almost exclusively defensive in nature and limited to these coastal areas. Many additional ships were non-operational, including a number of captured Italian submarines, but these vessels were little more than targets for the regular Allied air strikes and bombing raids that were now prevalent in all remaining portions of German-controlled territory.

The situation was more difficult regarding the local German ground forces, and the Allies faced many challenges in their quest to conclude the campaign in northern Italy. Foremost amongst these was a weakening strength ratio compared to the defending German forces. A primary reason for this was the recent transfer of three American and four French divisions, along with significant air and logistical assets from Italy to carry out Operation *Dragoon*. Contrasting this, during roughly the same period the Germans attained a net gain of five new divisions in Italy. As such, by mid-August the competing forces in Italy comprised 20 divisions for the Allies compared to 26 German and two Fascist Italian divisions for the Axis. Given the overriding events underway in France and Eastern Europe at the time, this result clearly contributed to the Allied goal of tying down German forces in Italy, but this strategic realisation came at the cost of making it more difficult for the Allies to attain local tactical success.

Making matters worse, unlike their counterparts in southern France and Greece, the Germans in Italy intended to stand and fight. Assisting them in this matter were the formidable defences of the newly established Gothic Line. Stretching some 200 miles from Pisa on the Ligurian coast to Pesaro on the Adriatic, most of the Gothic Line was built along the mountainous terrain of the northern Apennines. The exception to this was the easternmost portion where the mountains gradually gave way to a coastal plain that contained a series of spurs and rivers running perpendicular to the proposed line of advance. Likewise, much of this plain's low-lying terrain was susceptible to flooding when it rained. Utilising these natural barriers, the Germans constructed a series of strong defensive positions. By 28 August this effort included the construction of 2,375 machine gun posts, 479 artillery positions, 3,604 dugouts and shelters, 16,006 rifle positions, 8,944 metres of anti-tank ditches and the placement of 95,689 assorted mines and 117,370 metres of wire in just the eastern portion of the line defended by the German Tenth Army.[3] A second German army, the Fourteenth, defended the western portion of the line with a total of 19 divisions split between these two commands. The remaining nine Axis divisions garrisoned northern Italy where they countered growing partisan activity and defended against the prospect of further Allied amphibious landings.

For their part, the Allies were determined to maintain their forward progress despite the adversities arrayed against them. To carry this out, the Allies devised a massive new offensive, designated Operation *Olive*, to breach the Gothic Line. In this, Allied planners envisioned a one-two punch to dislodge the German defenders. Eighth Army would launch the first phase of this offensive by attacking along a 30-mile front on the Adriatic side of the Gothic Line. Taking advantage of the less inhospitable terrain, the British hoped to capitalise on their substantial armour and artillery resources to breach the Gothic Line and seize Rimini and the Rimini-Bologna road. Thereafter, the British would advance towards Bologna, threatening the rear of the German defences. To carry this out, Eighth Army possessed a total of four corps with 11 divisions, 1,200 tanks and 1,000 artillery pieces. Given this onslaught, the Allies anticipated that the Germans would shift forces from their western defences to meet the threat, and when conditions were right, the Allies would launch the second phase of their offensive with an attack by Fifth Army through the central Apennines. Utilising three corps (one of which was British), Fifth Army would advance towards Bologna, thus forming a pincer with the oncoming Eighth Army to destroy or dislodge the remaining German forces in the east.[4]

On 25 August Eighth Army opened its offensive with simultaneous attacks carried out by II Polish, I Canadian and V British Corps against the easternmost portion of the Gothic Line. This assault caught the Germans by surprise, and the British were able to make initial steady progress against the disjointed German defenders. By 2 September the British were through the main Gothic Line positions and advancing towards a secondary defensive line north of the Conca River. As anticipated, these actions caused the Germans to shift substantial reinforcements into the area, and on 5 September a British attempt to seize the Coriano ridge failed. This caused the British to pause and prepare a deliberate attack, which they successfully carried out on 12 and 13 September with the assistance of substantial artillery, air and naval gunfire support. Thereafter, the British continued their advance, and on 21 September elements of I Canadian Corps captured Rimini, thus achieving the first major milestone of the offensive. In 28 days, Eighth Army had advanced 30 miles and severely mauled the German LXXVI Panzer Corps, which suffered 16,000 casualties, including 8,170 men taken prisoner and the loss of just under 100 tanks and 124 artillery pieces.[5] Unfortunately, this success came at a heavy price as Eighth Army suffered some 14,000 casualties and 210 tanks irretrievably lost during the same period.[6]

For its part, Fifth Army launched its portion of the offensive on 10 September. This was mainly carried out by the US II Corps attacking with four divisions through the Il Giogo pass, supported by the British XIII Corps with three divisions attacking on its right flank towards Faenza. Given the transfer of reinforcements to stem Eighth Army's offensive, the Germans only had two divisions initially available to oppose this onslaught, but the terrain and formidable Gothic Line defences still slowed the Allied advance. This was particularly true for II Corps, which made little initial headway in its opening assault. Progress was better on XIII Corps' front, and the Americans quickly sent reinforcements to exploit this success. On 17 September a combined attack by the British 1st and American 85th Divisions split the German defences east of the Il Giogo pass, thus forcing a local withdrawal. Four days later the American 88th Division passed through the 85th Division and made rapid progress down the Imola road, eventually capturing Monte Battaglia on 27 September. However, here the advance stopped as the Germans launched a series of counter-attacks that blunted further progress.

By this stage in the offensive, the Allies were completely through the Gothic Line on both the Eighth and Fifth Army fronts, but they found the going behind this formidable barrier to be extremely difficult. When Fifth Army renewed its offensive towards Bologna in October, it took four weeks of heavy fighting for II Corps to advance ten miles, while progress on the flanks was even worse. Unfortunately, this meagre headway came at a heavy cost. From 10 September through 26 October the four American divisions of II Corps suffered a staggering 15,716 casualties, while British XIII Corps suffered a further 7,087 casualties through 14 October.[7] Things were moderately better on Eighth Army's front, where after the capture of Rimini, the British continued their northward advance. In this, the British were able to make steady, if unspectacular, progress, but a sustained breakthrough and pursuit eluded them. By the end of October a reinforced I Canadian Corps had advanced some 20 miles up the Adriatic coast while British V Corps had reached the vicinity of Forli, which was located roughly a third of the way between Rimini and Bologna along Route 9.

The reasons for these limited results were fivefold. First, harsh terrain continued to impede the Allied advances and follow-up logistical efforts. Second, heavy rain exacerbated this situation by swelling the rivers and turning much of the ground into muddy morass. Likewise, the rain mitigated the effectiveness of Allied air power. Third, despite their own heavy losses, the Germans doggedly mounted an effective defence that was bolstered by the arrival of fresh formations from northern Italy. Fourth, prolonged operations strained the Allied logistical system causing shortages of key commodities such as artillery ammunition. Finally, and perhaps most importantly, heavy casualties and a lack of adequate replacements progressively debilitated both Allied armies, thus reducing their combat effectiveness. By this stage in the war, all of the Allied nations were suffering varying degrees of manpower shortages, but this was particularly true in Britain where five years of conflict and substantial global commitments had strained the available manpower pool to a near breaking point. Exacerbating this problem was the fact that the campaign in Northwest Europe took priority for the resources that did exist. As such, by the autumn of 1944 the Allies in the Mediterranean were grossly short of reserve formations and replacement personnel, and this forced them to overuse and, in some cases, cannibalise existing units to make good their combat losses.

Given these realities, General Alexander, the Allied ground forces commander, realised he must soon halt the offensive to give his tired armies a chance to rest and regroup. However, before this happened, he wanted to capture Bologna and Ravenna so they could be used as winter bases. By this time Fifth Army was largely a spent force, so at the end of October Alexander ordered it to pause operations while Eighth Army continued its advance towards Ravenna. Over the next two months Eighth Army, despite its own exhaustion and diminishing strength, relentlessly pushed forward, not only capturing Ravenna, but also Faenza on Route 9 to Bologna. When Eighth Army finally ceased operations in early January 1945, it had advanced to the southern shores of Lake Comacchio, located some ten miles north of Ravenna, and added a further 5,000 prisoners to its cages. This, in turn, brought Eighth Army's total tally from the beginning of the offensive (25 August 1944) through 9 January 1945 to 14,805 German and roughly 3,000 non-German prisoners.[8] Meanwhile, in December Alexander (now promoted to Field Marshal) ordered Fifth Army to launch its offensive towards Bologna. However, before this could happen, German and Fascist Italian forces launched a spoiling attack on Fifth Army's Ligurian flank. With the help of the 8th Indian Division, which was rushed into the area, the Allies quickly restored the situation, but the action forced Fifth Army to cancel its Bologna offensive, thus curtailing further operations until the spring. For its part, Fifth Army had taken 13,573 prisoners during the offensive, of which 1,963 were collected by its attached British units.[9]

While this action signalled a temporary pause in the ground war, maritime operations continued at an unrelenting pace. Throughout this period Allied air and naval assets continued their interdiction efforts against the dwindling number of German vessels still present in the Ligurian and Adriatic Seas. The vast majority of these actions occurred against minor craft, but the Allies also scored numerous successes against sizable targets. In terms of the latter, in August and September USAAF aircraft sank 11 large merchant ships worth a combined 49,256 tons, along with the light cruiser *Taranto*, the torpedo boats *TA28* (ex-Italian *Rigel*) and *TA33* (ex-Italian *Squadrista*), the corvettes *UJ2223* (ex-Italian *Marangone*) and *UJ6085* (ex-Italian *Renna*) and the submarines *UIT15* (ex-Italian *Sparide*), *UIT16* (ex-Italian *Murena*) and *UIT20* (ex-Italian *Grongo*) in raids against local ports. Also in September, RAF Beaufighters sank the captured Italian passenger liner *Rex* off Capo d'Istria near Trieste. Weighing 51,062 tons, *Rex* represented the largest merchant ship sunk during the war, and its destruction denied the Germans the opportunity to use it as a blockship. In that same month British aircraft destroyed two further merchant ships, the 21,900-ton *Giulio Cesare* and the 1,979-ton *Mercurio*, at Vallone di Zaule and off Grado respectively.

The Allies continued their aerial onslaught in October and November, with British and Commonwealth aircraft moving to the forefront of the offensive. On 4 October South African aircraft attacked Genoa and destroyed the submarine *UIT1* (ex-Italian *R10*), which was under construction at the time. Three weeks later American bombers attacked the same port and damaged the torpedo boat *TA31* (ex-Italian *Dardo*) so extensively that it was rendered a total loss. Then on 4 November British aircraft sank the torpedo boat *TA49* (ex-Italian *Lira*), which was fitting out at La Spezia. The next day British aircraft bombed Fiume and destroyed the torpedo boat *TA21* (ex-Italian *Insidioso*), the 3667-ton minelayer *Kiebitz* and the auxiliary escort vessel *G104*. Following this, on 11 November British Beaufighters attacked and sank the 3,509-ton German hospital ship *Tübingen* off Cap Promontore. Finally, on 12 November South African aircraft sank the 834-ton war transports *KT35* and *KT36* at Genoa and off Moneglia respectively.

In related operations, this period also saw a continuation of the RAF's mining campaign against the barge traffic traversing the Danube River. As previously mentioned in Chapter 9, the Danube was a major transportation artery that not only supported the logistical needs of German forces confronting the Soviet Union, but was also the primary means by which petroleum products were dispersed from the Romanian oil fields. After a month-long pause in June, the Liberators and Wellingtons of No. 205 Group recommenced mining operations against the Danube in early July and continued their periodic drops for the next three months, concluding in early October. During the duration of this campaign, which started in April, the British carried out 392 mining and four flare-dropping sorties in which they laid a total of 1,375 mines. In turn, these mines sank an estimated 60 tugs and 200 barges with many more damaged.[10] Added to this, RAF Beaufighters carried out periodic sweeps over the river where they destroyed eight large oil barges and

The 51,062-ton Italian liner *Rex* on its side following an attack by RAF Beaufighters south of Trieste on 8 September 1944. *Rex* had the dubious distinction of being the largest merchant ship sunk during the war. Altogether, a total of 3,179 Axis merchant ships worth 4,147,523 tons were lost during the duration of the Mediterranean conflict. (Royal Air Force official photographer, public domain)

damaged 102 other craft. The net result of this combined onslaught was a 60 to 70 percent reduction in Danube barge traffic from April through August, which had a devastating effect upon German logistical efforts.[11] In fact, Albert Speer, the German minister of armaments and war production, later testified that the Danube mining had a greater impact in diminishing German oil supplies than did the acclaimed direct attacks against the Ploesti oil refineries.[12]

While on the subject, it is also worthwhile to touch upon the immense contributions that Allied bombers operating out of Italy had on the strategic bombing campaign. Primarily centred upon the activities of the American Fifteenth Air Force, this was overwhelmingly an American undertaking, although a number of British Liberator and Wellington squadrons from No. 205 Group also participated in the effort. Operating bombers out of Italy afforded the Allies a number of important benefits. Foremost amongst these was the ability to hit critical strategic targets that were beyond the range of bombers operating out of Britain, including multiple aircraft and armaments production facilities, oil refineries, synthetic oil plants and regional transportation assets. Other benefits included better flying weather generally prevalent within the region, a wider avenue of attacks that forced the Germans to spread their defences and the ability to use these attacks to directly support Soviet operations in Eastern Europe. Beginning operations on 2 November 1943, Fifteenth Air Force eventually flew 152,542 bomber and 89,835 fighter sorties throughout the duration of the campaign, concluding on 1 May 1945. During this time, it dropped 309,278 tons of bombs on targets ranging from eastern France to western Ukraine and as far north as southern Poland. Beyond the enormous damage these raids caused to ground facilities, Fifteenth Air Force claimed 3,946 aerial victories during the course of its operations for the cost of 3,410 aircraft in return.[13]

A major beneficiary of this immense onslaught was the Soviet Union. This support came in two primary forms. First, it helped deprive the German army and Luftwaffe of much needed fuel. During the last year of the war Mediterranean-based bombers destroyed or extensively damaged 46 crude-oil refineries and five synthetic oil plants located within their zone of operations that accounted for roughly 60 percent of all German oil supplies. In the Ploesti area alone, attacks from April through August 1944 destroyed 89 percent of the local production capacity and reduced gasoline and aviation fuel output by 91 percent.[14] These results had major implications for the entire German war effort, but were particularly consequential on the Eastern Front since most of the lost fuel was earmarked for use there. Adding to this already stark situation, Fifteenth Air force carried out extensive raids against regional transportation assets such as railway lines, marshalling yards and bridges that made it exceedingly difficult for the Germans to provide logistical support for their forward deployed units. From mid-1944 on, these two factors repeatedly assisted Soviet forces in outmanoeuvring and overcoming the largely immobile and emasculated German formations confronting them, thus greatly aiding the Soviet advance and hastening the end of the war.

Of course, this crucial aerial contribution was only made possible through the previous and ongoing successes attained in the Mediterranean. From the acquisition and maintenance of air bases in Italy and the surrounding islands to the ongoing efforts to keep the various aerial components abundantly supplied, this was all the result of an effective application of maritime power. Long gone were the days when the total air strength of the RAFME had numbered just a few hundred aircraft. Instead, the various Allied air commands now present in the theatre possessed an incredible 12,500 aircraft and some 325,000 personnel.[15] In turn, this was just part of about 1.7 million men making up the full force structure present within the region. Supporting this all was a constant flow of supply ships bringing in the fuel, ammunition, provisions and other materiel necessary to sustain the vast Allied effort. Putting this mammoth task into perspective, the amount of seaborne tonnage delivered to southern France alone each month was about seven times the average monthly tonnage the Axis had struggled to deliver to their forces in North Africa earlier in the war. While clearly an impressive achievement on its own, these French deliveries only constituted a fraction of the total Allied deliveries made within the region. Thus, it was sea power that provided the essential catalyst for the strategic bombing campaign and everything else underway within the theatre.

Returning now to the Allies' interdiction efforts within the Mediterranean, the Royal Navy also contributed to this ongoing campaign by dispatching various warships on regular forays into the waters off northern Italy and Yugoslavia where they destroyed a number of vessels of mostly minor tonnage. An exception to this occurred on the night of 1/2 November when the British Hunt class escort destroyers *Wheatland* and *Avon Vale* accompanied an assorted force of motor torpedo boats and motor gunboats to the waters between Rab and Premuda on the Dalmatian coast. Upon a sighting report from one of the motor torpedo boats, the British escort destroyers intercepted the German corvettes *UJ202* (ex-Italian *Melpómene*) and *UJ208* (ex-Italian *Spingarda*) off Pag Island at about 2015 hours and sank them both in a well-executed nocturnal engagement. Then at 2230 hours, while carrying out rescue operations, *Wheatland* and *Avon Vale* detected a third German warship, the torpedo boat *TA20* (ex-Italian *Audace*), entering the area and quickly engaged the new intruder in a devastating attack that resulted in its prompt destruction. Thus, in a period of little more than two hours the two British escort destroyers sank three equivalent German warships for no loss to themselves.

Rounding out the heavy toll inflicted upon the Kriegsmarine during this period were large numbers of ships sunk by other means. This included the torpedo boats *TA19* (ex-Italian *Calatafimi*) and *TA35* (ex-Italian *Giuseppe Dezza*), which were sunk by the Greek submarine *Pipinos* (ex-British *Veldt*) and mines off Samos and Pola on 9 and 17 August respectively. Likewise, the Germans scuttled large numbers of ships as they were forced to surrender territory. Already mentioned were the 279,305 tons of shipping scuttled or abandoned in southern France. Beyond this, from August through December the Germans scuttled a further 22 military and 60 commercial vessels worth 33,349 and 72,841 tons respectively. Of these, eight military and 40 commercial vessels worth 33,066 and 54,077 tons respectively were scuttled in the month of October alone (mostly in Greek waters).[16] When combined together and taking into account losses from all causes, the Germans lost a total of 340 military vessels and 304 merchant ships worth 79,271 and 519,985 tons respectively in the Mediterranean theatre from August through December 1944.[17] As bad as this was, this is still not a complete tally since it does not include U-boat losses or the destruction of certain non-operational French warships that were scuttled by the Germans. Against this immense toll, Allied losses were practically non-existent. In all, the Allies lost just four minor commercial vessels worth 4,976 tons and a single principal warship, the British escort destroyer *Aldenham*, that was mined off Pola, in the Mediterranean during the last five months of 1944.[18]

This period also saw the end of submarine operations in the Mediterranean. As already discussed, in August and September the last German-built U-boats were lost in the Mediterranean. After this, the Germans still possessed several captured Italian submarines, but none of these were operational or would become operational before the war's end. For their part, the ever-increasing scarcity of suitable targets and diminishing patrol areas convinced the British to suspend their own submarine operations by the end of 1944. In comparing the results of the competing submarine campaigns, in four years of Mediterranean combat the German U-boat arm sank 95 Allied merchant ships worth 449,206 tons and 28 principal warships, of which 23 were British. Included in the latter were the battleship *Barham*, the aircraft carriers *Ark Royal* and *Eagle*, four cruisers and 12 destroyers. Added to this were six merchant ships worth 23,393 tons, seven principal warships and an auxiliary anti-aircraft ship that were sunk by Italian submarines from June 1940 through September 1943.[19] Against these successes, 68 German, 64 Italian and 13 captured 'UIT' U-boats were sunk in the Mediterranean or the approaches to Gibraltar, thus constituting an exchange rate of less than one-to-one for the Axis.[20] Beyond this, a further four Italian submarines were sunk in the Red Sea. By comparison, in four and a half years of conflict British and British-affiliated submarines sank 286 primary Axis merchant ships and naval auxiliaries worth 1,030,960 tons in the Mediterranean, along with four cruisers, 17 destroyers/torpedo boats, one corvette and 21 submarines. In return, 45 British and seven Allied submarines were lost, constituting a favourable exchange rate of better than six-to-one.[21] Therefore, despite the notoriety of Germany's vaunted U-boat arm and the size of Italy's submarine force at the beginning of the war, the British had clearly attained the superior results in this underwater contest.

While the suspension of submarine operations signalled a definite winding down of the maritime conflict, the Allies continued their interdiction efforts against the slivers of coastal territory still under German control. During the first four months of 1945 the Allied Mediterranean air forces flew a total of 3,262 sorties in anti-shipping sweeps and attacks against German-held ports.[22] During this effort the Allies sank a total of 66 military and 12 commercial vessels worth 46,639 and 20,993 tons, of which the RAF and Commonwealth air forces sank or participated in the destruction of 44 military and eight commercial vessels worth 5,125 and 20,506 tons respectively.[23] In terms of principal warships, on 17 February RAF bombers attacked Trieste where they sank the torpedo boat *TA44* (ex-Italian *Antonio Pigafetta*) and damaged *TA41* (ex-Italian *Lancia*) so severely that it was rendered a total loss. Three days later USAAF bombers carried out similar raids against Monfalcone and Trieste that wrecked the torpedo boats *TA40* (ex-Italian *Pugnale*) and *TA48* (ex-Yugoslav *T3*).[24] Then on 16 March British bombers sank the incomplete submarines *UIT6* (ex-Italian *R9*), *UIT7* (ex-Italian *Bario*), *UIT8* (ex-Italian *Litio*) and *UIT9* (ex-Italian *Sodio*) at Monfalcone. Five days later British fighter-bombers attacked Venice and sank the torpedo boat *TA42* (ex-Italian *Alabarda*). Finally, on 27 March USAAF aircraft carried out a follow-up raid against Venice that sank the corvette *UJ205* (ex-Italian *Colubrina*).

Beyond this aerial onslaught, Allied warships also participated in the interdiction effort with numerous sweeps and shore bombardments conducted in the contested waters. By this stage in the war, there was little the Germans could do to blunt these incursions, but mines, E-boats and small battle units remained a persistent threat. In terms of the former, on 12 January a mine detonation sank the British minesweeper *Regulus* off Sista Island, thus representing the last principal Allied warship to be sunk in the Mediterranean. One month later six German explosive boats carried out an attack against Split that damaged the British anti-aircraft cruiser *Delhi*. Then in April Fascist Italian naval units scored a similar success when they damaged the French destroyer *Trombe* in the Ligurian Sea. This proved to be a final, fleeting success as Allied air attacks, operational hazards and the loss of their bases progressively rendered the small battle unit and other Axis surface threats impotent. Meanwhile, Allied warships sank a total of 15 German vessels worth 9,294 tons during the first four months of 1945.[25] Included in this were three principal warships that were sunk in two separate engagements.

The first of these occurred on the night of 17/18 March when the last three operational torpedo boats of the German 10th Flotilla (*TA24*, *TA29* and *TA32*) conducted an offensive mine-laying operation off Corsica. After completing the task, Allied shore radar at Livorno acquired the three German vessels as they were returning to Genoa and reported their presence to four Allied destroyers that were in the vicinity. While two of these destroyers, the French *Basque* and *Tempête*, remained behind to protect an Allied convoy nearing Cape Corse, the British destroyers *Lookout* and *Meteor* pressed forward to engage the retiring German warships. Although outnumbered, the British destroyers proceeded with great vigour, and at 0301 hours *Lookout* established radar contact with the German vessels. Nine minutes later *Lookout* opened fire at a range of 5,000 yards. Using radar to direct its gunfire, *Lookout* immediately scored hits on *TA24* and *TA29* that caused the latter to fall out of the line in a damaged state. As *Lookout* then finished off *TA29* (ex-Italian *Eridano*), *Meteor* continued forward to engage *TA24* (ex-Italian *Arturo*) and quickly scored additional hits with gunfire and a torpedo that sank the German torpedo boat. The third German warship, *TA32*, escaped the engagement with minimal damage. The same held true for the two British destroyers, which attained this victory for no appreciable damage to themselves.

Although unbeknown to the participants at the time, this constituted the last surface engagement between principal warships in the Mediterranean conflict. Yet, the fighting was not quite over as there was one final action pitting minor vessels against a principal German warship. On the night of 12/13 April a mixed force of British coastal craft conducted an anti-shipping patrol south of Fiume in the

Adriatic. At 0215 hours one of these vessels, *MGB658*, detected two large ships on radar approaching from the north, and *MTB670* and *MTB697* went forward to investigate the contact. The two motor torpedo boats soon visually identified the unknown ships as German destroyers and launched a torpedo attack at a range of 1,500 yards. One or more of these torpedoes hit the German torpedo boat *TA45* (ex-Italian *Spica*), which exploded and sank. The British force suffered no losses in return, and this would be Britain's final sole victory over a principal German warship in the theatre.

Beyond these anti-shipping successes, the Royal Navy also participated in numerous other offensive operations. As previously discussed in Chapter 10, the British were generally content to let the isolated Axis garrisons in the Aegean wither on the vine. Still, they did conduct periodic raids and bombardments to harass and keep these outposts subdued. Then in early March a small British force, supported by the escort destroyer *Liddesdale*, landed on the island of Piskopi and took the surrender of the local garrison. British naval forces conducted similar operations in the Adriatic where they landed partisan forces to occupy the Dalmatian islands, which were all cleared by 22 April. Throughout this process, British minesweepers were constantly active clearing routes for the assault and follow-up forces. Finally, as the Allies geared up to resume the offensive in Italy, a number of British warships, including the cruiser *Orion* and the destroyers *Meteor*, *Musketeer* and *Lookout*, joined French and American counterparts to bombard shore targets along the Riviera and Ligurian coastlines and to provide support for the Fifth Army.

Coinciding with these latter events was the resumption of Allied ground operations in northern Italy. By this point in the war Germany was clearly in a state of collapse with Russian, British, American and French armies all advancing deep within its national boundaries from both east and west. Yet, despite this ongoing conquest of their homeland, the Germans continued to allocate substantial forces for the defence of northern Italy. By April this included 21 German and four Fascist Italian divisions, plus large numbers of support and security personnel. For their part, Allied strength in Italy had waned with the departure of three British/Canadian divisions for service in Northwest Europe and three more British divisions sent to Greece to quell Communist unrest.[26] This left the Allies with just 17 divisions, plus various lesser formations to conduct their offensive. Fortunately, these forces were generally well rested and rejuvenated after their three-month pause in major combat operations. Likewise, the Allies continued to enjoy an overwhelming superiority in firepower, mobility and materiel abundance that far exceeded anything the Germans could hope to attain.

The Allied plan for this final offensive, codenamed Operation *Grapeshot*, closely resembled the strategy adopted to assault the Gothic Line seven months earlier. First, Eighth Army would open the offensive on the Adriatic sector with attacks across the Senio and Santerno rivers, followed by dual advances towards Budrio and the

Argenta Gap. A few days later Fifth Army would launch its own attack to the west of Bologna with the objective of advancing into the Po valley. Thereafter, the two armies would continue their converging assaults with the goal of meeting in the Bondeno area, thus completing the encirclement of German forces still south of the Po River. In the final phase of the offensive the Allied armies would cross the Po River and advance northward as conditions allowed. To carry this out, Eighth Army possessed four corps with eight divisions, but only three of these corps (V and XIII British and II Polish) would actually play an active role in the coming offensive. For its part, Fifth Army possessed two corps and nine divisions, including a single Commonwealth formation, the 6th South African Armoured Division, and an American-armed Brazilian division.[27]

After two successful preliminary operations that netted the British valuable staging terrain and 1,700 prisoners, Eighth Army launched its main attack across the Senio River on the evening of 9/10 April. Utilising three divisions (3rd Carpathian [Polish], 8th Indian and 2nd New Zealand) and an elaborate bombardment plan, the British successfully breached the German defences and advanced to the Santerno River, which they crossed by the 12th. With this, the British 78th Division passed through the 8th Indian Division and proceeded towards the Argenta Gap. Meanwhile, on 11 April the British 56th Division conducted an amphibious assault across Lake Comacchio that out-flanked the German defensive line along the Reno River. Over the next week these two British divisions continued to press forward against stiffening German resistance in the Argenta area, while New Zealand/Indian and Polish forces advanced towards Budrio and Bologna respectively. Likewise, on 14 and 15 April Fifth Army launched its portion of the offensive with consecutive attacks by US IV and II Corps in the area southwest of Bologna. After experiencing initial heavy resistance, the Americans were soon making steady progress through the last remaining mountains before the Po Valley.

This progress intensified in the second week of the Allied offensive. On 19 April Eighth Army broke through the Argenta Gap, and the British 6th Armoured Division passed through to spearhead a drive towards Bondeno and the Po River. The next day both American corps broke out of the Apennines Mountains and emerged onto the Plain of Emilia west of Bologna. From there, the Americans (including the South Africans) raced northward towards the Po River where they hoped to unite with the oncoming British to envelop the Germans. With their lines crumbling all around them, the Germans began a fighting withdrawal on the same day. On 21 April soldiers of II Polish Corps entered Bologna, thus attaining a prize that had eluded the Allies for the previous seven months. To their right, the six divisions of British XIII and V Corps continued their advance towards the northwest, and on 22 April the British captured Bondeno. For their part, the Americans reached the Po and attained a crossing on the 23rd. That same day the British 6th Armoured Division made contact with elements of the 6th South African Armoured Division in the village of Finale, thus linking the two armies and entrapping large numbers of Germans between the two pincers.

The speed of these events spelled disaster for the Germans. By 22 April the British Eighth Army had collected 10,447 prisoners since the beginning of the month, while a similar number of prisoners had been taken on the American front.[28] Now with the Allied advance to the Po River and the mass surrenders that followed, the influx of prisoners overwhelmed the Allies' ability to maintain an orderly count. By the evening of the 24th Field Marshal Alexander reported the capture of 54,000 men since the beginning of the offensive, but he acknowledged that this was just an estimate.[29] Examples of the ongoing rout included the activities of British V Corps, which by 25 April cleared a 25-mile stretch along the Po River from Stienta to Serravalle, having collected 14,000 prisoners and some 80 tanks, 300 guns and 1,000 vehicles found destroyed or abandoned.[30] Adding to this were thousands of prisoners taken by XIII British and II Polish Corps. Meanwhile, on Fifth Army's front, the American 88th Division alone took 11,000 prisoners in a two-day period up to the 25th.[31]

For the remainder of the month the Allies moved quickly to exploit their growing victory. As already mentioned, Fifth Army crossed the Po River on 23 April, and over the next two days the British followed suit. From there, the Allies raced forward to complete their liberation of northern Italy. By this stage in the campaign, order and discipline within the German army had largely disintegrated, and the Allies were able to make great gains against minimal or sporadic resistance. Assisting them in this process was a massive uprising by Italian partisans that exacerbated the situation for the Germans. One by one the major cities in northern Italy fell to the Allies as prisoners in the thousands and tens of thousands flowed into their cages each day.[32] This was particularly true for the American Fifth Army, which made widespread gains throughout the region. Spearheading the advance for the Eighth Army was a reinforced 2nd New Zealand Division, which made a dash to Monfalcone and Trieste on the Adriatic coast, collecting over 30,000 prisoners in the process.[33] On its left flank, the British 6th Armoured Division advanced to Vittorio Veneto, Udine and the border area adjoining Yugoslavia and Austria while collecting a further 20,000 prisoners.[34] On their right, the 8th Indian and British 78th and 56th Divisions made shorter advances, culminating with the latter's capture of Venice and the seizure of 3,000 additional prisoners located there.[35]

This period also saw the final acts of the local maritime struggle as the Germans scuttled or surrendered the remaining warships still under their control. Even before this occurred, on 19 April Italian-manned Chariot human torpedoes entered Genoa harbour and sank the nearly completed aircraft carrier *Aquila* to prevent it from being used as a blockship. Five days later the Germans carried out a mass scuttling in Genoa that accounted for the destruction of over 50 warships (most of which were non-operational or under construction) including seven destroyers/torpedo boats, nine corvettes and two submarines. While this represented the largest such demolition, the Germans carried out similar activities in other ports, including the scuttling of a fast escort at Oneglia, a destroyer at Imperia, a submarine at Monfalcone and four torpedo boats at Trieste. Finally, on 3 May the last seven German E-boats remaining in the region departed Pola and proceeded to Ancona to surrender. With this, the last semblances of German maritime power in the Mediterranean ceased to exist.

Coinciding with this event was an equally conclusive outcome for the German ground forces still present in northern Italy. On 27 April Italian partisans captured the Fascist dictator Benito Mussolini near Lake Como and summarily executed him the next day. On the 28th representatives from German Army Group C arrived at Field Marshal Alexander's headquarters in Caserta to negotiate an end to hostilities. The next day these authorities signed a document of unconditional surrender for all German forces in Italy to be effective at 1400 hours on 2 May. In the interim the Allied armies continued their northward advances, and by 2 May the Allies had taken 145,000 prisoners since the start of their spring offensive (including prisoners already mentioned).[36] Now with the advent of this comprehensive capitulation, a further 260,000 Germans laid down their arms.[37] Added to this were upwards of 160,000 Fascist Italians that were captured during the final offensive or its immediate aftermath.[38] Meanwhile, Axis equipment losses included 261 tanks, 475 self-propelled assault guns, 1,429 assorted artillery pieces, 345 heavy anti-tank guns and 572 infantry close support guns.[39]

These events concluded the struggle for Italy, and shortly thereafter the entire Mediterranean conflict came to an end. During the previous 20 months (beginning on 9 September 1943) the defence of Italy had cost the Germans some 735,000 casualties, including those sustained during the mass surrenders in late April and early May 1945.[40] Added to this loss were roughly 200,000 Fascist Italians and other Axis contributors who had provided security and logistical support to the Germans. Excluding enemy forces that were disarmed at the end of hostilities, Eighth Army's contribution to this combined total included 104,408 prisoners taken during the

Table 11.1 Warship Losses in the Mediterranean from 9 September 1943 through 2 May 1945

	Capital ships	Cruisers	Destroyers	Torpedo boats/ escorts/mine vessels	Submarines
British/Allied	-	3	13	16	7
German	1	3	8	55	44

Note: Only includes warships that were a total loss. These numbers do not include Italian warships that surrendered to the Allies or were otherwise lost when Italy capitulated in September 1943. Nor do they include certain German-controlled warships that were in the early stages of construction at the time of their demise. The old German light cruiser *Niobe* is counted in the escort category given its obsolete state and armament at the time of its destruction.

duration of the fighting (from 3 September 1943), while an additional 16,443 prisoners were taken by the British elements assigned to Fifth Army. For their parts, the American, French and Brazilian contingents within the Fifth Army combined to take a further 219,660 prisoners during the same period.[41] In achieving this substantial victory, the Allied armies in Italy suffered 313,495 casualties, of which 159,651 came from British or British-affiliated forces. This included 7,730 British and British-affiliated and 8,528 other casualties that were sustained during the final spring offensive ending the campaign.[42]

In considering the totality of operations within the theatre through the duration of the conflict, the scope of this victory was substantially larger. When including losses from Africa, Sicily, southern France, Yugoslavia, Greece and the Aegean Islands (the garrisons of which surrendered to British authorities in early May), the Germans suffered well over a million casualties within the theatre during the course of the war. This figure increases to more than three and a half million casualties when incorporating Italian losses into the calculation (which includes Italian forces lost to the Axis when Italy capitulated in September 1943).[43] Likewise, several hundred thousand additional prisoners were taken when elements of both the Fifth and Eighth Armies occupied portions of Austria following Germany's surrender, thus bringing this total number of Axis prisoners held in Italy and Austria by 17 May 1945 to more than 1.4 million, of which 1,134,000 were under British control.[44] By comparison, the total casualties suffered by the Western Allies during the duration of the Mediterranean conflict numbered about 650,000.[45]

In terms of the maritime struggle, the scope of the Allied victory was just as dramatic. In all, the Axis lost a total of 3,179 merchant ships and 1,817 military vessels worth 4,147,523 and 1,044,722 tons respectively within the Mediterranean from 10 June 1940 through 2 May 1945.[46] Added to this were a further 43 merchant ships and 15 military vessels worth 255,239 and 11,478 tons respectively that were sunk in the Red Sea.[47] In terms of major surface combatants, these losses included 179 principal warships that were sunk during the course of the conflict. Likewise, a further 74 principal warships surrendered to the Allies in September 1943 (including those initially interned by Spain), while 11 more were sunk by the Germans or scuttled off the Balearic Islands. Finally, beyond these surface vessels, the Axis also lost 183 submarines in and around the Mediterranean (including 34 that surrendered to the Allies in September 1943).[48] For their part, total Allied losses in the Mediterranean included 413 merchant ships worth 1,740,250 tons, along with 127 principal warships and 52 submarines.[49]

Of course, the true value of the Allied victory was based upon much more than the disparity of competing casualties. When viewed as a whole and despite periodic setbacks, the Western Allies were able to consistently attain their strategic objectives within the theatre while denying the same to the Axis. This, in turn, drove Italy out of the war, thus reducing the core Axis by a third and depriving Germany of

R. ESPLORATORE "PANCALDO„

With almost 6,000 vessels lost, World War II's Mediterranean campaign exacted a heavy toll on the participants involved. Pictured here is the Italian destroyer *Leone Pancaldo*, which had the distinction of being sunk twice, first by Swordfish torpedo-bombers in 1940 and then by Allied fighter-bombers in 1943. (Public domain)

its main European partner. Of even greater consequence, it forced Germany to add an additional front to its already overstretched war effort, which siphoned away substantial resources that were sorely needed in other theatres. This, in turn, helped ensnare the German empire in an ever-tightening vice that progressively squeezed the life blood from it and contributed to Germany's ultimate defeat. It was in this way that the theatre's impact was truly meaningful. Within a week following the surrender of all German forces in Italy, similar events occurred in Northern Europe, starting first on 4 May with the surrender of all German forces in the Netherlands, northwest Germany, Schleswig-Holstein and Denmark to the British 21st Army Group. This was followed a few days later with the surrender of Germany itself. After nearly six years of immense carnage, the war in Europe was over. Japan would surrender a few months later, thus completing the overall Allied victory. For the British and Allied servicemen who had fought in the Mediterranean theatre, they could now enter this new post-war world secure in the knowledge that their actions had contributed to this epic triumph.

CHAPTER 12

The Triumph of British Maritime Power

Amongst its many lessens, there are four things abundantly clear when viewing the totality of the struggle that took place in the Mediterranean and Middle East during the Second World War. First, the Allies were victorious in this endeavour. Second, the fighting was both materially and strategically consequential in advancing the overall Allied cause. Third, this was predominantly a British-run theatre in which the British Commonwealth was the ascendant power within the overall Allied effort in terms of leadership, forces employed and results attained. And fourth, sea power, and particularly British sea power, played an essential role in facilitating this victory. While there were many varied components to this conflict, the overall struggle can arguably be broken down into two major, consecutive campaigns. The first comprised the first three years of the conflict in which the competing forces vied for control over Africa. Included in this were the related peripheral operations concurrently underway, of which the struggle in the Mediterranean was paramount. The second covered the last two years in which the fighting moved to the domain of Southern Europe. The fact that the Allies were victorious during these endeavours is self-evident. The fact that these victories were materially and strategically consequential, that Britain was the dominant contributor and that sea power played an essential role in attaining these outcomes will now be discussed in the context of each of the above-mentioned campaigns.

The first of these was the battle for control over Africa and the Middle East. Although primarily centred in North Africa, this struggle also included peripheral operations in East Africa, the Mediterranean and Southwest Asia. Lasting almost three years (from June 1940 through May 1943), the campaign ended with the Allies in complete control over the African continent and entire Middle East, thus removing all threats to the Suez Canal and valuable Persian Gulf oil region. These actions also secured valuable bases for further operations against Southern Europe and an important logistical link to the Soviet Union. In the process of achieving this victory, the Allies inflicted heavy losses upon the Axis, which included the complete destruction of four Axis armies containing nine German and 31 Italian divisions as well as substantial air and maritime assets. In human and materiel terms, this equated to some 950,000 Axis casualties (mostly prisoners) and the loss of 183 principal warships, 2.4 million tons of merchant shipping, 8,000 aircraft, 2,500 tanks, 6,200 guns and 70,000 trucks. Given the magnitude of these losses, the Africa campaign clearly constituted a legitimate success in the effort to divert Axis resources away from the massive struggle underway against the Soviet Union.

In other benefits, the campaign severely eroded Italian resolve to continue fighting and provided the Allies with valuable aids that would serve them well during follow-up operations in Europe. In terms of the former, not only did the Italians lose all of their colonial possessions in Africa, but they also suffered the vast majority of the casualties listed above. In many cases, these losses came from Italy's best units, most of which were destroyed during the fighting. Together, the Italian Army, Regia Marina and Regia Aeronautica emerged from the conflict materially and psychologically prostrate, thus rendering them incapable or unwilling to offer meaningful resistance to further Allied ambitions. Given this reality, the Italians finished the campaign in an extremely demoralised state that would quickly lead to their exit from the war just four months later. As such, the demise of Italy as a major Axis partner had its origins firmly rooted in the Africa campaign.

By comparison, the Western Allies emerged from the conflict in a significantly strengthened state. From commanding generals to lower enlisted men, the Allies concluded the enterprise flush with the confidence and high morale born out of victory. As such, this triumph served as a transitional point, which Churchill described as 'the end of the beginning', in which the Allies went from a period of near perpetual struggle and malaise to a period of clear ascendancy. Beyond this, the Allies used the fighting in Africa as a means to learn the art of modern combined arms warfare along with its critical logistical components. Similarly, the campaign provided the training ground in which the Allies forged their fledgling coalition partnership and groomed many of their leaders for subsequent command positions. Finally, the campaign facilitated France's return to the Allied fold from its flirtation as a semi-Axis nation. Although the French homeland would remain under German control for another 16 months, French forces in the Mediterranean were now part of the Allied order of battle. Thus, unlike the Axis, the Allies emerged from the campaign in a substantially stronger and more proficient state that would help facilitate further victories during the final two years of the war.

In assigning credit for these many accomplishments, the Africa campaign was overwhelmingly a British-run affair. During the first two years of the campaign the British (including the Commonwealth) were the sole Allied participants, with the Americans and Free French only getting involved to any significant degree in the last six months of the fighting. Even then, the British Commonwealth still remained the predominant partner within the greater alliance. As such, the British engaged in the vast majority of the fighting and were responsible for inflicting more than 90 percent of the Axis casualties incurred during the three-year campaign. By comparison, their own losses were only about a quarter as high. Beyond these ground contributions, the British also provided the vast majority of maritime assets that were essential in bringing about this victory. This included the bulk of the shipping that provided the continuous flow of reinforcements and supplies needed to sustain the ground forces and the majority of air and naval resources used to interdict the corresponding Axis supply activities. In terms of the latter, the British were solely or partially responsible for roughly 81 and 84 percent of the theatre-wide Axis principal warship and merchant tonnage losses sustained during this period.[1]

As for the other Allied partners, the United States was the biggest contributor to this effort, while the Free French made smaller contributions during the closing days of the campaign. In a direct role, the Americans provided about half of the maritime assets and a majority of the landing forces involved in Operation *Torch*. Thereafter, American ground and air units made significant contributions during the subsequent fighting in Tunisia. This was particularly true of the latter as the USAAF actually surpassed the regional RAF in terms of numbers by the end of the campaign. Still, notwithstanding these operational inputs, America's greatest contribution to the Allied victory might have been in the form of materiel support since much of the aircraft, tanks and other weapons used by the Allies during the conflict were American-made. For their part, with the exception of the 1st Free French Brigade assigned to the Eighth Army, the French had little effective impact upon the fighting and were only relevant during the last few days of the conflict when they helped mop up defeated Axis formations stranded in Tunisia. Likewise, beyond these major Allied powers, small contingents from the conquered European nations, including the Poles, Dutch and Greeks, made contributions that were not substantial in the grand scheme of things, but still had a relative impact commensurate with the size of the forces involved.

Following this African triumph was the theatre's second major campaign, which encompassed all Allied operations in Southern Europe during the last two years of the war. Although primarily centred in Italy, this campaign also covered Allied actions in Pantellaria, Sicily, Sardinia, Corsica, Greece and southern France, as well as concurrent naval and aerial activities underway within the theatre. In pursuing these undertakings, the Allies had four initial objectives. These were to drive Italy out of the war, open the Mediterranean to Allied maritime traffic, secure bases for the strategic air offensive and force the Germans to divert resources into the theatre. Of these, the first three objectives were accomplished in less than six months while the final objective was an ongoing affair exercised through the remainder of the war. By accomplishing these goals, the Allies gained a direct route to the Indian Ocean, freed up substantial naval and shipping resources for use against Japan, exposed much of Germany's southern empire to the scourge of Allied bombing and forced the Germans to compensate for the loss of their Axis partner. In turn, this latter point eventually compelled the Germans to deploy more than 50 divisions to defend Italy and offset the loss of Italian garrison troops in the Balkans and southern France. By facilitating this outcome, the Allies precipitated a major diversion of forces away from the Eastern Front and provided the Soviets with substantial relief.

Later, as the campaign developed, the Allies attained additional benefits beyond their original objectives. This included the invasion of southern France, which helped facilitate a German collapse in that country and allowed the Allies to deploy and logistically support two armies in the subsequent Northwest Europe campaign. Eventually, these two armies, the American Seventh and the French First, were part of the Allied onslaught that advanced into Germany itself. In doing so, their logistical tails were still largely rooted in the Mediterranean. Meanwhile, on the other side of the theatre Allied air, logistical and commando support helped facilitate an effective guerrilla uprising in Yugoslavia that eventually transformed into a viable offensive that further challenged Germany's position within the region. Likewise, to the south the Allies secured an important post-war political victory with the establishment of a pro-western government in Greece and the subsequent defeat of Communist insurgents in that newly liberated country. Finally, in a contribution almost entirely overlooked by history, Mediterranean-based Allied air attacks against oil and infrastructure targets throughout central and Southern Europe severely degraded Germany's ability to logistically support their forces facing the Soviet Union. In doing this, Allied air power provided substantial assistance to Soviet operations during the last year of the war that almost certainly shortened the duration of the conflict and prevented many tens of thousands of additional Soviet and Allied casualties.

Beyond these strategic implications, the struggle for Southern Europe also exacted a heavy toll upon the Axis order of battle. Excluding prisoners collected in Austria after Germany's surrender, the campaign cost the Axis about three million men. Of these, roughly two million were Italians who either surrendered during the fighting or simply ceased operations when Italy capitulated. German casualties during operations in Sicily, Italy, southern France and Greece numbered about another 850,000 men, including those that surrendered at the close of hostilities. Added to this were a further 100,000 men who were left stranded on the Aegean islands or in the French Atlantic ports when the Allies bypassed their positions. In terms of materiel resources, these operations cost the Axis a heavy price, including the loss of thousands of assorted tanks, guns and aircraft as well as the Italian battle fleet and significant Kriegsmarine assets. Against this, the Allies suffered little more than 350,000 casualties during the two-year period, split almost equally between the British and American contingents.

This division of casualties was indicative of the shared roles played by both Allied powers throughout the Southern Europe campaign. Of the ground forces involved, both nations had general parity during the conquest of Sicily, but thereafter the British provided a slight preponderance of the units engaged during the duration of

The expansion of strategic bombing into central and Southern Europe was only made possible through Allied success in the Mediterranean. Through bombing and mining, this aerial assault severely degraded German industry and logistics and provided direct support to the Soviet Union. Pictured here is a Fifteenth Air Force Liberator bomber. (U.S. Air Force photo, public domain)

the fighting in Italy. As a result of the latter, British and Commonwealth formations usually comprised part of the American Fifth Army throughout most of the campaign as well as making up the vast bulk of their own British Eighth Army. By comparison, American and French ground forces almost exclusively carried out the invasion of southern France, with Britain's contribution being mainly limited to air and naval support. Of the local air strength, the majority came from the United States, although much of this was assigned to the strategic air campaign, thus leaving a greater degree of parity between the remaining forces earmarked for local tactical operations. Of the local naval strength, the British generally provided the bulk of the forces employed. The sole exception to this was during the invasion of southern France where the United States Navy was the dominant partner. On the other hand, operations in the Aegean and Adriatic were almost entirely British-run affairs. Similarly, the British were solely or partially responsible for 77 and 74 percent of the regional Axis principal warship and merchant shipping losses sustained during this period.[2] Thus, when viewing the campaign as a whole, it is clear that both nations played roughly equal roles in facilitating the victory in Southern Europe. However, when combined with the earlier Africa campaign, Britain was unmistakably the predominant partner during the collective five-year period.

At this time, it is worthwhile to further explore the breakdown of naval combat that occurred during this period. Of the naval events that transpired during the last two years of the Mediterranean conflict, the most impactful in terms of materiel results was the surrender of the Italian battle fleet. With this action, a total of 117 principal warships were lost to the Axis cause, and the Axis maritime coalition dropped from three nations to two. Of these lost vessels, 108 surrendered to the Allies while nine more were sunk by German forces to prevent this outcome. Several more vessels that could not get away were scuttled by the Italians, although many of these were subsequently raised and put back into service by the Germans. Likewise, 282 Italian merchant ships worth 259,889 tons surrendered or scuttled themselves in accordance with this event.[3] In assessing credit for this outcome, the British Commonwealth and United States were collective partners in bringing about Italy's demise as an Axis nation, but as earlier discussed here, as well as in Chapter 8, the British were the predominant players. As such, it is reasonable to give Britain shared (and arguably predominant) credit in facilitating the loss of these surrendered vessels.

Of course, as momentous as this capitulation was, it did not signal an end to the naval struggle in the Mediterranean. To the contrary, naval combat remained a consistent factor through the duration of the campaign in Southern Europe. In fact, during the last two years of the Mediterranean conflict more Axis warships (145) were lost through extended combat operations than the surrender of the Italian fleet. Beyond this, the Axis also lost some 1.6 million tons of regional merchant shipping, excluding the 259,889 tons associated with Italy's surrender. Britain's role in bringing about these losses was less dominant than it had been during the first phase of the war given America's increased participation in the maritime conflict. Nevertheless, British and affiliated forces still solely or partially accounted for 65 and 70 percent of these extended warship and merchant shipping losses. When including the ships lost due to Italy's capitulation, these numbers increase to the 77 and 74 percent specified above.

Moving beyond this materiel accounting, the successful application of British maritime power was an essential component to the theatre-wide victories scored throughout the conflict. The execution of this came in many forms. First and foremost was the provision of logistical support. From Egypt to Tunisia and Italy to southern France, nearly every man and item of equipment utilised by the Allied armies had to come in by sea. This was an enormous undertaking that compelled the Royal Navy, British Merchant Navy and their Allied counterparts to continually carry out various logistical operations throughout the region, eventually involving thousands of ships. In some cases, this effort included the maintenance of supply lines that stretched for

Table 12.1 Principal Axis Warship Losses by Period during the Mediterranean Conflict

	Africa Campaign 10 Jun 40–13 May 43		S. Europe Campaign 14 May 43–2 May 45		Italian Surrender Sep 43	
	Axis warship losses total (Br)	Percent lost solely or partially to British means	Axis warship losses total (Br)	Percent lost solely or partially to British means	Axis warship losses total (Br)	Percent lost solely or partially to British means
Capital ships	1(1)	100.0%	1(1)	100.0%	6(5)	83.3%
Cruisers	13(11)	84.6%	4(2)	50.0%	9(9)	100.0%
Destroyers, large torpedo boats	42(33)	78.6%	10(7)	70.0%	17(14)	82.4%
Small torpedo boats, escorts	35(26)	74.3%	43(25)	58.1%	27(24)	88.9%
Corvettes, sub-chasers	2(2)	100.0%	20(14)	70.0%	20(19)	95.0%
Submarines	85(73)	85.9%	64(42)	65.6%	34(34)	100.0%
Minelayers	1(1)	100.0%	2(2)	100.0%	4(3)	75.0%
Fleet minesweepers	4(2)	50.0%	1(1)	100.0%	-	-
Total	183(149)	81.4%	145(94)	64.8%	117(108)	92.3%

Note: As a point of comparison, the time periods covered here are different than those in the earlier tables. These figures only apply to Italian and German warships lost in the Mediterranean theatre and Red Sea. The first numbers delineate total losses while the numbers in parentheses indicate losses solely or partially attributable to British means. During the Italian Surrender period, surrendered Italian ships are partially credited to the British, but Italian ships sunk by the Germans are not.

more than 11,000 miles. Together, these activities resulted in the successful delivery of millions of men and many millions of tons of equipment and supplies. Just one example of this, for the duration of the conflict (3 September 1939 through 31 August 1945), the British delivered 3,309 tanks, 7,879 guns, 92,338 vehicles, 1,801 aircraft and 2,760,683 dead weight tons of stores into the theatre from the United Kingdom alone, with many more cargoes arriving from the United States or other parts of the world.[4] The British accomplished these movements with a minimal loss of life and materiel, and this success provided the Allied armies with the resources they needed to win on the battlefield. In fact, none of the great Allied victories discussed earlier would have been remotely possible without this support. Other than the United States, which often partnered with the British in these endeavours, no other nation in the world possessed the ability to carry out such an undertaking, which is ample testimony to the magnitude of this accomplishment.

The second major way in which Britain's maritime services contributed to the overall victory was through the execution of amphibious landings. These operations came in various sizes and fulfilled different functions. Of particular importance were the large strategic landings that ushered in new chapters in the regional conflict and changed the direction of the war. These consisted of the invasions of French North Africa, Sicily, Italy and southern France. Invariably carried out against defended coastlines, these assaults were complex, combined arms operations that involved hundreds, if not thousands, of vessels and the landings of tens, if not hundreds, of thousands of men. Essential tasks during these operations included the transportation of assault forces to their assigned landing zones, clearing minefields, conducting the landings, overcoming obstacles and fortifications, bringing in follow-up formations and providing fire support and security. Coupled with these strategic landings were smaller operations that were either carried out independently or as adjuncts to their larger counterparts. These included operations to capture Madagascar, Pantellaria, Anzio and Greece. All of these enterprises were successful, and with the exception

Allied ships approaching Sicily during Operation *Husky*. During the last three years of the war British maritime power facilitated or participated in the successful execution of nine major amphibious operations within the theatre ranging from North Africa to Greece. (Mason, H. A. (Lt), Royal Navy official photographer, public domain)

of the invasion of southern France, were carried out solely or predominantly by British maritime assets. Without these successes, the war would have taken a far different course.

Another form of amphibious warfare regularly employed by the British was the launching of raids into enemy-controlled territory. Throughout the war the British carried out a number of these forays against targets in Africa, the Aegean and the Adriatic. Although certainly less important than the major landing operations just described and far from universally successful, these raids still played a valuable role in weakening the enemy and forcing them to divert additional resources to defensive purposes. In many cases, these diversions of resources were quite substantial as impacted Axis commanders had to disperse their forces over wide areas to defend against the prospect of additional Allied incursions. In some cases, such as in the Adriatic, the British conducted these raids in conjunction with local partisan units that further enhanced their effectiveness and forced the Germans to deploy substantially greater resources to subdue these efforts. Thus, although extremely minor compared to the full scope of the Allied war effort, these raids generally attained results that more than justified their execution.

The next major way in which the Royal Navy provided assistance to ground operations was through the application of naval gunfire and aerial support. On literally thousands of occasions throughout the war British warships ranging from battleships to monitors and gunboats to minor auxiliary craft, carried out bombardments or answered calls for fire in support of their army brethren. Firing many tens of thousands of large-calibre shells, this proved to be a significant force multiplier for the Allied ground forces as time and again this naval cannonade reduced Axis fortifications, weakened their defences, repulsed counter-attacks and debilitated the enemy's willingness and ability to resist. This, in turn, saved thousands of Allied casualties and proved to be a decisive factor on numerous occasions, including at Salerno and Anzio where this fire support was instrumental in turning likely defeats into measured victories. It is also worth noting that this naval fire support was almost entirely one-sided as there were virtually no examples within the theatre where Axis warships provided similar support for their own forces. Finally, added to this was the role that the Fleet Air Arm played during many of these operations. Although certainly less consequential than the navy's heavy gunfire, British carrier aircraft did provide valuable close air support on a number of occasions, including during operations to secure Madagascar, French North Africa, southern France and the Aegean.

While maritime power clearly helped contribute to success on the battlefield, it was also there to mitigate the damage when fortunes faltered. This included times when Allied forces came under siege at Tobruk and Anzio, and all of their logistical support had to come in by sea. These proved to be long, arduous and costly undertakings, but in both cases the navy diligently performed this vital supply mission until the sieges were lifted. Of even greater consequence were times when conditions on the ground became hopeless and the navy was called upon to evacuate entrapped Allied forces. Invariably carried out in the face of strong opposition, these operations took a heavy toll on the participating maritime units, but the navy never faltered in fulfilling these vital tasks. In turn, at British Somaliland, Greece and Crete, these maritime elements successfully extricated some 74,000 military and civilian personnel who would have otherwise been lost if not for these evacuation efforts.

While this and the other discussed activities reflected the ways in which the Royal Navy and British Merchant Navy provided direct support for the Allied ground forces, the final contribution of this maritime power dealt with the denial of similar support for the Axis. In this, the British used both naval and air assets to interdict the flow of Axis seaborne transport and other support the Axis navies might have rendered for their ground forces. Through these efforts, they attained varying degrees of success that at times proved to be decisive. This latter point was particularly true in North Africa where success on the battlefield often correlated with how effectively the Allies interdicted the flow of supplies reaching the Axis armies. In the end, this supply deficit became so great that for the first time in the war, an otherwise intact German army lost its willingness to continue fighting, laid down its arms and surrendered en masse. With no chance for seaborne evacuation due to the strong Allied control of the adjacent waters, a total of 238,243 Axis personnel became prisoners, thus beginning a death spiral that would lead to Germany's total defeat two years later.

While these many inputs clearly played an essential role in facilitating victory in the Mediterranean theatre, to fully understand the scope and relevance of Britain's maritime contribution, it is necessary to view it in a global context. Of the six major powers that participated in the Second World War, only two, the British Commonwealth and the United States, conducted the war on a truly global basis. For the British, the Mediterranean and Middle East represented a single theatre in a multi-theatre war. Thus, even as the British were the prevailing Allied combatants in the Mediterranean and Middle East, this was not the centre of their overall maritime effort. Instead, the distinction for this went to the Atlantic and waters off Northwest Europe where the British confronted the Germans in the premier maritime struggle of the war. The execution of this crucial struggle tied directly into the Mediterranean conflict since there could never be any success in the Mediterranean without con-current success in the Atlantic. Similarly, while the Mediterranean conflict brought great benefit to the Allied cause as previously documented, the true apex of the Allied war effort was in the Atlantic and Northern Europe, and it was here that the outcome of the war was ultimately decided. In the end, the monumental successes attained in the Mediterranean theatre only served to support this greater victory.

In prosecuting the overall war at sea, Britain's maritime services fulfilled four primary roles. The first was to defend Britain against direct assault and invasion.

The second was to secure vital seaborne lines of communication. The third was to impose a maritime blockade against Germany. And the fourth was to use maritime power as a means to support the army. While these roles were consistent through the duration of the war, a fifth role was added a third of the way into the conflict regarding the provision of materiel support to the Soviet Union. In the end, the successful execution of these roles laid the foundation for the entire Allied war effort and provided an essential catalyst for the eventual Allied victory in Europe. Indeed, it was only through the successful application of maritime power that the alliance between the British Commonwealth, the Soviet Union and the United States was even able to exist. This is true if for no other reason than the obvious fact that Britain, which was the lynchpin of the alliance, would have fallen without success in the maritime realm. Thereafter, even if the United States had still opted to get involved in the European conflict, it is exceedingly difficult to envision how the Americans could have waged an effective war effort against Germany without the benefit of Britain's geographical location and military support.

Fortunately for the Allies and arguably the entire world, the British were successful in attaining their maritime objectives. To flesh this out further, we will now review each role in greater detail starting with the direct defence of the United Kingdom. This contribution is difficult to definitively quantify since it is largely measured against a non-event and is thus easy to overlook or take for granted. Still, one must remember that in the early summer of 1940, Britain faced its greatest invasion threat since 1805. The fact that this invasion never materialised was primarily due to the strength of the Royal Navy compared to the corresponding weakness of the Kriegsmarine. Given these force disparities, which were exacerbated by recent heavy German naval losses sustained off Norway (mostly at the hands of the Royal Navy), the Germans were extremely hesitant to actually attempt an invasion, and this reluctance was formalised when the Luftwaffe failed to gain air superiority over the RAF. As such, while the RAF gained deserved notoriety in winning the Battle of Britain, it was the Royal Navy that was the true deterrent to the proposed German invasion.

Beyond this, there was a second major component to the navy's defensive contribution. Even before the onset of the invasion threat, the Royal Navy and British Merchant Navy saved the vast bulk of the British Expeditionary Force from the clutches of the German war machine. In France alone during May and June 1940, this included the extraction of 558,032 Allied personnel, of which 368,491 were British.[5] In turn, this accounted for roughly 85 percent of the British Expeditionary Force. Tens of thousands more were rescued from Norway. This extraordinary achievement, which was executed in the face of severe adversity, provided both a practical and psychological boost to Britain's decision to fight on. Notwithstanding Churchill's fiery oratory to the contrary, British resolve would have been severely undermined had the expeditionary force been destroyed. Whether Churchill's government could have survived such an outcome or withstood calls for a negotiated settlement with

Germany is debatable. Fortunately, this did not occur, and the British stood firm against German intimidation. This accomplishment represented the key turning point of the war since it allowed Britain to survive, thus preserving the prospect of a viable Western Alliance that would eventually force Germany into a multi-front war. It was also the first time in the conflict that German strategic ambitions were checked and the aura of German invincibility was shattered. Again, while there were many contributors, an essential, but often overlooked, element in this victory was the existence and effective application of British maritime power.

The next two roles were accomplished concurrently during the longest running campaign of the war, spanning almost six years from September 1939 to May 1945. Often referred to as the battle of the Atlantic, this campaign was actually much larger in scope, being broken down into two concurrent parts. The first of these was defensive as the British fought to secure their own maritime lines of communication against the U-boat threat and other forms of Axis interdiction. This effort spanned the globe but was overwhelmingly centred in the North Atlantic where the battle derived its popular name. The stakes for this epic contest were extremely high as it represented Germany's best opportunity following its aborted invasion setback to drive Britain out of the war and derail the Western Alliance. By comparison, success for the Western Allies ensured the survival of the British nation as well as the means to employ America's vast military power into the European conflict. Concurrently, these same maritime lines of communication provided the conduits by which Britain and America supported combat operations throughout the world, including the Mediterranean theatre. As such, this colossal struggle was the most important campaign waged by the Western Allies during the war, with none of the other campaigns being remotely possible without the successful maintenance of these vital sea lanes.

The context behind this immense struggle was the fact that Britain lacked self-sufficiency in a number of key resources and commodities such as oil and foodstuffs, and had to depend upon seaborne commerce to make up the difference. In 1938 total British imports had amounted to 68 million tons, and although British authorities realised they could reduce this number through rationing and increased domestic production, they still determined that a minimum annual requirement of 27 million import tons was absolutely essential in meeting the nation's basic needs.[6] In attempting to sever this trade and starve Britain into submission, the Germans ultimately produced almost 1,200 U-boats along with an immense infrastructure to support this massive force. The Allies countered with a comprehensive convoy system supported by hundreds of escort vessels and patrol aircraft that eventually transported 85,775 merchant ships to and from the United Kingdom, and 175,608 ships in British coastal waters during the duration of the war.[7] In the resulting combat, the Germans initially inflicted heavy losses against the combined Allied merchant fleets, but ultimately failed to sever or significantly debilitate Britain's critical lines of communication. Invariably, enough men and materiel came through to ensure Britain's survival and America's effective participation in the European conflict. Then in 1943 the tide fully turned, and in the last two years of the war Allied shipping losses dropped to inconsequential levels while U-boat losses increased catastrophically, thus solidifying the Allied victory.

The second part of this maritime campaign was the offensive effort to blockade Germany and deprive it of all forms of seaborne commerce. Although often overlooked compared to the more publicised defensive struggle in the North Atlantic, this blockade ran just as long and encompassed numerous operations across the entire globe, with particular emphasis placed in the waters off Northwest Europe and the Baltic. The instruments of this offensive included aerial and ship-laid mines, maritime strike aircraft, bombers, submarines and surface warships. Together, these elements progressively diminished German maritime capacity until by war's end the

Table 12.2 Key Performance Indices from the Battle of the Atlantic

	Total Allied merchant shipping tonnage lost due to submarine attack	Total Allied merchant shipping tonnage lost due to other military means	Total import tons delivered to the United Kingdom	U-boat losses
Sep–Dec 1939	421,156	334,081	16,234,000	9
Jan–Dec 1940	2,186,158	1,805,483	55,009,000	22
Jan–Dec 1941	2,171,754	2,156,804	44,586,000	35
Jan–Dec 1942	6,266,215	1,524,482	34,090,000	86
Jan–Dec 1943	2,586,905	633,232	41,836,000	238
Jan–Dec 1944	773,327	272,302	46,093,000	254
Jan–May 1945*	270,277	142,656**	22,595,000	371***
Total	14,675,792	6,869,040	260,443,000	1,015

Source: The Central Statistical Office, *Statistical Digest of the War*, (London: Her Majesty's Stationery Office, 1975), pp. 184–185 and S. W. Roskill, *The War at Sea 1939–1945, Volume III, Part II*, (London: Her Majesty's Stationery Office, 1961), pp. 477, 479.
Note: Loss figures are compiled from all theatres of the war. The U-boat losses column only covers German losses. Italian and Japanese submarine losses are not included due to the limited role these boats played in the overall tonnage battle.
* Total import tons delivered to the United Kingdom are from January to June 1945.
** This includes two vessels worth 1,806 tons that were lost on unknown dates and are rolled into this period to capture their presence.
*** U-boat losses for 1945 consist of 163 U-boats sunk through combat or operational causes and 208 scuttled to avoid capture. A further 163 U-boats surrendered to the Allies, but these surrendered boats are not counted in the figures above. If added in, this would bring 1945's U-boat losses to 534.

German merchant fleet was all but destroyed and their seaborne trade (primarily with Scandinavia) had been reduced to a trickle. Given that Germany was already in a state of collapse by the time this occurred, the realisation of this goal came too late to be decisive on its own. Still, the effort was not in vain as the steady stream of attrition inflicted against the German merchant fleet caused inevitable disruptions to the German war economy and forced them to divert substantial resources to the maintenance and defence of their own seaborne lines of communication.

While these operations were underway, the British also embarked upon a new mission to materially support their Soviet allies. As discussed in Chapter 4, part of this effort was routed through Iran, but the main focus centred upon the running of a series of convoys through the Arctic to the Soviet ports of Murmansk and Archangel. Beginning in August 1941 and lasting through the duration of the war, the British ran a total of 75 convoys containing 1,526 merchant ships to and from the Soviet Union. This was no easy task as many of these convoys faced an array of threats as severe as the challenges encountered by British convoys travelling to Malta in 1942. Nevertheless, 1,400 of these vessels successfully completed their journeys. Added to this were a further 41 merchant ships that sailed independently, of which 32 reached their destinations.[8] In the process of these operations, the Western Allies shipped a total of 3,964,000 tons of weapons and materiel to the Soviet Union, of which 93 percent arrived.[9] The cost for this success consisted of 100 merchant ships worth 604,837 tons sunk (with the remaining unaccounted for ships having turned

Table 12.3 Axis Military and Commercial Surface Ships Sunk, Captured or Destroyed in European Waters outside of the Mediterranean and Black Sea

	Military Losses		Commercial Losses	
	No. of Ships	Tonnage	No. of Ships	Tonnage
Mines laid by Allied aircraft and naval vessels	255	168,271	631	683,630
Allied air attacks against ships and ports	437	405,656	689	1,150,319
Allied naval/submarine actions and seizures	181	206,777	344	950,405
Soviet actions, scuttling, accidents and other causes	385	161,024	831	1,633,310
Total	1,258	941,728	2,495	4,417,664

Note: The geographical area covered in this table consists of the waters from Archangel in the north to Gibraltar in the south, including the Baltic, and stretching out 350 miles to the west of the European coastline. Military losses include surface warships and naval auxiliary vessels. Commercial losses include civilian merchant ships and minor vessels such as tugs, fishing trawlers, harbour craft and barges. Included in these figures are a number of minor vessels of unknown, but presumably minimal tonnage.

back), while the Royal Navy lost two cruisers, six destroyers, ten assorted escort vessels and one submarine.[10] Corresponding German losses included the battlecruiser *Scharnhorst*, three destroyers and 38 U-boats sunk in operations directly related to these Allied convoy efforts.[11]

Success in these various operations, both defensive and offensive, laid the essential groundwork for the Allied victory, but the ultimate realisation of this victory occurred on the battlefields of Northern Europe. In bringing this about, British maritime power once again provided a vital contribution to the undertaking. The starting point for this was the Allied invasion of Normandy on 6 June 1944, which constituted the largest amphibious assault operation of the war, involving some 7,000 vessels. The maritime portion of this was overwhelmingly British with 79 percent of the combatant warships and at least 60 percent of the landing ships and assault craft coming from British or Canadian sources.[12] Once the initial assaults were successful, this British-dominated force then fulfilled the vital function of building up and logistically supporting the Allied ground armies while concurrently defeating German efforts to interdict this undertaking. By 31 August this resulted in the landing of 2,052,299 men, 438,471 vehicles and 3,098,259 tons of stores.[13] Throughout this massive endeavour, losses were exceedingly light, amounting to just 8,260 tons of materiel lost en route to France from 24 June through 12 September.[14] Meanwhile, throughout the campaign (into early September) British battleships, monitors and cruisers conducted over 750 fire support missions in which they fired 34,621 shells ranging from 16-inch to 5.25-inch in calibre, while British destroyers added another 24,000 shells to this onslaught.[15]

Bolstered by this massive execution of maritime power, the Allied armies won a decisive victory in Normandy that allowed them to push out into northern France and the Low Countries. In November the British conducted the last major amphibious operation of the European war when British forces captured Walcheren Island in the southern Netherlands, thus opening the approach to the vital port of Antwerp. Present at this endeavour, as well as the earlier Normandy invasion, was a venerable veteran from the Mediterranean Fleet, the battleship *Warspite*, which performed a fire support function.[16] Meanwhile, for the remainder of the campaign, British-led maritime forces continued in their all-important logistical support mission, which only increased in scope as the Allied armies expanded until ultimately containing 4,084,314 men (of which 1,053,147 were British or British-affiliated) by the end of April 1945.[17] Compared to the Axis' efforts to keep Rommel's forces in North Africa supplied in 1941 and 1942, this constituted an immense undertaking, eventually requiring the delivery of some 3.5 million tons of supplies per month.[18] The end result of this was a highly successful ground campaign in which the Allied armies, in conjunction with the oncoming Russians, pushed into and eventually captured most of Germany, thus fostering its unconditional surrender.

The maritime campaign that ultimately facilitated this outcome was a collective effort shared jointly between the forces of the British Commonwealth and the United States, with minor contributions made by the lesser navies. In this, both primary participants played essential roles, but Britain (with substantial support from Canada) was clearly the predominant partner in the undertaking. It was the British who provided the majority of resources, conducted the majority of related operations, suffered the majority of related losses and scored the majority of successes against the Kriegsmarine and German merchant fleet. In terms of the latter, Britain's share of German maritime losses (both sole and partial) included 100 percent of their capital ships, 75 percent of their cruisers, 86 percent of their destroyers, 75 percent of their torpedo boats and escort destroyers, 86 percent of their fleet minesweepers, 77 percent of their U-boats and 73 percent of their merchant and commercial vessels.[19]

This was no minor accomplishment given the eventual size of the Kriegsmarine, which proved to be Britain's greatest maritime nemesis during the war. This is clearly borne out by the fact that the Germans lost 1,634 principal warships during the war, of which 71.9 percent were lost solely or partially due to British action. By comparison, total Italian warship losses numbered just 418 vessels, of which 62.2 percent were solely or partially attributable to British means. However, this portion increases to 86.1 percent when just considering Italian losses incurred while facing the Allies.[20] Many of these combined Axis losses occurred in the Mediterranean, but the majority were sustained in the Atlantic and Northern European waters, thus attesting to the scale of the fighting that occurred there. Thus, by being the primary vanquisher of both the Kriegsmarine and Regia Marina, the British demonstrated their dominant position in these competing maritime conflicts.

The same was not true regarding the third Axis power, Japan. To the contrary, it was the United States that was the overwhelming architect of Japan's defeat. Still, even here British maritime power did contribute to the ultimate victory. Of particular importance was a series of British carrier-borne air strikes against the Palembang oil refineries in southern Sumatra in January 1945 that halved Japan's aviation fuel production for the remainder of the war. A few months before this the Australian cruiser *Shropshire* and destroyer *Arunta* joined American forces in destroying the Japanese battleship *Yamashiro* during the battle of Surigao Strait. In other joint actions, British and Commonwealth air and naval units participated in the destruction of the Japanese cruisers *Jintsu* and *Isuzu* along with American forces. Meanwhile, British submarines sank the Japanese cruisers *Kuma* and *Ashigara* in conventional attacks, while British X-craft submarines sank the cruiser *Takao* in 1944 and 1945. Likewise, in the last naval surface action of the war, British destroyers sank the Japanese cruiser *Haguro* off of Penang. Finally, in July and August 1945 British aircraft carriers launched a series of air strikes against the Japanese home islands that destroyed some 50,000 tons of shipping, including the Japanese auxiliary escort carrier *Shimane Maru* and at least five escort destroyers.

Table 12.4 Total German and Italian Warship Losses versus Losses Solely or Partially Due to British Means

	German Losses			Italian Losses		
	Total losses	Losses solely or partially due to British means	Percent of losses due to British means	Total losses	Losses solely or partially due to British means	Percent of losses due to British means
Capital ships*	11	11	100.0%	8	6	75.0%
Cruisers	12	9	75.0%	26	20	76.9%
Destroyers, large torpedo boats	74	64	86.5%	76	48	63.2%
Small torpedo boats, escorts	87	65	74.7%	98	52	53.1%
Corvettes, sub-chasers	21	16	76.2%	43	22	51.2%
Submarines	1,184	916	77.4%	151	104	68.9%
Minelayers	4	3	75.0%	10	5	50.0%
Fleet minesweepers	241	208	86.3%	6	3	50.0%
Total	1,634	1,292	79.1%	418	260	62.2%

Note: This includes warships that were sunk in direct action as well as those scuttled to avoid capture by Allied forces and those that surrendered at the end of hostilities (September 1943 for the Italians and May 1945 for the Germans).
* Capital ships consist of battleships, battlecruisers, pocket battleships (German) and aircraft carriers.

An important factor that allowed the British to make these contributions was their success in the Mediterranean. As previously discussed in Chapter 11, this assistance came in two primary forms. First, the opening of the Mediterranean greatly aided British logistical efforts to support operations in the Far East. Second, the triumph over the Regia Marina and surrender of the Italian fleet released numerous British ships for service against Japan. While these were tangible results that were clearly attained, it is also worthwhile to consider the potential consequences that might have occurred had the Axis prevailed and gained control over the Middle East. At a minimum, this would have greatly hindered British supply operations to the Far East and served as a potential western-based threat to the Indian Ocean. Finally, it is worth noting that many of the senior leaders who eventually fought against the Japanese were veterans from the Mediterranean conflict, including Admirals James Somerville, Bernard Rawlings, Philip Vian and Geoffrey Oliver.

So, what difference did this maritime effort make? When reviewing the record, it is abundantly clear that Britain (including the Empire and Commonwealth) played an indispensable role in bringing about the ultimate Allied victory. Of the major participants in this conflict, Britain was the only one engaged through its entire

Table 12.5 Japanese Warship Losses Solely or Partially Due to British Means

	Total losses	Losses solely due to British means	Losses partially due to British means	Percent of losses due solely or partially to British means
Battleships	12	-	1	8.3%
Aircraft carriers	24	1	-	4.2%
Cruisers	43	4	2	14.0%
Destroyers	143	-	9	6.3%
Escort destroyers*	305	8	4	3.9%
Submarines	232	9	2	4.7%
Minelayers	5	1	-	20.0%
Fleet minesweepers	9	1	-	11.1%
Total	773	24	18	5.4%

Note: Warships that surrendered at the end of hostilities are included in the total losses, but are not partially credited to the British. The reason for this is the limited role that Britain played in defeating Japan compared to the essential roles it played in defeating Germany and Italy. If the British were given partial credit for these surrendered ships, their overall success percentage would increase to 38.3%.
* Many of the escort destroyers were conversions from other warship types. In particular, large numbers of minesweepers were converted to serve as escort destroyers and are thus counted as such here.

duration waging war on a global scale against all three major Axis nations. To a large extent, Britain was the originator and cornerstone of the grand alliance that defeated the Axis. It served as the catalyst that brought the United States into the European war and gave America the structural means to effectively participate in the conflict. Without Britain, there would have been no effective Western Alliance, and the Soviet Union would have faced the full force of the European Axis alone. Beyond these geographical and political considerations, Britain actively participated in every major campaign waged by the Western Allies in the European war and usually served as the predominant or equal partner in these undertakings.

Many factors facilitated Britain's ability to make these contributions, but none was more important than the effective application of maritime power. This was true everywhere the British fought, be that in the Atlantic, Northwest Europe, Mediterranean, Middle East or Far East. Even the strategic bombing campaign had its roots firmly planted in the exploitation of sea power. Not surprisingly, these many successes came at a heavy cost. Through the duration of the war the British lost 377 principal warships, of which 86 percent came from the Royal Navy, while the remainder came from the various Commonwealth contingents or British-built ships manned by personnel from the lesser Allied nations. Roughly 45 percent of these warship losses occurred in the Mediterranean or in related operations, thus illustrating the scope of the combat there. Meanwhile, the British Commonwealth lost 2,627 merchant ships during the war worth a combined 11,396,900 tons. Altogether, this represented about 28 percent of the worldwide merchant tonnage lost during the war. However, unlike their warship counterparts, only about 10 percent of these losses were related to the Mediterranean conflict.

The war in the Mediterranean effectively ended on 2 May 1945. With this, the colossal contest that had ravaged the region for almost five years and resulted in the loss of some 6,000 assorted vessels entered the realm of history. In doing so, the war ended an era of naval combat that stretched back roughly 3,000 years. While it is certainly conceivable that more destructive wars might occur in the future, it seems highly unlikely that the Mediterranean will ever again experience a prolonged naval contest like World War II or play host to great naval battles such as Salamis, Actium, Lepanto, the Nile or Cape Matapan. Similarly, World War II also represented the swan song of Britain's maritime supremacy, as the mantle for this was handed over to the United States. Still, as Britain's maritime position now entered a state of

As momentous as the Mediterranean conflict was, it was only part of the vast global effort executed by Allied maritime power during World War II. Hundreds of Allied ships that fought in the Mediterranean also served in other theatres during the war. Amongst these was the cruiser *Sheffield*, which saw extensive action in the Atlantic and Arctic as well as the Mediterranean. (Coote, R. G. G. (Lt), Royal Navy official photographer, public domain)

decline, the war at least provided a fitting end to the glorious period making up the nation's naval legacy. As long as people review history, future generations will always be able to look back and understand the indispensable role that British maritime power played in triumphing over evil during World War II. They will also know that during a critical period in this conflict, the British thwarted Mussolini's dream to transform the Mediterranean into *Mare Nostrum*, and instead briefly turned this great body of water into Britannia's Sea.

Timeline of Significant Global Events during World War II

	Northwest Europe and Atlantic/Arctic	Africa/ Southern Europe	Mediterranean	Eastern Europe	Asia/Pacific and Indian Oceans
1939	Britain & France declare war on Germany.			Germany invades Poland.	
	Britain imposes naval blockade against Germany. Germany begins U-boat war against Britain.			USSR attacks Finland.	
1940	Germany attacks the West. British Expeditionary Force withdraws from France.				
	Fall of France.	Italy declares war on Britain and France.	Early Italian submarine losses. Naval action off Zante.		
	British conduct Operation *Catapult*.		Attack on Mers-el-Kébir. Naval actions off Calabria & Cape Spada.		

	Northwest Europe and Atlantic/Arctic	Africa/ Southern Europe	Mediterranean	Eastern Europe	Asia/Pacific and Indian Oceans
	Battle of Britain.	Italians invade British Somaliland.			
	Sea Lion postponed. Dakar Expedition.	Italians invade Egypt.	FAA strike against Benghazi.		French cede control of Indochina to Japan.
			Naval action off Cape Passero.		Convoy naval action in Red Sea.
	First U-boat Happy Time.	Italy invades Greece.	FAA strike against Taranto.		
	The Blitz.	British launch Operation *Compass*.			
1941		British destroy Italian Tenth Army & begin conquest of East Africa.	Luftwaffe intervenes. *Illustrious* damaged. Genoa bombarded.		British blockade Axis shipping in Red Sea and around East Africa.
	Five U-boats sunk. End of Happy Time.	British reinforce Greece.	Battle of Cape Matapan.		
		Germans attack Cyrenaica, Yugoslavia & Greece.	Force K formed. Destroys Axis convoy off Kerkenah Bank.		British capture Massawa securing the Red Sea. Heavy Axis naval losses.

Northwest Europe and Atlantic/Arctic	Africa/ Southern Europe	Mediterranean	Eastern Europe	Asia/Pacific and Indian Oceans
Bismarck sunk.	Invasion of Crete.	Crete evacuated. RN suffers heavy losses.		British suppress rebellion in Iraq.
Beginning of full convoy coverage in the Atlantic.	Operation *Battleaxe.*		Germany invades USSR.	British secure Syria.
British break U-boat Home Waters key.		Malta becomes offensive base.		
Beginning of Arctic convoys to USSR.			Battle of Kiev.	British & Soviets invade Iran.
		Germans send U-boats to assist Italians.	Siege of Leningrad begins.	
British attain temporary respite in the battle of the Atlantic.	British finish conquest of East Africa. Begin Operation *Crusader.*	Force K destroys convoy Beta. *Ark Royal* & *Barham* sunk.	Germans arrive on outskirts of Moscow.	
USA enters war.	British relieve Tobruk.	Naval action off Cape Bon. Alexandria attacked.	Soviets launch counter-attack.	Japan attacks British and American interests in Pacific. *Prince of Wales* & *Repulse* sunk.

	Northwest Europe and Atlantic/Arctic	Africa/ Southern Europe	Mediterranean	Eastern Europe	Asia/Pacific and Indian Oceans
1942	U-boats attack America. Beginning of Second Happy Time.	Rommel regains western Cyrenaica.	Beginning of renewed aerial assault against Malta.	The battles of Rzhev.	Loss of Malaya. The Philippines, Dutch East Indies & Burma invaded.
	Raid on St Nazaire.		Convoy MW.10. Second battle of Sirte.	Battle of the Demyansk Pocket.	
	U-boat assault shifts to Caribbean & Gulf of Mexico.		Height of Malta blitz. First Spitfires arrive.		Japanese raid Ceylon & inflict heavy losses on British Eastern Fleet.
	First 1,000-bomber raid against Cologne.			Second battle of Kharkov.	Operation *Ironclad*. Battle of the Coral Sea.
		Battle of Gazala. Fall of Tobruk.	*Harpoon* & *Vigorous* convoys.		Battle of Midway.
	Assault against Convoy PQ.17 in Arctic.	First battle of El Alamein.	Malta begins recovery.	Battle of Voronezh.	
	Raid on Dieppe.		*Pedestal* convoy.	Germans attack Caucasus.	Americans land on Guadalcanal. Battle of Savo Island.
	U-boats switch back to North Atlantic convoy routes.	Battle of Alam Halfa.	Raid on Tobruk. Resurgent Malta takes toll on Axis shipping.	Germans begin assault on Stalingrad.	Battle of Kokoda Trail.

	Northwest Europe and Atlantic/Arctic	Africa/ Southern Europe	Mediterranean	Eastern Europe	Asia/Pacific and Indian Oceans
		Second battle of El Alamein.	Malta mini-blitz.		Battle of Santa Cruz Island.
	USN landings in French Morocco.	Invasion of North Africa.	RN landings in Algeria.	Soviets counter-attack at Stalingrad.	Naval battles off Guadalcanal.
	British break Triton U-boat key. Battle of the Barents Sea.	Race to Tunisia.	Force Q destroys convoy H.		
1943		British capture Libya.	British interdict shipping around Tripoli.		
		Battle of Kasserine Pass.	Allies interdict Tunisian-bound shipping.	German Sixth Army surrenders at Stalingrad.	End of Guadalcanal campaign.
	Convoy battles SC.121 & SC.122/HX.229.	Battles of Mareth and Wadi Akarit.		Third battle of Kharkov.	Battle of the Bismarck Sea.
	Germans lose 40 U-boats in May. Withdraw from North Atlantic.	Operation *Strike.* Surrender of all Axis forces in Tunisia.	Operation *Retribution.*		Landing on Attu.
	Allies launch Bay of Biscay and mid-Atlantic offensives.		Operation *Corkscrew.* Capture of Pantelleria.		Landing on Rendova Island.
	RAF bombs Hamburg.	Invasion of Sicily. Mussolini deposed.	RN & USN conduct Operation *Husky.*	Battle of Kursk.	Naval actions at Kula Gulf and Kolombangara.

	Northwest Europe and Atlantic/Arctic	Africa/ Southern Europe	Mediterranean	Eastern Europe	Asia/Pacific and Indian Oceans
	USAAF Schweinfurt-Regensburg raids.	Capture of Sicily.	Axis evacuation across Strait of Messina.	Soviets launch counter-offensive.	Landing on Vella Lavella.
		Italy signs armistice. Allies land at Calabria & Salerno.	Surrender of the Italian fleet. Med open to Allied convoy traffic.	Battle of Smolensk.	Landings on Lae and Salamaua.
	Renewed U-boat offensive in the North Atlantic fails.	Capture of Naples. Advance to the Sangro and Garigliano Rivers.	Failed British Aegean expedition.	Battle of the Dnieper.	
		Activation of US 15th Air Force in Italy.		Second battle of Kiev.	Naval action in Empress Augusta Bay. Landing on the Gilbert Islands.
	Battle of North Cape. *Scharnhorst* sunk.			Dnieper-Carpathian offensive begins.	Landings on Arawe and Cape Gloucester.
1944		Landing at Anzio. Assault on Gustav Line.	RN & USN conduct Operation *Shingle*.		Landing on Kwajalein.
	Big Week bomber raids.	Assault on Cassino.	Maintenance of the Anzio beachhead.		Raid on Truk. Battle of Ngakyedauk Pass.
	Transportation Plan implemented.				Japanese invasion of India.

Northwest Europe and Atlantic/Arctic	Africa/ Southern Europe	Mediterranean	Eastern Europe	Asia/Pacific and Indian Oceans
	Mining of Danube River begins.		Crimean offensive.	BR Eastern Fleet begins offensive operations.
	Operation *Diadem*. Anzio breakout.			Landings on Wakde and Biak.
Invasion of Normandy.	Capture of Rome.	Crete convoy sunk. Landing on Elba.	Soviets launch Operation *Bagration*.	Landing on Saipan. Battle of the Philippine Sea.
Breakout from the Normandy lodgement.			German Army Group Centre routed.	Battle of Imphal & Kohima.
Battle of Falaise. Bay of Biscay evacuated.	Invasion of southern France.	USN & RN conduct Operation *Dragoon*.	Romania leaves Axis. Warsaw uprising.	
Liberation of France & Belgium.	Operation *Olive*. Gothic Line breached.	Interdiction operations in the Aegean.	Bulgaria & Finland leave Axis.	Landing on the Palau Islands.
		Greece Liberated. Heavy German naval losses.		Landing on Leyte & battle of Leyte Gulf.
Assault on Walcheren. Antwerp opened. Battleship *Tirpitz* sunk.		Naval action off Pag Island.	Budapest Offensive.	Mariana-based USAAF bombers begin aerial offensive against Japan.
Battle of the Bulge.				Beginning of third Arakan campaign.

	Northwest Europe and Atlantic/Arctic	Africa/ Southern Europe	Mediterranean	Eastern Europe	Asia/Pacific and Indian Oceans
1945				Visula-Oder Offensive.	FAA strikes against Palembang oil refineries.
	Battle of the Rhineland.		RAF & USAAF take toll on German shipping.		Landing on Iwo Jima.
	Rhine crossed. Advance into Germany.		Naval action off Corsica.	Operation *Spring Awakening*.	Battle of Meiktila & Mandalay.
	Battle of the Ruhr pocket. Advance to the Elbe River & Baltic.	Operation *Grapeshot*. Conquest of northern Italy. Death of Mussolini.	Fall of Genoa. Last German warships scuttled.	Battle of Berlin. Death of Hitler.	Landing on Okinawa. Kamikaze onslaught against USN and RN.
	Surrender of Germany.				Landing in Rangoon. Naval action off Penang.
					Landings in Borneo.
					USN & RN strike Japanese home islands.
					Atomic bombs dropped. USSR invades Manchuria. Japan surrenders.

Note: This timeline reflects general timeframes and the corresponding proximities of events to each other. It is not meant to be an exact representation of event dates.

Wartime Biographies of Prominent Royal Navy Officers Who Served in the Mediterranean Theatre

Vice-Admiral Sir William Gladstone Agnew, KCVO, CB, DSO. Born in London, England, on 2 December 1898. Died in Alverstoke, England, on 12 July 1960. Served in the Royal Navy from 1911 to 1950. Started the war as the commanding officer of the armed merchant cruiser HMS *Corfu*. In October 1940 assumed command of the light cruiser HMS *Aurora*. Participated in the hunt for the German battleship *Bismarck* and later helped destroy the German supply ship *Belchen* and the gunnery training ship *Bremse* on June 1941 and September 1941 respectively. Transferred to the Mediterranean in the autumn of 1941 and briefly commanded Force K stationed in Malta where he oversaw the destruction of convoy Beta and other Axis vessels in November/December of that year. In 1942 participated in the invasion of North Africa and the destruction of Convoy H and then later assumed command of the 12th Cruiser Squadron and participated in the invasions of Sicily and Italy in 1943. Ended the war as the commanding officer of the Royal Navy's gunnery school.

Admiral Sir Harold Martin Burrough, GCB, KBE, DSO. Born on 4 July 1888 in Easton Bishop, England. Died on 22 October 1977 in Hindhead, England. Served in the Royal Navy from 1903 to 1949. Started the war as Assistant Chief of the Naval Staff and was appointed Rear-Admiral commanding the 10th Cruiser Squadron in September 1940. Participated in the raid against Vågsøy and Måløy in Norway in December 1941. In 1942 commanded the close escort for Operation *Pedestal* and then served as the commanding officer of the Eastern Task Force during the invasion of North Africa. Became Flag Officer Commanding Gibraltar and Mediterranean Approaches in September 1943. Ended the war as Allied Naval Commander-in-Chief, Expeditionary Force (ANXF) following the death of Admiral Bertram Ramsay and was one of the signatories to the German surrender on 7 May 1945 in Rheims, France.

Admiral of the Fleet Andrew Browne Cunningham, 1st Viscount Cunningham of Hyndhope, KT, GCB, OM, DSO & Two Bars. Born on 7 January 1883 in

Rathmines, Ireland. Died on 12 June 1963 in London, England. Served in the Royal Navy from 1897 to 1946. Started the war as Commander-in-Chief, Mediterranean Fleet, and retained this position for most of the next four years (other than a short break to serve as the head of the British Naval Mission in Washington). Actions included the negotiated internment of the French fleet in Alexandria, the Fleet Air Arm strike against Taranto, the battle of Cape Matapan and the evacuation of Crete. Later served as the senior Allied naval commander for the invasions of North Africa, Sicily and Italy, and oversaw the surrender of the Italian fleet in September 1943. In October 1943 became First Sea Lord and Chief of the Naval Staff and retained this position for the remainder of the war.

Admiral of the Fleet Sir John Henry Dacres Cunningham, GCB, MVO, DL. Born on 13 April 1885 in Demerara, British Guiana. Died on 13 December 1962 in London, England. Served in the Royal Navy from 1900 to 1948. Started the war as the commanding officer for the 1st Cruiser Squadron. Participated in the Norwegian campaign and commanded the naval forces involved in the ill-fated attempt to capture Dakar in September 1940. After serving as Fourth Sea Lord and Chief of Supplies and Transport, became Commander-in-Chief, Levant, in June 1943 and Commander-in-Chief, Mediterranean Fleet, in October of that same year. Served in this capacity for the remainder of the war.

Admiral Sir Henry Harwood Harwood, KCB, OBE. Born on 19 January 1888 in London, England. Died on 9 June 1950 in Goring-on-Thames, England. Served in the Royal Navy from 1904 to 1945. Started the war commanding a cruiser squadron in the South Atlantic where he gained notoriety for his engagement against the German pocket battleship *Graf Spee* during the battle of the River Plate. After serving as the Lord Commissioner of the Admiralty and Assistant Chief of the Naval Staff, commanded the Mediterranean Fleet from April 1942 through February 1943. Thereafter, served a short time as the Commander-in-Chief, Levant, and then later became Admiral Commanding, Orkneys and Shetlands, in April 1944. Retired from active service on 15 August 1945 after being declared medically unfit for further duty.

Admiral of the Fleet Sir Rhoderick Robert McGrigor, GCB. Born on 12 April 1893 in York, England. Died on 3 December 1959 in Tarland, Scotland. Served in the Royal Navy from 1910 to 1955. Started the war as Chief of Staff to the Commander-in-Chief, China Station. In 1941 commanded the battlecruiser HMS *Renown* as part of Force H and participated in the bombardment of Genoa and the sinking of the German battleship *Bismarck*. Thereafter, served as Assistant Chief of the Naval Staff (Weapons) and then commanded the naval forces covering Operation *Corkscrew*, the invasion of Pantelleria, in June 1943. One month later commanded an assault group during the invasion of Sicily. Spent the last year and a half of the war assigned to the Home Fleet where he commanded the 1st Cruiser Squadron and participated in various Arctic convoy operations and strikes against German shipping, including the destruction of a German convoy off Listerfjord in November 1944 and the final Fleet Air Arm strike of the European War, Operation *Judgement*, in May 1945.

Admiral Sir Geoffrey Nigel Oliver, GBE, KCB, DSO & Two Bars. Born on 22 January 1898 in London, England. Died 26 May 1980 in Henfield, England. Served in the Royal Navy from 1915 to 1955. Started the war as deputy director of the Training and Staff Duties Division. From October 1940 to June 1942 commanded the light cruiser HMS *Hermione*, which participated in the *Bismarck* hunt and numerous Malta convoy operations and sank the Italian submarine *Tembien*. Thereafter, participated in the invasions of North Africa and Sicily and then commanded the British Northern Attack Force during the Salerno landings. In January 1944 appointed Naval Force Commander, Force J, which later participated in the Normandy invasion. Ended the war in command of the 21st Aircraft Carrier Squadron as part of the East Indies Fleet operating against the Japanese in the Indian Ocean.

Admiral Sir Henry Daniel Pridham-Wippell, KCB, CVO. Born on 12 August 1885 in Bromley, England. Died 2 April 1952 in Deal, England. Served in the Royal Navy from 1900 to 1948. Started the war as Director of Personal Services, Admiralty. From May 1940 through May 1942 served in various sea commands in the Mediterranean Fleet. Highlights of service include the destruction of an Italian convoy in the Strait of Otranto in November 1940, participation in the battle of Cape Matapan and seagoing command of the Greece and Crete evacuations. In November 1941 survived the sinking of the battleship HMS *Barham*. In August 1942 appointed Flag Officer Commanding Dover and held this position for the remainder of the war.

Admiral Sir Bertram Home Ramsay, KCB, KBE, MVO. Born on 20 January 1883 in London, England. Died on 2 January 1945 in Toussus-le-Noble, France. Served in the Royal Navy from 1898 to 1945. For the first two and a half years of the war served as Flag Officer Commanding Dover where he orchestrated the successful evacuation of the British Expeditionary Force from Dunkirk, Operation *Dynamo*, in May 1940. In 1942 served as the deputy naval commander for the Allied invasion of North Africa and then became Naval Commanding Officer, Eastern Task Force, for the invasion of Sicily in 1943. In 1944 appointed the Naval Commander-in-Chief of the Allied Expeditionary Force and oversaw the invasion of Normandy and subsequent support operations associated with the Northwest Europe campaign. Died while serving in this capacity in January 1945 as the result of a plane crash.

Admiral Sir Henry Bernard Hughes Rawlings, GBE, KCB. Born on 21 May 1889 in St Erth, England. Died on 30 September 1962 in Bodmin, England. Served in the Royal Navy from 1904 to 1946. Started the war as commander of the battleship HMS *Valiant* and participated in the bombardment of the French fleet at Mers-el-Kébir. Later commanded the 1st Battle Squadron and 7th Cruiser Squadron and participated in evacuation operations from Crete. In 1943 and 1944 served as Flag Officer, West Africa, and then later Flag Officer, Eastern Mediterranean. Ended the war as Second-in-Command of the British Pacific Fleet and the commander of Task Force 57/37 during strike operations against the Palembang oil refineries, Sakishima Gunto and the Japanese home islands.

Admiral of the Fleet Sir James Fownes Somerville, GCB, GBE, DSO, DL. Born on 17 July 1882 in Weybridge, England. Died on 19 March 1949 in Somerset, England. Served in the Royal Navy from 1897 to 1946. Started the war on special service to the Admiralty where he performed important work on naval radar development and helped organise the Dunkirk evacuation. From June 1940 through January 1942 served as Flag Officer Commanding Force H at Gibraltar where he led the attack against the French fleet at Mers-el-Kébir, the bombardment of Genoa and the conduct of multiple Malta convoys. Thereafter, spent the next two and a half years as Commander-in-Chief of the Eastern Fleet where he shepherded the fleet through a period of great danger and revitalised it to begin offensive operations against the Japanese. Ended the war as the head of the British naval delegation in Washington.

Admiral Sir Edward Neville Syfret, GCB, KBE. Born on 20 June 1889 in Newlands, South Africa. Died on 10 December 1972 in Highgate, England. Served in the Royal Navy from 1904 to 1948. Started the war as the commander of the battleship HMS *Rodney* and then became Naval Secretary to the First Sea Lord and commander of the 18th Cruiser Squadron. In January 1942 became Flag Officer Commanding Force H where he oversaw Operation *Ironclad*, the *Pedestal* convoy and the covering force for the invasion of North Africa. Spent the last two years of the war as a Lord Commissioner of the Admiralty and Vice-Chief of the Naval Staff.

Admiral of the Fleet John Cronyn Tovey, 1st Baron Tovey, GCB, KBE, DSO. Born on 7 March 1885 in Rochester, England. Died on 12 January 1971 in Funchal, Madeira. Served in the Royal Navy from 1900 to 1946. Spent the first 15 months of the war as a senior commander in the Mediterranean Fleet, eventually becoming Vice-Admiral Commanding Light Forces and Second-in-Command of the fleet. Led British naval forces in the first surface engagement of the Mediterranean conflict, resulting in the destruction of the Italian destroyer *Espero*. In late 1940 became commander of the Home Fleet and retained this position until May 1943, during which he presided over the destruction of the German battleship *Bismarck* and executed numerous Arctic convoys to the Soviet Union. Ended the war as Commander-in-Chief, Nore.

Vice-Admiral Sir Thomas Hope Troubridge, KCB, DSO & Bar. Born on 1 February 1895 in Southsea, England. Died 29 September 1949 in Hawkley, England. Served in the Royal Navy from 1908 to 1948. Other than a six-month stint in the Naval Intelligence Division, held consecutive commands of HMS *Furious*, HMS *Nelson* and HMS *Indomitable* during the first three years of the war, which included service in the Mediterranean and against Madagascar. In 1942 and 1943 commanded the Central Naval Task Force and an assault group during the invasions of North Africa and Sicily respectively. Then, in 1944 commanded the Northern Attack Force during the invasion of Anzio, Force N during the conquest of Elba, Task Force 88 during the invasion of southern France and Force 120 during the liberation of Greece. Ended the war as a Lord Commissioner of the Admiralty and Fifth Sea Lord (Air).

Admiral of the Fleet Sir Philip Louis Vian, GCB, KBE, DSO & Two Bars. Born on 14 June 1894 in London, England. Died on 27 May 1968 in Ashford Hill, England. Served in the Royal Navy from 1907 to 1952. Spent the first two years of the war as the commander of 11th and 4th Destroyer Flotillas where he led the rescue of British seaman from the German merchant ship *Altmark* and participated in the destruction of the battleship *Bismarck*. In mid-1941 briefly commanded Force A in the Arctic where he oversaw the destruction of the German gunnery training ship *Bremse*. In 1942 commanded the 15th Cruiser Squadron in the Mediterranean earning distinction during the Second Battle of Sirte. After holding various administrative positions, commanded an assault group and Task Force 88 during the invasions of Sicily and Salerno. In 1944 served as Commander, Eastern Task Force, during the Normandy invasion. Ended the war as Flag Officer Commanding, 1st Aircraft Carrier Squadron, British Pacific Fleet, during strike operations against the Palembang oil refineries, Sakishima Gunto and the Japanese home islands.

Admiral of the Fleet Sir Algernon Usborne Willis, KCB, DSO. Born on 17 May 1889 in London, England. Died on 12 April 1976 in Gosport, England. Served in the Royal Navy from 1904 to 1950. Held a number of administrative positions during the first two years of the war, including Chief of Staff to the Commander-in-Chief, Mediterranean Fleet. From February 1942 through January 1943 served as Vice-Admiral Commanding, 3rd Battle Squadron and Second-in-Command of the Eastern Fleet. Followed this with an eight-month stint as commander of Force H, providing coverage for the invasions of Sicily and Salerno. Thereafter, briefly served as the Commander-in-Chief, Levant Station, and then completed the war as a Lord Commissioner of the Admiralty and Chief of Naval Personnel (Second Sea Lord).

Selected Bibliography

Primary Sources

ADM 186/796, Battle Summaries, No. 43: Invasion of the South of France, Operation *Dragoon*, 15 August 1944.

ADM 186/797, Battle Summaries, Nos. 1, 6, 7 and 19: Operations against French Fleet at Mersel-Kebir (Oran) 3–6 July 1940, the bombardments of Bardia June 1940–Jan 1941, Genoa 9 Feb 1941 and Tripoli 21 Apr 1941.

ADM 199/2447, German Ships: Losses and Damages in North West European Waters.

ADM 199/2519, World War II Mediterranean Statistics.

ADM 223/34, Axis merchant shipping: enemy merchant shipping losses in the Mediterranean.

ADM 223/88, Admiralty Use of Special Intelligence in Naval Operations.

ADM 234/320, Battle Summaries, No. 4: Naval Operations of Battle of Crete, 20 May to 1 June 1941.

ADM 234/327, Battle Summaries, Nos. 2, 8, 9 & 10: Selected Operations in the Mediterranean, 1940.

ADM 234/331, Battle Summaries, No. 16: Naval Operations at the Capture of Diego Suarez (Operation *Ironclad*), May 1942.

ADM 234/334, Battle Summaries, No. 52: Tobruk Run June 1940–Jan. 1943.

ADM 234/335, Battle Summaries, Nos. 18 and 32: Selected Convoys Mediterranean 1941–1942.

ADM 234/356, Battle Summaries, No. 35: Invasion of Sicily (Operation *Husky*).

ADM 234/358, Battle Summaries, No. 37: Invasion of Italy: Landing at Salerno (Operation *Avalanche*) 9 Sept. 1943.

ADM 234/359, Battle Summaries, No. 38: Invasion of North Africa (Operation *Torch*), Nov. 1942–Feb. 1943.

ADM 234/364, Battle Summaries, No. 36: Aegean operations 7 Sept.–28 Nov. 1943: British occupation and German re-capture of Kos and Leros.

AIR 41/19, The RAF in Maritime War, Vol. VI.: The Mediterranean and Red Sea.

AIR 41/54, The RAF in Maritime War, Vol VII, Part I: Mediterranean Reconquest and the Submarine War May 1943–May 1944.

AIR 41/76, RAF in the Maritime War, Volume VII, Part II: Mediterranean; Naval Cooperation, the End of the Submarine War and Operations in the Adriatic, Greece and the Aegean, 1944–45.

AIR 41/79, RAF in the Maritime War, Volume VIII: Statistics.

WO 201/822, Operations: First Army and Second United States Corps in Tunisia.

WO 204/7846, Weekly Cumulative Return of Prisoners of War Captured.

WO 204/10505, 15th Army Group Administration: Report on Sicilian Campaign July–Aug. 1943.

WO 214/18, North African Campaign.

Secondary Sources

Bragadin, Mare' Antonio. *The Italian Navy in World War II* (Annapolis: United States Naval Institute Press, 1957).

Brown, David. *Carrier Operations in World War II, Volume One: The Royal Navy* (Annapolis: Naval Institute Press, 1968).

———. *The Seafire, The Spitfire that went to Sea* (Annapolis: Naval Institute Press, 1989).

———. *Warship Losses of World War Two* (London: Arms and Armour Press, 1990).

Buckley, Christopher. *Five Ventures: Iraq–Syria–Persia–Madagascar–Dodecanese* (London: Her Majesty's Stationery Office, 1954).

Cunningham, Andrew. *A Sailor's Odyssey, The Autobiography of Admiral of the Fleet, Viscount Cunningham of Hyndhope* (London: Hutchinson & Co Ltd., 1951).

Ehlers, Jr., Robert S. *The Mediterranean Air War, Airpower and the Allied Victory in World War II* (Lawrence: University Press of Kansas, 2015).

Great Britain Cabinet Office, Cabinet History Series. *Principal War Telegrams and Memoranda, 1940–1943, Middle East III* (Nendeln: KTO Press, 1976).

Great Britain War Office. *The Abyssinia Campaigns – The Official Story of the Conquest of Italian East Africa* (London, His Majesty's Stationery Office, 1942).

Greene, Jack and Massignani, Alessandro. *The Naval War in the Mediterranean 1940–1943* (London: Chatham Publishing, 1998).

Hinsley, F. H. *British Intelligence in the Second World War, Abridged Version* (New York: Cambridge University Press, 1993).

Ireland, Bernard. *The War in the Mediterranean 1940–1943* (South Yorkshire: Leo Cooper, 2004).

Jackson, William and Gleave, T. P. *The Mediterranean and Middle East, Volume VI: Victory in the Mediterranean, Part III, November 1944 to May 1945* (London: Her Majesty's Stationery Office, 1988).

Jackson, William and Gleave, T. P. *The Mediterranean and Middle East, Volume VI: Victory in the Mediterranean, Part II, June to October 1944* (London: Her Majesty's Stationery Office, 1987).

Jordan, Roger. *The World's Merchant Fleets 1939, The Particulars and Wartime Fates of 6,000 Ships* (Annapolis: Naval Institute Press, 1999).

Levine, Alan J. *The War Against Rommel's Supply Lines, 1942–1943* (Westport: Praeger Publishers, 1999).

Mawdsley, Evan. *The War for the Seas, A Maritime History of World War II* (New Haven: Yale University Press, 2019).

Molony, C. J. C. *The Mediterranean and Middle East, Volume V: The Campaign in Sicily 1943 and the Campaign in Italy 3rd September 1943 to 31st March 1944* (London: Her Majesty's Stationery Office, 1973).

———. *The Mediterranean and Middle East, Volume VI: Victory in the Mediterranean, Part I, 1st April to 4th June 1944* (London: Her Majesty's Stationery Office, 1984).

Morison, Samuel Eliot. *History of United States Naval Operations in World War II, Volume II: Operations in North African Waters, October 1942–June 1943* (Boston: Little, Brown and Company, 1947).

O'Hara, Vincent. *Struggle for the Middle Sea, the Great Navies at War in the Mediterranean, 1940–1945* (Annapolis: Naval Institute Press, 2009).

Playfair, I. S. O. *The Mediterranean and Middle East, Volume I: The Early Success against Italy* (London: Her Majesty's Stationery Office, 1954).

———. *The Mediterranean and Middle East, Volume II: The Germans come to the Help of their Ally* (London: Her Majesty's Stationery Office, 1956).

———. *The Mediterranean and Middle East, Volume III: British Fortunes Reach their Lowest Ebb* (London: Her Majesty's Stationery Office, 1960).

———. *The Mediterranean and Middle East, Volume IV: The Destruction of Axis Forces in Africa* (London: Her Majesty's Stationery Office, 1966).

Porch, Douglas. *The Path to Victory, The Mediterranean Theater in World War II* (New York: Farrar, Straus and Giroux, 2004).

Richards, Denis and Saunders, Hilary St. George. *Royal Air Force 1939–1945, Volume II: The Fight Avails* (London: Her Majesty's Stationery Office, 1954).

Rohwer, Jürgen. *Allied Submarine Attacks of World War Two, European Theatre of Operations 1939–1945* (Annapolis: Naval Institute Press, 1997).

———. *Axis Submarine Successes 1939–1945* (Annapolis: Naval Institute Press, 1983).

Rohwer, J. and Hummelchen G. *Chronology of the War at Sea 1939–1945* (Annapolis: Naval Institute Press, 1992).

Roskill, S. W. *The War at Sea, 1939–1945, Volume I: The Defensive* (London: Her Majesty's Stationery Office, 1954).

———. *The War at Sea, 1939–1945, Volume II: The Period of Balance* (London: Her Majesty's Stationery Office, 1956).

———. *The War at Sea, 1939–1945, Volume III, Part I: The Offensive, 1st June 1943–31 May 1944* (London: Her Majesty's Stationery Office, 1960).

———. *The War at Sea, 1939–1945, Volume III, Part II: The Offensive, 1st June 1944–14 August 1945* (London: Her Majesty's Stationery Office, 1961).

Sadkovich, James J. *The Italian Navy in World War II* (London: Greenwood Press, 1994).

Saunders, Hilary St. George. *Royal Air Force 1939–1945, Volume III: The Fight is Won* (London: Her Majesty's Stationery Office, 1954).

Smith, Peter C. and Walker, Edwin. *The Battles of the Malta Striking Forces* (Annapolis: Naval Institute Press, 1974).

Terraine, John. *The Right of the Line, The Royal Air Force in the European War 1939–1945* (London: Hodder and Stoughton, Sceptre edition, 1988).

Tomblin, Barbara Brooks. *With Utmost Spirit: Allied Naval Operations in the Mediterranean, 1942–1945* (Lexington: The University Press of Kentucky, 2004).

Warner, Oliver. *Admiral of the Fleet Cunningham of Hyndhope, The Battle for the Mediterranean* (London: John Murray, 1967).

Endnotes

Introduction

1   S. W. Roskill, *Naval Policy between the Wars, Volume I: The Period of Anglo-American Antagonism 1919–1929* (New York: Walker and Company, 1968), p. 586.

Chapter 1: Setting the Stage

1   These warship losses consisted of the aircraft carrier *Glorious*, the light cruiser *Effingham*, the anti-aircraft cruiser *Curlew*, 14 destroyers, three escort destroyers, five submarines, one sloop and two minesweepers.

2   S. W. Roskill, *The War at Sea 1939–1945, Volume I: The Defensive* (London: Her Majesty's Stationery Office, 1954), pp. 593–597.

3   I. C. B. Dear and M. R. D. Foot, *The Oxford Companion to World War II* (Oxford: Oxford University Press, 1995), pp. 593, 595.

4   Basil Liddell Hart (Editor In Chief), *World War II, An Illustrated History* (London: Purnell Reference Books, 1977), pp. 313, 333.

5   I. S. O. Playfair, The Mediterranean and Middle East, Volume I: The Early Success against Italy (London: Her Majesty's Stationery Office, 1954), pp. 93–94.

6   Ibid., pp. 95–96.

7   Dear and Foot, *The Oxford Companion to World War II*, p. 596.

8   Playfair, *The Mediterranean and Middle East, Volume I*, pp. 95–96.

9   Torpedo boats should not be confused with British-designated motor torpedo boats, which were small, fast coastal craft displacing less than 100 tons and generally armed with two or four torpedoes and small arms. Italian, German and American equivalents to these motor torpedo boats were known as MAS boats, E-boats and PT boats respectively.

10 Due to manufacturing delays in the 5.25-inch guns, the British substituted eight 4.5-inch guns on the *Dido*-class cruisers *Scylla* and *Charybdis*.

11 Roskill, *The War at Sea 1939–1945, Volume I*, p. 32.

12 James J. Sadkovich, *The Italian Navy in World War II* (London: Greenwood Press, 1994), p. 102.

13 Ibid.

14 ADM 199/2447, German Ships: Losses and Damages in North West European Waters and Roger Jordan, *The World's Merchant Fleets 1939, The Particulars and Wartime Fates of 6,000 Ships* (Annapolis: Naval Institute Press, 1999), pp. 530–539. The sunk/scuttled vessels include the 5,181-ton merchant ship *Madda*, which beached itself off Tenerife in the Canary Islands to avoid capture by British warships. The vessel was subsequently raised and interned by Spain.

15 Sadkovich, *The Italian Navy in World War II*, p. 102.

16 The distance from London to Alexandria via the Cape of Good Hope was 11,608 miles as compared to 3,097 miles directly through the Mediterranean. This represented a difference of 8,511 miles.

Of course, actual distances would vary depending upon the points of departure and arrival and any variations in routes. See Raymond De Beiot, *The Struggle for the Mediterranean, 1939–1945* (New York: Greenwood Press Publishers, 1951), p. 54.

17 These merchant fleet figures consist of British flagged merchant ships and British-controlled foreign time-charters of 1,600 gross registered tons or greater. See The Central Statistical Office, *Statistical Digest of the War* (London: Her Majesty's Stationery Office, 1975), pp. 173–174.

Chapter 2: Opening Moves

1 Playfair, *The Mediterranean and Middle East, Volume I*, pp. 118–119, 187.

2 Ibid., p. 170.

3 J. Rohwer and G. Hummelchen, *Chronology of the War at Sea 1939–1945* (Annapolis: Naval Institute Press, 1992), pp. 22–23.

4 Mare' Antonio Bragadin, *The Italian Navy in World War II* (Annapolis: United States Naval Institute Press, 1957), p. 16.

5 Jürgen Rohwer, *Axis Submarine Successes 1939–1945* (Annapolis: Naval Institute Press, 1983), pp. 223, 257.

6 Jürgen Rohwer, *Allied Submarine Attacks of World War Two, European Theatre of Operations 1939–1945* (Annapolis: Naval Institute Press, 1997), p. 126.

7 ADM 199/2447, German Ships: Losses and Damages in North West European Waters and Roskill, *The War at Sea 1939–1945, Volume I*, pp. 121, 599.

8 Roskill, *The War at Sea 1939–1945, Volume I*, p. 249.

9 ADM 186/797, Battle Summaries, Nos. 1, 6, 7 and 19: Operations against French Fleet at Mersel-Kebir (Oran) 3–6 July 1940, the bombardments of Bardia June 1940–Jan 1941, Genoa 9 Feb 1941 and Tripoli 21 Apr 1941, Appendix B.

10 ADM 234/579, Naval Staff History, Defeat of Enemy Attack on Shipping, 1939–1945: A Study of Policy and Operations, Volume IB (Plans and Tables), Table 21 and Rohwer and Hummelchen, *Chronology of the War at Sea 1939–1945*, p. 26.

11 Rohwer, *Allied Submarine Attacks of World War Two, European Theatre of Operations 1939–1945*, pp. 126–127.

12 Playfair, *The Mediterranean and Middle East, Volume I*, pp. 178–179.

13 Rohwer and Hummelchen, *Chronology of the War at Sea 1939–1945*, p. 36.

14 Rohwer and Hummelchen, *Chronology of the War at Sea 1939–1945*, p. 36 and Jordan, *The World's Merchant Fleets 1939, The Particulars and Wartime Fates of 6,000 Ships*, pp. 18, 449.

15 This includes vessels seized during Operation *Catapult*. See Jordan, *The World's Merchant Fleets 1939, The Particulars and Wartime Fates of 6,000 Ships*, pp. 456–464 and Rohwer and Hummelchen, *Chronology of the War at Sea 1939–1945*, pp. 47, 95.

16 This does not include Italian submarine successes in the Mediterranean. See Rohwer, *Axis Submarine Successes 1939–1945*, pp. 25–44.

17 David Brown, *Warships in Profile No. 11: HMS Illustrious, Aircraft Carrier, 1939–1956, Operational History* (London: Profile Publications Ltd., 1971), p. 264.

18 ADM 234/327, Battle Summaries, Nos. 2, 8, 9 & 10: Selected Operations in the Mediterranean, 1940, Appendix H.

19 Ibid., p. 45.

20 Playfair, *The Mediterranean and Middle East, Volume I*, pp. 245–246.

21 Peter C. Smith and Edwin Walker, *The Battles of the Malta Striking Forces* (Annapolis: Naval Institute Press, 1974), p. 13.

22   Churchill subsequently criticized Somerville's decision to break off the pursuit of the Italian fleet, and a Board of Inquiry was sent to Gibraltar to review the Force H commander's conduct during the engagement. This proved to be an unpopular move within the navy as a large number of officers, including Admiral Cunningham, came to Somerville's defence. In the end, the board cleared Somerville of any wrongdoing.

23   Playfair, *The Mediterranean and Middle East, Volume I*, p. 311.

24   Rohwer, *Allied Submarine Attacks of World War Two, European Theatre of Operations 1939–1945*, pp. 127–129.

25   AIR 41/79, RAF in the Maritime War, Volume VIII: Statistics.

26   Sadkovich, *The Italian Navy in World War II*, p. 103.

27   Sadkovich, *The Italian Navy in World War II*, p. 102 and Roskill, *The War at Sea 1939–1945, Volume I*, p. 537.

28   Sadkovich, *The Italian Navy in World War II*, p. 343.

29   7th Armoured was a British division. Unless stated otherwise, all unspecified Allied divisions listed in the remainder of the text can be assumed as British. 4th Indian Division, like all Indian divisions, was a combined British/Indian formation. In a typical Indian division, most of the officers, one-third of the fighting soldiers and many of the support personnel were British, with the remaining staffing coming from Indian sources.

30   Playfair, *The Mediterranean and Middle East, Volume I*, p. 271.

31   Ibid., p. 273.

Chapter 3: Germany Enters the Fray

1   Playfair, *The Mediterranean and Middle East, Volume I*, p. 312.

2   Ibid., p. 319.

3   ADM 186/797, Battle Summaries, Nos. 1, 6, 7 and 19: Operations against French Fleet at Mersel-Kebir (Oran) 3–6 July 1940, the bombardments of Bardia June 1940–Jan 1941, Genoa 9 Feb 1941 and Tripoli 21 Apr 1941, p. 25.

4   Playfair, *The Mediterranean and Middle East, Volume I*, p. 287.

5   Ibid., p. 293.

6   Ibid., p. 361.

7   Ibid., p. 362.

8   Ibid.

9   John Terraine, *The Right of the Line, The Royal Air Force in the European War 1939–1945* (London: Hodder and Stoughton, Sceptre edition, 1988), pp. 317–318.

10   Bragadin, *The Italian Navy in World War II*, p. 58.

11   The Great Britain War Office, *The Abyssinia Campaigns – The Official Story of the Conquest of Italian East Africa* (London: His Majesty's Stationery Office, 1942), p. 37 and W. E. Crosskill, *The Two Thousand Mile War* (London: Robert Hale, 1980), p. 136.

12   The 1st South African was a Commonwealth division while the 11th and 12th African were imperial divisions. These latter formations were British-officered with the bulk of their fighting troops coming from the native populations of Britain's African colonies.

13   The Great Britain War Office, *The Abyssinia Campaigns – The Official Story of the Conquest of Italian East Africa*, p. 85.

14   Rohwer and Hummelchen, *Chronology of the War at Sea 1939–1945*, p. 51.

15   Playfair, *The Mediterranean and Middle East, Volume I*, p. 418.

16 ADM 186/797, Battle Summaries, Nos. 1, 6, 7 and 19: Operations against French Fleet at Mersel-Kebir (Oran) 3–6 July 1940, the bombardments of Bardia June 1940–Jan 1941, Genoa 9 Feb 1941 and Tripoli 21 Apr 1941, p. 33.

17 Rohwer and Hummelchen, *Chronology of the War at Sea 1939–1945*, p. 50.

18 Rohwer, *Allied Submarine Attacks of World War Two, European Theatre of Operations 1939–1945*, pp. 130–133 and Rohwer and Hummelchen, *Chronology of the War at Sea 1939–1945*, pp. 47–55.

19 Roskill, *The War at Sea 1939–1945, Volume I*, p. 424.

20 ADM 223/88, Admiralty Use of Special Intelligence in Naval Operations, p. 325.

21 These prisoners consisted of 55 officers and 805 enlisted rescued by the British and 110 survivors later picked up by a Greek destroyer flotilla. See Jack Greene and Alessandro Massignani, *The Naval War in the Mediterranean 1940–1943* (London: Chatham Publishing, 1998), p. 159.

22 Barton Maughan, *Australia in the War of 1939–1945, Series 1 (Army), Volume III: Tobruk and El Alamein* (Canberra: Australian War Memorial, 1966), pp. 155, 163–165, 176–178, 182–184.

23 Ibid., p. 159.

24 I. S. O. Playfair, *The Mediterranean and Middle East, Volume II: The Germans come to the Help of their Ally* (London: Her Majesty's Stationery Office, 1956), p. 157.

25 Vincent O'Hara, *Struggle for the Middle Sea, the Great Navies at War in the Mediterranean, 1940–1945* (Annapolis: Naval Institute Press, 2009), p. 112.

26 Ibid., pp. 113–114.

27 Rohwer, *Allied Submarine Attacks of World War Two, European Theatre of Operations 1939–1945*, p. 134.

28 Playfair, *The Mediterranean and Middle East, Volume II*, pp. 104–105.

29 Gavin Long, *Australia in the War of 1939–1945, Series 1(Army), Volume II: Greece, Crete and Syria* (Canberra: Australian War Memorial, 1953), p. 183.

30 Playfair, *The Mediterranean and Middle East, Volume II*, p. 104.

31 Roskill, *The War at Sea 1939–1945, Volume I*, p. 446.

32 Maughan, *Australia in the War of 1939–1945, Series 1 (Army), Volume III*, p. 235.

33 These successes might have been higher. A number of sources credit the submarine *Urge* with the destruction of the 5,165-ton Italian merchant ship *Zeffiro* on 20 May. However, other sources indicate that the merchant ship actually sank in a newly laid Italian minefield off Cape Bon. Likewise, mines laid by the British submarine *Rorqual* in the Gulf of Salonica might have claimed the 2,000-ton Italian *Genova Perossi*, but Italian records cannot confirm this loss. Therefore, due to the uncertainty regarding the demise of these vessels, neither is included in May's total. See Rohwer, *Allied Submarine Attacks of World War Two, European Theatre of Operations 1939–1945*, pp. 134–136.

34 Various sources list different casualty totals ranging from 820 to 1,568 fatalities connected with the sinking.

35 Rohwer and Hummelchen, *Chronology of the War at Sea 1939–1945*, p. 64.

36 *Widnes* was later raised and put into service as the German corvette *UJ2109*.

37 Oliver Warner, *Admiral of the Fleet Cunningham of Hyndhope, The Battle for the Mediterranean* (London: John Murray, 1967), p. 152.

38 ADM 234/320, Battle Summaries, No. 4: Naval Operations of Battle of Crete, 20 May to 1 June 1941, Appendix F.

39 Playfair, *The Mediterranean and Middle East, Volume II*, p. 147.

40 ADM 234/320, Battle Summaries, No. 4: Naval Operations of Battle of Crete, 20 May to 1 June 1941, Appendix E.

41 Playfair, *The Mediterranean and Middle East, Volume II*, p. 147.

42 AIR 41/79, RAF in the Maritime War, Volume VIII: Statistics.

43 Playfair, *The Mediterranean and Middle East, Volume I*, p. 439.
44 These figures include European casualties only. There are no records for casualties sustained by Italian colonial troops at Keren. See A. J. Barker, *Eritrea 1941* (London: Faber and Faber LTD, 1966), pp. 172, 174.
45 Rohwer and Hummelchen, *Chronology of the War at Sea 1939–1945*, p. 57.
46 The Great Britain War Office, *The Abyssinia Campaigns – The Official Story of the Conquest of Italian East Africa*, p. 51.
47 This included the 40,000 prisoners taken in Eritrea, 50,000 prisoners taken during the conquest of Italian Somaliland and advance to Addis Ababa and 15,600 prisoners taken by an irregular formation known as Gideon Force in western Abyssinia.

Chapter 4: Stabilising the Middle East

1 Playfair, *The Mediterranean and Middle East, Volume II*, p. 171.
2 Ibid., pp. 157–158.
3 Christopher Shores, *Dust Clouds in the Middle East, The Air War for East Africa, Iraq, Syria, Iran and Madagascar, 1940–42* (London: Grub Street, 1996), p. 177.
4 Christopher Buckley, *Five Ventures: Iraq–Syria–Persia–Madagascar–Dodecanese* (London: Her Majesty's Stationery Office, 1954), p. 36 and Playfair, *The Mediterranean and Middle East, Volume II*, p. 193.
5 Buckley, *Five Ventures: Iraq–Syria–Persia–Madagascar–Dodecanese*, pp. 36–37.
6 Playfair, *The Mediterranean and Middle East, Volume II*, p. 196.
7 Buckley, *Five Ventures: Iraq–Syria–Persia–Madagascar–Dodecanese*, p. 21.
8 Playfair, *The Mediterranean and Middle East, Volume II*, p. 222.
9 Long, *Australia in the War of 1939–1945, Series 1(Army), Volume II*, p. 526.
10 Shores, *Dust Clouds in the Middle East, The Air War for East Africa, Iraq, Syria, Iran and Madagascar, 1940–42*, p. 269.
11 Rohwer and Hummelchen, *Chronology of the War at Sea 1939–1945*, p. 81.
12 Dispatch on Operations in Iraq, East Syria and Iran from 10th April, 1941 to 12 January, 1942 by General Sir Archibald P. Wavell, Commander-in-Chief, India, as reported in the London Gazette on 14 August 1946, p. 4100.
13 Paul Kemp, *Convoy, Drama in Arctic Waters* (London: Brockhampton Press, 1999), p. 235.
14 ADM 199/2519, World War II Mediterranean Statistics.
15 These casualty figures come from the Italian Ministry of Defence. See Angelo Del Boca, *The Ethiopian War 1935–1941* (Chicago: University of Chicago Press, 1969), p. 261.
16 Based upon equipment totals present at the beginning of the campaign as well as additional aircraft flown in as the campaign progressed. See Michael Glover, *An Improvised War, the Ethiopian Campaign 1940–1941* (London: Leo Cooper, 1987), p. 21.
17 Culmination of multiple inputs from Rohwer and Hummelchen, *Chronology of the War at Sea 1939–1945*.
18 Both the Italian prisoner and British casualty figures represent estimates based upon the culmination of multiple events throughout the campaign as documented by multiple sources.
19 Rohwer and Hummelchen, *Chronology of the War at Sea 1939–1945*, pp. 66, 73, 75.
20 Clay Blair, *Hitler's U-boat War, the Hunters, 1939–1942* (New York: Random House, 1996), p. 739.
21 This influx of manpower from January through July 1941 consisted of 144,000 troops from Britain, 60,000 from Australia and New Zealand, 23,000 from India and 12,000 from South Africa. It

did not include movements from other parts of the command. See Playfair, *The Mediterranean and Middle East, Volume II*, p. 223.

22 Sadkovich, *The Italian Navy in World War II*, p. 344.

23 ADM 234/334, Battle Summaries, No. 52: Tobruk Run June 1940–Jan. 1943, p. 14.

24 Roskill, *The War at Sea 1939–1945, Volume I*, p. 519.

25 Compiled from the results of Operations *Splice, Rocket, Tracer* and *Railway*. See Rohwer and Hummelchen, *Chronology of the War at Sea 1939–1945*, pp. 64, 66, 67, 71.

26 Playfair, *The Mediterranean and Middle East, Volume II*, p. 280.

27 Ibid., p. 269.

28 In fact, one of the motor torpedo boats, *MAS452*, was only damaged and was subsequently recovered by the British.

29 I. S. O. Playfair, *The Mediterranean and Middle East, Volume III: British Fortunes Reach their Lowest Ebb* (London: Her Majesty's Stationery Office, 1960), p. 324.

30 ADM 223/88, Admiralty Use of Special Intelligence in Naval Operations, pp. 331–332.

31 Of the minor vessels sunk during this period, 20 were of known tonnage totalling 4,804 tons. The remaining 12 vessels were small caiques and schooners of unknown and presumably limited tonnage. See Rohwer, *Allied Submarine Attacks of World War Two, European Theatre of Operations 1939–1945*, pp. 136–146.

32 The British sank *Albatros, Salpa* and *Jantina* in conventional submarine attacks while mines laid by the British submarine *Rorqual* claimed *Altair* and *Alderbaran*.

33 Playfair, *The Mediterranean and Middle East, Volume II*, p. 280.

34 Terraine, *The Right of the Line, The Royal Air Force in the European War 1939–1945*, p. 354.

35 AIR 41/79, RAF in the Maritime War, Volume VIII: Statistics. This does not include the 5,996-ton Italian merchant ship *Marigola*, which the British originally attributed as destroyed by shared means in September. Although British aircraft did damage and drive *Marigola* ashore in September, its final demise occurred in November as the result of gunfire from the British submarine *Utmost*. As such, I opted to include *Marigola*'s loss in November's tally for British submarine successes. Added in is the 5,219-ton Italian merchant ship *Zena*, which was initially attributed to a submarine loss, but was in fact sunk by Swordfish aircraft in October.

36 Ibid.

37 Sadkovich, *The Italian Navy in World War II*, p. 189.

38 Ibid., p. 344.

39 This includes one minor vessel of unknown but presumably limited tonnage. See Rohwer, *Allied Submarine Attacks of World War Two, European Theatre of Operations 1939–1945*, pp. 146–148.

40 AIR 41/79, RAF in the Maritime War, Volume VIII: Statistics and Rohwer and Hummelchen, *Chronology of the War at Sea 1939–1945*, pp. 99, 101.

41 Sadkovich, *The Italian Navy in World War II*, p. 344.

42 Bragadin, *The Italian Navy in World War II*, p. 141.

43 *Gnat* was towed back to Alexandria and beached to become a static anti-aircraft platform. For the merchant losses see ADM 234/579, Naval Staff History, Defeat of Enemy Attack on Shipping, 1939–1945: A Study of Policy and Operations, Volume IB (Plans and Tables), Table 21.

44 The major units available to the British included the 7th Armoured Division, 1st South African Division, 4th Indian Division, 2nd New Zealand Division, 2nd South African Division (held in army reserve), 22nd Guards Brigade, 1st Army Tank Brigade and 29th Indian Infantry Brigade Group.

45 The destruction of this vessel is already included in November's loss total.

46 Rohwer, *Allied Submarine Attacks of World War Two, European Theatre of Operations 1939–1945*, pp. 148–150. This includes a minor tonnage difference taken from other sources.

47 AIR 41/79, RAF in the Maritime War, Volume VIII: Statistics and Rohwer, *Allied Submarine Attacks of World War Two, European Theatre of Operations 1939–1945*, p. 150.

48 ADM 234/579, Naval Staff History, Defeat of Enemy Attack on Shipping, 1939–1945: A Study of Policy and Operations, Volume IB (Plans and Tables), Table 21.

49 Vincent O'Hara, *Six Victories, North Africa, Malta and the Mediterranean Convoy War, November 1941–March 1942* (Annapolis: Naval Institute Press, 2019), p. 267.

50 Sadkovich, *The Italian Navy in World War II*, p. 344.

51 ADM 234/334, Battle Summaries, No. 52: Tobruk Run June 1940–Jan. 1943, p. 16.

52 Rohwer and Hummelchen, *Chronology of the War at Sea 1939–1945*, p. 105.

53 ADM 234/334, Battle Summaries, No. 52: Tobruk Run June 1940–Jan. 1943, p. 24.

54 These figures have been rounded off and cover the period of serious fighting from November 1941 through the first half of January 1942. See Playfair, *The Mediterranean and Middle East, Volume III*, p. 97.

55 Estimate for Axis tank and gun losses comes from (1706 Susan 24/1) C.S. 652 24 January, Personal correspondence from the Commander-in-Chief of British Forces in the Middle East to the Prime Minister dated 24 January 1942. See Great Britain Cabinet Office, Cabinet History Series, *Principal War Telegrams and Memoranda, 1940–1943, Middle East III* (Nendeln: KTO Press, 1976). Estimate of Axis aircraft losses comes from Terraine, *The Right of the Line, The Royal Air Force in the European War 1939–1945*, p. 362.

56 Robert S. Ehlers, Jr., *The Mediterranean Air War, Airpower and the Allied Victory in World War II* (Lawrence: University Press of Kansas, 2015), p. 168.

57 Playfair, *The Mediterranean and Middle East, Volume III*, p. 97.

Chapter 5: Malta under Siege

1 (1700 Susan, 17/1) Personal and Most Secret for Prime Minister from General Auchinleck. See Great Britain Cabinet Office, Cabinet History Series, *Principal War Telegrams and Memoranda, 1940–1943, Middle East III*.

2 Roskill, *The War at Sea 1939–1945, Volume I*, p. 537.

3 O'Hara, *Six Victories, North Africa, Malta and the Mediterranean Convoy War, November 1941–March 1942*, p. 134.

4 Ibid., p. 36.

5 Sadkovich, *The Italian Navy in World War II*, pp. 228, 237, 344.

6 S. W. Roskill, *The War at Sea 1939–1945, Volume II: The Period of Balance* (London: Her Majesty's Stationery Office, 1956), p. 76.

7 Of the 1,455 passengers and crew aboard *Victoria* at the time of its demise, 409 were lost. See Christopher Shores and Brian Cull with Nicola Malizia, Malta: *The Hurricane Years, 1940–41* (London: Grub Street, 1987), p. 228.

8 Playfair, *The Mediterranean and Middle East, Volume III*, pp. 152–153.

9 This was the second British destroyer named *Gurkha* to be sunk during the war. Luftwaffe aircraft sank the first *Gurkha* off Norway on 9 April 1940.

10 ADM 223/548, Convoy MG 1 to Malta: Italian Fleet at Sea, p. 22.

11 Andrew Cunningham, *A Sailor's Odyssey, The Autobiography of Admiral of the Fleet, Viscount Cunningham of Hyndhope* (London: Hutchinson & Co Ltd., 1951), p. 454.

12 ADM 116/4559, Operation MG 1: Enemy Air Attacks on Ships in Grand Harbour, Malta, and Subsequent Recommendations for Awards, p. 38.

13 Various sources convey minor discrepancies regarding the number of Axis sorties flown per month against Malta. However, all sources agree upon a general trend of increased activity during this

period as spelled out in the text. Sortie data used in this book comes from Sadkovich, *The Italian Navy in World War II*, p. 223.

14   Denis Richards and Hilary St. George Saunders, *Royal Air Force 1939–1945, Volume II: The Fight Avails* (London: Her Majesty's Stationery Office, 1954), p. 194.

15   Ibid.

16   Roskill, *The War at Sea 1939–1945, Volume II*, p. 57.

17   AIR 22/165, A.M.W.R. Weekly Statistical Analysis: Mediterranean Area Nos. 1–63, "Summary 15.3.42 to 22.3.42".

18   For all Spitfire deliveries to Malta from March through June 1942, see Rohwer and Hummelchen, *Chronology of the War at Sea 1939–1945*, pp. 128, 130, 135, 138, 140, 143, 144.

19   Sadkovich, *The Italian Navy in World War II*, p. 224.

20   Ibid., p. 223.

21   Playfair, *The Mediterranean and Middle East, Volume III*, p. 155.

22   S. Woodburn Kirby, *The War against Japan, Volume V: The Surrender of Japan* (London: Her Majesty's Stationery Office, 1969), p. 542.

23   In Indochina, Vichy authorities succumbed to Japanese pressure and granted them basing rights that effectively put the colonies under Japanese control in 1940 and 1941. When Japan later attacked British interests in Southeast Asia, much of their effort was staged out of this strategically important area.

24   ADM 234/331, Battle Summaries, No. 16: Naval Operations at the Capture of Diego Suarez (Operation *Ironclad*), May 1942, Appendix A.

25   Ibid., Appendix F.

26   Ibid., Appendix G.

27   Evan Mawdsley, *The War for the Seas, A Maritime History of World War II* (New Haven: Yale University Press, 2019), pp. 289–290.

28   For personnel losses see Warren Tute, *The Reluctant Enemies, The Story of the last War between Britain and France 1940–1942* (London: Collins, 1990), p. 206. For naval losses see Rohwer and Hummelchen, *Chronology of the War at Sea 1939–1945*, p. 136.

29   ADM 199/1277, Madagascar and Jordan, *The World's Merchant Fleets 1939, The particulars and Wartime Fates of 6,000 Ships*, pp. 480, 526, 532.

30   Sadkovich, *The Italian Navy in World War II*, p. 344.

31   Ibid., pp. 237, 251.

32   Bragadin, *The Italian Navy in World War II*, p. 356.

33   Sadkovich, *The Italian Navy in World War II*, p. 256.

34   All submarine successes during this period are taken from Rohwer, *Allied Submarine Attacks of World War Two, European Theatre of Operations 1939–1945*, pp. 151–157. However, there are a few minor tonnage differences taken from other sources.

35   Ibid.

36   AIR 41/79, RAF in the Maritime War, Volume VIII: Statistics.

37   Tonnage of the three vessels destroyed during the Palermo raid is taken from AIR 41/79, RAF in the Maritime War, Volume VIII: Statistics. The number and tonnage of vessels damaged during this raid is from Christopher Shores, Brian Cull and Nicola Malizia, *Malta: The Spitfire Year 1942* (London: Grub Street, 1991), p. 679.

38   AIR 41/79, RAF in the Maritime War, Volume VIII: Statistics and Roskill, *The War at Sea 1939–1945, Volume II*, p. 76.

39   The loss of *Upholder* came as a particularly hard blow to the British. Under the leadership of Lieutenant-Commander M. D. Wanklyn, *Upholder* was Britain's highest scoring submarine during

the war with the destruction of one Italian destroyer, two Italian submarines and nearly 90,000 tons of Axis shipping to its credit.

40 A breakdown of the major formations of the competing armies is as follows:
Panzerarmee Afrika:
Deutsches Afrika Korps (15th Panzer Division, 21st Panzer Division, 90th Light Division and Reconnaissance Units 3, 33 and 580), XX Italian Corps (Ariete Armoured and Trieste Motorized Divisions), X Italian Corps (Pavia and Brescia Divisions), XXI Italian Corps (Trento and Sabratha Divisions) and the headquarters of the XV German Lorried Infantry Brigade plus two light infantry regiments.
British Eighth Army:
XIII Corps (50th Division, 1st and 2nd South African Divisions, 1st and 32nd Army Tank Brigades), XXX Corps (1st Armoured Division and 7th Armoured Division) and army reserve (5th Indian Division).

41 The Axis and British troop and equipment totals listed in the text only include forces and equipment immediately assigned to or in direct support of the competing armies. They do not include units and resources held in reserve or positioned in other parts of the theatre. See Hart, *World War II, An Illustrated History*, p. 935 and Playfair, *The Mediterranean and Middle East, Volume III*, p. 220.

42 Playfair, *The Mediterranean and Middle East, Volume III*, p. 274.

43 Winston S. Churchill, *The Second World War, Volume 4: The Hinge of Fate* (Boston: Houghton Mifflin Company, 1950), p. 383.

44 Sadkovich, *The Italian Navy in World War II*, p. 265.

Chapter 6: Turning Point

1 Playfair, *The Mediterranean and Middle East, Volume III*, p. 315.
2 Ibid., p. 343.
3 Terraine, *The Right of the Line, The Royal Air Force in the European War 1939–1945*, p. 376.
4 Maughan, *Australia in the War of 1939–1945, Series I (Army), Volume III*, pp. 568, 571, 574.
5 Sadkovich, *The Italian Navy in World War II*, pp. 275, 278.
6 (CS/1405 20/7) Personal and Most Secret for CIGS from General Corbett. See Great Britain, Cabinet Office, *Cabinet History Series, Principal War Telegrams and Memoranda, 1940–1943, Middle East III*.
7 (CST118 30/7) Personal and Most Secret for CGS and CIGS from General Auchinleck, Advanced Headquarters, 8th Army, 0430 GMT, 30 Jul 42. See WO 201/630, 8th Army Situation Reports.
8 Ibid. (CST121 31/7).
9 Sadkovich, *The Italian Navy in World War II*, p. 223.
10 Playfair, *The Mediterranean and Middle East, Volume III*, p. 327.
11 Ibid.
12 Rohwer, *Allied Submarine Attacks of World War Two, European Theatre of Operations 1939–1945*, pp. 157–161.
13 Sadkovich, *The Italian Navy in World War II*, p. 344.
14 Playfair, *The Mediterranean and Middle East, Volume III*, p. 327.
15 Ibid., pp. 371–372.
16 Ibid., pp. 458–459.
17 ADM 234/579, Naval Staff History, Defeat of Enemy Attack on Shipping, 1939–1945: A Study of Policy and Operations, Volume IB (Plans and Tables), Table 21.
18 Rohwer and Hummelchen, *Chronology of the War at Sea 1939–1945*, p. 151.

19 Greene and Massignani, *The Naval War in the Mediterranean 1940–1943*, p. 261.
20 Sadkovich, *The Italian Navy in World War II*, p. 283.
21 Ibid., p. 275.
22 Niall Barr, *Pendulum of War, The Three Battles of El Alamein* (New York: The Overlook Press, 2004), p. 222.
23 F. H. Hinsley, *British Intelligence in the Second World War, Abridged Version* (New York: Cambridge University Press, 1993), p. 236.
24 Playfair, *The Mediterranean and Middle East, Volume III*, p. 382.
25 Hinsley, *British Intelligence in the Second World War, Abridged Version*, p. 236.
26 For Axis fuel losses associated with the destruction of *Picci Fassio*, *Davide Bianchi* and *Padenna* see Sadkovich, *The Italian Navy in World War II*, p. 303.
27 Playfair, *The Mediterranean and Middle East, Volume III*, p. 391 and Bryn Evans, *The Decisive Campaigns of the Desert Air Force, 1942–1945* (Yorkshire: Pen & Sword Aviation, 2020), p. 35.
28 Playfair, *The Mediterranean and Middle East, Volume III*, p. 391.
29 Rohwer and Hummelchen, *Chronology of the War at Sea 1939–1945*, p. 164.
30 Sadkovich, *The Italian Navy in World War II*, p. 307.
31 Axis shipping losses during this period are compiled from a number of sources including Rohwer, *Allied Submarine Attacks of World War Two, European Theatre of Operations 1939–1945*, pp. 162–166; Sadkovich, *The Italian Navy in World War II*; AIR 41/79, RAF in the Maritime War, Volume VIII: Statistics and Playfair, *The Mediterranean and Middle East, Volumes III* and *IV*.
32 Hinsley, *British Intelligence in the Second World War, Abridged Version*, p. 237.
33 All data regarding opposing strengths, sorties and losses relating to the October mini-blitz comes from I. S. O. Playfair, *The Mediterranean and Middle East, Volume IV: The Destruction of Axis Forces in Africa* (London: Her Majesty's Stationery Office, 1966), p. 195.
34 Bernard Ireland, *The War in the Mediterranean 1940–1943* (South Yorkshire: Leo Cooper, 2004), p. 181.
35 Sadkovich, *The Italian Navy in World War II*, p. 78.
36 The Axis and British troop and equipment totals listed in the text only include forces and equipment immediately assigned to or in direct support of the competing armies. They do not include units and resources held in reserve or positioned in other parts of the theatre. For comparative strength figures on the eve of the battle see Barr, *Pendulum of War, The Three Battles of El Alamein*, p. 276.
37 The breakdown of corps and divisions for the competing armies on the eve of the battle is as follows:
    British Eighth Army:
    X Corps (1st, 8th and 10th Armoured Divisions), XIII Corps (7th Armoured Division, 44th and 50th Divisions), XXX Corps (51st Division, 2nd New Zealand Division, 9th Australian Division, 1st South African Division and 4th Indian Division).
    Panzerarmee Afrika:
    Deutsches Afrika Korps (15th Panzer Division, 21st Panzer Division, 90th Light Division, 164th Light Division), X Italian Corps (Pavia Division, Brescia Division and Folgore Parachute Division), XX Italian Corps (Ariete Armoured Division, Littorio Armoured Division and Trieste Motorized Division), XXI Italian Corps (Bologna Division and Trento Motorized Division).
38 When Rommel arrived back in Africa on the evening of the 25th, he found General Wilhelm Ritter von Thoma, the commander of the Deutsches Afrika Korps, in temporary command of the Panzerarmee since General Stumme had died from a heart attack on the previous day.
39 Playfair, *The Mediterranean and Middle East, Volume IV*, p. 79.
40 The first comes from British estimates based upon communication intercepts. The latter comes from estimates put out by General Alexander's staff. See Barr, *Pendulum of War, The Three Battles*

of El Alamein, p. 404 and Nigel Hamilton, *Master of the Battlefield, Monty's War Years, 1942–1945* (New York: McGraw-Hill Book Company, 1983), p. 39.

41 It's interesting to note how accurate Montgomery's predictions were regarding the duration and cost of the battle. It took precisely 12 days for the Eighth Army to achieve its breakthrough (23 October–4 November), and the army's casualty figure was only slightly higher than the 13,000 predicted by the British general. For these casualty figures see Playfair, *The Mediterranean and Middle East, Volume IV*, p. 78.

Chapter 7: Masters of the North African Shores

1 Although designated a British formation, the First Army was actually an Allied configuration that would ultimately contain British, American and French units. Of these, the British generally made up the largest contingent.

2 Samuel Eliot Morison, *History of United States Naval Operations in World War II, Volume II: Operations in North African Waters, October 1942–June 1943* (Boston: Little, Brown and Company, 1947), pp. 36–40.

3 ADM 234/359, Battle Summaries, No. 38: Invasion of North Africa (Operation *Torch*), Nov. 1942–Feb. 1943, pp. 14–16. During the course of operations, *Rodney*, *Furious* and the cruiser *Bermuda* were temporarily transferred from Force H to the Central and Eastern Task Forces, which explains why they are double listed in the order of battle of the Admiralty battle summary. This double listing is corrected in the strength totals presented here.

4 David Brown, *Carrier Operations in World War II, Volume One: The Royal Navy* (Annapolis: Naval Institute Press, 1968), pp. 80–81. This included some aircraft that were subsequently disembarked at Gibraltar upon the carriers' arrival in the Mediterranean.

5 ADM 234/359, Battle Summaries, No. 38: Invasion of North Africa (Operation *Torch*), Nov. 1942–Feb. 1943, p. 12.

6 Ibid.

7 Alan J. Levine, *The War Against Rommel's Supply Lines, 1942–1943* (Westport: Praeger Publishers, 1999), p. 58.

8 Roskill, *The War at Sea 1939–1945, Volume II*, p. 316.

9 Vichy naval losses at Casablanca included the destroyers *Fougueux*, *Boulonnais*, *Brestois* and *Frondeur* and the submarines *Amphitrite*, *La Sibylle*, *Méduse*, *Oréade*, *La Psyché*, *Sidi Ferruch*, *Le Conquérant* and *Le Tonnant* sunk and the destroyers *Milan* and *Albatros* damaged and beached.

10 George F. Howe, *United States Army in World War II, The Mediterranean Theater of Operations, Northwest Africa: Seizing the Initiative in the West* (Washington, D.C.: Office of the Chief of Military History, Department of the Army, 1957), p. 204.

11 Allied casualties during the first six days of Operation *Torch* (8–13 November 1942) consisted of 540 killed, 178 wounded and 33 missing for the British and 543 killed, 890 wounded and 41 missing for the United States. Additionally, 98 Dutch naval personnel were killed and 19 wounded when the Dutch destroyer *Isaac Sweers* was sunk on the 13th. See Playfair, *The Mediterranean and Middle East, Volume IV*, p. 155.

12 Jack Coggins, *The Campaign for North Africa* (Garden City: Doubleday & Company, Inc., 1980), p. 97.

13 Levine, *The War Against Rommel's Supply Lines, 1942–1943*, p. 60.

14 ADM 234/359, Battle Summaries, No. 38: Invasion of North Africa (Operation *Torch*), Nov. 1942–Feb. 1943, Appendix H1.

15 Of these losses, Axis submarines accounted for 12 merchant ships and eight warships while aircraft sank four merchant ships and three warships. Finally, the last warship, the corvette *Gardenia*, was lost to an accidental collision.

16 ADM 234/359, Battle Summaries, No. 38: Invasion of North Africa (Operation *Torch*), Nov. 1942–Feb. 1943, Appendix D.

17 Roskill, *The War at Sea 1939–1945, Volume II*, p. 340.

18 Levine, *The War Against Rommel's Supply Lines, 1942–1943*, p. 89 and O'Hara, *Struggle for the Middle Sea, the Great Navies at War in the Mediterranean, 1940–1945*, p. 199.

19 AIR 41/79, RAF in the Maritime War, Volume VIII: Statistics.

20 Playfair, *The Mediterranean and Middle East, Volume IV*, pp. 203, 208.

21 Rohwer, *Allied Submarine Attacks of World War Two, European Theatre of Operations 1939–1945*, pp. 167–172 and Playfair, *The Mediterranean and Middle East, Volume IV*, p. 210.

22 AIR 41/79, RAF in the Maritime War, Volume VIII: Statistics.

23 Ibid.

24 Sadkovich, *The Italian Navy in World War II*, p. 344.

25 Playfair, *The Mediterranean and Middle East, Volume IV*, p. 210.

26 Levine, *The War Against Rommel's Supply Lines, 1942–1943*, p. 84 and Playfair, *The Mediterranean and Middle East, Volume IV*, p. 210.

27 Playfair, *The Mediterranean and Middle East, Volume IV*, p. 226.

28 (CS/1786/2) Personal and Most Secret for the Chief of the Imperial General Staff from the Commander-in-Chief, 2 January 1943. See Great Britain Cabinet Office, Cabinet History Series, *Principal War Telegrams and Memoranda, 1940–1943, Middle East III*.

29 Playfair, *The Mediterranean and Middle East, Volume IV*, p. 222.

30 Roskill, *The War at Sea 1939–1945, Volume II*, p. 436.

31 Rohwer, *Allied Submarine Attacks of World War Two, European Theatre of Operations 1939–1945*, pp. 173–176 and Jordan, *The World's Merchant Fleets 1939, The Particulars and Wartime Fates of 6,000 Ships*, pp. 55, 470.

32 Rohwer and Hummelchen, *Chronology of the War at Sea 1939–1945*, pp. 187–188.

33 Playfair, *The Mediterranean and Middle East, Volume IV*, p. 238.

34 Rohwer and Hummelchen, *Chronology of the War at Sea 1939–1945*, p. 189.

35 Roskill, *The War at Sea 1939–1945, Volume II*, p. 486.

36 ADM 234/579, Naval Staff History, Defeat of Enemy Attack on Shipping, 1939–1945: A Study of Policy and Operations, Volume IB (Plans and Tables), Table 21.

37 Sadkovich, *The Italian Navy in World War II*, p. 103.

38 Playfair, *The Mediterranean and Middle East, Volume IV*, pp. 251, 417 and AIR 41/79, RAF in the Maritime War, Volume VIII: Statistics. The British total includes one vessel of unknown, but presumably limited tonnage.

39 AIR 41/79, RAF in the Maritime War, Volume VIII: Statistics.

40 Rohwer, *Allied Submarine Attacks of World War Two, European Theatre of Operations 1939–1945*, pp. 173–182. There are a few minor tonnage differences taken from other sources.

41 Rohwer and Hummelchen, *Chronology of the War at Sea 1939–1945*, pp. 188, 193.

42 AIR 41/79, RAF in the Maritime War, Volume VIII: Statistics.

43 Playfair, *The Mediterranean and Middle East, Volume IV*, pp. 240, 246, 250, 416, 417 and Coggins, *The Campaign for North Africa*, p. 192.

44 Ibid.

45 Playfair, *The Mediterranean and Middle East, Volume IV*, pp. 250, 417.

46 Gregory Blaxland, *The Plain Cook and the Great Showman – The First and Eighth Armies in North Africa* (London: William Kimber, 1977), p. 154.

47 Rick Atkinson, *An Army at Dawn, the War in North Africa, 1942–1943* (New York: Henry Holt and Company, 2002), p. 389.

48 David Rolf, *The Bloody Road to Tunis, Destruction of the Axis Forces in North Africa: November 1942–May 1943* (London: Greenhill Books, 2001), p. 158.

49 Despatch on Operations in North West Africa from 8th November 1942 to 13th May 1943 by Lieutenant-General K. A. N. Anderson, General Officer, Commander-in-Chief, First Army as reported in the London Gazette on 6 November 1946, p. 5458.

50 Rolf, *The Bloody Road to Tunis, Destruction of the Axis Forces in North Africa: November 1942–May 1943*, p. 162.

51 Letter from Lieutenant-General Bernard Montgomery to General Sir Harold Alexander dated 10 April 1943. See WO 214/18, North African Campaign.

52 Atkinson, *An Army at Dawn, the War in North Africa, 1942–1943*, p. 464.

53 Howe, *The US Army in World War II: Mediterranean Theater of Operations, Northwest Africa: Seizing the Initiative in the West*, p. 591.

54 Despatch on Operations in North West Africa from 8th November 1942 to 13th May 1943 by Lieutenant-General K. A. N. Anderson, General Officer, Commander-in-Chief, First Army as reported in the London Gazette on 6 November 1946, pp. 5458–5459.

55 The Allied divisions in Tunisia consisted of the British 1st Armoured, British 6th Armoured, British 7th Armoured, British 1st Infantry, British 4th Infantry, British 46th Infantry, British 50th Infantry, British 51st Infantry, British 56th Infantry, British 78th Infantry, 2nd New Zealand, 4th Indian, US 1st Armoured, US 1st Infantry, US 9th Infantry, US 34th Infantry, French d' Alger, French du Maroc and French d' Oran. German divisions in Tunisia consisted of the 10th Panzer, 15th Panzer, 21st Panzer, 90th Light, 164th Light, 999th Light, 334th Infantry, Hermann Göring Division and von Manteuffel Division. Italian divisions in Tunisia consisted of the 1st Superga, 16th Pistoia Motorized, 80th La Spezia Airborne, 101st Trieste Motorized and 136th Giovani Fascisti (Young Fascists). In addition, both sides possessed various independent brigades and battalions, and the Italians also possessed remnants of divisions destroyed in Egypt and Libya.

56 Playfair, *The Mediterranean and Middle East, Volume IV*, p. 417 and AIR 41/79, RAF in the Maritime War, Volume VIII: Statistics.

57 AIR 41/79, RAF in the Maritime War, Volume VIII: Statistics.

58 Levine, *The War Against Rommel's Supply Lines, 1942–1943*, p. 166.

59 Rohwer, *Allied Submarine Attacks of World War Two, European Theatre of Operations 1939–1945*, pp. 182–186. There is a minor tonnage difference taken from another source.

60 Playfair, *The Mediterranean and Middle East, Volume IV*, pp. 414–415 and AIR 41/79, RAF in the Maritime War, Volume VIII: Statistics.

61 AIR 41/79, RAF in the Maritime War, Volume VIII: Statistics.

62 Playfair, *The Mediterranean and Middle East, Volume IV*, p. 417 and Coggins, *The Campaign for North Africa*, p. 192.

63 Levine, *The War Against Rommel's Supply Lines, 1942–1943*, p. 177.

64 WO 201/822, Operations: First Army and Second United States Corps in Tunisia, p. 5.

65 Rohwer and Hummelchen, *Chronology of the War at Sea 1939–1945*, p. 209.

66 The British 4th Division took some 51,000 prisoners during its five weeks of combat operations in Tunisia, of which the vast majority were taken in the last few days of the campaign. See Hugh Williamson, *The Fourth Division 1939 to 1945* (London: Newman Neame, 1951), p. 93.

67 Howe, *United States Army in World War II, The Mediterranean Theater of Operations, Northwest Africa: Seizing the Initiative in the West*, p. 662.

68 Adrian Stewart, *Eighth Army's Greatest Victories, Alam Halfa to Tunis 1942–1943* (West Yorkshire: Leo Cooper, 1999), p. 201.

69 Winston S. Churchill, *The Second World War, Volume 4: The Hinge of Fate* (London: Cassell & Co. Ltd., 1951), p. 696.

70 Cunningham, *A Sailor's Odyssey, The Autobiography of Admiral of the Fleet, Viscount Cunningham of Hyndhope*, p. 529.

71 Playfair, *The Mediterranean and Middle East, Volume IV*, p. 460.

72 Message from General Sir Harold Alexander to Prime Minister Winston Churchill dated 13 May 1943. See WO 214/18, North African Campaign.

73 Thomas Parrish (ed.), *The Simon and Schuster Encyclopedia of World War II* (New York: Simon and Schuster, 1978), p. 446.

74 Paul Carell, *The Foxes of the Desert* (New York: E. P. Dutton & Company, Inc., 1961), p. 363 and Del Boca, *The Ethiopian War 1935–1941*, p. 261.

75 Italian naval fatalities through 8 September 1943 numbered 24,660 men. Meanwhile, the Italian merchant marine suffered 3,520 fatalities presumably during the same period. See Bragadin, *The Italian Navy in World War II*, p. 367 and Sadkovich, *The Italian Navy in World War II*, p. 329.

76 Coggins, *The Campaign for North Africa*, p. 167.

77 Ibid., p. 194.

Chapter 8: Italy Subdued

1 An estimated breakdown of Italian forces at this time included 200,000 men in southern France and Corsica, 579,000 in the Balkans, 217,000 in the Soviet Union and 800,000 at home. See W. G. F. Jackson, *The Battle for Italy* (New York: Harper & Row, 1967), p. 25.

2 Lt-Col. G. W. L Nicholson, *Official History of the Canadian Army in the Second World War, Volume II: The Canadians in Italy 1943–1944* (Ottawa: Roger Duhamel, F.R.S.C., 1966), p. 7 and Douglas Porch, *The Path to Victory, The Mediterranean Theater in World War II* (New York: Farrar, Straus and Giroux, 2004), p. 417.

3 ADM 234/356, Battle Summaries, No. 35: Invasion of Sicily (Operation *Husky*), p. 13 and S. W. Roskill, *The War at Sea 1939–1945, Volume III, Part I: The Offensive, 1st June 1943–31st May 1944* (London: Her Majesty's Stationery Office, 1960), p. 116.

4 ADM 234/356, Battle Summaries, No. 35: Invasion of Sicily (Operation *Husky*), pp. 12, 14.

5 Terraine, *The Right of the Line, The Royal Air Force in the European War 1939–1945*, p. 567.

6 Morison, *History of United States Naval Operations in World War II, Volume II*, p. 279.

7 Hinsley, *British Intelligence in the Second World War, Abridged Version*, p. 342.

8 Ehlers, *The Mediterranean Air War, Airpower and the Allied Victory in World War II*, p. 299.

9 AIR 41/79, RAF in the Maritime War, Volume VIII: Statistics. This total includes two vessels of unknown but presumably minimal tonnage.

10 Ibid.

11 Air 41/54, The RAF in Maritime War, Vol VII, Part I: Mediterranean Reconquest and the Submarine War, May 1943–May 1944, p. 78.

12 The British typically listed surface warship and submarine losses in separate categories. As such, the submarines *Mocenigo*, *U755* and *U97* are not included in the 56 military vessels sunk in May and June. Unless otherwise stated, similar tallies will only include losses of surface vessels, and any discussed submarine losses are in addition to these casualty figures.

13 This includes four vessels of unknown but presumably minimal tonnage. See Rohwer, *Allied Submarine Attacks of World War Two, European Theatre of Operations 1939–1945*, pp. 186–191 and Jordan, *The World's Merchant Fleets 1939, The Particulars and Wartime Fates of 6,000 Ships*, p. 458.

14 Roskill, *The War at Sea 1939–1945, Volume III, Part I*, p. 137.

15 WO 204/10505, 15th Army Group Administration: Report on Sicilian Campaign July–Aug. 1943.

16 Roskill, *The War at Sea 1939–1945, Volume III, Part I*, p. 138.

17 Ibid., p. 139.

18 Ehlers, *The Mediterranean Air War, Airpower and the Allied Victory in World War II*, pp. 299, 301.

19 Roskill, *The War at Sea 1939–1945, Volume III, Part I*, pp. 138–139.

20 This total includes two vessels of unknown but presumably minimal tonnage. See AIR 41/79, RAF in the Maritime War, Volume VIII: Statistics.

21 Ibid.

22 This includes several vessels of unknown but presumably minimal tonnage. See Rohwer, *Allied Submarine Attacks of World War Two, European Theatre of Operations 1939–1945*, pp. 191–197.

23 Ehlers, *The Mediterranean Air War, Airpower and the Allied Victory in World War II*, p. 304.

24 Roskill, *The War at Sea 1939–1945, Volume III, Part I*, p. 150.

25 Ibid.

26 Carlo D' Este, *Bitter Victory – The Battle for Sicily, 1943* (New York: E. P. Dutten, 1988), p. 552.

27 Nicholson, *Official History of the Canadian Army in the Second World War, Volume II*, p. 174.

28 WO 204/10505, 15th Army Group Administration: Report on Sicilian Campaign July–Aug. 1943.

29 Nicholson, *Official History of the Canadian Army in the Second World War, Volume II*, pp. 119, 174.

30 Barbara Brooks Tomblin, *With Utmost Spirit: Allied Naval Operations in the Mediterranean, 1942–1945* (Lexington: The University Press of Kentucky, 2004), p. 230.

31 Although designated an American army, Fifth Army contained British/Commonwealth formations throughout most of its combat history in Italy. At times this British presence was substantial, as was the case during Operation *Avalanche*.

32 ADM 234/358, Battle Summaries, No. 37: Invasion of Italy: Landing at Salerno (Operation *Avalanche*) 9 Sept. 1943, Appendix A. This listing does not include an unknown number of motor torpedo boats and motor gun boats that carried out diversionary activities during the invasion.

33 *Unicorn* was actually an aircraft maintenance carrier, but the British opted to give it a combatant role during Operation *Avalanche*. When used in this manner, *Unicorn* had a proscribed capacity of 35 aircraft thus making it a viable light carrier.

34 David Brown, *The Seafire, The Spitfire that went to Sea* (Annapolis: Naval Institute Press, 1989), p. 47.

35 Nicholson, *Official History of the Canadian Army in the Second World War, Volume II*, p. 206.

36 Roskill, *The War at Sea 1939–1945, Volume III, Part I*, p. 378.

37 AIR 41/79, RAF in the Maritime War, Volume VIII: Statistics.

38 Cunningham, *A Sailor's Odyssey, The Autobiography of Admiral of the Fleet, Viscount Cunningham of Hyndhope*, p. 565.

39 C. J. C. Molony, *The Mediterranean and Middle East, Volume V: The Campaign in Sicily 1943 and the Campaign in Italy 3rd September 1943 to 31st March 1944* (London: Her Majesty's Stationery Office, 1973), p. 318.

40 Brown, *The Seafire, The Spitfire that went to Sea*, p. 52.

41 ADM 234/358, Battle Summaries, No. 37: Invasion of Italy: Landing at Salerno (Operation *Avalanche*) 9 Sept. 1943, Appendix G.

42 Molony, *The Mediterranean and Middle East, Volume V*, p. 325.

43 Roskill, *The War at Sea 1939–1945, Volume III, Part I*, p. 182.

44 Ehlers, *The Mediterranean Air War, Airpower and the Allied Victory in World War II*, p. 323.

45 These figures only include Italian warships seized in the Mediterranean. They do not include French or Yugoslav warships that were under Italian control at the time of Italy's capitulation. See Rohwer and Hummelchen, *Chronology of the War at Sea 1939–1945*, pp. 231–232 and David Brown, *Warship Losses of World War Two* (London: Arms and Armour Press, 1990), pp. 94–97.

46 Rohwer and Hummelchen, *Chronology of the War at Sea 1939–1945*, p. 237.

47 *UJ2109* was the former British minesweeper *Widnes*, which had been sunk by German aircraft at Suda Bay on 20 May 1941. Raised and re-commissioned as a corvette, *UJ2109* was a rare example of a former British warship serving in the Kriegsmarine. It displaced 710 tons and possessed three 3.5-inch guns.

48 Rohwer and Hummelchen, *Chronology of the War at Sea 1939–1945*, p. 245.

49 Roskill, *The War at Sea 1939–1945, Volume III, Part I*, p. 203.

50 Molony, *The Mediterranean and Middle East, Volume V*, p. 557.

51 Ibid., pp. 381–382.

52 ADM 199/2519, World War II Mediterranean Statistics.

53 Roskill, *The War at Sea 1939–1945, Volume III, Part I*, p. 106.

54 Ibid., p. 210.

55 AIR 41/79, RAF in the Maritime War, Volume VIII: Statistics.

56 Roskill, *The War at Sea 1939–1945, Volume III, Part I*, p. 186.

57 AIR 41/79, RAF in the Maritime War, Volume VIII: Statistics.

58 Ibid.

59 The American total is taken from Blair, *Hitler's U-boat War, the Hunted, 1942–1945* (New York: Random House, 1998), p. 708 and the British total is taken from The Central Statistical Office, *Statistical Digest of the War*, p. 135.

60 AIR 41/79, RAF in the Maritime War, Volume VIII: Statistics.

Chapter 9: Supporting the Southern Flank

1 The divisions involved in this transfer were the 50th, 51st and 7th Armoured for the British and the 1st, 9th, 2nd Armoured and 82nd Airborne for the United States.

2 Molony, *The Mediterranean and Middle East, Volume V*, p. 509.

3 WO 204/7846, Weekly Cumulative Return of Prisoners of War Captured.

4 Roskill, *The War at Sea 1939–1945, Volume III, Part I*, p. 304.

5 Ibid.

6 Molony, *The Mediterranean and Middle East, Volume V*, p. 653.

7 Ibid., p. 620.

8 Roskill, *The War at Sea 1939–1945, Volume III, Part I*, p. 305.

9 Ibid., p. 307.

10 Martin Blumenson, *United States Army in World War II, Mediterranean Theater of Operations, Salerno to Cassino* (Washington, D.C.: United States Army Center of Military History, 1993), p. 391.

11 Porch, *The Path to Victory, The Mediterranean Theater in World War II*, p. 541 and Molony, *The Mediterranean and Middle East, Volume V*, p. 722.

12 This included some losses sustained in fighting not directly related to Cassino. See Molony, *The Mediterranean and Middle East, Volume V*, p. 722.

13 Ibid., pp. 749, 756.

14 Tomblin, *With Utmost Spirit, Allied Naval Operations in the Mediterranean, 1942–1945*, p. 352 and Molony, *The Mediterranean and Middle East, Volume V*, p. 757.

15 Molony, *The Mediterranean and Middle East, Volume V*, p. 759.

16 Roskill, *The War at Sea 1939–1945, Volume III, Part I*, p. 319.

17 Dominick Graham, *Cassino* (New York: Ballantine Books Inc., 1970), p. 138.

18 Roskill, *The War at Sea 1939–1945, Volume III, Part I*, pp. 320–321.

19 C. J. C. Molony, *The Mediterranean and Middle East, Volume VI: Victory in the Mediterranean, Part I, 1st April to 4th June 1944* (London: Her Majesty's Stationery Office, 1984), p. 359.

20 MAD stood for Magnetic Anomaly Detection, which used a magnetometer to detect anomalies in the earth's magnetic field caused by a U-boat's ferrous hull. This recently acquired device gave Allied aircraft a ground-breaking ability to detect submerged submarines, although this was limited to a range of only 400 to 600 feet. Given this range limitation, MAD was best suited for operations in confined areas such as the Strait of Gibraltar.

21 For merchant losses see Roskill, *The War at Sea 1939–1945, Volume III, Part I*, p. 327.

22 Ibid.

23 Ibid., p. 389.

24 All tallies include a number of vessels of unknown but presumably minimal tonnage. See AIR 41/79, RAF in the Maritime War, Volume VIII: Statistics.

25 Molony, *The Mediterranean and Middle East, Volume V*, p. 829 and *The Mediterranean and Middle East, Volume VI, Part I*, p. 388.

26 All tallies include a number of vessels of unknown but presumably minimal tonnage. See AIR 41/79, RAF in the Maritime War, Volume VIII: Statistics.

27 Particulars on the cited warships: *SG20* (ex-*Generale Achille Papa*, 635 tons, 3 × 4-inch guns), *TA15* (ex-*Francesco Crispi*, 970 tons, 4 × 4.7-inch guns), *UJ201* (ex-*Egeria*, 670 tons, 1 × 3.9-inch gun), *TA36* (ex-*Stella Polare*, 745 tons, 2 × 3.9-inch guns) and *TA23* (ex-*Impavido*, 1,204 tons, 3 × 3.9-inch guns).

28 Molony, *The Mediterranean and Middle East, Volume VI, Part I*, p. 373.

29 Hinsley, *British Intelligence in the Second World War, Abridged Version*, p. 337.

30 The breakdown of the competing division-sized forces on the eve of Operation *Diadem*:
British Eighth Army (excluding forces holding the Adriatic sector):
British 4th Division, British 6th Armoured Division, 8th Indian Division, British 78th Division, 1st Canadian Division, 5th Canadian Armoured Division, 3rd Polish Division, 5th Polish Division, 2nd New Zealand Division, 6th South African Armoured Division (Army Reserve).
American Fifth Army:
American 85th Division, American 88th Division, 1st (French) Motorized Division, 2nd (French) Moroccan Division, 3rd (French) Algerian Division, 4th (French) Moroccan Mountain Division.
VI Corps:
American 3rd Division, American 45th Division, American 1st Armoured Division, American 34th Division, American 36th Division, British 1st Division, British 5th Division.
German Tenth Army (holding Gustav Line excluding Adriatic sector):
15th Panzer Grenadier Division, 71st Division, 94th Division, 44th Division, 1st Parachute Division, 114th Jäger Division, 5th Mountain Division.
German Fourteenth Army (holding Anzio Perimeter):
4th Parachute Division, 65th Division, 3rd Panzer Grenadier Division, 362nd Division, 715th Division.
German Army Group C Reserves:
92nd Division, Hermann Göring Panzer Division, 29th Panzer Grenadier Division, 26th Panzer Division, 90th Panzer Grenadier Division.

31 Roskill, *The War at Sea 1939–1945, Volume III, Part I*, p. 322.

32 Molony, *The Mediterranean and Middle East, Volume VI, Part I*, p. 284.

33 Roskill, *The War at Sea 1939–1945, Volume III, Part I*, p. 323.

34 *TA34* was the ex-Yugoslav *T7*. It displaced 266 tons and was armed with two 66-millimetre guns and four 17.7-inch torpedo tubes. As such, it was not in the same category as most German torpedo boats, but was more akin to a large motor torpedo boat.

35 All tallies include a number of vessels of unknown but presumably minimal tonnage. See AIR 41/79, RAF in the Maritime War, Volume VIII: Statistics.

36 S. W. Roskill, *The War at Sea 1939–1945, Volume III, Part II: The Offensive, 1st June 1944–14th August 1945* (London: Her Majesty's Stationery Office, 1961), p. 109 and Jordan, *The World's Merchant Fleets 1939, The Particulars and Wartime Fates of 6,000 Ships*, pp. 45, 456.

37 Includes a number of vessels of unknown but presumably minimal tonnage. See AIR 41/79, RAF in the Maritime War, Volume VIII: Statistics.

38 Roskill, *The War at Sea 1939–1945, Volume III, Part II*, p. 478.

39 T. Dodson Stamps and Vincent J. Esposito, *A Military History of World War II, Volume II: Operations in the Mediterranean and Pacific Theaters* (West Point: USMA AG Printing Office, 1956), p. 167.

40 WO 204/7846, Weekly Cumulative Return of Prisoners of War Captured.

41 This casualty figure is an estimate based upon inputs from multiple sources. In particular, see Molony, *The Mediterranean and Middle East, Volume VI, Part I*, p. 284, William Jackson and T. P. Gleave, *The Mediterranean and Middle East, Volume VI: Victory in the Mediterranean, Part III, November 1944 to May 1945* (London: Her Majesty's Stationery Office, 1988), p. 400 and Stamps and Esposito, *A Military History of World War II, Volume II*, p. 167.

42 WO 204/7846, Weekly Cumulative Return of Prisoners of War Captured.

43 Ibid.

44 Of this total, 25 German divisions were located in Italy, 17 in the Balkans and 11 in southern France. See Nicholson, *Official History of the Canadian Army in the Second World War, Volume II*, pp. 678–679.

Chapter 10: Victory on the Peripheries

1   Roskill, *The War at Sea 1939–1945, Volume III, Part II*, p. 108.

2   ADM 186/796, Battle Summaries, No. 43: Invasion of the South of France, Operation *Dragoon*, 15 August 1944, pp. 7–8.

3   Ibid., Appendix A.

4   Brown, *The Seafire, The Spitfire that went to Sea*, p. 78.

5   William Jackson and T. P. Gleave, *The Mediterranean and Middle East, Volume VI: Victory in the Mediterranean, Part II, June to October 1944* (London: Her Majesty's Stationery Office, 1987), p. 221 and Jeffrey J. Clark and Robert Ross Smith, *The US Army in World War II: European Theater of Operations, Riviera to the Rhine* (Washington, D.C.: Office of the Chief of Military History, Department of the Army, 1993), p. 213.

6   This breaks down to roughly 1,700 aircraft from the Mediterranean Allied Tactical Air Force, 1,800 aircraft from the Mediterranean Allied Strategic Air Force, 300 aircraft from the Mediterranean Allied Coastal Air Force and 220 aircraft from Task Force 88. See ADM 186/796, Battle Summaries, No. 43: Invasion of the South of France, Operation *Dragoon*, 15 August 1944, pp. 10–11.

7   Ibid., p. 11.

8   Ibid.

9   Hinsley, *British Intelligence in the Second World War, Abridged Version*, p. 509.

10 Clark and Smith, *The US Army in World War II: European Theater of Operations, Riviera to the Rhine*, p. 122.

11 Rohwer and Hummelchen, *Chronology of the War at Sea 1939–1945*, p. 298.

12 Hinsley, *British Intelligence in the Second World War, Abridged Version*, p. 509.

13 Clark and Smith, *The US Army in World War II: European Theater of Operations, Riviera to the Rhine*, pp. 140, 142.

14 ADM 186/796, Battle Summaries, No. 43: Invasion of the South of France, Operation *Dragoon*, 15 August 1944, pp. 51–52.

15 Ibid., p. 42.

16 Roskill, *The War at Sea 1939–1945, Volume III, Part II*, p. 104.

17 Brown, *The Seafire, The Spitfire that went to Sea*, p. 83.

18 This is an estimate (conservative) based upon daily claims taken primarily from Brown, *The Seafire, The Spitfire that went to Sea*, pp. 80–83 and Kenneth Poolman, *Allied Escort Carriers of World War Two in Action* (Annapolis: Naval Institute Press, 1988), pp. 131–136.

19 Roskill, *The War at Sea 1939–1945, Volume III, Part II*, p. 99.

20 This monthly average is for the period of November 1944 through April 1945. See Clark and Smith, *The US Army in World War II: European Theater of Operations, Riviera to the Rhine*, p. 576.

21 These garrisons consisted of 24,700 men at Lorient, 29,900 men at St. Nazaire, 11,483 men at La Rochelle and 8,628 men on the Gironde estuary. See Lars Hellwinkell, *Hitler's Gateway to the Atlantic, German Naval Bases in France, 1940–1945* (Annapolis: Naval Institute Press, 2014), p. 167.

22 ADM 199/2447, German Ships: Losses and Damages in North West European Waters and Roskill, *The War at Sea 1939–1945, Volume III, Part II*, pp. 464–465.

23 Jackson and Gleave, *The Mediterranean and Middle East, Volume VI, Part II*, p. 199.

24 The first six vessels were the captured French warships *Bombarde*, *La Bayonnaise*, *Amiral Sénès*, *Enseigne Ballande*, *Ampère*, *La Curieuse* and the last two the converted French merchant ships *Djebel Dira* and *Cyrnos*. Most of these were in a non-operational or incomplete state at the time of their demise.

25 This total includes 20 vessels of unknown but presumably minimal tonnage. See AIR 41/79, RAF in the Maritime War, Volume VIII: Statistics.

26 For the ground losses see Jackson and Gleave, *The Mediterranean and Middle East, Volume VI, Part II*, p. 199.

27 ADM 186/796, Battle Summaries, No. 43: Invasion of the South of France, Operation *Dragoon*, 15 August 1944, pp. 56–57.

28 L. F. Ellis, *Victory in the West, Volume I. The Battle of Normandy* (London. Her Majesty's Stationery Office, 1962), p. 493 and AIR 41/74, The RAF in the Maritime War, Volume V: Atlantic and Home Waters; The Victory Phase, June 1944–May 1945, p. 52.

29 These nations were all minor powers, but still provided some assistance in combating the Soviets and garrisoning portions of Germany's European empire.

30 Brown, *The Seafire, The Spitfire that went to Sea*, p. 86.

31 Rohwer and Hummelchen, *Chronology of the War at Sea 1939–1945*, p. 305.

32 British aircraft had sunk or severely damaged both torpedo boats during earlier air raids. In the case of the former, British Beaufighters had sunk *TA15* at Crete on 8 March 1944. Raised and under repairs, *TA15* was hit again during the Piraeus raid and rendered a total loss. For its part, *TA17* had suffered severe damage on 18 September 1944 and was scuttled following further damage sustained during the follow-up raid on 12 October.

33 This prisoner count is an estimate compiled from a number of sources including J. Lee Ready, *Forgotten Allies, the Military Contribution of the Colonies, Exiled Governments and Lesser Powers to the Allied Victory in World War II, Volume I: The European Theatre* (Jefferson: McFarland & Company, 1985), pp. 380–381; John Lodwick, *Raiders from the Sea, the Story of the Special Boat Service in World War II* (Annapolis, Naval Institute Press, 1990), pp. 181–183, 194 and Jackson and Gleave, *The Mediterranean and Middle East, Volume VI, Part II*, p. 338.

34 Jackson and Gleave, *The Mediterranean and Middle East, Volume VI, Part II*, p. 440.

35 Air 41/76, RAF in the Maritime War, Volume VII, Part II: Mediterranean; Naval Cooperation, the End of the Submarine War and Operations in the Adriatic, Greece and the Aegean, 1944–45, p. 127 and Rohwer and Hummelchen, *Chronology of the War at Sea 1939–1945*, p. 305.

36 Air 41/76, RAF in the Maritime War, Volume VII, Part II: Mediterranean; Naval Cooperation, the End of the Submarine War and Operations in the Adriatic, Greece and the Aegean, 1944–45, p. 143.

37 Jackson and Gleave, *The Mediterranean and Middle East, Volume VI, Part II*, pp. 321–322.

Chapter 11: Britannia's Sea, Victory in the Mediterranean

1 Japanese casualties at Ngakyedauk Pass numbered 5,335 men including 3,106 fatalities compared to 3,506 casualties for the British. At Imphal and Kohima the Japanese suffered 53,505 casualties (including 30,502 killed or missing) out of 84,280 men committed. British losses numbered 16,667 casualties in return. See Dear and Foot, *The Oxford Companion to World War II*, p. 4 and S. Woodburn Kirby, *The War against Japan, Volume III: The Decisive Battles* (London: Her Majesty's Stationery Office, 1961), pp. 372, 526–527.

2 Dear and Foot, *The Oxford Companion to World War II*, p. 874.

3 Nicholson, *Official History of the Canadian Army in the Second World War, Volume II*, p. 497.

4 The breakdown of corps and divisions for the competing armies on the eve of Operation *Olive* is as follows:
British Eighth Army:
II Polish Corps (3rd Carpathian and 5th Kresowa Divisions), I Canadian Corps (1st and 5th [Armoured] Canadian Divisions), V British Corps (1st [Armoured], 4th, 46th and 56th British and 4th Indian Divisions), X British Corps (10th Indian Division) and 2nd New Zealand Division in army reserve.
Anglo-American Fifth Army:
II US Corps (34th, 85th, 88th and 91st US Divisions), XIII British Corps (1st and 6th [Armoured] British and 8th Indian Divisions), IV US Corps (1st US [Armoured] and 6th South African [Armoured] Divisions) and the Brazilian Expeditionary Force in army reserve.
German Tenth Army:
LXXVI Panzer Corps (1st Parachute, 71st, 5th Mountain, 162nd and 278th Divisions), LI Mountain Corps (114th Jäger, 44th, 305th, 334th and 715th Divisions) and 98th Division in army reserve.
German Fourteenth Army:
I Parachute Corps (356th, 4th Parachute and 362nd Divisions), XIV Panzer Corps (26th Panzer, 65th and 16th SS Panzer Grenadier Divisions) and 29th Panzer Grenadier and 20th Luftwaffe Field Divisions in army reserve.
Axis Forces in northern Italy:
Monte Rosa Mountain (Italian), San Marco (Italian), 42nd Jäger, 34th, 148th, 90th Panzer Grenadier, 157th Mountain, 94th and 188th Reserve Mountain Divisions.

5 Jackson and Gleave, *The Mediterranean and Middle East, Volume VI, Part II*, pp. 276, 302, 304.

6 Ibid., p. 303.

7 Ernest F. Fisher, Jr., *The US Army in World War II: Mediterranean Theater of Operations, Cassino to the Alps* (Washington, D.C.: Center of Military History, Department of the Army, 1989), p. 389 and Dominick Graham and Shelford Bidwell, *Tug of War – The Battle for Italy, 1943–1945* (New York: St. Martin's Press, 1986), p. 379.

8 WO 204/7846, Weekly Cumulative Return of Prisoners of War Captured.

9 Ibid.

10 Jackson and Gleave, *The Mediterranean and Middle East, Volume VI, Part III*, p. 138.

11 Hilary St. George Saunders, *Royal Air Force 1939–1945, Volume III: The Fight is Won* (London: Her Majesty's Stationery Office, 1954), pp. 227–228.

12 Hinsley, *British Intelligence in the Second World War, Abridged Version*, p. 578.

13 Ehlers, *The Mediterranean Air War, Airpower and the Allied Victory in World War II*, p. 361.

14 Ibid., pp. 370, 372.

15 Ibid., p. 362.

16 These totals include several vessels of unknown but presumably minimal tonnage. See AIR 41/79, RAF in the Maritime War, Volume VIII: Statistics.

17 Ibid.

18 Roskill, *The War at Sea 1939–1945, Volume III, Part II*, pp. 442, 478.

19 ADM 234/579, Naval Staff History, Defeat of Enemy Attack on Shipping, 1939–1945: A Study of Policy and Operations, Volume IB (Plans and Tables), Table 21; Roskill, *The War at Sea 1939–1945, Volume III, Part II*, pp. 439–447 and Brown, *Warship Losses of World War Two*, pp. 93, 97, 108.

20 All of the captured Italian 'UIT' boats were sunk in port due to Allied bombing or scuttling. None ever sailed operationally. Some of these losses occurred after the suspension of German U-boat activity in the Mediterranean.

21 Roskill, *The War at Sea 1939–1945, Volume III, Part II*, pp. 106–107.

22 Jackson and Gleave, *The Mediterranean and Middle East, Volume VI, Part III*, p. 310.

23 These totals include several vessels of unknown but presumably minimal tonnage. See AIR 41/79, RAF in the Maritime War, Volume VIII: Statistics.

24 Like *TA34* listed in Chapter 9, *TA48* was an ex-Yugoslav vessel of relatively small tonnage and was thus more analogous to a motor torpedo boat than a legitimate destroyer-type torpedo boat.

25 This includes three vessels of unknown but presumably minimal tonnage. See AIR 41/79, RAF in the Maritime War, Volume VIII: Statistics.

26 The units in question were the 1st and 5th (Armoured) Canadian and 5th British Divisions sent to northwest Europe and the 4th and 46th British and 4th Indian Divisions sent to Greece.

27 The breakdown of corps and divisions for the competing armies on the eve of the final offensive is as follows:
British Eighth Army:
V British Corps (56th and 78th British, 2nd New Zealand, 8th Indian Divisions), II Polish Corps (3rd Carpathian and 5th Kresowa Divisions), XIII British Corps (10th Indian Division) and 6th British Armoured Division in army reserve.
American Fifth Army:
II US Corps (34th, 88th and 91st US and 6th South African [Armoured] Divisions), IV US Corps (1st [Armoured] and 10th US and 1st Brazilian Divisions) and 85th and 92nd US Divisions in army reserve.
German Tenth Army (facing the British):
LXXVI Panzer Corps (42nd Jäger, 98th, 162nd and 362nd Divisions), I Parachute Corps (1st Parachute, 4th Parachute, 26th Panzer, 278th and 305th Divisions) and 29th Panzer Grenadier and 155th Divisions in army reserve.
German Fourteenth Army (facing the Americans):
XIV Panzer Corps (8th Mountain, 65th and 94th Divisions), LI Mountain Corps (114th Jäger, 148th, 232nd, 334th and Italia [Italian] Divisions) and 90th Panzer Grenadier Division in army reserve.

Axis Forces in northern Italy including Major Security Formations:
Littorio (Italian), Monte Rosa Mountain (Italian), San Marco (Italian), 5th Mountain and 34th
Divisions.

28 Jackson and Gleave, *The Mediterranean and Middle East, Volume VI, Part III*, p. 295 and
Headquarters 15th Army Group, *Finito – The Po Valley Campaign 1945* (Milano Rizzola, 1945),
p. 51.

29 Jackson and Gleave, *The Mediterranean and Middle East, Volume VI, Part III*, p. 295.

30 Eric Linklater, *The Campaign in Italy* (London: Her Majesty's Stationery Office, 1951), p. 465.

31 Fisher, *The US Army in World War II: Mediterranean Theater of Operations, Cassino to the Alps*, p.
494.

32 While Germans made up the vast majority of these prisoners, large numbers of Fascist Italians
and pro-German Yugoslav irregulars also surrendered to the Allies.

33 Robin Kay, *Official History of New Zealand in the Second World War 1939–45, Italy, Volume II:
From Cassino to Trieste* (Wellington: Historical Publications Branch Department of Internal Affairs,
1967), pp. 548–549.

34 This is an estimate (probably conservative) based upon various prisoner counts taken from Allied
Forces, Mediterranean Theatre, *Operations of British, Indian and Dominion Forces in Italy, 3
September 1943 to 2 May 1945, Part IV: The Campaign in Lombardy, 1 April to 2 May 1945,
Section D: 13 Corps Operations* (London: British Historical Section Central Mediterranean,
1945).

35 Richard Doherty, *A Noble Crusade, The History of Eighth Army 1941 to 1945* (Rockville Centre:
Sarpedon, 1999), pp. 312–313.

36 Fisher, *The US Army in World War II: Mediterranean Theater of Operations, Cassino to the Alps*, p.
512.

37 Officially the Germans reported their strength at the conclusion of hostilities as 207,425 men, but
this was certainly too low since some of their staffing data was missing. In particular, I Parachute
Corps, which had 66,438 divisional troops at the beginning of the spring offensive, was no longer
accounted for in their order of battle. Given the number of German soldiers assigned to Army
Group C at the beginning of the spring offensive (439,334) and the estimated casualties suffered
by the Germans through 2 May (5,000 dead and 27,000 wounded and sick), the figure of 260,000
men remaining seems appropriate. See Allied Forces, Mediterranean Theatre, *Operations of British,
Indian and Dominion Forces in Italy, 3 September 1943 to 2 May 1945, Part IV: The Campaign in
Lombardy, 1 April to 2 May 1945, Section G: German Strategy* (London: British Historical Section
Central Mediterranean, 1945).

38 Again, this is based on Italian strength in Army Group C at the beginning of the spring offensive
(160,180). Most of these men (108,114) were police or security personnel, while only 52,066
were actually assigned to combat divisions. See Allied Forces, Mediterranean Theatre, *Operations
of British, Indian and Dominion Forces in Italy, 3 September 1943 to 2 May 1945, Part IV: The
Campaign in Lombardy, 1 April to 2 May 1945, Section G: German Strategy*, Table 5.

39 Ibid.

40 The German Army in Italy suffered 295,650 casualties from 9 September 1943 to 31 March 1945.
Thereafter, Army Group C, which contained 439,334 German soldiers, was entirely destroyed in
the final Allied offensive and subsequent capitulation. See Jackson and Gleave, *The Mediterranean
and Middle East, Volume VI, Part III*, pp. 399–400 and Allied Forces, Mediterranean Theatre,
*Operations of British, Indian and Dominion Forces in Italy, 3 September 1943 to 2 May 1945, Part
IV: The Campaign in Lombardy, 1 April to 2 May 1945, Section G: German Strategy*.

41 WO 204/7846, Weekly Cumulative Return of Prisoners of War Captured.

42 Jackson and Gleave, *The Mediterranean and Middle East, Volume VI, Part III*, pp. 334–335.

43　These war-long Axis casualty figures represent estimates based upon the culmination of multiple events throughout the theatre as documented by multiple sources.

44　Field Marshal Alexander to SHAEF Fwd dated 9 June 1945 REF No. 383.7/4. NARS, Washington and In-Log, 8 May and 17 May, 1945.

45　Estimate based upon the culmination of multiple events throughout the theatre as documented by multiple sources.

46　These totals include 524 vessels of unknown but presumably minimal tonnage. See AIR 41/79, RAF in the Maritime War, Volume VIII: Statistics.

47　Culmination of multiple inputs from Rohwer and Hummelchen, *Chronology of the War at Sea 1939–1945* and David Brown, *Warship Losses of World War Two*.

48　These tallies of principal warship and submarine losses are based upon inputs from multiple sources.

49　Allied merchant ship losses taken from Jackson and Gleave, *The Mediterranean and Middle East, Volume VI, Part III*, p. 314. The tallies of principal warship and submarine losses are based upon inputs from multiple sources. They do not include vessels sunk by Vichy French forces, but do include certain vessels sunk in the Atlantic while supporting the Allied invasion of French North Africa.

Chapter 12: The Triumph of British Maritime Power

1　Author's calculation based upon inputs from a variety of sources. Warship losses are calculated through to 13 May 1943 while the tonnage losses are calculated through to the end of that same month.

2　Ibid. This includes 100 percent of surrendered Italian warships and 64.8 percent of Allied-inflicted Axis warship losses from 14 May 1943 to 2 May 1945. It does not include Italian warships sunk by the Germans in September 1943.

3　This includes 13 vessels of unknown but presumably limited tonnage. See AIR 41/79, RAF in the Maritime War, Volume VIII: Statistics.

4　ADM 199/2519, World War II Mediterranean Statistics.

5　Roskill, *The War at Sea 1939–1945, Volume I*, p. 239.

6　Friedrich Ruge, *Der Seekrieg, The German Navy's Story, 1939–1945* (Annapolis, Naval Institute Press, 1957), p. 43 and C. B. A. Behrens, *Merchant Shipping and the Demands of War* (London: Her Majesty's Stationery Office and Longmans, Green and Co., 1955), p. 363.

7　ADM 234/579, Naval Staff History: Defeat of the Enemy Attack on Shipping, 1939–1945: A Study of Policy and Operations, Volume IB (Plans and Tables), Tables 12(ii) and 12(iii).

8　ADM 234/369, Battle Summaries, No. 22: Arctic Convoys 1941–1945, Appendix A, Sections I, II and III.

9　Kemp, *Convoy, Drama in Arctic Waters*, p. 235.

10　ADM 234/369, Battle Summaries, No. 22: Arctic Convoys 1941–1945, Appendix A, Sections V and VII.

11　Ibid., p. 129.

12　For a general listing of the British and Allied ships assigned to Operation *Neptune* see ADM 234/367, Battle Summaries, No. 39, Volume II: Landings in Normandy (Operation *Neptune*) June 1944: Appendices, Appendixes A(1), A(2), B(2) and C.

13　L. F. Ellis, *Victory in the West, Volume I*, p. 478.

14　ADM 234/363, Battle Summaries, No. 49: Campaign in North-West Europe June 1944–May 1945, p. 12.

15　Roskill, *The War at Sea 1939–1945, Volume III, Part II*, p. 135.

16 This proved to be *Warspite*'s final operation in an illustrious career that had begun 28 years earlier at the Battle of Jutland and earned the great warship more battle honours than any other ship in Royal Navy history.

17 L. F. Ellis, *Victory in the West, Volume II: The Defeat of Germany* (London: Her Majesty's Stationery Office, 1968), p. 406.

18 Ibid., p. 408.

19 Brian E. Walter, *The Longest Campaign, Britain's Maritime Struggle in the Atlantic and Northwest Europe, 1939–1945* (Oxford: Casemate, 2020), p. 269. These percentages consist of vessels lost solely or partially as a result of British means. Warship losses are from all theatres while merchant/commercial losses are solely from European waters (excluding the Mediterranean and Black Sea).

20 Ibid., pp. 274, 279, 280. In breaking down the Italian numbers, 45.8 percent were lost during the period of Italy's Axis partnership (10 June 1940 to 8 September 1943), while 25.2 percent surrendered to the Allies and 29 percent were sunk or seized by the Germans following Italy's capitulation. Of this latter category, all of the seized vessels were subsequently sunk or scuttled while operating under German service. As such, these losses are counted twice being first tallied against the Italians and then later against the Germans.

Index of Warships

Abdiel British minelayer, 15, 65, 154, 182

Abercrombie British monitor, 177

Abingdon British minesweeper, 99

Acciaio Italian submarine, 174

Achates British destroyer, 143

Actéon French submarine, 143

Admiral Hipper German heavy cruiser, 27

Admiral Scheer German pocket battleship, 27

Adrias Greek escort destroyer, 186

Adua Italian submarine, 7, 10, 81

Airedale British escort destroyer, 111

Airone Italian torpedo boat, 39

Ajax British light cruiser, 39, 41, 54, 55, 62, 63, 73

Ajax French submarine, 37

Alabastro Italian submarine, 130

Alagi Italian submarine, 121

Albatros French destroyer, 295

Albatros Italian corvette, 83, 290

Alberico da Barbiano Italian light cruiser, 87

Alberto di Giussano Italian light cruiser, 87

Alcione Italian torpedo boat, 87

Aldebaran Italian torpedo boat, 83

Aldenham British escort destroyer, 238

Alessandro Malaspina Italian submarine, 78

Algerine British minesweeper, 146

Alpino Italian destroyer, 158

Altair Italian torpedo boat, 83, 290

Alvise da Mosto Italian destroyer, 86

Ambra Italian submarine, 57

Ammiraglio Millo Italian submarine, 105

Ammiraglio St. Bon Italian submarine, 95

Amphitrite French submarine, 295

Andrea Doria Italian battleship, 5, 6, 178, 179

Andromeda Italian torpedo boat, 53

Anfitrite Italian submarine, 53

Angelo Bassini Italian torpedo boat, 171

Antares Italian torpedo boat, 171

Anthony British destroyer, 103

Antonio da Noli Italian destroyer, 178

Antonio Sciesa Italian submarine, 146

Antoniotto Usodimare Italian destroyer, 121

Aphis British gunboat, 218

Aquila Italian aircraft carrier, 184, 243

Aquilone Italian destroyer, 39

Arethusa British light cruiser, 80, 110, 148

Argento Italian submarine, 174

Argonaut British light cruiser, 148

Argonauta Italian submarine, 26

Argonaute French submarine, 143

Argus British aircraft carrier, 11, 35, 42, 94, 100, 101, 109, 140

Ariane French submarine, 143

Ariel Italian torpedo boat, 39

Ark Royal British aircraft carrier, 11, 27, 30, 31, 35, 36, 43, 52, 59, 77, 80–82, 85, 239, 269

Arkansas American battleship, 214

Armando Diaz Italian light cruiser, 52

Artigliere Italian destroyer, 39

Arunta Australian destroyer, 262

Ascianghi Italian submarine, 174

Ashanti British destroyer, 124

Ashigara Japanese heavy cruiser, 262

Asteria Italian submarine, 153

Attacker British escort carrier, 177, 213, 223, 224, 226

Attilo Regolo Italian light cruiser, 178

Auckland British sloop, 70

Auricula British corvette, 103, 104

Aurora British light cruiser, 84, 86, 100, 143, 148, 169, 182, 186, 223, 275

Australia Australian heavy cruiser, 36

Avenger British escort carrier, 146, 159

Aviere Italian destroyer, 85, 150

Avon Vale British escort destroyer, 238

Avorio Italian submarine, 153

Axum Italian submarine, 124, 204

Babr Iranian sloop, 75

Bagnolini Italian submarine, 23, 25

Baleno Italian destroyer, 58

Barham British battleship, 8, 36, 37, 40, 49, 54, 55, 59, 63, 85, 239, 269, 277

Bari Italian light cruiser, 171

Bartolomeo Colleoni Italian light cruiser, 34

Battler British escort carrier, 177

Béarn French aircraft carrier, 28, 31
Beatty American destroyer, 188
Bedouin British destroyer, 110
Berenice Italian corvette, 178
Berillo Italian submarine, 44
Bermuda British light cruiser, 295
Bersagliere Italian destroyer, 154
Bévéziers French submarine, 37, 103
Birmingham British light cruiser, 110
Bismarck German battleship, 77, 82, 269, 275–279
Biter British escort carrier, 143
Blean British escort destroyer, 146
Boise American light cruiser, 182
Bolzano Italian heavy cruiser, 32, 54, 125, 184, 207
Bombardiere Italian destroyer, 154
Bonaventure British light cruiser, 47,48, 57
Borea Italian destroyer, 39
Bougainville French armed merchant cruiser, 103
Bougainville French sloop, 37
Boulonnais French destroyer, 295
Brecon British destroyer, 223
Bremse German gunnery training ship, 275, 279
Brestois French destroyer, 295
Bretagne French battleship, 28, 30
Brilliant British destroyer, 143
Brin Italian submarine, 7, 10
Bristol American destroyer, 188
Broke British destroyer, 142, 143
Bronzo Italian submarine, 174
Brooklyn American light cruiser, 201, 205
Buck American destroyer, 188
Bulgaria German minelayer, 186
Cachalot British submarine, 83
Cagni Italian submarine, 7, 10
Caïman French submarine, 73
Caio Duilio Italian battleship, 41, 178
Cairo British anti-aircraft cruiser, 109, 110, 121, 124
Calcutta British anti-aircraft cruiser, 35, 62, 63, 111
Caledon British light cruiser, 52
Calipso Italian torpedo boat, 44
Calypso British light cruiser, 23, 25, 26
Calypso French submarine, 159
Canberra Australian heavy cruiser, 51
Canopo Italian torpedo boat, 61
Capetown British light cruiser, 51, 66
Carlisle British anti-aircraft cruiser, 62, 96, 97, 100, 186, 187
Carlo Mirabello Italian destroyer, 65
Cassiopea Italian torpedo boat, 158
Castore Italian torpedo boat, 171
Centauro Italian torpedo boat, 150
Ceres British light cruiser, 51
Cérès French submarine, 143

Cesare Battisti Italian destroyer, 66
Charybdis British light cruiser, 121, 124, 285
Chevalier Paul French destroyer, 73
Ciclone Italian escort destroyer, 154
Cicogna Italian corvette, 174
Cigno Italian torpedo boat, 158
Circe French submarine, 159
Circe Italian torpedo boat, 48, 150
Clacton British minesweeper, 188
Cleopatra British light cruiser, 96, 110, 148, 174
Climene Italian torpedo boat, 158
Cobalto Italian submarine, 123, 125
Cockchafer British gunboat, 74
Commandant Teste French seaplane tender, 28, 146
Conte di Cavour Italian battleship, xviii, 5, 6, 33, 40, 41
Corallo Italian submarine, 146
Corfu British armed merchant cruiser, 275
Courbet French battleship, 27, 29
Coventry British anti-aircraft cruiser, 35, 73, 110, 130
Cricket British gunboat, 70
Cromarty British minesweeper, 188
Curlew British anti-aircraft cruiser, 285
Curtatone Italian torpedo boat, 65
D'Entrecasteaux French sloop, 103
Da Recco Italian destroyer, 149
Dagabur Italian submarine, 123, 125
Dainty British destroyer, 52
Danae French destroyer, 143
Daniele Manin Italian destroyer, 66
Dasher British escort carrier, 143
Defender British destroyer, 80
Delfino Italian submarine, 153
Delhi British anti-aircraft cruiser, 240
Dessie Italian submarine, 146
Diamante Italian submarine, 26
Diamond British destroyer, 60
Diana Italian sloop, 81, 119
Diane French submarine, 143
Dido British light cruiser, 9, 62, 63, 96, 110, 148, 182, 205, 285
Dolfijn Dutch submarine, 153
Drache German minelayer, 223
Duca degli Abruzzi Italian light cruiser, 54, 85
Duke of York British battleship, 140
Dulverton British escort destroyer, 135, 187
Dunedin British light cruiser, 77
Dunkerque French battlecruiser, 28, 30, 31, 146
Durazzo Italian minelayer, 174
Durbo Italian submarine, 44
Eagle British aircraft carrier, 2, 3, 11, 24, 33–35, 40, 43, 66, 77, 100, 101, 109, 121, 123, 125, 239
Eclipse British destroyer, 185, 186

Effingham British light cruiser, 285
Elan French sloop, 73
Emanuele Pessagno Italian destroyer, 105
Emerald British light cruiser, 71
Emo Italian submarine, 146
Emperor British escort carrier, 213, 223–226
Endicott American destroyer, 218
Enrico Cosenz Italian torpedo boat, 178
Enrico Tazzoli Italian submarine, 78
Enterprise British light cruiser, 71
Epervier French destroyer, 143
Erebus British monitor, 15, 173, 177
Escort British destroyer, 35
Eso Italian minesweeper, 154
Espero Italian destroyer, 24, 278
Eugenio di Savoia Italian light cruiser, 110
Euro Italian destroyer, 24, 84, 185
Euryalus British light cruiser, 96, 110, 148, 169
Evangelista Torricelli Italian submarine, 25
Faa di Bruno Italian submarine, 38
Falmouth British sloop, 71, 74
Faulknor British destroyer, 185
Fearless British destroyer, 80
Fechteler American destroyer escort, 202
Felixstowe British minesweeper, 188
Fermoy British minesweeper, 61
Fiji British light cruiser, 61, 62
Fiume Italian heavy cruiser, 54, 55
Flores Dutch gunboat, 201
Flutto Italian submarine, 174
Foca Italian submarine, 44
Folgore Italian destroyer, 149
Foresight British destroyer, 36, 123
Formidable British aircraft carrier, 51, 54–56, 62–64, 103, 105, 140, 144, 167, 177, 230
Fortune British destroyer, 37
Fougueux French destroyer, 295
Francesco Nullo Italian destroyer, 39
Francesco Stocco Italian torpedo boat, 178
Fratelli Cairoli Italian torpedo boat, 44
Freccia Italian destroyer, 106, 174
Frondeur French destroyer, 295
Fulmine Italian destroyer, 84
Furious British aircraft carrier, 11, 80, 81, 121, 123, 132, 140, 143, 279, 295
Galatea British light cruiser, 88
Galileo Ferraris Italian submarine, 78
Galileo Galilei Italian submarine, 25
Gallant British destroyer, 48, 99
Gardenia British corvette, 146, 296
Garland Polish destroyer, 223
Gemma Italian submarine, 44
Generale Antonio Cantore Italian torpedo boat, 119

Generale Antonio Chinotto Italian torpedo boat, 52
Generale Marcello Prestinari Italian torpedo boat, 154
Geniere Italian destroyer, 154
Giacomo Medici Italian torpedo boat, 157
Giosue Carducci Italian destroyer, 55
Giovanni Acerbi Italian torpedo boat, 66
Giovanni Berta Italian gunboat, 23
Giovanni da Verazzano Italian destroyer, 130
Giovanni delle Bande Nere Italian light cruiser, 34, 99, 105
Giulio Cesare Italian battleship, 33, 43, 178
Giuseppe La Farina Italian torpedo boat, 61
Giuseppe Sirtori Italian torpedo boat, 178
GK32 German harbor patrol boat, 224
Glasgow British light cruiser, 52
Glauco Italian submarine, 77
Glavkos Greek submarine, 99
Glorious British aircraft carrier, 285
Gloucester British light cruiser, 24, 33, 47, 49, 54, 62
Gnat British gunboat, 85, 290
Gneisenau German battlecruiser, 27
Gondar Italian submarine, 35
Gorizia Italian heavy cruiser, 184, 207
Graf Spee German pocket battleship, 276
Granito Italian submarine, 146
Grecale Italian destroyer, 84
Greyhound British destroyer, 55, 62
Griffin British destroyer, 55
Grimsby British sloop, 58
Groppo Italian escort destroyer, 171
Guépard French destroyer, 73
Guglielmotti Italian submarine, 105
Guiseppe Garibaldi Italian light cruiser, 54
Gurkha British destroyer, 81, 96, 291
H8 Italian submarine, 174
Haguro Japanese heavy cruiser, 262
Hartland British sloop, 142
Hasty British destroyer, 47, 111
Havock British destroyer, 55, 100
Hawkins British light cruiser, 51
Hebe British minesweeper, 188
Hereward British destroyer, 47, 48, 63
Hermes British aircraft carrier, 11, 31, 51, 71
Hermes German destroyer (ex-*Greek Vasilevs Georgios I*), 60, 159
Hermione British light cruiser, 80, 110, 112, 277
Hero British destroyer, 47
Heythrop British escort destroyer, 96, 98
Holcombe British escort destroyer, 188
Hood British battlecruiser, 8, 9, 27, 30, 31
Howe British battleship, 167, 168, 230
Hunter British escort carrier, 177, 213, 224
Huntley British minesweeper, 52

Hursley British destroyer, 186
Hurworth British destroyer, 135, 186
Hyperion British destroyer, 34, 44
Hythe British minesweeper, 188
Ibis British sloop, 146
Ilex British destroyer, 34, 73
Illustrious British aircraft carrier, 11, 35, 39–43, 48,
    49, 53, 102–104, 177, 230, 268
Imperial British destroyer, 63
Impero Italian battleship, 184
Indomitable British aircraft carrier, 102–104,
    121–123, 125, 167, 173, 230, 279
Inglefield British destroyer, 36, 201
Intrepid British destroyer, 185
Iride Italian submarine, 35
Isaac Sweers Dutch destroyer, 87, 146, 295
Isis British destroyer, 73
Isuzu Japanese light cruiser, 262
Italia (ex-*Littorio*) Italian battleship, 178
Ithuriel British destroyer, 123, 146
Jackal British destroyer, 106
Jaguar British destroyer, 47, 106
Jamaica British light cruiser, 143
Jantina Italian submarine, 83, 290
Janus British destroyer, 58, 73, 197
Jean Bart French battleship, 28, 140, 142
Jersey British destroyer, 61
Jervis British destroyer, 56, 58, 106, 171, 186, 197
Jintsu Japanese light cruiser, 262
Juno British destroyer, 62
Kandahar British destroyer, 51, 52, 88
Kanimbla British armed merchant cruiser, 74
Kasaan Bay American escort carrier, 214
Kashmir British destroyer, 62
Katsonis Greek submarine, 189
Kelly British destroyer, 9, 62, 64
Kent British heavy cruiser, 39
Kenya British light cruiser, 121, 124
Khartoum British destroyer, 26
Khedive British escort carrier, 213, 223, 224
Kiebitz German minelayer, 235
Kilkis Greek battleship, 60
Kimberley British destroyer, 39, 226
King George V British battleship, 8, 9, 77, 110, 167,
    168, 230
Kingston British destroyer, 52, 66, 99
Kipling British destroyer, 106
Kujawiak Polish escort destroyer, 110
Kuma Japanese light cruiser, 262
L'Audacieux French destroyer, 36, 159
La Curieuse French sloop, 26, 303
La Psyché French submarine, 295
La Sibylle French submarine, 295

La Surprise French sloop, 143
Ladybird British gunboat, 58
Lafolè Italian submarine, 44
Laforey British destroyer, 9, 202
Lamerton British escort destroyer, 145
Lampo Italian destroyer, 58, 159
Lance British destroyer, 84, 99
Lanciere Italian destroyer, 99
Lansdale American destroyer, 202
Lanzerotto Malocello Italian destroyer, 154
Latona British minelayer, 80
Lawrence Indian sloop, 71
Le Conquérant French submarine, 295
Le Héros French submarine, 104
Le Tonnant French submarine, 295
Leander New Zealand light cruiser, 9, 34, 39, 51,
    71, 76
Legion British destroyer, 81, 87, 97, 98
Legnano Italian minelayer, 185
Lemnos Greek battleship, 60
Leonardo da Vinci Italian submarine, 78
Leone Italian destroyer, 66
Leone Pancaldo Italian destroyer, 33, 159, 246
Libeccio Italian destroyer, 41, 85
Liddesdale British escort destroyer, 241
Lightning British destroyer, 155
Lince Italian torpedo boat, 175
Littorio Italian battleship, 5, 6, 40, 41, 97, 111, 112,
    178
Liuzzi Italian submarine, 7, 25
Lively British destroyer, 84, 86, 106
Liverpool British light cruiser, 24, 109
Lookout British destroyer, 240, 241
Lorraine French battleship, 28, 214
Luca Tarigo Italian destroyer, 58
Luigi Galvani Italian submarine, 25
Lupo Italian torpedo boat, 62, 149
Lützow German pocket battleship, 27
M6062 German converted minelayer, 221
M6063 German converted minelayer, 221
Macalle Italian submarine, 26
Maddox American destroyer, 173
Maestrale Italian destroyer, 84
Maggiori Baracca Italian submarine, 78
Malachite Italian submarine, 153, 154
Malaya British battleship, 2, 3, 8, 33, 52, 94, 109
Malcolm British destroyer, 142
Manchester British light cruiser, 121, 124
Manxman British minelayer, 80, 101, 148, 149
Maori British destroyer, 87, 99
Marcello Italian submarine, 7, 38
Marconi Italian submarine, 7, 10
Marigold British corvette, 146

Marsouin French submarine, 73
Martin British destroyer, 146
Massachusetts American battleship, 140, 142
Matteucci Italian gunboat, 65
Mauritius British light cruiser, 199, 201
Medusa Italian submarine, 95
Méduse French submarine, 295
Meteor British destroyer, 240, 241
MGB658 British motor gunboat, 241
Miaoulis Greek destroyer, 186
Michele Bianchi Italian submarine, 78
Milan French destroyer, 295
Milford British sloop, 37
Mocenigo Italian submarine, 171, 298
Mogador French destroyer, 30
Mohawk British destroyer, 41, 58, 59
Monge French submarine, 104
Monsone Italian escort destroyer, 154
Montecuccoli Italian light cruiser, 110
MTB276 British motor torpedo boat, 190
MTB298 British motor torpedo boat, 190
MTB670 British motor torpedo boat, 241
MTB697 British motor torpedo boat, 241
Musketeer British destroyer, 241
Muzio Attendolo Italian light cruiser, 125, 150
Naiad British light cruiser, 61, 62, 106
Naiade Italian submarine, 44
Nani Italian submarine, 38
Narval French submarine, 53
Narvalo Italian submarine, 152, 153
Nautilus French submarine, 159
Nazario Sauro Italian destroyer, 66
Neghelli Italian submarine, 53
Nelson British battleship, 8, 9, 81, 121, 167, 168, 177, 230, 279
Nembo Italian destroyer, 34
Neptune British light cruiser, 24
Nereide Italian submarine, 174
Nestor Australian destroyer, 111
Nevada American battleship, 137, 214
New York American battleship, 140
Newcastle British light cruiser, 110, 111
Newfoundland British light cruiser, 169, 174
Nigeria British light cruiser, 121, 124
Niobe German old light cruiser (ex-Yugoslav *Dalmacija*), 190, 244
Nordstern German auxiliary minesweeper, 223
Nubian British destroyer, 41, 58, 63, 159, 169
O21 Dutch submarine, 88
Odin British submarine, 26
Olympus British submarine, 101
Ondina Italian submarine, 121
Onice Italian submarine, 121

Oréade French submarine, 295
Orion British light cruiser, 24, 41, 54, 55, 62, 63, 148, 169, 201, 241
Orione Italian torpedo boat, 88
Orpheus British submarine, 26
Ostia Italian minelayer, 66
Ostro Italian destroyer, 34
Oswald British submarine, 35
P32 British submarine, 83
P33 British submarine, 83
P36 British submarine, 97, 99
P38 British submarine, 105, 106
P39 British submarine, 99
P48 British submarine, 150
P222 British submarine, 150
P311 British submarine, 150
Pakenham British destroyer, 135, 158
Paladin British destroyer, 158
Palang Iranian sloop, 75
Palestro Italian torpedo boat, 6, 35
Pallade Italian torpedo boat, 174
Pallas French submarine, 143
Pandora British submarine, 30, 99
Pantera Italian destroyer, 66
Panther British destroyer, 186
Paris French battleship, 27, 29
Parthian British submarine, 25, 73, 174
Partridge British destroyer, 110, 146
Pathan Indian sloop, 26
Pelagosa Italian minelayer, 178
Pelikan German minelayer, 223
Penelope British light cruiser, 84, 86, 97, 99, 100, 169, 182, 186, 201, 202
Penn British destroyer, 186
Perla Italian submarine, 7, 121
Persée French submarine, 36
Perseo Italian torpedo boat, 159
Perseus British submarine, 88
Perth Australian light cruiser, 54, 62, 63
Petard British destroyer, 135, 159
Philadelphia American light cruiser, 205
Phoebe British light cruiser, 73, 121, 201
Phoenix British submarine, 35
Pier Capponi Italian submarine, 52, 53
Pietro Calvi Italian submarine, 78
Pietro Micca Italian submarine, 174
Pipinos Greek submarine, 238
Platino Italian submarine, 97
Pleiadi Italian torpedo boat, 83
Plunkett American destroyer, 198
Pola Italian heavy cruiser, 54
Polluce Italian torpedo boat, 54–56
Poncelet French submarine, 37

Porcupine British destroyer, 146
Porfido Italian submarine, 146
Portent American minesweeper, 196, 202
Primauguet French light cruiser, 141, 142
Prince of Wales British battleship, 81, 269
Procellaria Italian corvette, 154
Procione Italian torpedo boat, 149
Protée French submarine, 204
Proteus Greek submarine, 44
Provana Italian submarine, 26
Provence French battleship, 28, 30, 146
Puckeridge British escort destroyer, 188
Pursuer British escort carrier, 213, 220, 223, 224
Quail British destroyer, 188
Queen Elizabeth British battleship, 8, 9, 61, 88, 230
Quentin British destroyer, 148, 149
Quiberon British destroyer, 148
Quintino Sella Italian destroyer, 178
Rainbow British submarine, 44
Ramillies British battleship, 2, 43, 102, 213, 214, 218
Ranger American aircraft carrier, 140, 142
Regent British submarine, 158
Regulus British minesweeper, 240
Regulus British submarine, 44
Remo Italian submarine, 174
Renown British battlecruiser, 8, 9, 43, 52, 140, 230, 276
Repulse British battlecruiser, 8, 269
Resolution British battleship, 27, 30, 36, 37
Richelieu French battleship, 28, 31, 37, 141, 147, 230
Rigault de Genouilly French sloop, 30
Roberts British monitor, 15, 140, 177
Rodney British battleship, 8, 19, 77, 81, 121, 140, 144, 167, 168, 177, 278, 295
Roma Italian battleship, 178
Romolo Italian submarine, 174
Rorqual British submarine, 26, 44, 52, 149, 154, 288, 290
Rowan American destroyer, 182
Royal Sovereign British battleship, 2, 8, 9, 33
Royalist British light cruiser, 223, 226
Rubino Italian submarine, 26
Saetta Italian destroyer, 154
Sahib British submarine, 158
Salpa Italian submarine, 83, 290
Salvia British corvette, 88
San Giorgio Italian armoured cruiser, 6, 23, 24, 50, 68
Santorre Santarosa Italian submarine, 152, 153
Saracen British submarine, 174
Savannah American light cruiser, 181
Savorgnan de Brazza French sloop, 39
Scarab British gunboat, 218
Scharnhorst German battlecruiser, 27, 261, 272

Scirè Italian submarine, 88, 121
Scirocco Italian destroyer, 99
Scorpion British destroyer, 19
Seafire British destroyer, 19
Searcher British escort carrier, 213, 223
Selve Italian minesweeper (ex-Yugoslav *Galeb*), 150
Sentinel American minesweeper, 173
Seraph British submarine, 171
Severn British submarine, 78
SG10 German fast escort, 174
SG11 German fast escort, 207
SG14 German fast escort (ex-French *Matelot Leblanc*), 174
SG15 German fast escort (ex-French *Rageot de la Touche*), 204
SG16 German fast escort (ex-French *Amiral Sénès*), 221
SG20 German fast escort (ex-Italian *Generale Achille Papa*), 204, 301
SG21 German fast escort (ex-French *Chamois*), 218
SG22 German fast escort (ex-French *Enseigne Ballande*), 221
SG24 German fast escort (ex-French *Ampère*), 221
SG25 German fast escort (ex-French *La Curieuse*), 221
Shakespeare British submarine, 180
Sheffield British light cruiser, 52, 77, 145, 265
Shimane Maru Japanese auxiliary escort carrier, 262
Shoreham British sloop, 51, 74
Shropshire British/Australian heavy cruiser, 51, 262
Sickle British submarine, 208
Sidi Ferruch French submarine, 295
Sikh British destroyer, 87, 130
Simone Schiaffino Italian torpedo boat, 61
Simoon British submarine, 189
Sirius British light cruiser, 121, 148, 182, 186
Skill American minesweeper, 182
Snapdragon British corvette, 74
Soemba Dutch gunboat, 201
Somers American destroyer, 218
Souffleur French submarine, 73
Southampton British light cruiser, 47, 49
Southwold British escort destroyer, 98
Spartan British light cruiser, 198
Sparviero Italian aircraft carrier, 184
Splendid British submarine, 150, 158
Stalker British escort carrier, 177, 213, 224, 226
Strale Italian destroyer, 119
Strasbourg French battlecruiser, 28, 30, 32, 146
Stuart Australian destroyer, 35, 55
Swerve American minesweeper, 208
Sydney Australian light cruiser, 24, 34, 41
TA9 German torpedo boat (ex-French *Bombarde*), 221
TA10 German torpedo boat (ex-French *La Pomone*), 185, 190

TA11 German torpedo boat (ex-French *L'Iphigénie*), 178

TA12 German torpedo boat (ex-French *Baliste*), 190

TA13 German torpedo boat (ex-French *La Bayonnaise*), 221

TA14 German torpedo boat (ex-Italian *Turbine*), 207, 223

TA15 German torpedo boat (ex-Italian *Francesco Crispi*), 204, 225, 301, 303

TA16 German torpedo boat (ex-Italian *Castelfidardo*), 207

TA17 German torpedo boat (ex-Italian *San Martino*), 207, 223, 225, 303

TA18 German torpedo boat (ex-Italian *Solferino*), 224

TA19 German torpedo boat (ex-Italian *Calatafimi*), 238

TA20 German torpedo boat (ex-Italian *Audace*), 238

TA21 German torpedo boat (ex-Italian *Insidioso*), 235

TA22 German torpedo boat (ex-Italian *Giuseppe Missori*), 207

TA23 German torpedo boat (ex-Italian *Impavido*), 204, 301

TA24 German torpedo boat (ex-Italian *Arturo*), 240

TA25 German torpedo boat (ex-Italian *Ardito*), 207

TA26 German torpedo boat (ex-Italian *Intrepido*), 207

TA27 German torpedo boat (ex-Italian *Auriga*), 207

TA28 German torpedo boat (ex-Italian *Rigel*), 235

TA29 German torpedo boat (ex-Italian *Eridano*), 240

TA30 German torpedo boat (ex-Italian *Dragone*), 207

TA31 German torpedo boat (ex-Italian *Dardo*), 235

TA32 German torpedo boat (ex-Italian *Premuda*), 240

TA33 German torpedo boat (ex-Italian *Squadrista*), 235

TA34 German torpedo boat (ex-Yugoslav *T7*), 207, 302, 305

TA35 German torpedo boat (ex-Italian *Giuseppe Dezza*), 238

TA36 German torpedo boat (ex-Italian *Stella Polare*), 204, 301

TA37 German torpedo boat (ex-Italian *Gladio*), 224

TA38 German torpedo boat (ex-Italian *Spada*), 225

TA39 German torpedo boat (ex-Italian *Daga*), 226

TA40 German torpedo boat (ex-Italian *Pugnale*), 239

TA41 German torpedo boat (ex-Italian *Lancia*), 239

TA42 German torpedo boat (ex-Italian *Alabarda*), 240

TA44 German torpedo boat (ex-Italian *Antonio Pigafetta*), 239

TA45 German torpedo boat (ex-Italian *Spica*), 241

TA48 German torpedo boat (ex-Yugoslav *T3*), 239, 305

TA49 German torpedo boat (ex-Italian *Lira*), 235

Takao Japanese heavy cruiser, 262

Talisman British submarine, 150

Tarantini Italian submarine, 38

Taranto Italian light cruiser, 184, 235

Teazer British destroyer, 223

Tembien Italian submarine, 80

Tempest British submarine, 106

Termagant British destroyer, 224

Terpsichore British destroyer, 223

Terre Neuve French patrol vessel, 31

Terror British monitor, 45, 49, 52, 68

Tetrach British submarine, 83

Texas American battleship, 137, 140, 214

Thorn British submarine, 119

Thrasher British submarine, 129

Thunderbolt British submarine, 38, 150, 154

Tifone Italian escort destroyer, 159

Tigre Italian destroyer, 66

Tigris British submarine, 154

Torbay British submarine, 186

Tornade French destroyer, 143

Tramontane French destroyer, 143

Traveller British submarine, 150

Trento Italian heavy cruiser, 6, 41, 54, 111, 112

Triad British submarine, 44

Tricheco Italian submarine, 105

Trieste Italian heavy cruiser, 54, 85, 157

Triton British submarine, 44

Triton Greek submarine, 150

Tritone Italian submarine, 153

Triumph British submarine, 106

Trombe French destroyer, 240

Trooper British submarine, 150, 189

Troubridge British destroyer, 223

Tulagi American escort carrier, 214

Turbulent British submarine, 154

Turquoise French submarine, 159

Tuscan British destroyer, 223–225

Tynedale British escort destroyer, 188

Tynwald British anti-aircraft ship, 146

Typhon French destroyer, 143

U73 German submarine, 123, 188

U74 German submarine, 121

U75 German submarine, 88

U77 German submarine, 153, 154

U79 German submarine, 88

U81 German submarine, 85, 202

U83 German submarine, 153, 154

U95 German submarine, 88

U97 German submarine, 171, 298

U98 German submarine, 146

U133 German submarine, 96, 121

U205 German submarine, 112, 153

U223 German submarine, 202

U224 German submarine, 153

U230 German submarine, 218

U259 German submarine, 146

U301 German submarine, 153, 154

U303 German submarine, 171

U331 German submarine, 85, 146

U340 German submarine, 188

U343 German submarine, 202

U371 German submarine, 202

U372 German submarine, 115, 121

U374 German submarine, 121

U375 German submarine, 174

U380 German submarine, 202

U392 German submarine, 202

U407 German submarine, 224

U409 German submarine, 174

U410 German submarine, 201, 202

U411 German submarine, 146

U414 German submarine, 171

U421 German submarine, 202

U431 German submarine, 188

U433 German submarine, 88

U443 German submarine, 159

U450 German submarine, 202

U453 German submarine, 202

U455 German submarine, 202

U458 German submarine, 188

U466 German submarine, 218

U471 German submarine, 207

U557 German submarine, 88

U559 German submarine, 135, 136

U561 German submarine, 174

U562 German submarine, 153

U565 German submarine, 106, 224

U568 German submarine, 88, 121

U573 German submarine, 121

U577 German submarine, 121

U586 German submarine, 207

U593 German submarine, 188

U595 German submarine, 146

U596 German submarine, 224

U602 German submarine, 153,

U605 German submarine, 146

U616 German submarine, 202

U617 German submarine, 154, 188

U642 German submarine, 207

U652 German submarine, 96, 106, 121

U660 German submarine, 146

U731 German submarine, 202

U755 German submarine, 171, 298

U761 German submarine, 202

U952 German submarine, 207

U960 German submarine, 202

U967 German submarine, 218

U969 German submarine, 207

Uarsciek Italian submarine, 146

Uebi Scebeli Italian submarine, 25

Uganda British light cruiser, 181

Ugolino Vivaldi Italian destroyer, 110, 178

UIT1 German submarine (ex-Italian *R10*), 235

UIT4 German submarine (ex-Italian *R7*), 202

UIT5 German submarine (ex-Italian *R8*), 202

UIT6 German submarine (ex-Italian *R9*), 239

UIT7 German submarine (ex-Italian *Bario*), 239

UIT8 German submarine (ex-Italian *Litio*), 239

UIT9 German submarine (ex-Italian *Sodio*), 239

UIT15 German submarine (ex-Italian *Sparide*), 235

UIT16 German submarine (ex-Italian *Murena*), 235

UIT19 German submarine (ex-Italian *Nautilo*), 202

UIT20 German submarine (ex-Italian *Grongo*), 235

UJ201 German corvette (ex-Italian *Egeria*), 204, 301

UJ202 German corvette (ex-Italian *Melpómene*), 238

UJ205 German corvette (ex-Italian *Colubrina*), 240

UJ208 German corvette (ex-Italian *Spingarda*), 238

UJ2101 German auxiliary sub-chaser, 206

UJ2102 German auxiliary sub-chaser, 224

UJ2104 German auxiliary sub-chaser, 184

UJ2105 German auxiliary sub-chaser, 206

UJ2107 German auxiliary sub-chaser, 223

UJ2108 German auxiliary sub-chaser, 224

UJ2109 German corvette (ex-British *Widnes*), 186, 190, 228, 300

UJ2111 German auxiliary sub-chaser, 186

UJ2142 German auxiliary sub-chaser, 223

UJ2223 German corvette (ex-Italian *Marangone*), 235

UJ6081 German corvette (ex-Italian *Camoscio*), 218

UJ6082 German corvette (ex-Italian *Antilope*), 218

UJ6085 German corvette (ex-Italian *Renna*), 235

Ulpio Traiano Italian light cruiser, 150

Umbra British submarine, 105, 112

Unbeaten British submarine, 121

Unbroken British submarine, 125

Undaunted British submarine, 61

Unicorn British aircraft repair ship, 11, 177, 299

Unie Italian minesweeper, 154

Union British submarine, 83

Unique British submarine, 82

Unruly British submarine, 186

Upholder British submarine, 61, 83, 85, 106, 292

Upright British submarine, 47, 52

Uragano Italian escort destroyer, 154

Urge British submarine, 65, 87, 99, 100, 288

Usk British submarine, 61

Usurper British submarine, 189

Utmost British submarine, 150, 290

Valiant British battleship, 8, 27, 30, 35, 39, 43, 49, 54, 55, 59, 62, 88, 167, 168, 177, 181, 230, 278

Valmy French destroyer, 73
Vasilevs Georgios I Greek destroyer, 60, 159
Vasilissa Olga Greek destroyer, 171, 185
Vauquelin French destroyer, 73
Vega Italian torpedo boat, 48
Velella Italian submarine, 180
Veniero Italian submarine, 109
Vetch British corvette, 171
Victorious British aircraft carrier, 80, 121–123, 140, 230
Vincenzo Gioberti Italian destroyer, 174
Vincenzo Giordano Orsini Italian torpedo boat, 66
Vittorio Alfieri Italian destroyer, 55
Vittorio Veneto Italian battleship, 43, 53–56, 87, 111, 178
Vivid British submarine, 207
Walney British sloop, 142
Warspite British battleship, 2, 8, 19, 33, 43, 49, 54, 55, 59, 62, 64, 103, 105, 167, 168, 177, 181, 182, 261, 308,

Wasp American aircraft carrier, 100, 132
Waterhen Australian destroyer, 70
Welshman British minelayer, 101, 109, 148, 154
Westcott British destroyer, 143
Wheatland British escort destroyer, 145, 238
Widnes British minesweeper, 62, 288, 300
Wolverine British destroyer, 123
Wryneck British escort destroyer, 60
Yamashiro Japanese battleship, 262
Yarra Australian sloop, 71, 74
York British heavy cruiser, 39, 57, 62, 64
Zaffiro Italian submarine, 109
Zara Italian heavy cruiser, 6, 54–56
Zeffiro Italian destroyer, 24
Zetland British destroyer, 143, 223
Zeus German minelayer, 224, 226
Zirona Italian minelayer, 85
Zulu British destroyer, 130

Index of Merchant Ships and Support Vessels

Aagtekerk Dutch merchant ship, 111

Abruzzi Italian merchant ship, 129

Achaia German merchant ship, 106

Adriatico Italian auxiliary, 86

Alicante German merchant ship, 65

Almeria Lykes American merchant ship, 124

Alstertor German merchant ship, 77

Altmark German merchant ship, 279

Antonietta Lauro Italian merchant ship, 59

Apuania Italian merchant ship, 130

Ariosto Italian merchant ship, 105, 106

Arlesiana Italian merchant ship, 159

Askari German merchant ship, 51

Assiria Italian merchant ship, 59

Belchen German merchant ship, 275

Belluno Italian merchant ship, 159

Bertrand Rickmers German merchant ship, 51

Bhutan British merchant ship, 111

Biscayne American headquarters ship, 195

Breconshire British transport, 88, 96–98

Brioni Italian naval auxiliary, 134

Brisbane Star British merchant ship, 124, 125

Bulolo British headquarters ship, 140, 195

Burdwan British merchant ship, 110

Campobasso Italian merchant ship, 159

Capitano A Cecchi Italian merchant ship, 61

Capo Faro Italian merchant ship, 86

Carola German merchant ship, 223

Centurion British demilitarized battleship, 110

Chant American merchant ship, 110

Città di Agrigento Italian merchant ship, 117

Citta di Napoli Italian merchant ship, 150

Citta di Trapani Italian merchant ship, 150

Citta di Tunisi Italian merchant ship, 150

City of Calcutta British merchant ship, 111

Clan Campbell British merchant ship, 96, 97

Clan Chattan British merchant ship, 96

Clan Cumming British merchant ship, 47

Clan Ferguson British merchant ship, 124

Clan MacDonald British merchant ship, 47

Coburg German merchant ship, 51

Conte Rosso Italian troopship, 61

Cuma German merchant ship, 106

D'Annunzio Italian merchant ship, 152

Davide Bianchi Italian merchant ship, 129, 294

Denbydale British tanker, 88

Deucalion British merchant ship, 123

Donizetti German merchant ship, 185

Dorset British merchant ship, 124

Duca degli Abruzzi Italian merchant ship, 51, 104

Durham British merchant ship, 88

Egeo Italian merchant ship, 59

Elba German merchant ship, 77

Elli German tanker, 223

Empire Hope British merchant ship, 124

Empire Song British merchant ship, 47, 61

Esperia Italian troopship, 82

Essex British merchant ship, 47

Etiopia Italian merchant ship, 134

Favor German merchant ship, 154

Fiona Shell British merchant ship, 88

Friedrich Breme German tanker, 77

Garaventa Italian training ship, 52

General Duquesne French merchant ship, 104

Genova Perossi Italian merchant ship, 288

Gertrud German merchant ship, 206, 207

Gino Allegri Italian merchant ship, 106

Giulio Cesare German-controlled merchant ship, 235

Giuseppe Mazzini Italian merchant ship, 51

Glengyle British landing ship, 73

Glenorchy British merchant ship, 124

Gloria Stella Italian merchant ship, 39

Gradisca German hospital ship, 226

Helly German transport, 223

Imperial Star British merchant ship, 81

Ingeborg German merchant ship, 186

Ingo German merchant ship, 53

Iridio Mantovani Italian tanker, 86

Irma Italian tanker, 152

Jiul Romanian merchant ship, 65

Juventus Italian merchant ship, 53

Kari German merchant ship, 186

Kentucky British tanker, 110

Ketty Brovig German prize tanker, 51

Knyaguinya Marie Louisa Bulgarian merchant ship, 65

KT4 German military transport, 223

KT5 German military transport, 159
KT7 German military transport, 158
KT9 German military transport, 159
KT21 German military transport, 159
KT26 German military transport, 223
KT35 German military transport, 235
KT36 German military transport, 235
Kybfels German transport, 65
Largs British headquarters ship, 140, 169
Le Tre Marie Italian merchant ship, 106
Leinster British troop transport, 80
Liguria Italian troopship, 24, 50
Loasso Italian merchant ship, 26
Lola German merchant ship, 226
Lothringen German tanker, 77
LST282 American landing ship tank, 218
Luisiano Italian merchant ship, 134
Mannheim German military transport, 223
Manzoni Italian merchant ship, 24
Marburg German transport, 65
Marguerite German merchant ship, 186
Maria Italian merchant ship, 24
Maria Eugenia Italian merchant ship, 39
Marigola Italian merchant ship, 290
Marocchino Italian merchant ship, 59
Medway British depot ship, 115
Melbourne Star British merchant ship, 124
Mercurio German-controlled merchant ship, 235
Moncalieri Italian merchant ship, 51
Monte Gargano Italian depot ship, 35
Napoli Italian merchant ship, 105, 106
Neptunia Italian troopship, 83
Newfoundland British hospital ship, 182
Norge Italian merchant ship, 43
Oceania Italian troopship, 83
Oder German merchant ship, 51
Ohio American tanker, 121, 124–126
Olympos German merchant ship, 186
Orari British merchant ship, 110
Orion German merchant ship, 223
Ostia German coaster, 134
Padenna Italian merchant ship, 129, 294
Pampas British merchant ship, 96
Panuco Italian tanker, 84
Paula German merchant ship, 185
Pensilvania Italian merchant ship, 51
Perla Italian merchant ship, 95
Persiano Italian merchant ship, 59
Peuceta Italian merchant ship, 43
Picci Fassio Italian tanker, 129, 294
PLM20 French tanker, 105
Plumleaf British tanker, 99
Pluto German merchant ship, 185

Pomezia German merchant ship, 224
Port Chalmers British merchant ship, 124
Princess Beatrix British transport, 169
Proserpina Italian tanker, 134
Queen Emma British transport, 169
Ramb I Italian auxiliary cruiser, 51
Rex German-controlled merchant ship, 235, 236
Rochester Castle British merchant ship, 124, 125
Rowallan Castle British merchant ship, 96
Royal Ulsterman British transport, 169
Sabine German merchant ship, 206
Sagona Norwegian tanker, 88
Saint Didier French merchant ship, 73
Samuel Huntington American merchant ship, 198
San Giovanni Battista Italian merchant ship, 95
Sant' Antonio Italian merchant ship, 159
Santa Elisa American merchant ship, 124, 124
Securitas Italian merchant ship, 106
Serenitas Italian merchant ship, 24
Sereno Italian merchant ship, 34
Sinfra German merchant ship, 186
Somalia Italian merchant ship, 51, 104
Soudan British merchant ship, 120
St. David British hospital ship, 198
Stella Sirius British trawler, 37
Stromboli Italian naval transport, 152
Tacoma French merchant ship, 37
Talabot Norwegian merchant ship, 96
Tanais German merchant ship, 206, 207
Tanaro Italian naval transport, 152
Tanimbar Dutch merchant ship, 109
Tarquinia German merchant ship, 186
Tenace Italian merchant ship, 61
Tergestea Italian merchant ship, 134
Thermopylae Norwegian merchant ship, 96
Ticino Italian merchant ship, 52
Toni German transport, 223
Trapani German merchant ship, 186
Tripolino Italian merchant ship, 134
Tübingen German hospital ship, 235
Uckermark German merchant ship, 51
Ulster Queen British fighter direction ship, 224
Veloce Italian merchant ship, 149
Verde Italian merchant ship, 52
Vettor Pisani Italian merchant ship, 117
Victoria Italian troopship, 95, 291
Viminale Italian transport, 150
Waimarama British merchant ship, 124
Wairangi British merchant ship, 124
Wartenfels German merchant ship, 104
Zara Italian naval auxiliary, 134
Zeffiro Italian merchant ship, 65, 288
Zena Italian merchant ship, 290

Index of Operations

Agreement, 130

Appearance, 52

Avalanche, 180, 194, 220

Battleaxe, 69, 70, 269

Baytown, 176, 177

Bellows, 121

Bowery, 100

Brevity, 60

Calendar, 100

Catapult, 29, 32, 267

Collar, 43

Compass, 45, 50, 53, 93, 94, 268

Corkscrew, 169, 170, 271, 276

Crusader, 85, 86, 89, 93, 94, 96, 104, 162, 269

Diadem, 201, 204–206, 209, 273, 301

Dragoon, 212–215, 219–222, 231, 273

Excess, 47, 48

Flax, 158

Grapeshot, 241, 274

Halberd, 81

Harpoon, 109, 112, 122, 125, 270

Hats, 35

Hercules, 101, 118

Hurry, 35

Husky, 166–168, 170–174, 176, 188, 194, 254, 271

Insect, 121

Ironclad, 103–105, 270, 278

Judgement (1945), 277

Judgment (1940), 40, 41

Lightfoot, 133, 134

Lustre, 53

Manna, 226

Mincemeat, 171

Olive, 232, 273, 304

Outing, 223

Overlord, 191, 192, 194, 206

Pedestal, 121, 123, 125, 126, 148, 270, 275, 278

Pinpoint, 121

Portcullis, 148

Railway, 290

Retribution, 160, 271

Rocket, 290

Shingle, 192–198, 200, 272

Slapstick, 182

Sledgehammer, 139

Splice, 290

Stoneage, 148

Strike, 159, 271

Style, 80

Substance, 80

Supercharge, 134

Tiger, 60, 61, 69, 70

Torch, 139, 142, 144, 146, 194, 220, 249

Tracer, 290

Train, 132

Vigorous, 110–112, 270

Vulcan, 158

Zitadelle, 176

Index of Personalities

Agnew, Captain W. G., 84, 275
al Gailani, Rashid Ali, 71, 72
Alexander, General Harold, 128, 160, 166, 198, 234, 243, 244, 294, 297, 298, 307
Anderson, Lieutenant-General K. A. N., 140, 297
Auchinleck, General Claude, 70, 86, 115–117, 128, 291, 293
Badoglio, Marshal Pietro, 176–178, 183
Beresford-Peirse, Lieutenant-General Noel, 69
Bradley, Lieutenant-General Omar, 192
Burrough, Rear-Admiral Harold, 121, 124, 140, 275
Campioni, Admiral Inigo, 33
Castellano, General Giuseppe, 177
Churchill, Winston, 16, 37, 41, 70, 108, 136, 160, 191, 193, 248, 257, 287, 298
Clark, Lieutenant-General Mark, 176, 181, 193, 197, 205
Coningham, Air Marshal Arthur, 192
Cooke, Captain G. C., 85
Cunningham, Lieutenant-General Alan, 50, 51, 86
Cunningham, Vice-Admiral Andrew, 18–21, 23, 24, 26, 29, 33, 35, 36, 39–41, 43, 48, 51, 52, 54–56, 63, 97, 111, 140, 160, 166, 171, 179, 192, 275, 287
Cunningham, Vice-Admiral John, 36, 192, 276
Darlan, Admiral François, 27, 144, 145
de Gaulle, General Charles, 32, 36
Dentz, General Henri, 74
Devers, Lieutenant-General Jacob, 212
Duke of Aosta, 75
Eisenhower, Lieutenant-General Dwight, 140, 151, 166, 177, 192, 193, 220
Emmanuel III, King Victor, 176, 178
Freyberg, Major-General Bernard, 63
Fusson, Lieutenant Anthony, 135, 136
Gensoul, Admiral Marcel-Bruno, 29, 30
Giraud, General Henri, 141, 145
Godfroy, Admiral René-Émile, 29
Grazier, Able Seaman Colin, 135, 136
Hall, Rear-Admiral J. L., 177
Hardy, Captain C. C., 110
Harwood, Vice-Admiral Henry, 111, 276

Hewitt, Rear-Admiral Henry Kent, 140, 168, 176, 212, 214
Hitler, Adolf, xvii–xix, 48, 49, 85, 101, 109, 145, 157, 176, 185, 217, 222, 274
Holland, Captain C. S., 29
Iachino, Admiral Angelo, 53–56, 111
Kai-shek, Chiang, 191
Kesselring, Field Marshal Albert, 100, 117, 196–198, 206
Lowry, Rear-Admiral F. J., 195
Lucas, Major-General John, 194, 197, 198
McGrigor, Rear-Admiral R. R., 168, 169, 276
Messe, Field Marshal Giovanni, 160
Montgomery, Lieutenant-General Bernard, 128, 133, 134, 151, 156, 166, 176, 192, 295, 297
Morshead, Major-General L. J., 57
Mussolini, Benito, xvii–xix, 1, 2, 4, 5, 16, 21, 37, 38, 101, 176, 183, 244, 266, 271, 274
O'Connor, Lieutenant-General Richard, 45
Oliver, Commodore G. N., 176, 263, 277
Papandreou, Georgios, 226
Patton, Lieutenant-General George, 166, 192
Pavesi, Vice-Admiral Gino, 169
Platt, Lieutenant-General William, 50
Pridham-Wippell, Vice-Admiral H. D., 41, 54, 60, 277
Ramsay, Admiral Bertram, 168, 192, 275, 277
Rawlings, Rear-Admiral Bernard, 63, 263, 278
Ritchie, Lieutenant-General Neil, 108
Rommel, General Erwin, 57, 58, 60, 78, 79, 84, 86, 89–91, 94, 95, 104, 106–109, 115–119, 126–130, 133, 134, 150–152, 156, 157, 161, 270, 294
Roosevelt, Franklin, 108, 139, 191
Somerville, Vice-Admiral James, 27, 29, 30, 43, 52, 263, 278, 287
Speer, Albert, 236
Stalin, Joseph, 191
Stumme, General Georg, 133, 294
Sturges, Major-General R. G., 103
Syfret, Rear-Admiral E. N., 100, 103, 123, 140, 278

Tedder, Air Chief Marshal Arthur, 166, 192
Tovey, Vice-Admiral John, 24, 278
Troubridge, Commodore Thomas, 140, 168, 195, 209, 214, 223, 279
Vian, Rear-Admiral Philip, 97, 111, 168, 177, 181, 192, 263, 279

von Arnim, General Hans-Jürgen, 160
von Thoma, General Wilhelm Ritter, 294
Wanklyn, Lieutenant-Commander M. D., 61, 292
Wavell, General Archibald, 63, 70, 289
Willis, Vice-Admiral A. U., 168, 177, 279
Wilson, General Henry Maitland, 192